A N C I E N T   C I T I E S   C

INDUS VALLEY CIVILIZATION

This Catalogue accompanied the exhibition *Great Cities, Small Treasures: The Ancient World of the Indus Valley* held at the Asia Society, New York, 11 February through 3 May 1998; the Elvehjem Museum of Art, Madison, Wisconsin, September through November 1998; and the Pacific Asia Museum, Pasadena, California.

OXFORD
UNIVERSITY PRESS

Great Clarendon Street, Oxford ox2 6DP

Oxford University Press is a department of the University of Oxford.
It furthers the University„s objective of excellence in research, scholarship, and education by publishing worldwide in

Oxford New York

Auckland Cape Town Dar es Salaam Hong Kong Karachi
Kuala Lumpur Madrid Melbourne Mexico City Nairobi
New Delhi Shanghai Taipei Toronto

With offices in

Argentina Austria Brazil Chile Czech Republic France Greece
Guatemala Hungary Italy Japan Poland Portugal Singapore
South Korea Switzerland Turkey Ukraine Vietnam

Oxford is a registered trademark of Oxford University Press
in the UK and in certain other countries

ISBN 978-0-19-577940-0

Ninth Impression 2011

Designer: David Alcorn, Museum Publication Design, Blairsden California

Editor: Patricia Powell, Elvehjem Museum of Art, Madison, Wisconsin

Dimensions are given in centimeters, except where otherwise indicated.

Front cover: See Cat. no. 23 (also text Figure 6.18) Square seal depicting a nude male deity with three faces, seated in yogic position on a throne.

Printed in Pakistan by
Kagzi Printers, Karachi.
Published by
Ameena Saiyid, Oxford University Press
No. 38, Sector 15, Korangi Industrial Area, PO Box 8214,
Karachi-74900, Pakistan.

and

American Institute of Pakistan Studies
House 2, Street 84, Ataturk Avenue, G-6/4, PO Box 1128
Islamabad, Pakistan.

MAJOR SPONSORS OF THE EXHIBITION

Golden Jubilee Committee, Ministry of Culture, Sports, Tourism and Youth Affairs, Government of the Islamic Republic of Pakistan

Pakistan International Airlines

MetLife is a proud sponsor of Pakistan 1997-98,
Asia Society programs in Celebration of Pakistan's 50th anniversary.

Harappa Archaeological Research Project

Smithsonian Institution, Foreign Currency Program Grant

Association of Pakistani Physicians of North America (APPNA)

Pakistan's Arts Council

OTHER SPONSORS

Favrot Fund

Caltex Oil Pakistan Ltd.

IBM

WWW.HARAPPA.COM

Alastair B. Martin

Dr. Q.D. and Mrs. M.J. Kenoyer

Barbara A. Dales

Richard H. Meadow

ANCIENT CITIES OF THE
INDUS VALLEY CIVILIZATION

JONATHAN MARK KENOYER

Dedicated to the memory of

George F. Dales, Jr. (1927-1992) and Walter A. Fairservis, Jr. (1924-1994)

AMERICAN INSTITUTE OF PAKISTAN STUDIES

OXFORD
UNIVERSITY PRESS

Contents

Foreword

*A*ncient Cities of the Indus Valley Civilization introduces the general public to one of the most important civilizations of the ancient world, the Indus Valley civilization of Pakistan and northwestern India (2600-1900 B.C.). The primary purpose of this book and the associated exhibition is to underscore the importance of South Asia as the birthplace of a unique and highly developed urban culture. Because the ancient Indus writing is still undeciphered, our only way to understand the nature of the early cities and their inhabitants is through the archaeological record, supplemented by comparative studies with other contemporaneous civilizations and later cultures of South Asia.

This book has been written as an introductory text. It begins with the discovery of the Indus civilization in Chapter 1, followed by a general discussion of the theoretical frameworks currently used to understand the complex processes leading to the establishment of the first cities of South Asia. A short discussion of the climate and geographical setting is presented in Chapter 2, along with a discussion of the regional cultural developments that provided the foundation for the emergence of the later urban centers and the Indus culture. This is followed by the main body of the text, which focuses on the character of the Indus Valley civilization. Chapter 3 deals with the character and organization of Indus cities, towns and villages. In Chapter 4 the enigmatic Indus script is presented along with a new perspective on the contexts in which this writing was used, based on new discoveries at Harappa and other sites. Chapter 5 is devoted to examining the nature of the ruling elites and traders using as evidence the archaeological remains left by those communities. New analyses of specific artifacts are interpreted in relation to factors of socio-economic control and integration. A similar approach is used in Chapter 6 for understanding religious art and symbols that represented the ideology of Indus culture and reinforce the structure of Harappan society. Discussion of the many different social classes and ethnic communities that made up the Indus cities are presented in Chapter 7, using as a principal source studies of the many diverse types of artifacts found in the cities. Specific sets of artifacts are used to characterize the nature of the daily life of the men and women living in the Indus region, beginning with childbirth and concluding with death and burial. Chapter 8 focuses on the crafts and technologies that were developed in the Indus cities, with a special emphasis on the crafts that were used to create symbols of wealth and power. The many factors leading to the decline of the Indus cities and the localization of socio-economic interaction networks are presented in Chapter 9, followed by a discussion of the legacy of the Indus Valley civilization and it contributions to later cultures of the subcontinent.

Additional details about the Indus civilization are presented at the end of the text in a catalogue of important objects from the Indus civilization. These include artifacts from the excavations of the 1920s and 1930s at the major cities of Mohenjo-daro and Harappa and at the town of Chanhudaro. Other objects in the catalogue section have been excavated in the past three decades at the sites of Harappa, Mehrgarh, Nausharo, Allahdino and Miri Qalat. Most of the objects pictured in the text and the catalogue section have been selected for display in the exhibition Great Cities, Small Treasures: The Ancient World of the Indus Valley which is being organized in the United States of America in conjunction with the Golden Jubilee Celebration of the independence of Pakistan (14 August 1947). Bibliographic references are cited for the text as endnotes to each chapter and for the catalogue as a bibliography. A comprehensive bibliography of all references cited in the text and catalogue section is provided at the end of the book where it precedes a comprehensive index of important topics, names and places mentioned in the book.

In writing this book I have tried to present a balanced perspective of the Indus Valley civilization using the most recent data and a contextual archaeological analysis of the archaeological materials. Nevertheless, many of the interpretations presented in this text will be different than those that might be made by my colleagues. Each of us has our own unique perspective informed by our life experiences, education and field research. As an archaeologist who has himself revised many earlier interpretations of the Indus civilization, I am confident that future archaeological excavations and the eventual decipherment of the Indus script will change many of the interpretations presented in this book. Nevertheless, my sincere hope is that what I have written here will in some measure be a stimulus for these future endeavors by scholars from Pakistan, South Asia, and around the world.

Jonathan Mark Kenoyer
Madison, Wisconsin
September 30, 1997

Preface

by Richard H. Meadow

I first met Jonathan Mark Kenoyer in 1975 at the archaeological site of Balakot. It was the third year of excavations being carried out by the late George Franklin Dales, Jr. (1927-1992) at this small Harappan and pre-Harappan settlement situated near the Arabian Sea coast some 50 miles north-northwest of Karachi. All my recent fieldwork and study had been focused on eastern Iran and Oman, both areas that had strong prehistoric ties to Baluchistan and beyond it to the Indus alluvium. It was thus a logical step for me to turn toward the 3rd millennium colossus of the east — the Indus Valley civilization, and I joined the Balakot excavations in 1974.

During that long and hot 1974-75 field season we inhabited tents laid out in military precision at the foot of the site in a dusty field. Well into the season we were visited by Jean-François and Catherine Jarrige, who had been working with Jean-Marie Casal at the site of Pirak near Sibi on the north Kachi Plain. They were in Karachi making arrangements to begin excavations at a new site — Mehrgarh — that appeared on the basis of sherds gathered from the surface to have remains contemporary with those from the early period at Balakot. I remember that George gave them a copy of the report of the previous season, and I believe that it was on this occasion that some remarks were made about the high quality of the artifact drawings. Perhaps this was the first time that I heard Mark Kenoyer's name — as the source of these depictions of lithics, bone and ceramic implements. Mark had just finished his undergraduate degree at Berkeley and had entered the M.A./Ph.D. program as George's student. I was told that, if his academic progress was good, Mark would be coming to Balakot for the next field season.

Sure enough, next season there he was, thrilled to once again be back in South Asia. Born in Shillong, India, where his father was the head doctor of a mission hospital, Mark had spent most of his first eighteen years either in Assam or at the Woodstock School in Mussoorie in northern Uttar Pradesh. His first language had been the Kuki language of his ayah, but he soon learned Bengali and then English followed by Hindi, and now he was making the adjustments to Urdu. And he loved to make things.

He immediately recognized that the Harappans at Balakot had made shell bangles using a variety of species and more than one technique. He proceeded to investigate the process by attempting to replicate it. The results formed the basis of his first article coauthored with George Dales. He subsequently expanded this research as a part of his doctoral dissertation, which remains the definitive study of Harappan shellworking as well as being a milestone in the fields of experimental archaeology and ethnoarchaeology. Thus, already at the very beginning of his career — grinding bivalve shells in the camp at Naka Kharai with a mongoose on his shoulder — Mark had settled on those aspects of the past that were be his principal focus — ancient technologies — and on those approaches he would use to study them — careful excavation of workshop areas, detailed analysis of the debris from all stages of manufacture and comparison with like materials from his own manufacturing attempts and those of traditional craftsmen in South Asia.

Excavations at Balakot were completed in early 1977, the year Mark took his M.A. The following years saw him frequently in Pakistan and India. He worked with George Dales in Karachi documenting the Mohenjo-daro material excavated in 1964 and completed with George a monograph on the pottery from that site. He spent three seasons in India with Desmond Clark and G. R. Sharma excavating at Baghor I, an Upper Paleolithic site in the Son Valley of Madhya Pradesh, where they uncovered a feature that can convincingly be identified as an ancient shrine. He searched out shell materials in archaeological collections across the length and breadth of both India and Pakistan and studied the traditional shell manufacturing groups of Bengal, working all of this into his dissertation which he completed at the University of California at Berkeley in 1983.

He nelped the joint German-Italian team to record surface indicators of craft activities at Mohenjo-daro, where he struck up a close working relationship with Massimo Vidale that in the late 1980s was to develop into a project along with Kuldeep K. Bhan studying the modern carnelian beadmakers of Khambhat, India. Then, in 1985, he joined the faculty at the University of Wisconsin - Madison, and at the end of his first semester, went back to Pakistan with his mentor, George Dales, to begin exploration and excavations at Harappa as field director of the University of California, Berkeley, Harappa Project. Now 12 years later, the renamed Harappa Archaeological Research Project continues under the joint direction of Mark and myself assisted by Rita Wright from New York University.

Some of the finds and much of what we have learned at Harappa are represented in this volume. More than that, however, the author's long attachment to South Asia — both personal and professional — are reflected in his presentation and interpretation of artifacts, archaeological features and architectural configurations. What begins as a largely descriptive exposition of the "dead dry bones" of Harappan archaeology transforms itself as the volume proceeds into an increasingly vibrant picture of ancient life. This picture represents one man's view of the past informed by 23 years of archaeological and ethnographic research in Pakistan and India and by 18 years of growing up in India. But the paints, often applied with a broad brush necessarily in an impressionistic manner, are tempered by Western academic skepticism. Thus we do not see those wild flights of fancy or long leaps of faith that characterize some literature of the region. What flights and leaps are there do not require a suspension of disbelief to entertain.

Whether the mix of exposition and interpretation found here suits the individual reader, he or she must decide. When I first examined the book two incarnations ago (and it has improved since then), I was put off by what seemed to be rather awkward attempts in the early chapters to put flesh on the bones. I decided, however, to persist and see if things got any better. By the end I had been drawn into the author's embrace and was no longer struggling. I was particularly impressed by the effort to examine the interplay of technology, ornamentation, social structure and ideology which I was obliged to look at in a new light. And if I still am not willing to entertain all that is written here, I do believe that the story is better than any propounded in the past two decades about a literate civilization that we still can only know from archaeology. And even my most skeptical professional colleagues can profitably mine the text and especially the catalogue of objects that follows for new data on the Indus civilization. Many objects from the excavations at Harappa are presented here for the first time; previously unappreciated and even unpublished objects from Chanhu-daro are highlighted, and the horde of gold and silver jewelry from Allahdino finally sees the light of day after more than 20 years of darkness in a Karachi vault.

I would like to express my hope that this book and the exhibition that it accompanies will serve to make the American public better informed about and more appreciative of South Asia's first urban civilization. It was very different than its better known contemporaries in Mesopotamia and Egypt, and than its later peers in the Aegean, China, and the New World. Mark Kenoyer argues that what made it different is similar to some of what makes modern South Asia different from the rest of the world. With the recent South Asian diaspora around the globe and especially across America, and with the increasing importance of the region to us all, efforts such as this one to promote better public understanding are welcome indeed. In particular, the role of Pakistan as custodian of much of the archaeology of the Indus civilization needs to be better appreciated. The cooperation of the Government and the warmth and generosity of the people of Pakistan have made it a real pleasure for us to work with them over the past quarter of a century — half of that young country's history.

Richard H. Meadow

Peabody Museum, Harvard University

28 September 1997

Acknowledgements

This book would not have been possible without the support of numerous individuals and institutions. My first thanks must be to the Government of the Islamic Republic of Pakistan, Ministry of Culture, Sports, Tourism and Youth Affairs and Department of Archaeology and Museums for providing me with the opportunity to study aspects of the Indus Valley civilization over the past 23 years at the sites of Balakot, Mohenjo-daro and Harappa. I would also like to acknowledge the support of the Golden Jubilee Committee, Ministry of Culture, and Pakistan International Airlines for providing essential logistic and financial support for the exhibition *Ancient Cities of the Indus Valley* that is being held in the United States of America in conjunction with the 50th anniversary of the independence of Pakistan. The Department of Archaeology and Museums, Government of Pakistan has facilitated the object photography. I would like to thank the numerous staff members for their unreserved assistance at the Exploration Branch in Karachi, the National Museum in Karachi, the Mohenjo-daro Museum, the Islamabad Museum and the Harappa Museum. I am greatly indebted to the Directors General of Archaeology who have facilitated my work on this project: Dr. Ishtiaq Khan, Dr. Ahmed Nabi Khan, Dr. Mohammad Rafique Mughal and Mr. Niaz Rasool. The Lahore Museum has also provided access to important objects, and I would like to thank the director, Dr. Saif-ur-Rahman Dar, and the curator, Miss Humera Alam, for their willingness to allow me access to the necessary objects. Most of the artifacts from the site of Chanhudaro pictured in this book are in the collections of the Museum of Fine Arts, Boston, and I thank that institution for permitting me to use these images in the book and the objects in the exhibition.

Support for my ongoing research at Harappa and the Indus Civilization has been provided by numerous organizations; I am grateful to thank the National Science Foundation, the National Endowment for the Humanities, the National Geographic Society, the Smithsonian Institution, the American School of Prehistoric Research (Peabody Museum of Archaeology and Ethnology, Harvard University), American Institute of Pakistan Studies, the Fulbright Foundation and the University of Wisconsin for their long term commitments to my research. Additional major support has come through private donations from individuals who have taken an interest in my work and the study of early civilizations in the subcontinent. I offer special thanks to Henry C. and Mary E. Meadow, Celie Arndt, Alastair B. Martin and other anonymous sponsors.

In writing this book I have drawn on the research of many different scholars who have studied the Indus civilization from a variety of perspectives. Archaeologists, physical anthropologists, art historians, linguists, ethnographers and historians have provided the major new interpretations and data sets, but material scientists, modern craftsmen of Pakistan and India, and the people living in villages and cities throughout South Asia have also made significant contributions.

I would like to acknowledge my great debt to my mentor, the late Dr. George F. Dales, for his guidance and encouragement in my early research, first at the site of Balakot and later at the site of Harappa where he invited me to work with him as field director. Dr. Walter Fairservis also provided considerable intellectual stimulation and encouragement as I immersed myself in the field of Indus studies, and I have dedicated this book to the memory of these two great scholars and teachers.

I am also grateful to my colleagues Dr. Richard H. Meadow (Harvard University and Co-Director at Harappa), Dr. Rita P. Wright (New York University and assistant director at Harappa) and Mrs. Barbara A. Dales for their considerable discussion and constructive criticisms of my investigations of the Indus cities. It would be impossible to list all of the many scholars who have influenced my interpretations of the Indus civilization, but I would especially like to thank some of the people who have been willing to share information and provide important feedback on my work: Drs. Mohammad Rafique Mughal, Farzand Durrani, Farid Khan, Bridget Allchin, F. Raymond Allchin, Jim G. Shaffer, Gregory L. Possehl, M. Usman Erdosy, Maurizio Tosi, Michael Jansen, Massimo Vidale, Kuldeep K. Bhan, Ute Frank-Vogt, Ravindra Singh Bisht and Alexandra Ardeleanu-Jansen, Robert H, Dyson, Jr., Vince C. Piggott, Gerald Berreman, J. Desmond Clark and Carla Sinopoli. Special thanks go to Jean-François Jarrige, Catherine Jarrige, Monique Lechevallier and Gonzaque Quivron for sharing information on the recent work of the French Archaeological Mission at Mehrgarh and Nausharo. I would also like to thank Asko Parpola for his contributions to the study of the Indus script.

Much of the data presented in this book derives from recent excavations at Harappa by the Harappa Archaeological Research Project, and I would like to thank all of the colleagues who have participated in the research at Harappa and have helped to collect and analyze the data. These individuals include: Mohammad Siddique, Bahadur Khan, and Habibullah Nasir, curators at Harappa Museum; and the physical anthropologists who worked at Harappa in 1987 and 1988: Drs. Kenneth A. R. Kennedy, John R. Lukacs, Brian Hemphill and Nancy Lovell and Many interpretations presented in this book derive from teaching classes at the University of Wisconsin - Madison; I thank my students for their stimulating discussions and comments on my various papers and lectures which form the foundation of the interpretations presented in this book. Special thanks go to Seetha Reddy, William R. Belcher, Heather M.-L. Miller, and P. Christy Jenkins.

My work on crafts of the Indus Valley civilization would not have been possible without the assistance of numerous master craftsmen in both Pakistan and India. Of these, the most important are Mohammad Nawaz, master potter from Harappa, Pakistan, and Aswini Kumar Nandi, shell bangle maker from Bishnupur, West Bengal, India and Inayat Hussain, agate bead maker from Khambhat, India. My work on the crafts and cultures of the subcontinent has been greatly influenced through interaction and support from numerous colleagues and friends from around the world. Special thanks goes to Francine Berkowitz, Jeffrey T. LaRiche, Richard Kurin, Rajeev Sethi, Renée Altman and Willam Miller.

The editorial assistance of Patricia Powell at the University of Wisconsin - Madison, has been invaluable in preparing the manuscript and organizing the numerous illustrations for this book. I would specifically like to thank her for helping to ensure that the text and illustrations present a concise and easily understood text on the Indus Valley civilization. The excellent design of this book is due to the patience and hard work of David Alcorn, whose artistic sensitivity is revealed in the presentation of images and accompanying text in manner that leads the reader from one section to the next in an uninterrupted flow.

Finally I would like to acknowledge the invaluable support from my parents, Dr. Quentin D. and Mrs. Marleah J. Kenoyer, and family, who have provided unflagging moral support throughout the long and difficult process of doing research, writing, compiling, editing and fundraising for this book and the exhibition.

J. M. K.

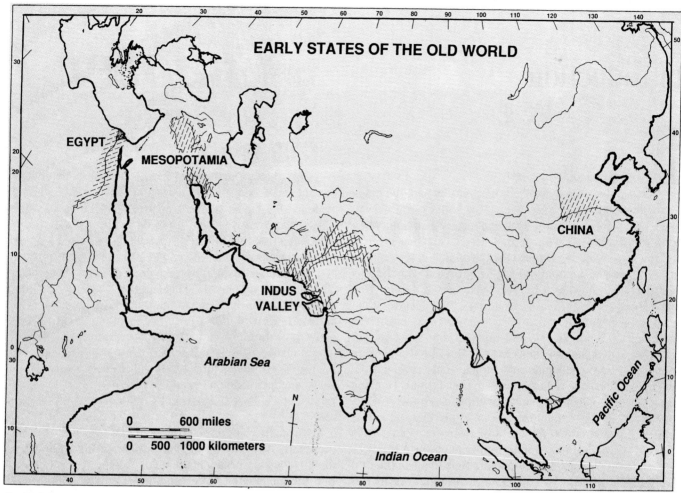

EARLY STATES OF THE OLD WORLD

EGYPT

MESOPOTAMIA

INDUS VALLEY

CHINA

Arabian Sea

Pacific Ocean

Indian Ocean

0   600 miles

0   500 1000 kilometers

N

Fig. 1.3. Early states of the Old World.

how to resolve conflicts, what to do with surplus food and wealth and how to pass on knowledge from one generation to the next. In each region of the world people made choices and established cultural patterns that set a framework for each succeeding generation.

For example, during the Neolithic period at the site of Mehrgarh, Pakistan (6500-4500 B.C.) burials were often accompanied by grave offerings of sacrificed animals, ornaments and/or tools.[2] In some cases young children had more elaborate ornaments than adults. Then, during the later Chalcolithic (Period III, 4500-3500 B.C.) something changed. Although the settlement had become a center for craft production and trade, producing ornaments and decorated ceramics, few of these valuable commodities are found in the graves, which consisted of simple burials with only a few minor ornaments. In the later Indus cities (2600 to 1900 B.C.) we also see the production of valuable ornaments and fancy ceramics, but the burials remain relatively simple.[3]

The change in burial customs at Mehrgarh and the relatively simple burial practices of the Indus cities represent cultural choices that differed from those we see in Mesopotamia. In the Indus cities, valuable ornaments and wealth were not buried with the dead but continued in circulation to be enjoyed or used for profit by succeeding generations. Whereas subsistence and technology are limited

or influenced by the environment in which people live, burial customs and religious beliefs, as well as forms of political organization, result more from choices made by individuals or communities. Nine-thousand years ago, such communities were made up of farmers, herders and artisans as well as spiritual and political leaders. Scattered along the piedmont and the Indus plains, these communities built the foundation for the eventual rise of the distinct culture known as the Indus Valley civilization.

While the origins of the Indus Valley civilization can be traced to much earlier periods, the specific events that led to its rise remain obscure in part because its writing remains undeciphered. Most of the ancient languages of Egypt and Mesopotamia have long since been deciphered. Their inscribed monuments and extensive libraries have provided scholars with unique perspectives on the history of these regions, and the daily life, religion and political organization of their peoples. In contrast, the language of the Indus Valley civilization remains a mystery. The thousands of short inscriptions were written in a script that has no ancient parallels and cannot be connected to any known script of a later period.[4] In spite of not being able to read what the Indus people wrote about themselves, a few scholars from around the world working in Pakistan and India have begun to unravel some mysteries of the Indus cities.

Table 1.1. Comparative timeline for early states of the Old World.

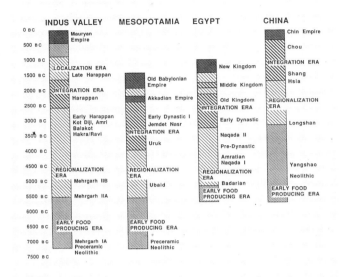

	INDUS VALLEY	MESOPOTAMIA	EGYPT	CHINA
0 BC	Mauryan Empire			Chin Empire
500 BC				Chou
1000 BC	LOCALIZATION ERA		New Kingdom	INTEGRATION ERA
1500 BC	Late Harappan	Old Babylonian Empire		Shang / Hsia
2000 BC	INTEGRATION ERA / Harappan	Akkadian Empire	Middle Kingdom	REGIONALIZATION ERA
2500 BC			Old Kingdom / INTEGRATION ERA	
3000 BC	Early Harappan, Kot Diji, Amri, Balakot, Hakra/Ravi	Early Dynastic I, Jemdet Nasr	Early Dynastic	Longshan
3500 BC		INTEGRATION ERA / Uruk	Naqada II	
			Pre-Dynastic	
4000 BC			Amratian Naqada I	
4500 BC	REGIONALIZATION ERA	REGIONALIZATION ERA	REGIONALIZATION ERA	Yangshao
5000 BC	Mehrgarh IIB	Ubaid	Badarian	Neolithic
5500 BC	Mehrgarh IIA		EARLY FOOD PRODUCING ERA	EARLY FOOD PRODUCING ERA
6000 BC				
6500 BC	EARLY FOOD PRODUCING ERA	EARLY FOOD PRODUCING ERA		
7000 BC	Mehrgarh IA Preceramic Neolithic	Preceramic Neolithic		
7500 BC				

The major contribution to this success has been through archaeological excavations and studies of many different types of artifacts—the objects, architecture and physical remains of the people who lived in the cities and villages. Studies of crafts, social organization and belief systems among modern communities in South Asia also have contributed to a better understanding of the past. Additional insights into the complex patterns of continuity and change are provided by historians, linguists and physical anthropologists. Together, these multidisciplinary approaches have succeeded in revealing the accomplishments of the Indus people in a way that was hardly conceivable when the cities were first discovered in the 1920s.

Today, over 1500 settlements of the Indus Valley civilization have been discovered, and they are spread out over 680,000 square kilometers of northwestern South Asia, an area twice the size of ancient Egypt or Mesopotamia. For 700 years, from around 2600 to 1900 B.C., the Indus cities and the intervening networks of smaller settlements dominated the regions of what are now Pakistan and northwestern India. The establishment of large cities, where people from many different social classes and occupational backgrounds lived side by side, created the need for new forms of social organization. Maintaining law and order within the city would have been a major concern to the rulers, along with establishing mechanisms for the distribution of food and water and the disposal of waste. Without the aid of written texts we find it difficult to understand fully how these early Indus cities functioned, but we can learn much by studying specific types of archaeological objects. For example, we know that specialized crafts and new technologies were developed to create painted pottery, elaborate ornaments, seals, writing and new forms of ritual objects. Some objects may have been used to differentiate the various classes of peoples living in the cities. Gold and precious stones were probably worn by the rulers, whereas the common people most likely adorned themselves with imitations made of clay and soapstone. Painted pottery with important religious symbols and decorative motifs appears to have been available to all of the different classes and may have served as one of the unifying cultural symbols (see fig. 1.1). Disposable pottery drinking cups were made in the urban centers, possibly to address the new problems, such as hygiene or even ritual purity (fig. 1.4). Along with the general similarities in style and symbol over this vast area, specific regional styles also give us some insight into the many different communities that were integrated in these first cities of the subcontinent.

We do not know who the actual rulers of these cities were, but they may have been wealthy merchants, powerful landlords or spiritual leaders. These rulers controlled vast trade networks that funneled raw materials from distant Central Asia, Oman and peninsular India to urban workshops. Local exchange networks redistributed the finished goods; agricultural and pastoral communities provided food for the urban centers. The early farmers of the Indus Valley raised a variety of grains and cash crops, such as cotton. They kept herds of livestock, including the water buffalo and the famous humped cattle known as the zebu. Artisans living in these cities developed elegant objects out of bronze,

Fig. 1.4. Terracotta disposable drinking cups with seal impressions, Mohenjo-daro, cat. nos. 193, 194 (left and center).

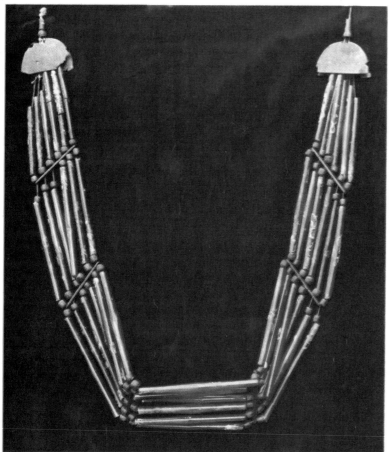

Fig. 1.5. Belt or necklace made from carnelian and bronze beads from Mohenjo-daro, cat. no. 47.

gold and sliver, terracotta, glazed ceramic and semiprecious stones. Many of the most exquisite objects are extremely small and were often made from raw materials that were transformed through complex techniques of manufacture. Their craftsmanship demonstrates a total control of the medium and the ability to capture the essence of a symbol or figure with a few delicate strokes. The small scale of Indus art objects suggests that craftsmanship and technical qualities were more desirable than gross monumentality. Fired steatite seals with animal motifs and the undeciphered script are perhaps the most commonly known objects, but elaborately decorated terracotta figurines, carved ivory dice, ornaments of gold and semiprecious stones (fig. 1.5), as well as miniature squirrels and monkeys made in glazed faience clearly reflect the versatility and technical expertise of the ancient artisans.

Another way to understand this society is to study the burials that have been uncovered in several cemeteries located at some of the larger towns and cities. The types of objects included with the dead give an insight into beliefs of an afterlife, and the careful study of the skeletal remains themselves help us to understand more about the health and physical characteristics of the people living in the cities.

Perhaps the most intriguing aspects of the ancient Indus culture are the religion and politics, which appear to have been closely intertwined. The mythical unicorn commonly illustrated on seals may have been a symbol of a

merchant clan as well as an object of veneration (fig. 1.6). Stone sculptures such as the famous "priest-king" from Mohenjo-daro may represent some of the ruling elites or elders of this large city. The clay female figurines found at the large sites are often described as mother goddesses (fig. 1.7), and the male figures with horned headdresses may represent gods. Clay animal figurines may represent sacrificial animals, whereas carved animal motifs could indicate totemic animals or clan symbols. Other geometric symbols such as the swastika and many distinctive floral motifs also probably represent specific ritual symbols.

Many scholars have tried to correlate Indus symbols and ritual objects with those used by later Hindu and Buddhist cultures. Although some characters and narrative scenes on the Indus seals and tablets are similar to those used in later times, as long as we do not understand the writing, we can never be certain about their precise meaning. Some meanings may have changed, but given the continuities in the archaeological and historical record, we can see long-term patterns in the use of specific objects and symbols. These patterns in themselves are significant and can help us to begin to understand the nature of early Indus religion and the political systems.

Until the 1970s, scholars thought that this civilization along with its spectacular achievements evolved quite mysteriously and then disappeared, leaving little or no legacy for later cultures. However, as new sites have been discovered and previously excavated sites restudied, scholars are now able to show how this civilization disintegrated gradually, leaving the field open for the development of a second major urban civilization during the first millennium B.C.

Although there were some important changes in social and religious organization, we have no evidence for new populations entering into the subcontinent and replacing the indigenous people of the Indus Valley. In fact, there are significant continuities in subsistence activities, technologies, economic networks, urban organization and possibly socio-ritual as well as political structures.

Fig. 1.6. Steatite pendant from Mohenjo-daro depicting the mythical unicorn and many sacred symbols of the Indus religion, cat. no. 10.

Contrary to the common notion that Indo-Aryan-speaking peoples invaded the subcontinent and obliterated the culture of the Indus people, we now believe that there was no outright invasion; the decline of the Indus cities was the result of many complex factors. Overextended economic and political networks, the drying up of major rivers as well as the rise of new religious communities all contributed in some way to the creation of a new social order. More than one-thousand years later, between 600 and 300 B.C. as new cities grew up in the Ganga and Yamuna river valleys and peninsular India, the classical Hindu and Buddhist civilizations of ancient India were established. Many of the technologies, architectural styles, artistic symbols and aspects of social organization that characterize these later cities can be traced to the earlier Indus culture.[5]

Even today, in the modern cities and villages of Pakistan and India, we see the legacy of the Indus cities reflected in traditional arts and crafts, as well as in the layout of houses and settlements. These remnants of the past do not represent a stagnation of culture but rather highlight the optimal choices made by the Indus people. Given the availability of similar natural resources and raw materials, modern potters and glazemakers use many of the same production processes and firing techniques (fig. 1.8). The goldsmiths and agate beadmakers who make ornaments for modern city dwellers still use many techniques that were first discovered by the ancient Indus jewelers. Bronzeworkers who make utensils and sculptures have preserved many ancient techniques. Bone carvers of today have replaced the ivory workers of the past, but they continue to produce similar ornaments, gaming pieces and inlay.

Archaeologists studying the manufacturing techniques and artistic styles of these modern artisans have been able to reconstruct how the ancient artisans produced their striking objects. We can also study some relationships between these crafts and traditional trading practices in order to understand better the economic organization of the ancient Indus cities.[6] By combining the results of these craft studies with similar information on agricultural, pastoral and fishing communities, archaeologists are just beginning to bring to light the hidden faces of the ancient Indus people and provide voices for the mute artifacts that they have left behind.

Fig. 1.7. Terracotta mother goddess figurine with flower headdress and elaborate ornaments, Harappa, cat. no. 133.

Fig. 1.8. Master craftsman Mohammed Sajid Ansari of Multan, Pakistan, uses a squirrel-hair brush and copper oxide pigments to decorate a large tile with complex floral motifs. After being coated with a transparent glaze and fired, the design will become dark blue and light blue on white, like the minaret and tiles in the background. The first use of blue-glazed ceramics in this region, in the form of amulets, ornaments and miniature vessels, can be traced back over 5000 years to the faience technology of the Indus Valley cities.

Discovering the Indus Civilization

The discovery of the Indus Valley civilization reads like a mystery novel about archaeologists and historians who were looking for one thing and discovered something totally different and immensely more significant. In the early 1800s after the collapse of the Mughal Empire, the British East India Company had extended its control from Bengal in the east to the borders of the Punjab, which was ruled by the charismatic Sikh military leader, Maharaja Ranjit Singh.

In 1826, British Army deserter James Lewis, posing as an American engineer named Charles Masson, recorded the existence of mounded ruins at a small town in the Punjab called Harappa. Masson was not an archaeologist and only noted the presence of a vast ruined city with the remains of a "ruinous brick castle" and fragments of walls and buildings.[7] He was followed by the energetic young explorer Alexander Burnes in 1831, who was scouting out the region for its commercial and strategic potential.

The Punjab came under British control after 1849, and, with the building of canals, roads and bridges, it became one of the most prosperous agricultural provinces of the empire. During this period Alexander Cunningham, the director of the recently formed Archaeological Survey of India, visited the mounds in 1853 and 1856 as he searched for the cities of the Buddhist period that had been visited by early Chinese pilgrims.[8] Over the next fifty years numerous other scholars and officials passed by the site and confirmed the presence of an ancient city, but no one had any idea of its age or importance.

In the meantime British railway engineers were preparing to connect the northern city of Lahore to Multan some 320 kilometers to the south. Usually railway beds are constructed with crushed rock and gravel, but due to the lack of stone in the plains, they were prepared to use crushed brick rubble instead. There were many mounds along the ancient trade route from Lahore to Multan, and the massive brick buildings and vast quantities of brick rubble that lay scattered across the surface of sites such as Harappa were a convenient and cheap source of raw material for the contractors. The site had already been used to supply bricks for buildings in the modern town of Harappa, but beginning as early as the 1850s the contractors began the systematic removal of brick buildings and rubble from the site for constructing the railway bed.

Many of the largest mounds were situated approximately one day's walking journey apart (10 to 15 kilometers), and each represented a large walled city built primarily with baked bricks. Some mounds could easily be identified as cities mentioned in ancient Buddhist and Hindu texts as well as in later Greek accounts. The largest collection of mounds is found at Harappa, which is situated approximately halfway between Lahore and Multan (figs. 1.9 and 1.10). Cunningham thought that Harappa might have been the city

Fig. 1.9. In 1920, the northeastern corner of the highest mound at Harappa was still littered with brick rubble and huge pits left by brick robbers. The mud-brick core is all that is left of what was one of the massive brick walls reported by Charles Masson. © Archaeological Survey of India, New Delhi.

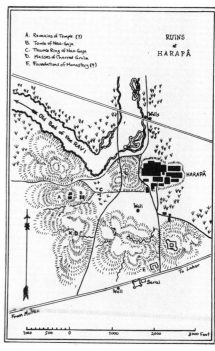

Fig. 1.10. Map of Harappa in 1873, after Cunningham 1875.

of *Po-fa-to*, which was described by the early Chinese Bud- dhist pilgrim Hsüang-tsang (A.D. 625 to 645). This city, which was said to be over three miles in circumference (5 kilome- ters) was a thriving urban center with four Buddhist stupas and twelve monasteries with over 1000 monks. The city also had at least twenty Brahmanical temples. Although there has been some controversy about the identification of Harappa with *Po-fa-to*,[9] the ancient mounds of Harappa did cover a three-mile circuit and consisted of massive ruins of baked brick buildings.

Cunningham made several small excavations at Harappa between 1856 and 1872 to search for more clues, but he was unable to stop the devastation of brick-robbing, and the upper layers of the site had been virtually destroyed

by 1872 (fig. 1.11). His own excavations were disappointing because he did not find the Buddhist remains for which he was looking. Instead, he grudgingly reported meager discoveries of ancient pottery, a few stone tools, some worked shell and a badly preserved stone seal with curious motifs. The seal had a knob on the back with a small hole. On the front was a strange one-horned animal resembling a bull that did not have a hump. Above the animal was a short inscription in a script that did not relate to any other known writing of the ancient world.[10]

After Cunningham had published his finds and the unique seal with its strange motifs, many scholars became interested in learning more about Harappa. In 1920, John Marshall, the director of the Archaeological Survey of India,

Fig. 1.11. The modern city of Harappa is built on part of the ancient site, and many houses built before the 1920s were constructed with bricks robbed from the high mounds that still rise over 13 meters above the plain.

sent his field officer Daya Ram Sahni to begin new excavations at Harappa (fig. 1.12). One year later another archaeologist, R. D. Banerji, began excavating at the site of Mohenjo-daro, some 570 kilometers to the south, in what is now Sindh, Pakistan (fig. 1.13). Banerji was also in search of Buddhist remains, and even though he did discover a ruined Buddhist stupa, he also found numerous seals and ceramics similar to those recovered at Harappa. In addition to the writing and the seals, excavations at Mohenjo-daro revealed a well-planned city with elaborate drainage systems, massive brick buildings, stone sculptures, bronze tools, gold ornaments and cubical chert weights (fig. 1.14).

Fig. 1.12.Deep digging to reveal the massive structure known as the great granary at Harappa, Pakistan. Punjab Vol. 35, No. 3826.© Archaeological Survey of India, New Delhi.

John Marshall thought that the evidence at both sites was sufficient to announce to the world the discovery of a new civilization that was older than any previously known in the subcontinent. At that time he did not venture to say how old it was, but suggested that it lasted for several centuries and had disappeared before the rise of the early historic Mauryan Empire in the third century B.C. Concerning the origins of this civilization, he was the first to propose that it had developed in the Indus Valley itself and was not intrusive from regions to the west. He published his findings with photographs of the seals and other objects in the *Illustrated London News* (20 September 1924), and within

Fig. 1.13. Hundreds of workmen were employed during the 1925-26 season to excavate and expose the well-preserved brick houses in the DK-E area of Mohenjo-daro. © Archaeological Survey of India, New Delhi.

Fig. 1.14. Dating between 2600-1900 B.C. the city of Mohenjo-daro is composed of many different mounds such as the HR area with its vast neighborhoods built of baked brick. In the distance is a higher mound referred to as the citadel, on top of which the remains of a Buddhist period stupa (2nd century A.D.) can be seen.

a week had responses from scholars who had discovered similar seals at ancient Susa dating to the mid-third millennium B.C. At that time, Susa, the capital of a region of southwestern Iran known as Elam, was often at war with the Sumerian cities in the southern Tigris and Euphrates river valley in southern Iraq. When seals and comparable objects were reported from excavations in the Sumerian cities, it became clear that the relationships between the Indus Valley, Elam and Sumer were not simply coincidental. To complicate the story, excavations along the Arabian Gulf in Bahrain, Oman and the United Arab Emirates began turning up seals and other Indus-related objects as well.

Instead of resolving the mystery of the Indus Valley civilization, these discoveries raised new and more intriguing questions. How old are the Indus cities? Who were the Indus people, and how did they relate to the peoples of ancient Mesopotamia? How did they build such magnificent cities? What was their language? And finally, what led to the decline and disappearance of their unique civilization? New excavations were undertaken, and different research strategies were developed to answer these questions. Each generation of scholars has added to our understanding of these ancient cities, but every now and then a new discovery revives the mystery, and a new wave of investigation begins.

Chronology

The scribes of ancient Mesopotamia, writing in the distinctive wedge-shaped script known as cuneiform, were the first to make lists of kings along with the years that they reigned. After cuneiform writing was deciphered in the nineteenth century, these texts were translated, and the dates were soon correlated to later known historical events. On the basis of this information, archaeologists were able to reconstruct general chronologies for the early cities in Mesopotamia. Consequently, when Indus seals and motifs began turning up in Mesopotamian cities (fig. 1.15), it was not long before a general time frame for the Indus Valley civilization had been proposed.

Sir John Marshall thought that the Indus seals found at Mesopotamian cities of Ur and Kish belonged to the Intermediate Period at Mohenjo-daro, and in 1931 he suggested that the Indus cities flourished between 3250 and 2750 B.C.[11] This dating was provisional, and after more than twenty years new discoveries combined with revisions of the Mesopotamian chronologies led Sir Mortimer Wheeler to propose 2500 B.C. as the beginning of the Indus cities and 1500 B.C. as their demise. This terminal date was based on the approximate dating of the Rig Vedic hymns, but he later revised it to around 1700 B.C.[12]

Fig. 1.15. Steatite cylinder seal from Susa, Iran. The motifs on this seal, typical of Harappan square seals, depict a short-horned bull bison with head lowered, feeding from a basin. A second bull bison figure is visible, and a long inscription appears above the two animals. Louvre, Sb 2425. © Musee du Louvre and Pierre and Maurice Chuzeville.

Table 1.2. General Chronology of South Asia.

ARCHAEOLOGICAL / HISTORICAL EVENTS	GENERAL DATES
Palaeolithic	
Earliest stone tools	+ 2MYA to 700,000
Lower Palaeolithic	+700,000 - 100,000
Middle Palaeolithic	100,000 to 30,000
Upper Palaeolithic	30,000 to 10,000
Epi-Palaeolithic	10,000 +/-1000
"Mesolithic" transition	10,000 to 6500 B.C.
INDUS VALLEY TRADITION	
Early Food Producing Era	
Neolithic/Chalcolithic	ca. 6500 to 5000 B.C.
Regionalization Era	
Early Harappan Phase	ca. 5000 to 2600 B.C.
Integration Era	
Harappan Phase	2600 to 1900 B.C.
Localization Era	
Late Harappan Phase	1900 to 1300 B.C.
POST-INDUS OR INDO-GANGETIC TRADITION	
Regionalization Era	
Painted Grey Ware	ca. 1200 to 800 B.C.
Northern Black Polished Ware	700 or 500 to 300 B.C.
Early Historic Period begins around 600 B.C.	
Buddha (Siddhartha Gautama)	563-483 B. C. (or 440-360 B. C.)
Panini (Sanskrit grammarian)	ca. 500-400 B. C.
Alexander of Macedon receives "submission" and becomes the "ally" of Ambhi, King of Taxila, 326 B. C.	
Integration Era	
Mauryan Empire	
Chandragupta Maurya	ca. 317 - 298 B. C.
Kautilya (Minister of Chandragupta, possible author of Arthashastra)	
Bindusara	298-274 B. C.
Ashoka	274-232 B. C.

Many scholars were not satisfied with these relative dating methods, which relied on distant Mesopotamian chronologies, but it was not until after the introduction of the radiocarbon dating technique in the 1950s that the situation began to change. During his excavations at Mohenjo-daro in 1964-65, George F. Dales collected the first series of samples for radiocarbon dating from the latest levels of the city. Unfortunately, he was unable to reach the earliest levels because they were submerged beneath the high water table. No further major excavations have been undertaken at Mohenjo-daro, and the origins of this city remain obscure, but Dales was able to fulfill his goals through excavations at the city of Harappa.

From 1986 to 1996, excavations at Harappa have produced over seventy new radiocarbon dates that help to refine the chronology of the urban centers.[13] Other excavations at smaller towns and villages throughout the Indus Valley and beyond have produced hundreds of additional radiocarbon dates.[14] Taken all together, these dates indicate that the origin and spread of this civilization were not a uniform process and that there were time lags in some regions.[15]

In general the formation of large urban centers such as Mohenjo-daro and Harappa, located in the core areas of the Indus Valley, can be dated from around 2600 to 1900 B.C. In speaking of cultures, however, 700 years is an extremely long time, spanning nearly 30 generations. Many important changes in social organization, politics, language and even religion took place during the lives of these cities. We know that in Mesopotamia and Egypt many kingdoms rose and fell within a period of even 100 years, and along with changes in politics there was often a change in the religious order. The recent studies at the site of Harappa are helping to rectify this problem, so that it is now possible to identify and date several major phases in the growth and development of the city. Changes in artifact styles and painted pottery motifs are also being identified. However, it is still premature to apply these findings to other cities such as Mohenjo-daro, and for the purposes of this book we must be content with the big chronological picture.

After around 1900 B.C. the centralized economic and political power of the Indus cities weakened, and the regions controlled by their rulers began to fragment into smaller units. There was no longer any trade contact with distant Mesopotamia or the Gulf regions, and the focus of interaction shifted to the east, towards the Ganga river valley.

Terminology and Theoretical Frameworks

Although it is now possible to date reliably the Indus Valley civilization, we still have only limited consensus regarding terminology and the theoretical framework within which to study the origin and decline of this culture. This is partly due to the fact that scholars working in the region are scattered among Pakistan, India, Europe, America and Japan, each with differing academic traditions and historical perspectives. In this book I use the general term *Indus Valley civilization* to refer to the period of urban expansion and cultural integration that encompassed a very large geographical region. When speaking more specifically about the processes of cultural development, I will use a more complex terminology that has been developed over the past ten years through the efforts of Jim Shaffer and other scholars. This terminology reflects a comprehensive theoretical and chronological framework that is both meaningful and at the same time flexible enough to accommodate the ever-changing archaeological data base.[16]

Instead of seeing the Indus cities as an isolated phenomenon associated with a brief phase of urbanism, Shaffer proposed the term *Indus Valley Tradition*, using a concept borrowed from American archaeology.[17] The Indus Valley tradition refers to the total phenomenon of human adaptations, beginning with the domestication of plants and animals, that resulted in the integration of diverse communities throughout the greater Indus Valley and adjacent regions.[18] Shaffer identifies two other cultural traditions in Baluchistan and the Helmand basin that evolved alongside the developments in the Indus Valley. As more research is conducted in peninsular India, we can expect to see additional cultural traditions being defined to the east of the Indus Valley.

The Indus Valley tradition can be divided into four different eras that are distinguished by the following characteristics.

Early Food-producing Era: During this period people lived in scattered villages and nomadic camps, with an economy based on food production. No elaborate ceramic technology had been developed at this time.

Regionalization Era: This is a long period during which numerous crafts were invented, including ceramics, metallurgy, lapidary arts, glazed faience and sealmaking. Distinct artifact styles evolved in specific regions, and different regions were connected by trade networks.

Integration Era: This relatively short period of time saw the integration of many different regional cultures, resulting in a pronounced homogeneity in material culture over a large geographical area.

Localization Era: Comparable to the *Regionalization Era*, this period sees the breakdown of the previously integrated culture into smaller localized groups. Local trade networks and artifact styles show a continuity from the previous period.[19]

Each era can also be subdivided into phases, which are characterized by specific types of artifacts, painted pottery and technologies. A phase is limited to a specific region and period of time, but there can be some overlap and linkage between phases through exchange networks. This analytical framework allows archaeologists to organize and compare cultural developments in adjacent regions and understand changes over time.

The Early Food-producing Era of the Indus Valley tradition is represented at the site of Mehrgarh Periods IA, IB, and IIA (around 6500 to around 5000 B.C.), where there is conclusive evidence for the use of domestic wheat and barley and domestic cattle, sheep and goats. The small rectangular mud-brick houses of this site were subdivided into rooms and cubicles that could have been used for storage of grain and other necessities. Baskets coated with bitumen have been discovered in the houses and graves. The first coarse chaff-tempered ceramics begin to appear at the very end of this period. Numerous ornaments made from sea shells and colorful stones were buried with the dead along with ground stone axes and chert blades.

The Regionalization Era is much longer, extending from about 5000 B.C. to about 2600 B.C. It includes many different phases characterized by different pottery designs, ornaments, architectural developments and methods of farming and animal herding. During this era we see the development of such new technologies as hand-built and then wheel-thrown pottery, copper metallurgy, stone beadmaking and seal carving. Geometric seals were made from terracotta, bone and ivory, and the beginning of writing is seen in the form of graffiti on pottery. Extensive trade networks were established along the major river routes and across mountain passes to connect settlements to each other and facilitate the movement of goods and raw materials.

The later part of the Regionalization Era, often referred to as the Early Harappan Period, represents a phase of formative urbanism. The building of walled settlements, the use of specific types of painted pottery and ornaments, the appearance of seals and rudimentary writing and the expanded trade networks are thought to represent the initial step towards urbanism.

During the Integration Era of the Indus Valley tradition, the Harappa Phase, dating from approximately 2600 to 1900 B.C., features the synthesis of all the different cultural groups into a single overarching system. Unifying symbols appear on painted pottery, ornaments and ritual objects. This is also the phase of urbanism, characterized by large cities and their satellite settlements, writing, the use of standardized weights and measures, taxation and a hierarchical social order.

The main focus of this book is on the Harappa Phase, Integration Era, but in order to clarify the connection between the Indus cities and later cultures of the subcontinent we must summarize briefly the rest of the terminology and chronological framework.

The Localization Era of the Indus Valley tradition is a time of decline and disintegration for the Indus economic and political structure. Each phase during this era represents the emergence and consolidation of localized states or chiefdoms with smaller scale social and political interaction. As the cultures of each region became disconnected from each other, the unifying styles of artifacts of the earlier Indus cites disappeared. Seals and writing were no longer needed, neither were the chert weights that may have been used for taxation. The Localization Era is also the period during which major changes occurred in burial practices and ritual objects. This is also the time when Indo-Aryan languages were becoming common in the northern subcontinent along with the religious traditions that set the foundation for later Hinduism, Jainism and Buddhism. However, the Indus techniques of farming and herding continued to be used along with many of the technologies, such as ceramics, beadmaking, shellworking and metallurgy.

The Localization Era of the Indus Valley tradition links up with a new trajectory of cultural development that encompasses a much larger geographic region extending over both the Ganga-Yamuna river valley as well as the greater Indus river valley (see map). This transformation, generally associated with the rise of early historic states between 600 B.C. and 300 B.C., is focused primarily in the Ganga-Yamuna river valley. I have called this the Indo-Gangetic tradition following the framework outlined above.

The Indo-Gangetic tradition is a more complex phenomenon than the earlier Indus Valley tradition, because it incorporates a larger geographical area as well as new forms of subsistence, technology and political organization. The Regionalization Era of the Indo-Gangetic tradition, 2000 B.C. to 300 B.C., overlaps the localized cultural networks of the Indus Valley tradition. New settlements spread throughout the northern Punjab, the Ganga-Yamuna river valley and the Malwa Plateau. This was a period of synthesis and new inventions. Rice and millet agriculture became widespread in regions watered by the monsoon rains, the use of iron tools and the horse became commonplace. As was the case during the Regionalization Era of the Indus Valley tradition, this period set the foundation for the subsequent developments in the Integration Era.

The Integration Era of the Indo-Gangetic tradition begins around 300 B.C. with the establishment of the Mauryan Empire, after which it is possible to link up with the well-known chronologies of the historical period. We see for the first time an emerging writing system that was used for long

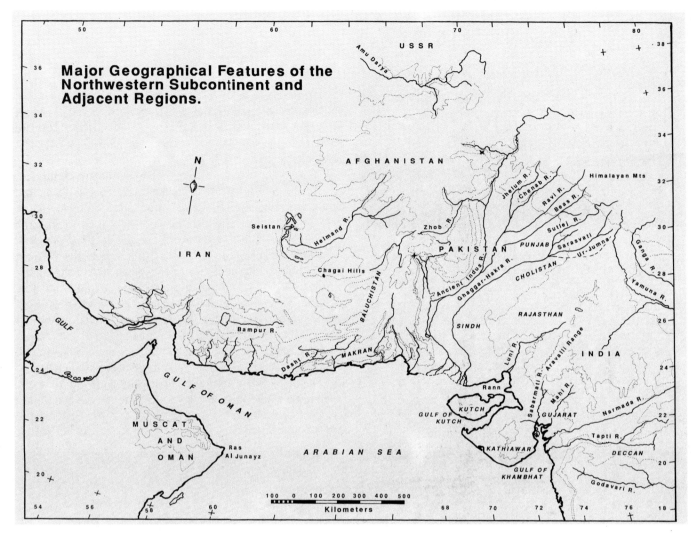

Fig. 1.16. Map of major geographic regions.

texts carved on monumental columns or boulders. The first coins were minted, and standardized weights and measures were introduced. The horse, which had already been known for many centuries, came to be used for long-distance communication and war. Iron technology became quite common for making tools and weapons. Although many aspects of the Indus civilization had disappeared during the intervening period, some technologies, symbols and possibly even religious beliefs had been absorbed and adapted to the newly evolving social order. Although some continuities represent cultural choices, others can be attributed to the environment, which limits the choices that humans can make.

Environmental Setting

On January 21, 1831 Alexander Burnes, a subaltern of the elite British political service, set sail from Kutch on a historic voyage, 1610 kilometers, up the Indus and Ravi rivers to Lahore (fig. 1.16).[20] The official objective of his journey was to bring a gift of five giant English dray horses and a magnificent state carriage to Maharaja Ranjit Singh, the Sikh ruler of the Punjab. Although this was disguised as a courtesy call, no one was fooled about his main goal, secretly to map the river and determine the commercial and strategic importance of the Indus river and its tributaries. Local observers exclaimed that with the knowledge of the Indus river the British would soon be able to control the entire region. Their predictions came true, and within twelve years the British had conquered Sindh; by 1850 they controlled the Punjab as well, thereby adding the entire Indus river valley to their empire.

Some five-thousand years earlier, this vast river plain with its rich agricultural resources was the heartland in which the cities of Indus Valley civilization arose. When British scholars first discovered the ancient cities along the Indus and Ravi rivers, they did not consider the fact that another ancient river, the Saraswati or Ghaggar-Hakra had taken its course along the eastern edge of the plain.[21] Numerous surveys in the deserts of Cholistan and Rajasthan made it clear that large numbers of settlements dating from the fourth to the first millennium B.C. were situated along the banks of this other major river system.[22]

The ancient Indus river, fed by numerous tributaries emerging from the mountains to the north, flowed along the western edge of the vast alluvial plain and ended in a marshy delta near the modern city of Karachi. In the east, the ancient

Fig. 1.17. The mineral-rich mountains of Baluchistan are cut by the Bolan river, which leads to a pass connecting the Quetta Valley and central Baluchistan with the Kachi Plain, a small extension of the greater Indus Valley. The sites of Mehrgarh, Nausharo and Pirak are located in the Kachi Plain at the foot of the pass.

Saraswati (or Ghaggar-Hakra) river ran parallel to the Indus, and some scholars suggest that it reached the sea coast in what is now a swampy salt flat known as the Greater Rann of Kutch. Another explanation is that it joined the Indus at the head of the expansive delta.

Both of these river systems, with their many tributaries, were fed by melting snows and glaciers high in the Himalayan mountains. During the summer rainy season known as the monsoon, the rivers flooded vast tracts of land with fertile silts and left numerous natural reservoirs in the form of oxbow lakes as the waters receded. The tributaries of these rivers provided important links to adjacent regions, connecting the settlements on the plains to important resources and raw materials. From the Indus river, tributaries such as the Bolan, Gomal and Kabul rivers extended to low-altitude passes on the west that led to the plateaus of Baluchistan (fig. 1.17). To the north the Indus itself along with the Jhelum, Chenab and Beas tributaries snaked their way into the forested mountain valleys (fig. 1.18) eventually connecting with the Valley of Kashmir and high-altitude passes into Central Asia and China. In the east, the ancient Saraswati and its major tributaries, the Sutlej and Drishadvati rivers led through the flat plains

Fig. 1.18. Isolated stands of Deodar, pine and oak cling to the rugged slopes enclosing Chitral Valley in the Hindu Kush mountains. During the 3rd millennium B.C. these slopes would have been covered with thick forests.

of north central India into the teak forests of the Siwalik foothills and eventually to the core of the central Himalaya. Although some scholars have suggested that the Yamuna river also flowed into the Saraswati, recent satellite image analysis and geological studies indicate that it always flowed to the east joining with the Ganga system. Nevertheless, the plain between the Saraswati and Yamuna is flat and narrow, providing an important link with the vast plains of the Ganga river valley to the east.

Following the rivers to the south, the Indus originally hugged the western edge of the plain but gradually, through silting and changes in water flow, began creeping to the east (fig. 1.19). The ancient Satluj river also gradually became silted and slowly moved to the west, eventually becoming captured by the Beas to join the Indus system. Toward the end of the Indus Valley civilization, the ancient Saraswati had totally dried up and its original tributaries were captured by two other mighty rivers.

When British scholars first discovered the cities of Mohenjo-daro and Harappa, the Indus river dominated the alluvial plain, hence the name Indus Valley civilization. However, now that we know of the presence of the ancient Saraswati river (also known as the Ghaggar-Hakra along its central stretches), some scholars refer to this culture as the Indus-Saraswati civilization.

The ancient Indus and Saraswati rivers provided the cities with life-giving water that ensured bountiful harvests, rich riverine resources and essential communication routes. These two mighty rivers and their tributaries linked the

Fig. 1.19. The Indus river near Mohenjo-daro still serves as a link between the communities along its banks, and its silt-laden waters renew the fertility of the soil much as it did during the period of the Indus cities.

largest cities with smaller regional towns and distant resource areas, both coastal and inland. Unlike most Mesopotamian city-states, which remained focused on the lands directly watered by the rivers, the Indus cities also extended their direct control to the adjacent regions that were rich in such resources as copper, semiprecious stones and minerals as well as timber.

These regions include the highlands and plateaus to the west of the modern Indus river valley, generally referred to as Baluchistan and located in the modern countries of Pakistan, Afghanistan and Iran. To the northwest and north of the Indus are the mountainous regions of northern Pakistan, Afghanistan, the former provinces of Soviet Central Asia and China.

To the east, the ancient Saraswati (Ghaggar-Hakra) river is bordered by the great Thar desert and the north-

The gradual drying up of the Saraswati river is an event documented both geologically as well as in the sacred Vedic and Brahmanical literature of ancient India. The Rig Veda is a compilation of sacred hymns that was codified in its present form during the mid-second to first millennium B.C. at around the same time as the Indus cities were declining. These hymns tell of a mighty river, the sacred Saraswati, that flowed from the mountains to the sea. Many episodes described in the Vedic literature take place along the sacred Saraswati, but eventually the river disappeared beneath the sands. A later text, the Mahabharata, says that the river, which was personified as a goddess, kept changing its course and adding new channels and oxbow curves to

accommodate all of the sages and righteous people who lived along her banks. The Sutlej river, a tributary of the Saraswati, also figures in some stories recounted in the Mahabharata. The shifting courses of the Sutlej are attributed to an event associated with the sage Vashishta, one of the most important clan leaders of the Vedic period. Although a great man, he had his weaknesses and on one occasion committed incest with his daughter. This led him to try to commit suicide by jumping into the Sutlej river, but the river goddess split herself into a hundred streams to avoid drowning him.[23]

As early as 1887 geologists such as Oldham had begun mapping the ancient beds of the Punjab rivers to show how the drying up of the Saraswati had led to numerous stream channels.[24] Later studies by Wilhelmy

confirmed that the Sutlej did in fact change its course and probably split into hundreds of streams in the process.[25] Eventually the waters of the Sutlej were captured by the Indus system, where they still flow today. The geological and archaeological evidence also confirms that the Saraswati kept changing its course, in the process creating numerous streams. The presence of many archaeological sites along their banks attests to the fact that people continued to live along the river as it shifted its course. Eventually however, the sacred river became totally dry, and tradition says that it disappeared beneath the sands and flowed east to join with the Ganga and Yamuna in a confluence called Tribeni Sangam at the city of Prayag (modern Allahabad, India).

Fig. 1.20. The sea coast west of Karachi provided the Indus cities with shells, fish and harbors. Travel along this coast is not easy because it is extremely rugged and there is little water. Sail boats, however, can follow the coast and eventually cross over to Oman or enter the Persian Gulf.

south Aravalli ranges. To the west of the Indus delta is the arid and rugged coastal region of Pakistan and Iran that is generally referred to as the Makran (fig. 1.20). East of the delta in modern India is the region of Kutch, which was made up of many islands during the prehistoric period, and the larger peninsula of Saurashtra. These two regions are generally grouped together with the mainland coastal plains of Gujarat, but they are in fact three distinct subregions. To the north, the Gujarat plains are bordered by the southern Aravalli ranges and to the east the Vindhya, Satpura and Sahyadripar ranges of central India.

Climate

This vast area is dominated by two different weather systems that sometimes overlap, the winter cyclonic system of the western highlands and the summer monsoon system in the peninsular regions. In the northern subcontinent, the traditional division of the year is in six seasons, beginning with the spring equinox. Spring lasts from the end of February through March, summer covers the hot months of April, May and June. The rainy season begins at the end of June and continues through September when it is followed by the autumn season. Winter and the dewy season are the last two seasons that extend from November through February.

Sometimes these six seasons are grouped as three major seasons with many variations depending on the specific region. Along the southern Indus river in Sindh there is often little or no rain, but the rivers bring down the flood waters from the north and cover the land with rich silts. If the winter and dewy season rains from the western highlands are timely, abundant harvests and vast grazing becomes available along the piedmont and northern Punjab in the spring. These same rains fall as snow in the highlands and water the fields and highland pastures, where the growing season begins in the spring and fields are harvested at the end of summer. When both the winter and summer rains are bountiful, the land is extremely rewarding. Usually one or the other system will provide enough water to sustain agriculture and herding from one year to the next; it is extremely rare for both systems to fail.

The climatic cycle in place today is probably not much different from that experienced by the Indus cities, although evidence suggests that there may have been a stronger summer monsoon and more seasonal fluctuation of temperatures. In July it would have been warmer than at present and in January slightly cooler.[26]

The environmental and climatic diversity of these regions is extremely important; the two complement one another and provide a wide range of resources that are relatively accessible to human communities living in any one region. The Indus cities established settlements in most of these regions and connected them to each other and the urban centers with trade networks. In this way, when harvests or resources in one region were poor, people had the option of obtaining support from other sources. The juxtaposition of mountains, river plains and coasts provides a unique pattern of seasonally available resources and abundant raw materials that is quite different from the situation in either Mesopotamia or Egypt.

■

Endnotes

1. Jonathan Mark Kenoyer, "The Indus Valley Tradition of Pakistan and Western India," *Journal of World Prehistory* 5.4 (1991): 331-85.

2. Pascal Sellier, "The Contribution of Paleoanthropology to the Interpretation of a Functional Funerary Structure: The Graves from Neolithic Mehrgarh Period IB," in *South Asian Archaeology, 1989*, ed. Catherine Jarrige (Madison, Wis.: Prehistory Press, 1992), 253-66; Jean-François Jarrige, "Continuity and Change in the North Kachi Plain (Baluchistan, Pakistan) at the Beginning of the Second Millennium B.C.," in South Asian Archaeology, 1983, ed. J. Schotsmans and M. Taddei (Naples: Istituto Universitario Orientale, 1985), 35-68.

3. George F. Dales and J. Mark Kenoyer, "Excavation at Harappa—1988," *Pakistan Archaeology* 24 (1989): 68-176.

4. Asko Parpola, *Deciphering the Indus Script* (Cambridge: Cambridge University Press, 1994).

5. J. Mark Kenoyer, "Interaction Systems, Specialized Crafts and Culture Change: The Indus Valley Tradition and the Indo-Gangetic Tradition in South Asia," in *The Indo-Aryans of Ancient South Asia: Language, Material Culture and Ethnicity*, ed. George Erdosy (Berlin: de Gruyter, 1995), 213-57.

6. Kenoyer, "The Indus Valley Tradition of Pakistan and Western India"; J. Mark Kenoyer, "Socio-Economic Structures of the Indus Civilization as Reflected in Specialized Crafts and the Question of Ritual Segregation," in *Old Problems and New Perspectives in the Archaeology of South Asia*, ed. J. Mark Kenoyer (Madison, Wis.: UW-Madison Department of Anthropology, 1989), 183-92; Kuldeep K. Bhan, Massimo Vidale and J. Mark Kenoyer, "Harappan Technology: Methodological and Theoretical Issues," *Man and Environment* 19.1-2 (1994): 141-57.

7. Charles Masson, *A Narrative of Various Journeys in Balochistan, Afghanistan and the Punjab* (London: Richard Bently, 1842), vol. 1, 452-55.

8. Sir Alexander Cunningham, "Harappa," *Archaeological Survey, Report 1872-73* (1875): 105-8.

9. Sir John H. Marshall, *Mohenjo-daro and the Indus Civilization* (London: Probsthain, 1931), vol. 1, 102-7.

10. Cunningham, "Harappa."

11. Marshall, *Mohenjo-daro and the Indus Civilization.*

12. R. E. Mortimer Wheeler, *The Indus Civilization,* supplementary volume to *Cambridge History of India* (Cambridge: Cambridge University Press, 1953), 93; R. E. Mortimer Wheeler, *The Indus Civilization,* supplementary volume to *Cambridge History of India* 3rd ed. (Cambridge: Cambridge University Press, 1968), 124-25.

13. J. Mark Kenoyer, "Urban Process in the Indus Tradition: A Preliminary Model from Harappa," *Harappa Excavations 1986-1990,* ed. Richard H. Meadow (Madison, Wis.: Prehistory Press, 1991), 29-60.

14. Gregory L. Possehl, *Radiometric Dates for South Asian Archaeology. An Occasional Publication of the Asia Section* (Philadelphia: University of Pennsylvania Museum, 1994).

15. Gregory L. Possehl, "Revolution in the Urban Revolution: The Emergence of Indus Urbanism," *Annual Review of Anthropology* 19 (1990): 261-82; Gregory L. Possehl, "The Date of Indus Urbanization: A Proposed Chronology for the Pre-urban and Urban Harappan Phases," in *South Asian Archaeology, 1991,* ed. Adalbert J. Gail and Gerd J. R. Mevissen (Stuttgart: Steiner, 1993), 231-49; Jim G. Shaffer, "The Indus Valley, Baluchistan and Helmand Traditions: Neolithic Through Bronze Age," in *Chronologies in Old World Archaeology,* ed. Robert W. Ehrich, 3rd ed. (Chicago: University of Chicago Press, 1992), vol. 1, 441-64.

16. Kenoyer, "Indus Valley Tradition of Pakistan and Western India"; Shaffer, "Indus Valley, Baluchistan and Helmand Traditions: Neolithic Through Bronze Age."

17. Gordon R. Willey and Philip Phillips, *Method and Theory in American Archaeology* (Chicago: University of Chicago Press, 1958), 167-82.

18. Kenoyer, "Indus Valley Tradition of Pakistan and Western India"; Shaffer, "Indus Valley, Baluchistan and Helmand Traditions: Neolithic Through Bronze Age."

19. Kenoyer, "Indus Valley Tradition of Pakistan and Western India"

20. Sir Alexander Burnes, *Travels into Bokhara, Together with a Narrative of a Voyage on the Indus,* 4th ed. (London: John Murray, 1834; reprint Karachi: Oxford University Press, 1973).

21. R. D. Oldham, "On Probable Changes in the Geography of the Punjab and Its Rivers," *Journal of the Asiatic Society of Bengal* 55.2 (1887): 305-67.

22. M. Rafique Mughal, "The Harappan Settlement Systems and Patterns in the Greater Indus Valley (circa 3500 -1500 B.C.)," *Pakistan Archaeology* 25 (1990): 1-72.

23. D. P. Agrawal and R. K. Sood, "Ecological Factors and the Harappan Civilization," in *Harappan Civilization: A Recent Perspective,* ed. Gregory L. Possehl (New Delhi: Oxford and IBH, 1993), 445-54.

24. Oldham, "Probable Changes in the Geography of the Punjab and Its Rivers."

25. Herbert Wilhelmy, "Das Urstromtal am Ostrand der Indusebene und das Sarasvati-Problem," *Zeitschrift fur Geomorphologie* Supplement 8 (1969): 76-93.

26. John E. Kutzbach and COHMAP Members, "Climatic Changes of the Last 18,000 Years: Observations and Model Simulations," *Science* 241 (August 1988): 1043-52.

Fig. 2.1. Tall jar with polychrome geometrical motifs, Mehrgarh, Period V, ca. 3300 B.C., cat. no. 6.

Origins of Urban Society

For over a hundred years, scholars have tried to understand how the first urban civilizations evolved and why they only developed in specific regions of the world. No written records are available from these early stages of urban development, and since archaeological data is the only source of information, it is unlikely that *specific* explanations will ever be possible. However, we can identify factors that set the stage for the establishment of the first cities, and the presence of such factors can explain why early cities developed only in certain regions of the world.

Some factors result from patterns of human adaptation that have their roots in the first stone tool technologies and hunting strategies of the earliest human populations living in the subcontinent. Other factors can be traced to the time when communities began producing their own food by cultivating plants and raising animals. The development of specialized technologies for creating elaborate painted ceramics and ornaments also reflects important economic and social changes that are closely tied to status and ritual beliefs (fig. 2.1). Political and religious changes occurring in conjunction with these other developments helped set the stage for the final rise of cities and state level political organization. This scale of integration occurred only in four geographical regions of the Old World: between 3500 and 2600 B.C. in Mesopotamia, Egypt and the Indus Valley, and around 1500 B.C. in China. In the New World the first integrated state-level societies evolved between 900 and 500 B.C. in Central America and around 900 B.C. in Peru.

When archaeologists first discovered the cities of the Indus civilization, they focused primarily on understanding the nature of the cities and the period immediately preceding their development. Later, as new sites such as Mehrgarh and Nausharo were discovered and excavated, the earlier stages of indigenous development were revealed. Although considerable research remains to be undertaken, we can now follow the long thread of human adaptation in the subcontinent from the first small bands of Stone Age hunters and gatherers to the earliest farming villages and finally the large cities along the Indus and Saraswati rivers.

First Settlers of the Indus Valley

The earliest inhabitants of South Asia belonged to the hominid species *Homo erectus*, the ancestor of modern *Homo sapiens*. These stone tool-using hominids lived in the Potwar plateau region of northern Pakistan over two million years ago where the oldest stone tools have been discovered near the town of Riwat (figs. 2.2, 2.4).[1] Most of the Stone Age or Palaeolithic sites in this part of the subcontinent, however, date to a much later time, between 30,000 and 10,000 years ago. Cave sites, such as Sanghao, and temporary camps of Middle Palaeolithic and Upper Palaeolithic hunters and gatherers have been found along the eastern edge of the Saraswati river in Rajasthan and Gujarat and in the highlands of Baluchistan and Afghanistan to the west of the Indus river. Hundreds of additional camp sites of these mobile hunting bands must lie buried beneath the silts of the Indus and Saraswati river flood plains, but a few have survived on the limestone and chert escarpments of the Rohri hills and at Jerruk in central and southern Sindh (figs. 2.3, 2.4). Perched high above the river plain, bands of hunters and gatherers mined huge nodules of yellow-brown and grayish chert from the soft limestone deposits of these outcrops. Using rounded chert hammerstones and antler punches, they fashioned sharp stone blades and scrapers for making weapons and tools.

Thousands of years later, the chert tools needed by the Indus cities were made on these same rocky hills using techniques that had been developed during the Upper Palaeolithic

Fig. 2.2. Two million year-old stone tool from Riwat, Pakistan.

Fig. 2.3. Chert blades and cores from 5,000 year-old Harappan Phase workshops on the Rohri hills.

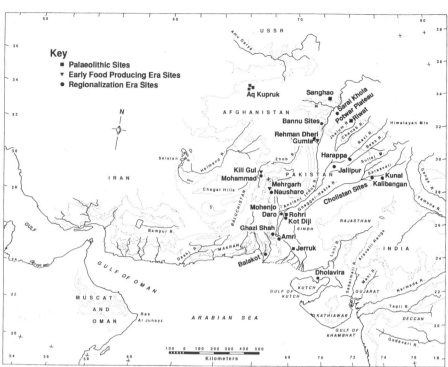

Fig. 2.4. Palaeolithic, Neolithic and Chalcolithic sites of the greater Indus valley.

period. The most important technique was the preparation of prismatic cores from which long parallel-sided blades could be removed. These long stone blades with straight, sharp edges were then snapped into shorter segments or chipped into geometric shapes to make cutting tools or barbed arrow points. During the Upper Palaeolithic, the prismatic cores and hundreds of blades were carried away by the wandering bands for use in their seasonal travels across the stoneless alluvial plains. Other smaller escarpments similar to the Rohri hills are found to the south near the Indus delta; bands of hunters and gatherers traveled to these quarries whenever they needed raw materials for tools. These migration patterns between rocky highlands and quarries established an adaptive strategy for obtaining necessary raw materials that were the basis for the extensive trade networks during later periods.

Stone Tool Technologies

Chert or flint is one of the most important raw materials used in the prehistoric period for making tools. The techniques used in flaking or knapping vary depending on the nature of the raw material and the type of tool needed. Slow heating can remove moisture from the nodule and make it easier to flake rocks that have impurities, but the chert from the Rohri hills, relatively free of impurities, can be flaked easily without heating. When a nodule is first removed from the ground, it is covered with a thick layer of weathered stone or cortex that must be removed to reach the better quality stone in the center of the nodule. A stone hammer made from any handy pebble is used to flake away this cortex layer. This technique is called direct percussion, because the hammer is struck directly against the nodule. Hard-hammer direct percussion prepares a blocklet, or core, from which thin sharp flakes or long blades can then be removed.

During the Upper Palaeolithic period specialized cores were prepared so that fairly uniform, long, thin blades could be removed. The long blades were removed by a more refined technique called indirect percussion, where a small punch made from antler was placed against the core and then struck with a hammer-stone. This technique permitted better control of the force and resulted in longer and thinner blades that had straight parallel sides, with sharp edges. Pressure-flaking, another method used to produce long blades, requires a steady hand and a strong force from a shoulder-held crutch that has a pointed end made from antler.[2]

After a series of blades is removed, the core looks like a many-sided prism, hence the term prismatic core (see fig. 2.3). Parallel-sided blades can be used for cutting or scraping without further modification, but they also can be snapped into shorter segments and hafted with bitumen or resin in a handle to make a sickle (fig. 2.5). Some segments can be chipped to make pointed tools for piercing or drilling, and others can be made into barbs for arrows, harpoons or spears. Blade production was a major revolution in technology because it provided a standardized form that could be modified into many different tools.

Hard-hammer direct percussion, indirect percussion and pressure-flaking are techniques used throughout the world for making blades, but in the Indus Valley and peninsular India a unique technique called inverse indirect percussion was developed (fig. 2.6). This procedure is perhaps the most efficient technique for chert-knapping. A wooden stake with an antler tip is set in the ground, and the core is held at a specific angle against the stake. In this technique the core is struck and pushed against the pointed stake, which is firmly set in the ground. One sharp blow against the core from a wooden or antler hammer can quickly detach a long, parallel-sided blade, and without much effort additional blades can be removed in quick succession. This technique, which may have been invented during the Upper Palaeolithic period in South Asia,[3] was used during the later Indus period, probably with a copper or bronze pointed stake.[4] Today this technique is still used in the agate beadmaking center of Khambhat in western India, where people use iron stakes and buffalo-horn hammers to make roughly shaped beads that are then ground, polished and drilled.[5]

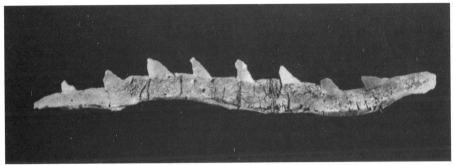

Fig. 2.5. Sickle made of chert blades set in bitumen (natural tar). The original wooden handle is not preserved. Mehrgarh, Period V, ca. 3300 B.C.

No Upper Palaeolithic sites with animal bones have been found in the Indus Valley, but on high rocky outcrops near modern Karachi piles of oyster shells associated with scattered stone blades suggest that some bands fished and collected shellfish from the estuaries and delta of the Indus river. Further to the east, inland camps of Upper Palaeolithic hunters and gatherers in the jungles and deserts of Gujarat and Rajasthan reveal the continuous occupation of these regions from 30,000 B.C. to after 10,000 B.C.[6] Thousands of years later, as village communities became established in the central and northern Indus Valley, the descendants of the early coastal hunter-gatherers supplied marine resources such as shell and dried fish for inland trade. In much the same way, the later communities living in the eastern deserts and jungles provided raw materials that were needed for the workshops in the villages and cities of the Indus Valley.

To the west of the Indus, in the rocky piedmont and highlands of Baluchistan and Afghanistan, there is ample stone suitable for making tools and grinding implements. Rivers filled with rounded pebbles of gray black chert, sandstone and quartzite made it unnecessary for people to congregate at a single locality for essential raw materials. However, during the cold glacial periods people probably migrated to the highlands only during the spring and summer, when game and wild plants were available.

In the 1960s Louis Dupree found stone tools and animal bones at two cave sites and an open-air camp site at Aq

Fig. 2.6. Inverse indirect percussion technique used to make blades in Khambhat, India.

Kupruk in northern Afghanistan (fig. 2.4), enabling archaeologists to reconstruct the general lifestyle of these communities. Between 30,000 and 15,000 B.C. during the Middle and Upper Palaeolithic periods, the hunters went after a wide range of game but were most successful with the wild mountain sheep, goats, and possibly cattle (*Bos primigenius*).[7] Grinding stones and mullers or pestles provide indirect evidence for the processing of plant foods, as they may have been used for grinding nuts or roasted wild grain. Evidence for wild barley has been found in the earliest Neolithic levels at Mehrgarh, which suggests that it would have been present during the preceding Palaeolithic period, and may have been indigenously domesticated.[8] Although domesticated einkorn and emmer wheat must have originated further to the west in the Zagros mountains, bread wheat may have been indigenously domesticated from them, based on the distribution of the wild progenitors of bread wheat. Native fruits such as the wild apricot, pomegranate and apple would also have been abundant in these regions in the spring and summer and may have been used to sweeten their diet.

At the end of the Pleistocene glacial period between 12 and 10,000 years ago, some communities may have lived all year around in the highland valleys, but many bands continued to move back to the plains in the cold winters. Numerous archaeological sites have been found at springs along the piedmont or in the river valleys at the foot of the passes, where fish and game as well as edible wild plants were available.

Further to the west in the Zagros mountains (Iran and Iraq), as well as in the Levant (Israel, Syria and Palestine) similar patterns of seasonal movement and dependence on specific animals and plants were going on during this same period. Some hunting-and-gathering bands returned to the same locality each year and eventually constructed more permanent houses out of mud or stone, reeds and thatch. They began systematically to exploit specific types of plants (wheat, barley, lentils) and animals (sheep, goats, cattle and pigs), which eventually became domesticated.

Almost every excavation reveals a slightly different pattern of subsistence. At the site of Jericho in the Levant (Pre-pottery Neolithic A around 8350-7350 B.C.) hunting was supplemented by planting wheat (emmer) and barley (two-row hulled). Further east at the site of Ali Kosh (southwest Iran) from 8000 to 6500 B.C. the dependence on wild resources gradually shifted to domestic plants and animals.[9]

Scholars once thought that the domestication of plants and animals began in one small region and spread throughout the Near East, but continued research and better dating techniques have shown that, in fact, domestication of some plants and animals began independently in different areas at approximately the same time.

However, until the 1970s we had little evidence for the early use of domesticated plants and animals in South Asia, and many scholars still thought that the use of domesticated wheat and barley, cattle, sheep and goats originated in the Near East and gradually spread across the highlands of eastern Iran and through the passes of Baluchistan to the Indus Valley. This perspective was changed forever after 1976 with the excavations at Mehrgarh, a site in the Indus Valley beginning around 6500 B.C.[10]

At Mehrgarh, situated at the base of the Bolan Pass, the first settlers cultivated barley and grew domestic wheat. At first they relied heavily on hunted game, but gradually turned to domestic sheep and goat. Most significantly they began to domesticate the cattle unique to the subcontinent, the humped zebu (*Bos indicus*).[11] In time, the newly developed skills of agriculture and animal husbandry led to a decrease in the dependence on wild plants and animals. Mehrgarh and probably many other unexplored sites of the Indus Valley and Baluchistan represent the first early food-producing communities of the subcontinent.

The Early Food-producing Era established the subsistence base on which the later Indus cities were sustained. The humped zebu and later the domestic water buffalo along with wheat and barley became the basic staples during this period and continued to be of central importance in the later Indus cities. But perhaps even more significant is that many other important changes occurred as these first settlers became less and less mobile. Population increased and settlements grew in size and complexity; new technologies were invented (fig. 2.7), and trade networks were established between different regions; social and ritual organization evolved and, eventually, new political organizations came into power.[12]

Mehrgarh

The site of Mehrgarh was excavated by the French Archaeological Mission to Pakistan under the direction of Jean-François Jarrige from 1974 to 1986, and excavations have resumed again in 1996-97. A major contribution of these excavations is that the cultural sequence provides a fairly clear picture of the process of settling down and establishing domestic plants and animals as the major source of subsistence. The transition to food production can be seen as an indigenous event[13] that probably occurred

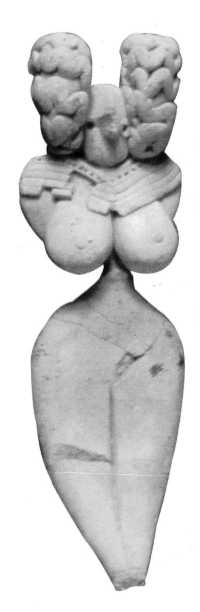

Fig. 2.7. Terracotta female figurine with elaborate coiffure and ornaments, Mehrgarh, Period VI, ca. 3000 B.C., cat. no. 1.

simultaneously in the highland regions and all along the piedmont zone of Baluchistan. These early food-producing communities appear to have had trade networks extending from the highlands to the west, out into the Indus Plains to the east and south to the Makran coast.[14]

In Baluchistan itself the early highland villages have not yet been located or excavated, possibly because they are hidden under large mounds or modern villages. Kili Gul Mohammed in the Quetta valley is the only known site in the highland areas where there is possible evidence for the early exploitation of cereals. The extent of the excavation was extremely limited, but in the lowest levels, just above natural soil, there were traces of mud-built houses, the bones of sheep, goats, and cattle, stone blades with sickle gloss (assumed to be related to cutting grasses/grain), and ground stone tools. No pottery was found in the lowest levels, but subsequent levels, called KGM II, yielded low-fired, handmade and basket-impressed pottery.[15]

On the basis of this admittedly slight evidence we can assume that communities in the highlands harvested cereal grains and possibly managed sheep/goat and cattle herds. As winter approached, the communities may have moved through the passes with their herds and bags filled with grain to the rivers or springs along the piedmont. Mehrgarh is one camp along the Bolan river at the base of a major pass that became a permanently reoccupied settlement.[16] At Mehrgarh the initial settlement may have been seasonal, but eventually some of the population appear to have lived there year round. Since there has been no significant change in climate and rainfall, the annual migration to the highlands would have taken place after the spring harvest in much the same pattern as we see today among agricultural/pastoral communities living in the Kachi plain.

Early Food-Producing Era: Mehrgarh, Aceramic Neolithic

The earliest levels at Mehrgarh, Period IA date from around 6500 to 6000 B.C., and because no pottery or copper tools have been found in these levels, they are said to belong to the nonceramic or aceramic Neolithic period.[17] An irregular scatter of mud-brick houses separated by refuse dumps and passageways made up the first village. The square or rectangular houses, made of hand-formed, plano-convex mud bricks with finger impressions, were subdivided into four or more internal compartments, some of which may have been used as storage areas (fig. 2.8). Later buildings had increasing numbers of internal subdivisions, and some of these may have been purely for storage. The upper portions of these houses may have been made of mud bricks along with wood, branches and grass. While the internal layout of each structure is divided into rooms or storage compartments, the location of individual houses in the settlement is not uniform and shows no overall site planning.

There is no evidence for pottery in the earliest levels. Some foods may have been cooked in skins or baskets with hot rocks, as there are numerous ash layers filled with fire-cracked rock.[18] The earliest inhabitants were, however, familiar with the plastic properties of clay; they made small clay figurines and small unfired clay containers.[19]

The subsistence of the earliest inhabitants was focused primarily on hunting-gathering, supplemented by some agriculture and animal husbandry. The domestic cereals found in these levels include some wheat (einkorn and emmer) (*Triticum monoccum, T. turgidum*, subsp. *dicoccum, T. turgidum* cf. conv. *durum*), but mostly barley (*Hordeum vulgare spontaneum* (wild two-row barley), *H. v. distichum* (cultivated two-row barley), *H. v. vulgare* (six-row hulled barley), *H. v. vulgare* var. *nudum* (six-row naked "shot" barley).[20]

In the earliest period these grains could have been cultivated either locally or brought from the highlands, but eventually as the settlement became more established they were cultivated on the Bolan river flood plain. The growing season is different from that in the highlands, where the

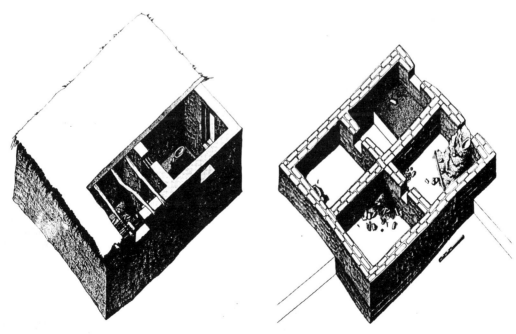

Fig. 2.8. Mud-brick house with internal divisions, Mehrgarh, Period IA, ca. 6500 B.C.

grain would be watered by the winter snow melt and spring rains, and depending on the altitude, harvested in late summer (May-July) or in the early fall (August-September). In the piedmont zone the grain would have been planted in the late fall (November) and then harvested in the spring (March-April). The early farming probably would have been done in moist areas near the rivers, and there is some indirect evidence for irrigation later, possibly by flooding the field with diverted water.[21]

Jarrige suggests that the cultivation of these plants may have begun after the last flooding of the summer monsoon.[22] Planted in the fall (October-November), these crops were watered by the winter rains, which can be derived either from the retreating southwest monsoon or because of the winter cyclonic weather system that dominates the highlands of Baluchistan. The harvest for these crops, called *rabi* or winter crops, occurs in the spring. An important wild fruit that also ripens in the spring is the jujube, a small, nutritious plumlike fruit. Today the jujube is eaten fresh, dried or preserved as a sweet chutney.

The only evidence for summer crops at Mehrgarh comes from impressions of date seeds and actual date seeds. Dates ripen in the summer after the monsoon, but we cannot tell if the date seeds belong to wild or domesticated plants. Today dates are grown throughout southern Pakistan and along the Makran coast and Oman.

Wild animals were extensively hunted at Mehrgarh during the initial phase of the settlement, and only a small proportion of the animal bones seem to have come from domestic goats. The wild game included gazelle, deer, pig, sheep and goat as well as larger animals such as cattle, nilgai, water buffalo and onager. Large tusks of elephant ivory indicate that they may have hunted or trapped this extremely large and dangerous animal as well.

By the end of period IA, around 5500 B.C., the percentage of wild animals decreased and the use of sheep, goat and cattle increased, with the humped variety of cattle, *Bos indicus* being the most important.[23] By documenting a decrease in body size of cattle through Periods I and II at Mehrgarh, at the same time that their bones were becoming increasingly better represented in the archaeological record, Richard Meadow has been able to propose that humped zebu cattle (*Bos indicus*) were domesticated locally in the area of the Indus Valley itself.[24]

The human population of Mehrgarh I-IIA is well represented through numerous burials found between the mud-brick structures. After carefully studying the shape of the teeth in these early burials, John Lukacs feels that they do not reflect peoples who have moved into the region from the west because they do not have strong morphological relationships to known Neolithic populations of West Asia.[25] On the contrary their dental morphology associates them with a distinctively Asian gene pool. This early pattern is the more significant because there is a distinct change in tooth shapes during the later Chalcolithic period (Mehrgarh III) when the skeletal remains show greater similarity to West Asian populations.[26] This change could be explained

by the increase in trade, communication and corresponding gene flow between the Indus region and West Asian cultures during the fifth and fourth millennia B.C.

In Neolithic Mehrgarh, the dead were buried with considerable quantities of funerary offerings comprising animal sacrifices and utilitarian objects such as tools, baskets, grinding stones and many varieties of ornaments. In two of the earliest burials dating to about 6500 B.C. five young goats were slaughtered and buried with the dead (fig. 2.9).[27] This practice of goat sacrifice with burials was found not just at Mehrgarh but has been noted at many other Neolithic sites in Baluchistan, Afghanistan and Central Asia.[28]

Ornaments in the Neolithic burials included beads and pendants made from exotic raw materials: azure blue lapis lazuli, blue-green turquoise, white and black steatite, red-orange carnelian, banded agate and white marine shell as well as locally available yellow-brown limestone. A single copper bead was also found in one of the burials.[29] The colors of these ornaments and the materials from which they were manufactured became the foundation for later ornaments used in the Indus cities.

Wide shell bangles made from the large conch shell *Turbinella pyrum* were also found in the Neolithic burials (fig. 2.10). The nearest source for this species of shell is along the Makran coast near modern Karachi, some 500 km to the south. Pendants made from mother-of-pearl (*Pinctada* sp.) may have come from even more distant sources across the Arabian Gulf in Oman.

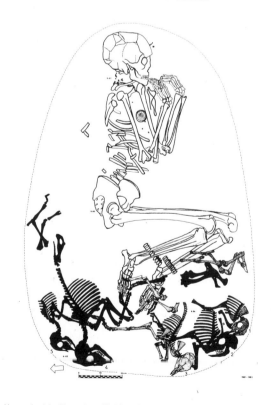

Fig. 2.9. Human burial with goat sacrifice from Mehrgarh, Period IA, ca. 6500 B.C., Tomb MR3.287.

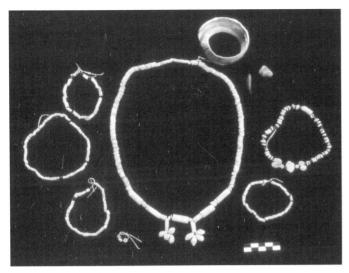

Fig. 2.10. Burial ornaments made of shell and stone disc beads, and Turbinella pyrum bangle, Tomb MR3T.21, Mehrgarh, Period 1A, ca. 6500 B.C. © Catherine Jarrige.

Fig. 2.11. Painted sherd with stylized bull motif, Mehrgarh, Period III, Kili Gul Mohammed ware (Togau A), ca. 4500 B.C.

The exotic raw materials such as shell, lapis lazuli, turquoise and steatite can be traced to the coast or to the highland regions to the west, indicating the presence of long-distance trade networks.[30] Although there was local production of limestone and soft steatite beads during the Neolithic at Mehrgarh, the other exotic ornaments, particularly the marine shell, do not appear to have been manufactured at the site. This trade in finished objects suggests that somewhere along the coast and somewhere in the highland regions, contemporaneous communities were manufacturing special status items for trade and exchange. These specialized crafts of the Early Food-producing Era were to become of major importance during the following Regionalization Era.

While neither the coastal nor the highland production sites have been identified yet, numerous sites dating to approximately the same period have now been located in Oman on the southern perimeter of the Gulf.[31] Some objects produced at the sites in Oman were probably carried across the Gulf to the Makran coast and eventually brought inland by migrating herders or traders. These early maritime connections between the Makran coast and the further coast of Oman later developed into full- scale sea trade during the period of the Indus cities.

In summary, the aceramic Neolithic occupation at Mehrgarh during the Early Food-producing Era shows how the basic subsistence economy of the Indus Valley became established and how the fundamentals of trade and craft specialization began. During the next 2500 years these communities developed new technologies to produce pottery and figurines of terracotta, elaborate ornaments of stone and metal, tools and utensils, and architectural styles that together reflect regional cultures. Of the many animals and materials these people began to use, a few became more important than others, not simply for utilitarian purposes, but also in iconography, presumably reflecting their role as symbols of cultural identity and religious beliefs. The bull (fig. 2.11), the water buffalo, the ram; beads and bangles of conch shell, carnelian, and gold; red-slipped and black-painted pottery; blue-green glazed faience and glazed steatite, all may have played a role in defining the different communities in the Indus Valley and representing their beliefs.

Regionalization Era: New lifestyles and new technologies

After the initial domestication of plants and animals, settled communities developed regional cultures that were centered in different geographical areas. This process is not unique to the Indus Valley but was common throughout the world, because human communities use material objects and religious symbols to create their own identity. The Regionalization Era of the Indus Valley begins with the elaboration of ceramic technology, around 5000 B.C. and ends around 2600 B.C. with the integration of various regional cultures into a single urban civilization.

In order to understand the processes that led to the rise of cities and state-level society, archaeologists have developed many complementary research strategies and interpretive models. Limited funds and time make it possible to excavate only a small section of an ancient village or city and from this small sample it is necessary to make interpretations about the rest of the settlement. Stratigraphic levels filled with cultural debris, including pot-sherds, architectural units and other artifacts are studied to define the degree of change or stability over time. When archaeologists find several sites in a single region with similar sequences and artifacts, they group them together as a single culture. In the Indus Valley itself, Shaffer has identified four important cultural phases: the Balakot Phase, the Amri Phase, the Hakra Phase and the Kot Diji Phase.[32] During these phases of development the final set of critical factors or preconditions for the formation of cities and state-level society were fulfilled.

Many other distinctive cultural phases can be identified at Mehrgarh relating to the highland communities, which Shaffer groups with the Baluchistan tradition. Changes occurring in all of the phases contributed in one way or another to the development of the Indus cities, but the main focus falls on the Amri and Kot Diji phases because many styles of painted pottery and other artifacts of these cultures eventually became incorporated in the later urban society of the Integration Era.

The Amri Phase, named after the site of Amri in Sindh, refers to the geographical region of southern Pakistan and possibly extends as far as the Rann of Kutch. The Kot Diji Phase, named after a small site near Mohenjo-daro, covers a much larger area including the northern Indus and Saraswati river plains as well as parts of Baluchistan to the west. Both the Amri and the Kot Diji phases fall within the later part of the Regionalization Era, approximately 3300 to 2600 B.C., prior to the rise of large urban centers.

During the Regionalization Era, the preconditions for the development of cities and state-level societies were fulfilled in each of these cultures or phases in slightly different ways and different combinations. When taken all together, they present a fairly clear picture of the origin of Indus cities and culture. Although the Western audience has become infatuated with a quest for the earliest city or the oldest copper tool, etc., it is not necessary in this context to focus on specific dates and sites. My main objective is to present an overview of the oftentimes confusing array of evidence that archaeologists have been digging up for over a hundred years.

Resources for Food and Raw Materials

The first precondition is a diverse agricultural and pastoral subsistence base that can produce enough surplus to feed cities in a secure manner regardless of short-term problems such as drought, flood or war. This was easily met in the Indus Valley due to the presence of two river systems with rich agricultural lands, abundant fishing resources in the rivers and coastal zone, extensive grazing lands on the plains and in the highlands and the forests and jungles filled with wild plants and animals. Because of the proximity of these different zones, failure in one area could always be supplanted by obtaining food from a different source. This is often done though social and economic contacts with other communities.

It is also necessary to have diverse and abundant resources for building and maintaining large settlements and supplying workshops with raw materials for making tools, ornaments and religious objects. During the Regionalization Era, explorers from villages in the different regions searched out the sources of precious materials such as lapis lazuli and carnelian, copper and tin, gold and silver. Timber from the northern mountain slopes was floated down the rivers to supplement the locally available lumber. Boulders from mountain streams or chert nodules from the central Rohri hills were used for making tools and grinding stones. Many essential raw materials were available in different localities of the greater Indus Valley. This pattern of distribution may have played an important role in stimulating competition between different regions and the search for additional sources.

Trade and Communication

A second major precondition for the rise of cities is the establishment of trade and communication networks that link settlements to each other and to their agricultural hinterlands, as well as to distant resource areas. Four major spheres of interaction and exchange can be documented during the Regionalization Era: 1) the southern Indus plain and adjacent western highlands; 2) the islands of Kutch, Saurashtra and mainland Gujarat; 3) the northern Indus and Saraswati river valleys and 4) the highland valleys of Baluchistan and Afghanistan.

Beginning in the seventh millennium B.C. as the first farmers settled down, and continuing through the Regionalization Era, these networks gradually enveloped the newly discovered resource areas and the new settlements that spread out across the Indus plain. At the major crossroads of these trade routes, new villages sprang up and eventually became the large towns and cities of the Indus civilization.

Two-wheel carts pulled by oxen were used for heavy transport across the plains while flat-bottomed boats and rafts were probably used on the rivers. Human porters or pack animals such as oxen, sheep and goat could have moved goods back and forth from the highlands. The Bactrian or two-humped camel and the horse were domesticated in the highlands of Central Asia by about 3000 B.C., but we have no evidence of their use in the Indus Valley until the end of the Integration Era.[33]

Most goods probably consisted of staple foods, such as salt and grain, but luxury items such as ornaments and metal tools were also being traded. The major new development at this time was the importing of raw materials from distant source areas to workshops in the larger settlements. Whereas the initial processing of raw materials such as copper, stone and shell occurred at the source areas, final processing was done in workshops located at the settlements, where it was easier to control the style of objects being produced and was also economically more profitable.

For example, by 4800 B.C. during Mehrgarh Period III, the site no longer consumed finished products made in other regions, but rather it produced them. Copper, shell, agate, chert and minerals for pigments were obtained from distant resource areas and processed by highly skilled artisans at the site itself. Mehrgarh producers soon made superior painted pottery (see fig. 2.1), glazed steatite and faience ornaments, metal tools, agate and carnelian beads and inlaid objects. In addition to supplying all the local needs their surplus could be traded back to the outlying regions for more raw materials.

Technology

New technologies that developed in conjunction with trade begin to fulfill the third major precondition for the rise of urbanism, which is the presence of appropriate technologies to build and maintain a city. Many basic technologies were developed during the initial phase of settling down, but cities are different from villages, both in scale and complexity. More varieties of distinctive ornaments are required to differentiate the many different classes of people who live in cities. Specialized technologies were invented to create new materials just for the elite: high-fired ceramics, higher qualities of glazed steatite and faience, stoneware, decorated carnelian and bronze.

Clay from the river banks was made into handsome vessels that were painted and fired in special kilns to produce red or gray ceramics (see fig. 2.1, fig. 2.12).[34] The high temperatures and special pigments allowed these early artisans to develop the first glazing technology using steatite to make white (fig. 2.13) or blue-green colored beads. Eventually powdered quartz was fired to create a new material known as faience, which could be coated with silica

Fig. 2.12. Faiz Mohammed Gray Ware bowl with swirling fish motif, Mehrgarh, Period VII, ca. 2800-2600 B.C., cat. no. 7.

and copper minerals to produce a shiny turquoise glaze. Copper spears and ornamental pins reflect uses for metal, from weapons and tools to ornaments. The alloying of copper with tin or arsenic may have begun during this period; it was well established during the later urban phase. Alloys may have first been used to produce different color tones in metal, but metalsmiths soon came to appreciate that alloys also increased the hardness and working life of a metal tool.

Along with these craft technologies was the beginning of abstract designs that may be the predecessors of writing. Many pottery vessels had marks carved into their base before firing. These marks, often referred to as potters' marks, may have been necessary to distinguish pottery made by different individuals when they were all put together in a single kiln for firing. Other signs, called graffiti, were scratched onto pottery after it had been fired. These signs may have indicated the contents of a vessel, the owner of a vessel, or possibly magical symbols related to religious beliefs. Although some early potters' marks and graffiti are identical to signs of the later Indus script, the invention of the Indus script probably did not evolve from potters marking their wares. Such identification marks are found on pottery from all of the early village cultures from the Indus Valley to Mesopotamia and to Egypt; when writing did develop in these regions, it was probably invented by or for the people who controlled the cites and not the artisans who labored in the workshops.

With the invention of new techniques and the production of specialized objects came the problem of protecting and controlling these valuable commodities (fig. 2.14). At some sites, houses were built around a central courtyard that provided an open space for working, but was private from the streets and lanes of the settlement. Villages were surrounded by thick walls made from sun-dried brick. These walls served as protection against raiding and wild animals, but they also defined a boundary around the village to which access could be controlled. By having walls and gateways, anyone carrying goods or commodities into or out of a settlement could be monitored. We do not know if taxation developed during this preurban period, but the basic structure of control had become well established before the appearance of the first cities.

These walls also protected the villages from annual floods, and as the site grew, they had to be extended. Many surrounding walls became retaining walls for large platforms on top of which new houses were constructed. Entire settlements were gradually raised higher and higher above the plain level. This technology for raising and protecting a

Fig. 2.13. Necklace made of black, unfired steatite and white, fired steatite disc beads, Nausharo, Period I, 2800-2700 B.C.

Fig. 2.14. Large compartmented mud-brick structures that may have been used for storage, Mehrgarh, Period II, ca. 5500-4800 B.C. © Catherine Jarrige.

settlement against floods became essential for large cities that were located on important crossroads in the middle of the alluvial plains.

As settlements became larger during the last phase of the Regionalization Era, such as at the site of Kalibangan, we see the first evidence for building latrines, drains and washing areas. This pattern of waste disposal came to be a defining characteristic in the larger cities of the Indus Valley. We have not yet identified wells from the early settlements, but this is possibly due to the fact that wells are usually maintained for hundreds of years and are often repaired by later inhabitants. Some of the wells in the later Indus cities may have been first constructed by the earlier villagers.

Irrigation technology, invented during this period, was practiced primarily along the piedmont zone and in areas where the tributaries of the larger rivers could be exploited. Out on the active flood plain there was no possibility of controlling the mighty rivers, and, in fact, there was little need to do so. The annual flooding created ponds and oxbow lakes that served as reservoirs for agriculture, for watering herds and for fishing.

One technology that does not seem to have grown or flourished during the Regionalization Era is that of war. Although many settlements did have walls around them for protection, we have not found evidence for massive destruction levels or slaughtered inhabitants at any of the sites. Ash layers at the site of Kot Diji may represent the intentional destruction of the site, but the fire could just as well have been an accidental. The settlement was soon rebuilt and the strong continuities in ceramics and other artifacts suggests that the inhabitants were not replaced by a new culture (figs. 2.15). A similar pattern of burning and rebuilding has been documented at the site of Nausharo, but here too there is no evidence for killing or intentional destruction of the town.[35] In contrast to these smaller towns, at Harappa there is no evidence for discontinuity of

occupation between the early settlement and the Harappan Phase, but over several hundred years, artifact styles such as ceramics and figurines gradually changed (figs. 2.16, 2.17).

The presence of copper spears and knives, bone points and stone mace heads indicates that weapons existed, and raiding or local feuds were probably quite commonplace. But there are no figurines of warriors or captives or painted scenes of battles and human conflict. Such artifacts are present in Mesopotamia and Egypt during the period just prior to the establishment of cities and are prominent in the art of the later urban phases.

The process of urbanization and cultural integration in the Indus Valley probably did result in battles over control of resources and the destruction of some villages, but we have little archaeological evidence for this. What we do see are symbols of status and power that indicate the presence of different classes of people living within a single site or region, fulfilling the final precondition for the rise of cities and early states.

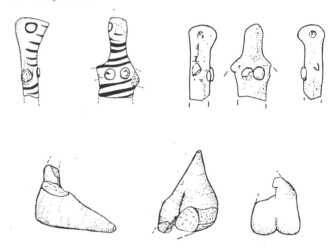

Fig. 2.16. Terracotta female figurines from the preurban settlement at Harappa, Period 2, ca. 2800-2600 B.C. (top left H89-1542/1200-1, top right H96/7423-1, bottom H89-1541/1101-2.

Fig. 2.15. The fortified site of Kot Diji situated at the edge of the Indus flood plain in Sindh, Pakistan.

Fig. 2.17. At Harappa is evidence for continuity of ceramic production in one area for over 500 years. The small kiln in the upper right dates to before 2800 B.C., while the other two kilns in the foreground date to about 2400-2300 B.C. during the Harappan Phase.

Status and Power

The final precondition for urbanism and state-level society is the ability to control access to essential resources, which include both food items and material goods that define status and power. As cities evolved, some individuals or communities gained control over the basic resources needed for subsistence and economic development. These dominant communities or social classes emerged from a milieu of communities which over the centuries had developed different levels of status and power based on occupational specialization, kin relations, religion and ideology.

Complex processes of social change resulting in stratified classes and occupational specialists set the foundation for later social organization in the Indus cities. These processes can be characterized by two different models of social fragmentation and agglomeration. As individual artisans or their families became more specialized in one occupation, such as herding, fishing, shellworking or potterymaking, they would become socially and economically separated from the rest of the community. Over time this process of fragmentation[36] within a community eventually led to the formation of distinct social classes based on occupational specialization. The other process that leads to the development of stratified social classes is agglomeration,[37] where individuals or entire communities of specialists become attached to a larger community. With the creation of distinct communities through fragmentation or agglomeration, new relationships emerged, and social classes were ranked on the basis of complex social, economic, political and religious factors.

The diverse agricultural and resource zones of the Indus Valley were not accessible to all communities or individuals, and during the Regionalization Era certain settlements located at important crossroads of trade networks with access to rich agricultural lands grew. For example, from 3300 to 2600 B.C. the small agricultural village at the site of Harappa grew into a large town of over 15 hectares. Other settlements of the same time located in the hinterland around Harappa are all much smaller.

The early town at Harappa had trade connections with the chert quarries at the Rohri hills in the central Indus and the shell collectors of the distant Makran coast. Precious stones, such as carnelian and agate, lapis lazuli and steatite, were brought to the site from mines to the southeast in Gujarat and from the highlands to the west. Copper that was made into tools and weapons could have been obtained from the highland mining and smelting areas or from the mines to the east in Rajasthan. Harappa was no longer just a small agricultural village like scores of other villages dotting the plains; it had become a large town that must have had considerable political power over the trade and economics of the region.

Many occupational specialists at Harappa may have evolved through the process of social fragmentation as the need for potterymaking, brickmaking, woodworking, etc. made these crafts a viable profession. Other communities of occupational specialists may have agglomerated to the settlement from other regions: shellworkers from the coast, metalworkers from the highland regions, and beadmakers from the mining areas. The relative ranking of these occupational and craft specialists would have been closely tied to the importance of their products for reinforcing and maintaining social status.

In every society, social status is defined by material possessions and the power to act in certain ways. However, which objects are determined to have high value differs in each region depending on the availability of materials as well as ritual beliefs. For example, lapis lazuli was an important symbol of wealth and power in Mesopotamia because it was brought from the distant regions of Baluchistan, while in the Indus Valley, this more easily available stone was relatively unimportant. In contrast the Indus elites preferred objects made of materials that were transformed by complex technology, such as faience, stoneware and red carnelian. With the rise of Indus cities, crafts that produced these materials and elaborate objects became more important as a means for reinforcing and maintaining the social order. Consequently, the control of these crafts and their products would have been essential for maintaining political and economic power.

In some communities, the highest status is given to people who acquire goods that are then redistributed to everyone in the community. Usually these goods consist of consumable items, such as livestock or produce, but occasionally they include exotic ornaments or tools made from rare materials. In other societies status and power is represented by the accumulation of wealth and the display of valuable ornaments and clothing. When people died, it was a common practice to bury their wealth along with food items as a sign of respect or for their use in the after life. A person who was buried with considerable wealth is assumed to have been of high status in life.

We think that ornaments made of precious stones, painted ceramics and metal tools found in the houses and streets of sites such as Harappa (during Period 1 and 2, ca. 3300-2600 B.C.) and Nausharo reflect the presence of high-status individuals. Similar styles of ornaments made in clay, undecorated pottery and stone tools may represent less important people. This pattern may represent the beginnings of social stratification and a hierarchy of classes living in the larger settlements during the Regionalization Era.

Unlike the funerary practices of Mesopotamia and Egypt, no Indus burials from this period reveal individuals interred with great wealth. Although Mehrgarh is the only site where the cemetery from this period has been excavated, the burials show a smaller amount of wealth compared with the burials of the earlier Neolithic inhabitants of the site. This dramatic change in burial customs is intriguing because it suggests that unlike other communities to the west, the people of Mehrgarh chose to keep their wealth in circulation rather than burying it with the dead. This distinctive burial pattern is also seen in the cemeteries of the later urban phase that have been excavated at Harappa and other sites.

Some scholars have argued that because of the absence of elite burials the society was not really divided into classes of elites and commoners, but many other categories of evidence do not support this argument. For example, many settlements became separated into two or more mounded areas, with one mound often being much higher than the others. The separation may represent the division of different communities into separate neighborhoods or the elevation of a sacred temple to a high place overlooking the main settlement.[38] Both explanations assume that the society was segregated into distinct living areas defined by ethnic affiliation, social status or ritual status.

Excavations at the sites of Amri and Kot Diji found two distinct habitation areas, one of which may have been surrounded by a massive wall. At Amri the wall was made of sun-dried brick, and at Kot Diji it was built with stone. At both sites, the process of segregation was not abrupt but occurred over hundreds of years and many phases of rebuilding. Recent excavations at the site of Ghazi Shah in Sindh have shown that the higher mounded area is made up of layer upon layer of habitations,[39] and at Harappa one kitchen area shows six successive hearths rebuilt one above the other for over 200 years.

House size and complexity is another indicator of different classes or social stratification. At Mehrgarh and also at Nausharo, some six kilometers to the south of Mehrgarh, large houses with many rooms are distinct from smaller structures, indicating different classes of people and a hierarchical division of classes.[40] The most convincing evidence for different classes of people and different ethnic groups is economic and technological specialization, combined with regional styles of artifacts such as pottery (fig. 2.18). Farmers were probably becoming distinct from fisherfolk and herders, and rural populations were becoming distinct from people living in large settlements. Each of the major crafts probably developed into specific ethnic or social classes; shellworkers, potters, bead makers, etc. Even within these crafts there would have been a hierarchy of communities: miners, laborers, skilled artisans and traders. Society was gradually divided into those who had access and control of crafts and the artisans who were producing various commodities.[41]

Rare painted terracotta figurines provide a glimpse of how some people dressed and what ornaments they wore (figs. 2.19, 2.20). Many female figurines have a streak of

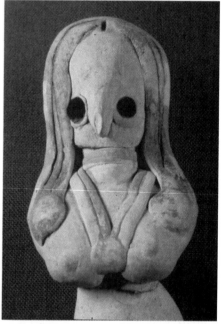

Fig. 2.19. Female figurine with traces of red pigment in the hair part, Nausharo, Period IB, 2800-2600 B.C., cat. no. 2.

Fig. 2.20. (Below right) Male figurine wearing an elaborate headdress and carrying a male infant, Nausharo, Period ID, ca. 2600 and 2500 B.C., cat. no. 4.

Fig. 2.18. Large painted storage jar found in burned rooms at Nausharo, Period ID, ca. 2600 and 2500 B.C., cat. no. 8.

vermilion painted in the middle part of their hair, and the male figurines show heavy black eye liner or kohl. Both forms of adornment are still practiced by many ethnic communities throughout the subcontinent.

An important indicator of social stratification is the presence of seals during the later phases of the Regionalization Era. Seals from Mehrgarh and Naushari are made of clay, bone or ivory and, rarely, copper (fig. 2.21). They are generally composed of geometric designs, but occasionally an abstract animal or human shape is incorporated. These signs may have had specific ritual meaning signifying control, ownership or protective powers. At Rehman Dheri, a large walled settlement in the Gomal plain, seals have been found made from ivory (fig. 2.22) as well as from fired steatite and shell. Some square steatite seals from Rehman Dheri and Harappa have a small knob on the back that is perforated for hanging on a string. This style of fired steatite seal became common in the later Indus cities as an important indicator of status and power.

Seals are generally used to stamp documents or bundles of goods to verify ownership. The people who used seals in these early settlements controlled the access and distribution of essential resources. In Mesopotamia and Central Asia, the earliest seals were made as cylinders instead of squares and were rolled on a lump of clay, rather than being stamped. These two different methods of identifying ownership and control suggest that the newly emerging elites of the Indus Valley and Mesopotamia invented their own systems of economic and political power. The symbols of their power were derived from their own cultures and were distinctive of their own religious beliefs.

The characteristic intersecting-circle motif that becomes a marker of Harappan culture (see fig. 1.1) can be traced to the earlier periods, and at Harappa, this design appears on the earliest hand-built pottery, from about 3300 to 2800 B.C. (fig. 2.23). Another motif that appears with increased frequency on pottery (figs. 2.24, 2.25) and even carved into a terracotta cake is a human figure wearing a horned headdress representing the wide curving horns of the water buffalo (fig. 2.26).[42] The bull water buffalo was one of the most powerful animals found in the marshes along the river banks. He ensured the growth of his herd through reproductive virility and protected his herd of females and young with ferocious strength. A headdress made from the horns of the water buffalo probably symbolized the power and virility of a deity that protected and ensured the fertility of the fields and the herds. There is little doubt that this deity was feared and worshiped throughout the Indus and Saraswati valleys before the rise of cities. This and other shared beliefs may have played an important role in the eventual integration of the many regional cultures.

Fig. 2.21. Geometric button seals from Mehrgarh, Period V, 3300 B.C. to Period VII 2800 B.C.

Fig. 2.22. Ivory seal or amulet with script and two mountain goats on one face and two scorpions on the other, Rehman Dheri, Period IB, ca. 3100-2850 B.C., after Durrani 1988, figs. XVIIIa, b.

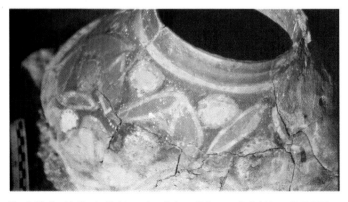

Fig. 2.23. Hand-built pot with intersecting-circle motif, Harappa, Period 1A, ca. 3300-2900 B.C., cat. no. 204.

Fig. 2.24. Horned deity painted on Kot Dijian jars from Rehman Dheri, ca. 2800-2600 B.C., after Shah and Parpola 1991, color photographs 13, 14; see also Durrani 1988, fig. LVI.

Fig. 2.25. Buffalo-horned deity painted on a jar from Kot Diji, 2800-2600 B.C., after Khan 1965, pl. XVIIb.

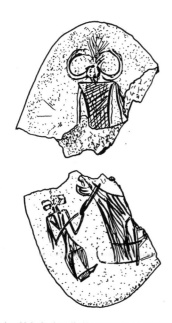

Fig. 2.26. Terracotta cake with incised motif of horned deity on one side and a figure with a tied animal on the other, Kalibangan, Period I, 2800-2600 B.C., after Lal 1979, pl. XII.

Endnotes

1. Robin W. Dennell, Linda Hurcombe, Rogan Jenkinson and Helen Rendell, "Preliminary Results of the Palaeolithic Programme of the British Archaeological Mission to Pakistan, 1983-1987," in *South Asian Archaeology, 1987*, ed. Maurizio Taddei (Rome: IsMEO, 1990), 17-30.

2. Jacques Pelegrin, "Lithic Technology in Harappan Times," in *South Asian Archaeology, 1993*, ed. Asko Parpola and Petteri Koskikallio (Helsinki: Suomalainen Tiedeakatemia, 1994), 2:587-98.

3. J. Desmond Clark, "Why Change? An Example of the Technology from India's Enduring Past," *Bulletin of the Deccan College* 49 (1990): 83-98.

4. J. Mark Kenoyer, "The Indus Bead Industry: Contributions to Bead Technology," *Ornament* 10.1 (1986): 18-23.

5. J. Mark Kenoyer, Massimo Vidale and Kuldeep K. Bhan, "Contemporary Stone Bead Making in Khambhat India: Patterns of Craft Specialization and Organization of Production as Reflected in the Archaeological Record," *World Archaeology* 23.1 (1991): 44-63.

6. Virendra N. Misra and S. N. Rajguru, "Palaeoenvironment and Prehistory of the Thar Desert, Rajasthan, India," in *South Asian Archaeology, 1985*, ed. Karen Frifelt and Per Sørensen (London: Curzon Press, 1989), 296-320.

7. Dexter Perkins, "The Fauna of Aq Kupruk Caves: A Brief Note," *Prehistoric Research in Afghanistan* (1959-1966), ed. Louis Dupree. *Transactions of the American Philosophical Society*, ns 62.4 (1972): 73; Jim G. Shaffer, "The Later Prehistoric Periods," in *The Archaeology of Afghanistan: From Earliest Times to the Timurid Period*, ed. F. Raymond Allchin and Norman Hammond (London: Academic Press, 1978), 71-90 ff.

8. Richard H. Meadow, "The Origins and Spread of Agriculture and Pastoralism in South Asia," in *The Origins and Spread of Agriculture and Pastoralism in Eurasia*, ed. David R. Harris (Washington, D.C.: Smithsonian Institution Press, 1996), 390-412.

9. James Mellaart, *The Neolithic of the Near East* (New York: Scribner's, 1975).

10. Jean-François Jarrige and Richard H. Meadow, "The Antecedents of Civilization in the Indus Valley," *Scientific American* 243.2 (1980): 122-33; Jean-François Jarrige, "Excavations at Mehrgarh: Their Significance for Understanding the Background of the Harappan Civilization," in *Harappan Civilization*, ed. Gregory L. Possehl (New Delhi: Oxford and IBH, 1982), 79-84.

11. Richard H. Meadow, "The Origins and Spread of Agriculture and Pastoralism in South Asia," in *The Origins and Spread of Agriculture and Pastoralism in Eurasia*, ed. David R. Harris (Washington, D.C.: Smithsonian Institution Press, 1996), 390-412.

12. David R. Harris, "Settling Down: An Evolutionary Model for the Transformation of Mobile Bands into Sedentary Communities," in *The Evolution of Social Systems*, ed. J. Friedman and M. J. Rowlands (Pittsburgh: University of Pittsburgh Press, 1978), 401-17.

13. Lorenzo Costantini, "The Beginning of Agriculture in the Kachi Plain: The Evidence of Mehrgarh," in *South Asian Archaeology, 1981*, ed. Bridget Allchin (Cambridge: Cambridge University Press, 1984), 29-33.

14. Jean-François Jarrige, "Towns and Villages of Hill and Plain," in *Frontiers of the Indus Civilization*, ed. B. B. Lal and S. P. Gupta (New Delhi: Books and Books, 1984), 289-300.

15. Walter A. Fairservis, Jr., "Excavations in the Quetta Valley, West Pakistan," *Anthropological Papers of the American Museum of Natural History* 45 (part 2) (1956).

16. Jean-François Jarrige, "Continuity and Change in the North Kachi Plain (Baluchistan, Pakistan) at the Beginning of the Second Millennium B.C.," in *South Asian Archaeology, 1983*, ed. Janine Schotsmans and Maurizio Taddei (Naples: Istituto Universitario Orientale, 1985), 35-68.

17. Jean-François Jarrige, "Chronology of the Earlier Periods of the Greater Indus as seen from Mehrgarh, Pakistan," in *South Asian Archaeology, 1981*, ed. Bridget Allchin (Cambridge: Cambridge University Press, 1984), 21-28.

18. Monique Lechevallier and Gonzaque Quivron, "Results of the Recent Excavations at the Neolithic Site of Mehrgarh, Pakistan," in *South Asian Archaeology, 1983*, ed. Janine Schotsmans and Maurizio Taddei (Naples: Istituto Universitario Orientale, 1985), 69-90.

19. Jean-François Jarrige and Monique Lechevallier, "Excavations at Mehrgarh, Baluchistan: Their Significance in the Prehistoric Context of the Indo-Pakistan Borderlands," in *South Asian Archaeology, 1977*, ed. Maurizio Taddei (Naples: Istituto Universitario Orientale, 1979), 463-536.

20. Costantini, "Beginning of Agriculture in the Kachi Plain"; Richard H. Meadow, "Continuity and Change in the Agriculture of the Greater Indus Valley: The Palaeoethnobotanical and Zooarchaeological Evidence," in *Old Problems and New Perspectives in the Archaeology of South Asia*, ed. J. Mark Kenoyer (Madison, Wis.: UW-Madison Department of Anthropology, 1989), 61-74.

21. Jarrige, "Excavations at Mehrgarh."

22. Jarrige, "Continuity and Change in the North Kachi Plain."

23. Richard H. Meadow, "A Camel Skeleton from Mohenjo Daro," in *Frontiers of the Indus Civilization*, ed. B. B. Lal and S. P. Gupta (New Delhi: Books and Books, 1984), 137-40; Meadow, "Continuity and Change in the Agriculture of the Greater Indus Valley," 67-68.

24. Meadow, "The Origins and Spread of Agriculture and Pastoralism in South Asia."

25. John R. Lukacs, "Biological Affinities from Dental Morphology: The Evidence from Neolithic Mehrgarh," in *Old Problems and New Perspectives in the Archaeology of South Asia*, ed. J. Mark Kenoyer (Madison, Wis: UW-Madison Department of Anthropology, 1989), 75-88.

26. John R. Lukacs, "On Hunter-Gatherers and Their Neighbors in Prehistoric India: Contact and Pathology," *Current Anthropology* 31.2 (1990): 183-86.

27. Richard H. Meadow, "Prehistoric Wild Sheep and Sheep Domestication on the Eastern Margin of the Middle East," in *Animal Domestication and its Cultural Context*, ed. P. J. Crabtree, D. V. Campana and K. Ryan (Philadelphia: University Museum, University of Pennsylvania, MASCA, 1990), 24-36.

28. Louis Dupree, ed., *Prehistoric Research in Afghanistan 1959-1966*, Transactions of the American Philosophical Society ns 62.4 (1972).

29. Jarrige, "Continuity and Change in the North Kachi Plain"; Lechevallier and Quivron, "Results of the Recent Excavations at the Neolithic Site of Mehrgarh, Pakistan."

30. J. Mark Kenoyer, "Shell Trade and Shell Working during the Neolithic and Early Chalcolithic at Mehrgarh," in *Mehrgarh Field Reports 1975 to 1985*, ed. Catherine Jarrige, Jean-François Jarrige, Richard H. Meadow and Gonzaque Quivron (Karachi: Government of Sindh Department of Culture and Tourism, 1995), 566-81.

31. Daniel T. Potts, *The Arabian Gulf in Antiquity: From Prehistory to the Fall of the Achaemenid Empire* (Oxford: Clarendon Press, 1990).

32. Jim G. Shaffer, "The Indus Valley, Baluchistan and Helmand Traditions: Neolithic Through Bronze Age," in *Chronologies in Old World Archaeology*, ed. Robert Ehrich, 3rd ed. (Chicago: University of Chicago Press, 1992), vol. 1: 441-64.

33. Richard H. Meadow, "Animal Domestication in the Middle East: A Revised View from the Eastern Margin," in *Harappan Civilization: A Recent Perspective*, ed. Gregory L. Possehl, 2nd ed. (New Delhi: Oxford and IBH, 1993), 295-320.

34. Jarrige, "Continuity and Change in the North Kachi Plain"; Jean-François Jarrige, "Economy and Society in the Early Chalcolithic/Bronze Age of Baluchistan: New Perspectives from Recent Excavations at Mehrgarh," in *South Asian Archaeology, 1979*, ed. Herbert Härtel (Berlin: Dietrich Reimer, 1981), 93-114; Rita P. Wright, "New Perspectives on Third Millennium Painted Grey Wares,"in *South Asian Archaeology, 1985*, ed. Karen Frifelt and Per Sørensen (London: Curzon Press, 1989), 137-49.

35. Catherine Jarrige, "The Mature Indus Phase at Nausharo as Seen from a Block of Period III," in *South Asian Archaeology, 1993*, ed. Asko Parpola and Petteri Koskikallio (Helsinki: Suomalainen Tiedeakatemia, 1994), 1:281-94.

36. Harold A. Gould, *Caste and Class: A Comparative View* (Reading, Mass.: Addison Wesley Modular Publication, 1971); Harold A. Gould, The Hindu Caste System (Delhi: Chanakya, 1987).

37. Irawati Karve, Hindu Society—An Interpretation (Poona: Deccan College, 1961).

38. Louis Flam, "Recent explorations in Sind: Paleography, Regional Ecology and Prehistoric Settlement Patterns," in *Studies in the Archaeology of India and Pakistan*, ed. Jerome Jacobson (New Delhi: Oxford and IBH, 1986), 65-89; Louis Flam, "Excavation at Ghazi Shah, Sindh, Pakistan," in *Harappan Civilization: A Recent Perspective*, ed. Gregory L. Possehl (New Delhi: Oxford and IBH, 1993), 457-67.

39. Flam, "Excavation at Ghazi Shah, Sindh, Pakistan."

40. Jean-François Jarrige, "Les Cités oubliées de l'Indus: Introduction," in *Les Cités oubliées de l'Indus*, ed. Jean-François Jarrige (Paris: Musée Guimet, 1988), 13-37.

41. Kuldeep K. Bhan, Massimo Vidale and J. Mark Kenoyer, "Harappan Technology: Methodological and Theoretical Issues," *Man and Environment* 19.1-2 (1994): 141-57; Marielle Santoni, "Potters and Pottery at Mehrgarh during the Third Millennium B.C. (Periods VI and VII)," in *South Asian Archaeology, 1985*, ed. Karen Frifelt and Per Sørensen (London: Curzon Press, 1989), 176-85; Massimo Vidale, "On the Structure and the Relative Chronology of a Harappan Industrial Site," in *South Asian Archaeology, 1987*, ed. Maurizio Taddei and Pierfrancesco Callieri (Rome: IsMEO, 1990), 203-44; Rita P. Wright, "Patterns of Technology and the Organization of Production at Harappa," in *Harappa Excavations 1986-1990*, ed. Richard H. Meadow (Madison, Wis.: Prehistory Press, 1991), 71-88.

42. Farzand A. Durrani, "Excavations in the Gomal Valley: Rehman Dheri Excavation Report No. 1." *Ancient Pakistan* 6 (1988): 1-232; F. A. Khan, "Excavations at Kot Diji." *Pakistan Archaeology* 2 (1965): 13-85; Braj Basi Lal, "Kalibangan and the Indus Civilization," in *Essays in Indian Protohistory*, ed. D. P. Agrawal and D. K. Chakrabarti (Delhi: B. R. Pub. Corp., 1979), 65-97.

Fig. 3.1. The baked brick buildings of Mohenjo-daro are grouped into different neighborhoods linked by wide streets, such as First Street in DK-G area, which is over 9 meters wide.

Indus Cities, Towns and Villages

The First Cities

Chapter 3

Emerging from the scrub forest after a long journey from the copper mines in highland Baluchistan, an early trader would have immediately recognized the first cities of the Indus by their imposing mud-brick walls and massive red brick gateways. Located at the cross roads of important trade routes and surrounded by rich agricultural lands, these cities were powerful economic and political centers. Landowners or entrepreneurial merchants may have been the first leaders to take administrative control of the cities, but religious leaders must have legitimized their position. Seasonal rituals or religious celebrations involving the ruling elites would have made the cities an important focus for surrounding communities, but possibly even more important were the tools and utensils, ornaments and decorated ceramics that were produced in the city workshops. The many different communities and classes of people who came to live and trade in the cities provided a totally new context for the development of the arts and technology throughout the Indus region (see figs. 3.1-3.2).

These cities were not created in a short time by visionary rulers or architects, but rather grew out of earlier villages that had existed in the same locality for hundreds of years. Beginning with a relatively small population, they grew in size and density to become the largest settlements of the region, surrounded by numerous smaller towns and villages.

All these settlements were linked by trade and economic activities, as well as by religious beliefs and social relations.

At the site of Harappa, archaeologists have traced the development of the settlement from its origins as a small agricultural village to its glory as one of the largest cities of the Indus Valley civilization. Many of the crafts that began in the early village set the foundation for the attractive ornaments and pottery of the urban center. The precise time when the settlement changed from village to city is hard to define, just as it is difficult to determine when a child becomes an adult. But recent excavations at Harappa indicate that the earliest city may have been formed prior to the Integration Era, during what is called the Kot Diji Phase, between 2800 and 2600 B.C. During this phase the settlement grew to around 25 hectares in size and became a center for trade networks extending from Baluchistan and Afghanistan to the west to the distant sea coast in the south. Raw materials such as carnelian for beads, chert and copper for tools and sea shells for ornaments began to flow to the workshops at Harappa. Within a few hundred years the thriving town had grown six times larger, covering an area of over 150 hectares.

Most of the 1500 settlements found in the Indus and Saraswati regions can be classified as small villages or hamlets (less than 1 and up to 10 hectares) with a few larger towns and small cities (10 to 50 hectares) (fig. 3.3). Each settlement contributed to support and maintain the larger urban centers that grew up along the major trade routes. Five large cities have been identified as the major urban centers of the Indus Valley civilization: Mohenjo-daro (+200 ha), Harappa (+150 ha), Ganweriwala and Rakhigarhi (+80 ha) and Dholavira (100 ha). The first four are inland centers located at approximately equivalent distances in a zigzag pattern that covers the Indus and Saraswati river plain.[1] The fifth, Dholavira, is situated on a small island in the Rann of Kutch, where it would have controlled the movement of goods between the resource areas of Gujarat and the core areas of the Indus plain.

Fig. 3.2. Beneath the disturbed upper layers of Mound AB at Harappa, a row of bathing platforms and a large well may have been used for public washing and bathing (partially reconstructed with modern drains for conservation).

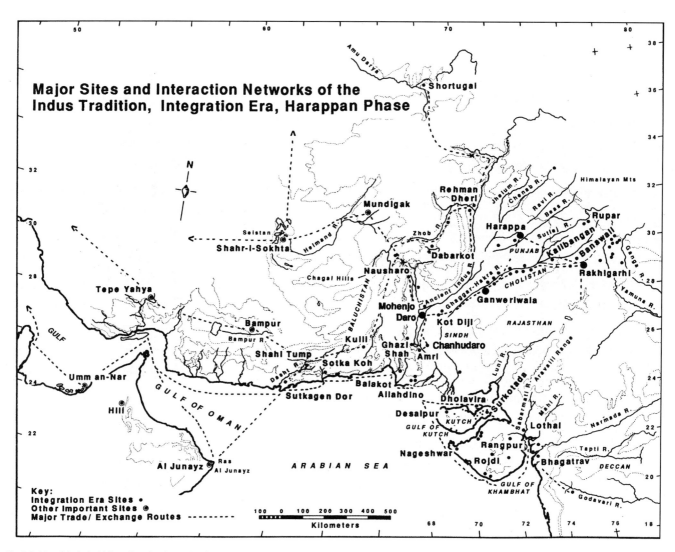

Fig. 3.3. Map of the Indus Valley with major sites and trade routes.

Major excavations have been undertaken at Mohenjo-daro, Harappa and Dholavira, but only a small proportion of each site has been excavated. Based on the density of houses in the excavated areas at Mohenjo-daro, the late Walter Fairservis proposed that as many as 41,250 people lived in the lower town at Mohenjo-daro, which he calculated as being 76.6 hectares of the total site.[2] The inhabited area of Mohenjo-daro is actually greater than 250 hectares and therefore may have held considerably more people than calculated by Fairservis. However, it is unlikely that the entire city was continuously occupied to its maximum capacity, and the population probably fluctuated considerably when people from the surrounding countryside and distant villages came to the city for special festivals or during trading seasons.

Each city was surrounded by vast agricultural lands, rivers and forests that were inhabited by scattered farming and pastoral communities, fisher folk and bands of hunters and gatherers. The cities may not have had direct control over all of these different communities, but they certainly controlled the movement of trade goods passing through the territory into and out of the city markets. A rough estimate of the hinterland for each of the inland cities ranges from approximately 100,000 to 170,000 square kilometers (Table 3.1). City states of this magnitude did not emerge again in the northern subcontinent until the Early Historical period (ca. 600-300 B.C.) and only the largest Greek city state, Sparta (ca. 550-450 B.C.), controlled an equivalent amount of area (168,000 sq. kms).[3]

Table 3.1: Distances Between the Major Urban Centers.

Cities	Total Area	Distance between	km	Hinterland sq. km
Rakhigarhi	+80 ha	RKG-HAR	350	106,225
		RKG-GNW	407	
Harappa	+150 ha	HAR -GNW	280	128,800
Mohenjo-daro	+250 ha	MD-GNW	308	169,260
		MD-HAR	570	
Ganweriwala				
	+80 ha	GNW-DLV	558	108,280
Dholavira	100 ha	DLV-MD	448	?
		DLV-GNW	523	

Site Plan of Mohenjo-daro, Sindh, Pakistan

Museum Campus

Bund

"Citadel"

DKg

Site Continues

SD
W

"Lower Town"

DKb

Washed out by river
no cultural remains

DKc

Bund

N

VS

M

HR

D (UMP)

Bund

Key
D (UMP)   Dales (University Museum, Pa)
DK   Dikshit
HR   Hargreaves
L
M
SD   Siddiqui
VS   Vats
W   Wheeler

Bund

Site Continues

0   100   200 meters   Site Continues

Fig. 3.4. Site plan of Mohenjo-daro.

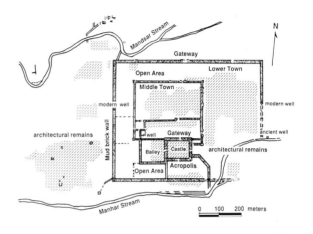

Site Plan of Dholavira, Gujarat, India

Mandsar Stream

Gateway

N

Open Area

Lower Town

Middle Town

modern well

modern well

architectural remains

well

Gateway

ancient well

Mud brick wall

Bailey

Castle

architectural remains

Open Area

Acropolis

Manhar Stream

0   100   200 meters

Fig. 3.6. Site plan of Dholavira.

Fig. 3.5. Site plan of Harappa.

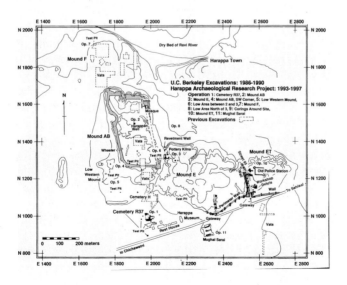

U.C. Berkeley Excavations: 1986-1990
Harappa Archaeological Research Project: 1993-1997
Operation 1: Cemetery R37, 2: Mound AB
3: Mound E, 4: Mound AB, SW Corner, 5: Low Western Mound,
6: Low Area North of 3, 7: Mound F,
8: Low Area between 2 and 3,7: Mound F, 9: Corings Around Site,
10: Mound ET, 11: Mughal Sarai
Previous Excavations

Dry Bed of Ravi River

Harappa Town

Mound F

Test Pit

Op. 7

Vats

N

Mound AB

Tomb

Mosque

Op. 2

Harappa
Well

Vats

Op. 8

Wheeler

Op. 6

Revetment Wall

Pottery Kilns

Mound ET

Op. 3

Test Pit

Op. 10

Low
Western
Mound

Op. 4

Old Police Station

Test Pit

Workshop
Debris

Op. 5

Vats

Mound E

Wall

To Sahiwal

Cemetery H

Test Pit

Gateway

Cemetery R37

Op. 1

Harappa
Museum

Test Pit

Rest House

Gateway

Vats

Op. 11

0   100   200 meters

Mughal Sarai

to Chichawatni

City Planning

The overall layout of Indus cities and villages is distinguished by the orientation of streets and buildings according to the cardinal directions—east and west, north and south. The resulting grid pattern of the cities is not unlike the plan of the compartmented houses of Neolithic Mehrgarh or the geometric seals from the Early Chalcolithic period. Even though there may not be a direct connection between these early patterns and the layout of Indus cities, they probably do reflect what is called a cultural template for the organization of space. Each culture develops specific styles or patterns that are repeated in many different objects or contexts. The division of space into separate blocks organized on a grid is seen not only in the layout of city streets and neighborhoods, but also in house plans, the panels of painted designs on pottery, the ritual diagrams on seals and individual signs of the Indus script. In contrast, the layout of early Mesopotamian cities was quite irregular, and temples or important buildings were oriented with the corners (instead of walls) pointing to the cardinal directions.

This idea of settlement planning did not appear suddenly with the first large cities of Mohenjo-daro and Harappa, but was already well established in the earlier Kot Diji Phase, prior to 2600 B.C. At the site of Harappa, during Period 2 (2800-2600 B.C.), the basic layout of the settlement was established along a grid that was defined by large streets running north-south and presumably also east-west. A similar pattern is seen in other settlements throughout the Indus and Saraswati regions dating to the same time period: at Kalibangan to the northeast, Rehman Dheri to the northwest, Naushero in the west and at the site of Kot Diji in the south. Because of the high water table at Mohenjo-daro, it has not been possible to investigate the lowest levels of the site, but it is not unlikely that this same pattern will be found there as well.

Indus cities are often misrepresented in the popular literature as having a standard division into a high western citadel and a lower town to the east, reflecting the division of the cities into rulers' and service communities, with the craft workshops located in the lower city. But this interpretation is not correct, because large public buildings, market areas, large and small private houses, as well as craft workshops have been found in all of the different mounds.

Each city is composed of a series of walled sectors or mounds, oriented in different directions. Harappa and Mohenjo-daro both have a high rectangular mound on the west and extensive mounds to the north, south and east (figs. 3.4, 3.5). At Mohenjo-daro the western mound stands high above the others, but at Harappa it is only slightly higher than two of the eastern mounds (Mound E and modern Harappa town).[4] Dholavira has a single walled mound internally subdivided into three or four walled sectors (fig. 3.6), the highest being in the southern portion and not in the west as at Mohenjo-daro and Harappa. To the west and northwest, outside of the walled city are low mounds with remains of Harappan houses that represent suburban areas of the city.[5]

Astronomy and City Planning

The orientation of Indus cities along the cardinal directions is not simply a coincidence but is probably linked to religious beliefs, reflecting the development of precise astronomical observations of the movement of the sun, moon and stars across the heavens. Early astronomical texts from Mesopotamia, ancient India and China indicate the primary directional reckoning was not based on the north star, but rather on the rising and setting in the east or west by the sun, moon or bright stars. In modern astronomy we usually think of Polaris, the North Star, as being a constant unwavering point for sighting direction, but around 2300 B.C., Polaris was not at the center of the heaven, that place was taken by a relatively dim star called Draconis.[6]

Establishing an east-west line for marking out the foundation of a building could have been done by sighting on the stars that rise in the east or set in the west, or by mapping the movements of the sun. An early Vedic text (ca. 700 B.C.) recommends sighting on the rising constellation of the Pleiades for establishing an east-west line. Later texts explain how to make a true east-west line by placing a peg in the ground and drawing a circle around the peg using a string that is as long as the peg itself (fig. 3.7). Stakes placed at the point where the shadow of the peg enters and leaves the circle define the east-west line. Another method is to sight on the rising of the constellation called *krittikah*, which in the Greek tradition is called the Pleiades.[7]

The architects during the Kot Diji Phase and on into the Harappa Phase may have taken their bearings using the simple solar technique or by more complex sightings using the rising star Aldebaran or the constellation Pleiades. Dr. Michael Jansen, a German architect who has documented the architecture of Mohenjo-daro, has determined several different orientations of buildings within the city that may indicate construction episodes that used different sightings.[8] Hundreds of years after the first streets were laid out, as new suburbs or neighborhoods were established, architects sighting on the same traditional points would have ended up with slightly different angles due to the changing position of the earth's axis and its position with relation to the sun.

By making complex calculations, astronomers have determined which stars or clusters of stars would have risen above the horizon at dusk during specific seasons in the past. During the spring equinox, the brightest single star

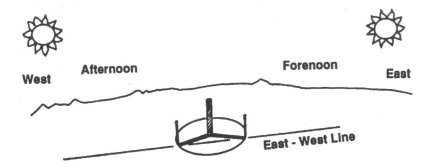

Fig. 3.7. Drawing of east-west sighting technique.

was called *rohini* by Vedic astronomers and is known to us as Aldebaran, part of the constellation of Taurus. Next in line is the cluster of stars known as *krittikah* or the Pleiades. Astronomers think that the Pleiades rose exactly at the equinoctial point during the spring or vernal equinox around 2240 B.C., at the height of the Indus cities. But to the naked eye it would have arisen in approximately this same spot during each vernal equinox from 2720 to 1760 B.C. The Pleiades is the first constellation in the Vedic calendar and is also the first in the Arabic and Chinese calendars. Even in Mesopotamian calendrical texts dating to around 700 B.C. the Pleiades are listed as the first stars in the path of the moon as it progresses across the sky.[9]

Although the Indus architects used the cardinal directions to lay out houses, streets and large public buildings, they were not fettered by these parameters, and the actual layout of streets and smaller lanes is defined as an irregular net pattern. The walls of the houses were rebuilt at different angles and even the city walls were often built curving instead of along the cardinal directions. These irregularities demonstrate that while specific directions may have had some spiritual or social meaning, the people living in the cities were willing to break the rules when it became more expedient to build a wall at an angle or to enclose an area with a curving wall.

City Walls and Gateways

Archaeologists have discovered massive foundations of eroded mud-brick walls and traces of large brick gateways around the edges of the now eroded mounds of Mohenjo-daro and Harappa, attesting to the power and wealth of these cities. The lofty stone walls and imposing gateways of Dholavira provide a hint of the spectacular walls that must have once been the pride of these cities.

Dholavira, Kutch

Dholavira (Kotada) is located on Kadir island in the Rann of Kutch, just north of the large island of Kutch, India.[10] This city's strategic position permitted it to control shipping through the Rann between Saurashtra and the delta of the Indus and Ghaggar-Hakra rivers.

The first phase of occupation at the site began during the Kot Diji Phase, before the rise of the large urban centers in the central valley, but soon the settlement was culturally

and economically integrated into the greater Indus system. Like most sites in Kutch and Gujarat, the houses and drains were made with sandstone blocks (dressed and undressed) combined with some mud-brick superstructures.

This city is oriented in the traditional cardinal directions, but the layout of the walls and sectors of the city is very different from that of other Indus settlements. Three nested rectangular city walls enclose the habitation areas, with the highest area located to the south, on top of a low hill (figs. 3.6, 3.8). The outer wall covers an area approximately 771 m x 616.8 m (47 hectares)[11] and is constructed entirely of mud brick, with large square bastions and two major gateways located at the center of the northern and southern walls.

The fortified middle town (360 x 250 m) has four gateways, one in the center of each wall. The acropolis (300 x 300 m) sits approximately 13 meters above the lower town and has one gateway in the center of each of its four walls. The north gateway of the acropolis may have been the most important because of the large rectangular open area or plaza and entrance ramp associated with it (fig. 3.8). The northern gate has two side rooms that may have had large wooden pillars set on heavy ringstone bases (fig. 3.9). The discovery of these ringstones in situ help to explain the numerous ringstones found out of context in the streets and dumps of Mohenjo-daro and Harappa (fig. 3.10). A large inscription, possibly a fallen sign board was found in one of the side rooms (fig. 3.11). This inscription, the largest example of writing ever discovered in the Indus cities, is made from a white gypsum paste inlay set into a wooden plank. Ten symbols, each measuring approximately 37 cm high and 25 to 27 cm wide, proclaimed some name or title, and mounted above the gateway this sign would have been visible throughout the city.

Large buildings in the acropolis area may represent administrative or ritual structures, and some open areas in the city could have functioned as markets or public gathering places. Various types of craft activity areas have been located within the lower town, including agate beadmaking, shellworking, and ceramic production. Habitation and craft activity areas in the lower sectors of the city are organized in blocks divided by north-south and east-west streets.

Cisterns and reservoirs located in the citadel and lower town would have been filled with seasonal rainwater. The reservoirs account for 17 hectares (36 percent) of the walled areas, and an additional reservoir has been identified outside

Fig. 3.8. The northern gateway of the citadel at Dholavira is approached by a wide procession way that overlooks an open public space. © Archaeological Survey of India, New Delhi.

Fig. 3.10. Massive ringstones made of white limestone were found discarded along one street in the HR area of Mohenjo-daro.© Archaeological Survey of India, New Delhi.

Fig. 3.9. Ringstone bases for wooden columns are found in several of the side verandahs in the gateways of the citadel at Dholavira © Archaeological Survey of India, New Delhi.

Fig. 3.11. Inscription found on the floor of a side room in the north gateway at Dholavira.© Archaeological Survey of India, New Delhi.

of the city wall.[12] To the west, outside the walled city, additional areas of habitation and for burials bring the total area of the site to approximately 100 hectares.

Harappa

At Harappa the different walled areas were spread around a central depression that may have been a large tank or reservoir (fig. 3.5). Each major mound was surrounded by a massive mud-brick wall, with brick gateways and bastions located at intervals along each face. Mound E, oriented along an east-west axis, is one of the oldest parts of the ancient city that grew up on top of the early village settlement. This mound is surrounded by a large mud-brick wall that was faced with baked brick in some sections. A major gateway was constructed along the south wall at the center of a large curve that extends out onto the plain as if to encompass a large market or open space. At the gateway itself, the mud-brick city wall is over 9 meters wide and may have had additional bastions making it up to 11 meters wide. The gate itself is made from baked brick with one meter thick walls firmly bonded to the mud-brick city wall. A small projection on the inner eastern edge of the brick gate may indicate stairs leading to the top of the wall. The opening in the gate is only 2.8 meters wide, just large enough to allow one ox cart at a time to pass into or out of the city. The wall and gate are now badly eroded, but the calculation of the height from the width of the doorway and fallen portions of the wall suggests that it stood between three and four meters high. The top of the gate was probably covered and may have had rooms or lookout posts, which are commonly depicted in gateways of the historical cities.

The large open area inside the gateway may have been used as a market or checkpoint for taxing goods being brought into the city. To the east of the gateway is a large street leading north into the center of the city, where there is evidence for shell and agate workshops. On the west is another neighborhood that had evidence for copperworking. This gateway was probably used as a means of controlling access into and out of this section of the city.

Outside of the city wall and only some 30 meters due south of the gateway is a small mound dating to the Harappan Phase, with houses, drains, bathing platforms and possibly a well. This cluster of houses may represent a temporary rest stop or caravansarai, for travelers who were passing by the city or who had arrived after the city gates were closed. In the historical period, caravansarais were set up outside of major cities and along the major trade routes to accommodate traders and postal relays. Travelers could leave their goods in the rest stop while negotiating taxes or trading privileges.

The modern road which runs along the southern edge

of the mound past this gateway was probably first established by Harappan traders 4500 years ago. The small mound outside the ancient gateway of Mound E was used during historical times as a caravansarai and a stable for horses used in postal relays between Lahore and Multan. The historical well in the center of the caravansarai was probably a reused Harappan well, because it was next to an ancient Harappan bathing platform that had been repaired and reused by the travelers of the historical caravansarai thousands of years later.

The second major gateway of Mound E is much more complex and is located some 200 meters to the east, at the juncture between the corner of the old city wall of Mound E and a new wall that encircled the suburb on Mound ET. The actual gate opening is only about 2.6 meters wide, but the gate pylons and side rooms cover an area over 25 meters across and some 15 meters deep. Rebuilt and modified, on several occasions, this gateway controlled access into the new suburb of the city, where numerous workshops were producing ornaments and trade goods. Outside of this gateway and about 50 meters to the south is another low mounded area that may have been a separate rest stop or caravansarai for merchants who were trading with this part of the city.

The other mounds at Harappa probably had their own walls and separate gates, but only the wall around Mound AB has been excavated. This wall, much larger and higher than the wall around Mound E, was up to 14 meters wide at the base and faced on the exterior with baked bricks, gently tapering to the top, more than 11 meters above the plain level. Three small gateways built at different periods were found by Wheeler along the western face of the wall, and in the north was a larger gate with a ramp leading down to a lower suburb in the north, called Mound F. This northern suburb contained an area with numerous house structures associated with craft manufacturing debris and a series of circular platforms that were thought to be working platforms. To the north of this area was an extremely large building with twelve sections that may have been a palace or storehouse. The area of Mound F was enclosed by a mud-brick wall like the suburb of Mound ET in the east.[13]

The different mounds or walled neighborhoods at Harappa were established at different times as the city grew, but they all were inhabited by people who shared the same culture. Characteristic styles of painted ceramics, clay figurines, inscribed seals and ornaments have been recovered from all of the excavated mounds, and there is evidence for the movement of goods from one sector to the other. However, it still is not clear why the different mounds continued to be walled or how they were politically united into a single city.

Most scholars have assumed that the walls were

constructed for military defense, but it is impractical to have so many separate walled areas next to each other, and we have found no evidence of damage from battles. None of the gateways found at Harappa was constructed for defense from frontal military attack. In later historical cities, major city gateways had a sharp turn just inside the gate to expose attackers to the defenders on the top of the gate. A fortified city also had a moat and double or triple walls like those seen at Dholavira. The lack of such defensive planning suggests that the gates and walls of Harappa were never intended to withstand battle, but were more symbolic in nature and intended to control the trade and commerce which was the life blood of the city. Whatever the precise function of the walls and gateways, their presence made the city stand out from other smaller settlements. They demonstrate the high level of architectural skills and civic control in the Indus cities.

Fig. 3.12. Looming brick pylons mark the spot where Wheeler excavated a possible gateway at the southeastern corner of the citadel mound at Mohenjo-daro.

Mohenjo-daro

At Mohenjo-daro the presence of city walls and gateways has been controversial, but recent studies seem to confirm that like Harappa, each major mound was surrounded by an enormous mud-brick wall with gateways at key locations. The western citadel mound, the highest habitation area at Mohenjo-daro, rises up to 12 meters above the plain in the north, where a Buddhist stupa and monastery of the historical period have been found (see fig. 3.4). This mound is encircled by a massive mud-brick wall or platform which is now eroded down to the modern plain level. Wheeler identified what might be a gateway at the southeast corner of the citadel mound, but he never fully published his report (fig. 3.12).

In contrast to the high citadel mound, the so-called lower town to the east consists of low mounds covering over 80 hectares. These mounds (comprising of DK-G area, VS area, HR area and Moneer area) are divided into major blocks by four major north-south streets and four equally wide east-west streets, with numerous smaller streets and alleyways.[14] Recent corings along the eroded perimeter of HR area have revealed the presence of great mud-brick walls or platforms. If these structures are indeed the foundations for city walls, they would be even more impressive than those recovered at Harappa.

Architectural Materials and Crafts

Houses built by people from different communities usually show considerable variation in the raw materials used, the style of construction, the bonding techniques for laying bricks and the ways in which materials are combined. In the Indus cities there is a remarkable uniformity in both the raw materials used and the style of construction. Because most Indus settlements were located in the alluvial plains, the most common building materials were mud bricks and baked bricks, wood and reeds. However, in the rocky foothills and on the islands of Kutch and in Saurashtra where stone is commonly available, dressed stone replaced baked brick.

An average size of mud brick and baked brick (7 x 14 x 28 cm) was used in house construction, and a different size (10 x 20 x 40 cm) was used in the building of city walls. Both sizes of brick have identical proportions—thickness (=1), width (=2 x 1) and length (= 4 x 1). This ratio is commonly expressed as 1:2:4; both sizes of bricks appeared during the Kot Diji Phase and become standard at all of the settlements during the Harappan Phase. The uniformity is probably not the result of a state decree or federal building codes, but rather the rise of a class of brickmakers whose craft tradition spreads to all of the different settlements. This diffusion of an idea could have been accomplished through marriages or by moving to new settlements to set up shop.

These same brickmakers may have also branched out as masons and architects, filling an important niche in the rapidly growing urban centers. The result is a fairly uniform building tradition with variations depending on the availability of materials and the plot of land on which a house was being built. Mud brick and baked brick or stone were used for the foundations and walls of the houses; the doors and windows were made with wood and mats. The floors of a house were generally hard-packed earth that was often replastered or covered with clean sand. Bathing areas and drains were made with baked brick or stone. Some rooms were paved with bricks or fired terracotta cakes. Very few actual roof fragments have been recovered, but they were probably made of wooden beams covered with reeds and packed clay.

The wooden components in the Indus houses would have been made by a different set of artisans, carpenters, who used totally different techniques and tools. In later historical cities, the protective designs and decorative carvings on door frames and windows designated status and wealth. Pottery replicas of houses with carved and painted windows and doorways attest to the beginnings of such embellishments during the first cities (fig. 3.13).

Some of the largest public buildings at Mohenjo-daro and Harappa appear to have been made entirely of wood, and specialized tools would have been needed to shape and fit the huge timbers for gateways and columns. Copper and bronze were used for axes, adzes, chisels, drills and saws. Stone tools were used for drilling, scraping and finishing. Tropical hard woods and aromatic cedar were used for buildings and furniture. One locally available hard wood that became famous in trade to Mesopotamia is known as "shisham" (*Dalbergia sisoo*). The dark heartwood is termite proof and used extensively today for making doors, windows and furniture. A type of cedar, "deodar" (*Cedrus deodara*), was also used by the Indus artisans, but it is not native to the hot plains. Some cedar may have been intentionally floated down from the Himalayas by traders, but landslides and storms in the mountains would have tumbled many trees into the river naturally.

Dressed stone blocks and architectural components represent a third major craft associated with the architecture of cities. Most dressed stone would have been made by direct hard hammer percussion, similar to that used in flaking chert, but some immense ringstones and square column bases reflect a much more refined stone-working tradition (figs. 3.9, 3.10). Hammerstones and chisels were used to shape the large discs and square blocks. Abrasive drills were used for hollowing out the center of the ringstones and for making the dowel holes. Fine-grained quartzite and sandstone were used for grinding and polishing the carefully finished surfaces. All these techniques were used on a much finer scale to produce polished alabaster grillwork that would have been set into windows or dividing walls.

Incorporating different qualities of materials and variations of style, these architectural crafts helped create a unique living environment. Enclosed within massive city walls, many different social and economic classes were able to live in close proximity and still maintain their status and identity.

Architectural Styles

Excavations have uncovered many types of houses and public buildings at both large and small settlements. The major difference between the cities and the smaller towns and villages is the type and combination of raw materials used. In the rural areas houses were made almost entirely of mud brick with occasional bricks or stone used in the foundations or drains. Although a few houses in the larger urban centers were made in the same manner, most buildings in the cities were constructed either entirely or partially with baked brick.

Most of the architecture can be grouped into three categories with some variations resulting from rebuilding and

Bricks

Bricks hand formed from clay or mud had been manufactured since the aceramic Neolithic at Mehrgarh, but not until the Kot Diji Phase were the first mold-made bricks of standard proportions used. Two sizes of sun-dried mud bricks were manufactured at Harappa during Period 2 (Kot Diji Phase). The smaller sized bricks, 7 x 12 x 34 cm, were used in houses, whereas the larger size 10 x 20 x 40 cm, were used to make the large perimeter walls that protected the settlement. While the smaller size of brick is slightly irregular, the larger bricks have the standard thickness to width to length ratio of 1:2:4.

At Harappa itself, during the subsequent Harappan Phase, the smaller mud bricks used to build house walls measure 7 x 14 x 28 cm; the larger mud bricks used in building the city walls measure 10 x 20 x 40 cm. At around 2600 B.C. we see the first use of kiln-baked bricks, almost always made in the smaller size, around 7 x 14 x 28 cm.

In recent excavations at the city gateway at the juncture of Mound E and Mound ET, we identified three phases of building that showed a gradual decrease in the absolute size of baked bricks over time. In the earliest gateway bricks were 7 x 14 x 28 cm, but by the final phase of rebuilding the size had become reduced to 5 x 12 x 24 cm. Similar patterns had been observed at Mohenjo-daro by Dr. George F. Dales that he was unable to confirm, because many later structures reused bricks from earlier periods. He was unable to reach the lowest levels of the site due to the high water table.

The fact that this size ratio had been in existence long before the rise of large cities indicates that brick masons had probably developed these size proportions in order to build structurally sound walls with strong corner joins. Scholars originally thought the uniformity of brick sizes represented a strong centralized government, but it is probably the result of concepts of measurement and proportion that were passed from one generation of builders to the next and gradually spread to distant communities along with the specialized artisans. It is also possible that the ratios of 1:2:4 were defined by some unknown ritual, since these ratios are not limited to bricks alone, but are reflected in the rooms of houses, in the overall plan of houses and in the construction of large public buildings. Dr. Michael Jansen has pointed out that this ratio is reflected in the overall plan of the large walled sector at Mohenjo-daro called the citadel mound.

modifying original structures. In the first category are private houses with rooms arranged around a central courtyard that offer privacy from the public passing along the city streets. Doorways and windows rarely opened out onto the main street, but faced side lanes. The view into the house was blocked by a wall or hallway, so that activity in the central courtyard was protected from the view of passersby, a pattern still maintained in traditional homes throughout the northern subcontinent. Several rooms were situated around the courtyard; stairs led up to the roof or second story from one room or the courtyard. Many houses were at least two stories high, and based on the thickness of some house walls at Mohenjo-daro, there may have been three-storied buildings as well. On the average, walls were 70 cm thick, and most ceilings were probably over 3 meters high.

Fig. 3.13. Fragments of carved toy houses or shrines from Harappa provide a glimpse of architectural woodworking (top H87-378/73-18, bottom H87-379/73-19).

The doors were made with wooden frames, and a brick socket set in the threshold served as a door pivot. Clay models of houses show that some of the doors frames were painted and possibly carved with simple ornamentation (fig. 3.13). A hole at the base of the door frame may have allowed a rope to secure or lock the door. Two holes at the top of the door frame may have been used to hang a curtain. The lock at the base of the door and a curtain to cover the doorway is still a common practice in cities and villages throughout the subcontinent.

Windows situated on both the first and second stories had shutters with latticework grills above and below the shutters. This allowed air and light into the room when the shutters were closed and maintained the privacy of the room from outsiders. The shutters and grillwork were probably made of wood, but some may have been made of reeds or matting. A few examples of carved alabaster and marble lattice work have been found at Mohenjo-daro and Harappa. Set into the red-fired brick walls these lattices may have adorned the houses of wealthy merchants or rulers. These early artisans combined the functional features of architecture with patterned beauty, a tradition that anticipated the elegant marble screens of the Mughal period

and the more mundane wooden screens on highrise apartment buildings of modern Karachi.

Buildings in the second category include large houses surrounded by smaller units. Complex passageways gave access to interior rooms, and numerous rebuilding phases indicate repeated reorganization of space. Outer units may have been the houses of relatives or service groups attached to the original house.

The third category of structures includes large public structures that have many access routes or provide a thoroughfare from one area of the site to another. Markets or public meetings may have been held in large open courtyards, while other buildings may have had specific administrative or religious functions.

Groups of houses or public buildings were built close together with shared walls and formed larger blocks that were bordered by wide streets. Most houses or groups of houses had private bathing areas and latrines as well as private wells.

Wells and Sanitation

Water for drinking and bathing was an important commodity in the first cities. Although nearby rivers may have provided water for some inhabitants they could not have been convenient for the entire population. Depending on the geographical setting, wells, reservoirs or cisterns were built within the cities to ensure drinking and bathing water. At Mohenjo-daro numerous wells were dug throughout the city and maintained for hundreds of years (fig. 3.14). When the early excavators had cleared some of these wells, they once again began to fill with water, although much of the ground water around the site today is quite brackish. These 10 to 15 meter deep wells were lined with specially made wedge-shaped bricks to form a structurally sound cylinder that would not cave in under pressure from the surrounding soil. Deep grooves on the bricks at the top edge of the well show that ropes were used to lift the water out, probably with leather or wooden buckets.

At Mohenjo-daro, most houses or blocks of houses had at least one private well (fig. 3.14), and many neighborhoods had public wells along the main streets for travelers and the general public (fig. 3.15). On the basis of the number of wells found in the excavated areas, Michael Jansen has calculated that the city may have had over 700 wells. In contrast, Harappa may have had as few as 30, since only 8 wells have been discovered in the areas excavated so far. The difference between these two cities may be that Mohenjo-daro had less winter rain and may have been situated far away from the Indus river. At Harappa a large depression in the center of the city may represent a large tank or reservoir accessible to the inhabitants from all the different neighborhoods. The site of Dholavira has only a few wells, and most water for the city was collected during the rainy season in large stone-lined cisterns. The drains for collecting rain water were built separately from drains used to take away dirty sewage water.

The wells in private houses at Mohenjo-daro and Harappa were probably built by people living in these houses and not by the state government. The abundance of private as opposed to public wells suggests that at Mohenjo-daro water purity and pollution had become an important issue in the increasingly congested urban setting. There is no evidence for a highly stratified caste society in the Indus cities, but such perceptions about water do become an important feature of the caste divisions in Brahmanical Hinduism. Members of the higher castes will not drink water that has been touched or carried by individuals of a lower caste. And because water is used to wash away physical and spiritual impurities, it is important to keep the source of water itself from being polluted.

In the Indus cities, the top of the well would have stood above the ground level with a small drain nearby to keep

Fig. 3.14. Wells in some parts of Mohenjo-daro have been excavated in such a way that they appear to be towers. This is a private well in DK-G area.

dirty water from running back into the well itself. Bathing platforms with drains were often situated in rooms adjacent to the well (fig. 3.16). The floor of the bath was usually made of tightly fitted bricks, often set on edge, making a water-tight floor. A small drain cut through the house wall out into the street directed the dirty water to a larger sewage drain. Much care was taken to ensure that water from the bathing area and latrines did not flow into the rest of the house. Drains and water chutes from the second story were often built inside the wall with an exit opening just above the street drain. At Mohenjo-daro and Harappa tapered terracotta drain pipes were used to direct the water out to the street.

Latrines

Many urban dwellers may have walked outside the city wall to the nearby fields to relieve themselves, as is commonly done today in much of Asia. But many houses had latrines that were distinct and separate from the bathing areas. The early excavators at both Mohenjo-daro and Harappa did not pay much attention to this essential feature of the Indus cities, but current excavations at Harappa are finding what appear to be latrines in almost every house. The commodes were made of large jars or sump pots sunk into the floor, and many of them contained a small jar (fig. 3.17) similar to the modern water jar or *lota* used throughout Pakistan and India for washing after using the toilet. Sometimes these sump pots were connected to a drain to let sewage flow out, and most had a tiny hole at the bottom to let water seep into the ground. Clean sand was scattered on the floor of the latrine and periodically an entire new floor was installed. These sump pot latrines were probably cleaned out quite regularly by a special class of laborers who also would have periodically cleaned out the large garbage bins and sewage drains in the city streets.

Fig. 3.15. Public wells that were accessible from the street have been found in HR area at Mohenjo-daro.

Fig. 3.16. A bathing platform in SD area at Mohenjo-daro with a drain leading out to the street.

Fig. 3.17. Several sump pots and latrines built one above the other were uncovered on Mound ET at Harappa. A small water jar dropped into one pot was never retrieved. The hole in the foreground is the beginning of another latrine that turned out to be a complete black-slipped jar, cat. no. 178.

Streets and Drains

Well laid-out streets and side lanes equipped with drains are one of the most outstanding features of the Indus cities. The fact that even smaller towns and villages have impressive drainage systems indicates that removing polluted water and sewage was an important part of the daily concerns of the Indus people. The drains, made of baked brick, connected the bathing platforms and latrines of private houses to medium-sized open drains in the side streets. These open drains flowed into larger sewers in the main streets which were covered with bricks or dressed stone blocks.

Corbeled arches allowed the larger drains to cut beneath streets or buildings until they finally exited under the city wall, spewing sewage and rainwater onto the outlying plain. At Harappa a sequence of four drains, built one after the other, has been found exiting the city at the main gateway between Mound E and Mound ET (figs. 3.18, 3.19). Some drains appear to have been provided with wooden sluice gates or perhaps a grill to keep people from secretly entering into the walled city. One completely preserved drain has a magnificent corbeled arch that is 1.6 meters high, 60 cm wide and extends for 6.5 meters beneath a major city street.

At intervals along the main sewage drains were

Fig. 3.18. A large corbeled drain was built in the middle of an abandoned gateway at Harappa to dispose of rainwater and sewage.

Fig. 3.19. An artist's reconstruction of the gateway and drain at Harappa. Courtesy of Chris Sloan.

rectangular sump pits for collecting solid waste. These sump pits were cleaned out on a regular basis; otherwise the entire drainage system would have become blocked. Separately built garbage bins were also found along the major streets. At Harappa there were periods when the city drain cleaners did not do their job, causing the drains throughout part of the city to become totally clogged. Sewage ran along a general depression in the street until finally, fifty to a hundred years later, the city once again took control and built new drains directly above the old ones. These fluctuations in street and drain maintenance resulted in the rapid build up of street levels. Many doorways and walls had to be raised above the level of the street to keep sewage from flowing into the house. Eventually, entire rooms would be filled with dirt and a new house built well above the street level (figs. 3.20, 3.21). Over hundreds of years this process of mound buildup raised the entire city high above the original plain level.

Public Buildings

Many of the largest and best-known buildings of the Harappa Phase are located on the citadel mound at Mohenjo-daro. Perched high above the surrounding plain, these important buildings would have been visible from all parts of the city to legitimize the power and authority of the rulers. On the northern half of the mound are three large buildings that have been the focus of attention since their discovery in the 1920s: the so-called granary, the great bath, and the college. Protruding fragments of walls indicate that other potentially important buildings still lie buried beneath the Buddhist stupa which covers the eastern quarter of the mound. The southern part of this mound has a large building called the assembly hall, which has a double row of square columns and lines of bricks set into the floor. In Buddhist monasteries or Brahmanical ashrams, monks or students often sit in lines on the floor; these lines of bricks may also have been used to define where people should sit.

Other important public buildings have been found in different neighborhoods of the lower mounds. In DKG area is an expansive courtyard that may have been a large market or public assembly area. Located nearby is a large complex of houses, which the early excavators called the house of a chief. To the south at the other end of the lower mound in the HR area another important building was discovered. This building, called House A1 may have been a temple or the house of an important leader. Two doorways lead to a narrow courtyard at a lower level. In the courtyard was a circle of bricks which might have been the site of a sacred tree. A double staircase led to an upper courtyard surrounded by several rooms. This house had numerous seals and fragments of a stone sculpture depicting a seated man wearing a cloak over the left shoulder. Other pieces of this bearded figure were found scattered in nearby houses. This sculpture closely resembles the so-called priest-king image (cat. no. 118) which was found far to the north in the DK area.

Fig. 3.20. Brick buildings in HR area at Mohenjo-daro showing a blocked-up doorway and numerous building levels.

Fig. 3.21. In modern Harappa City, rising street levels gradually covered the thresholds of older doorways (background), and new doors were built above the level of the street (foreground).

Great Bath

The great bath, located to the east of the granary is without doubt the earliest public water tank in the ancient world (fig. 3.22). Some visitors to Mohenjo-daro refer to it as the first swimming pool, but it is unlikely that it was ever used for swimming laps or diving. The tank measures approximately 12 meters north-south and 7 meters wide, with a maximum depth of 2.4 meters. Two wide staircases lead down into the tank, one from the north and one from the south. Small sockets at the edges of the stairs could have held wooden planks or treads. At the foot of the stairs is a small ledge with a brick edging that extends the entire width of the pool. People coming down the stairs could move along this ledge without actually stepping into the pool itself.

The floor of the tank is water-tight due to finely fitted bricks laid on edge with gypsum plaster; the side walls were constructed in a similar manner. To make the tank even more water-tight, a thick layer of bitumen (natural tar) was laid along the sides of the tank and presumably also beneath the floor. The floor slopes down to the southwest corner where a small outlet leads to a brick drain, which takes the water to the edge of the mound. This small drain first passes through a large rectangular space that was originally covered with wooden beams and then through a corbeled arch drain that curves along the edge of the northern terrace of the granary.

A detailed analysis of symmetry of the building and comparison with other buildings has led Michael Jansen to suggest that the architects who designed and constructed this building and water tank were constrained by the limited area between the main north south street and the granary.[15] Brick colonnades were discovered on the eastern, northern and southern edges, but due to erosion of the mound, the western edge was missing. Marshall assumed that there would have been colonnades running along the west edge, and subsequent reconstructions have shown these hypothetical columns. The preserved columns have stepped edges that may have held wooden screens or window frames. Two large doors led into the complex from the south, with

Fig. 3.22. The great bath at Mohenjo-daro.

additional access from the north and east (fig. 3.23).[16] Rooms are located along the eastern edge of the building; in one room is a well that may have supplied some of the water needed to fill the tank. Rainwater also may have been collected for this purposes, but no inlet drains have been found.

It is unlikely that this elaborate building was used simply for public bathing, because just to the north is a substantial building containing eight small rooms with the more common bathing platforms.[17] Most scholars agree that this tank was used for special religious functions where water was used to purify and renew the well being of the bathers.

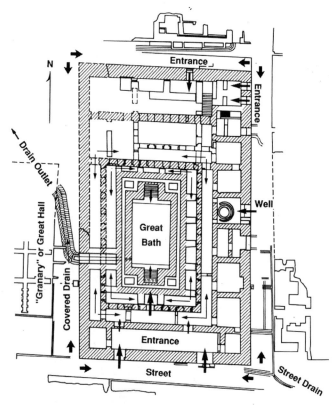

Fig. 3.23. Plan of the great bath of Mohenjo-daro showing access routes, after Jansen 1993, fig. 50.

"Granaries" or "Great Halls"?

Whereas the earliest excavators of Mohenjo-daro were unable to confirm the identity of any structure as a palace or temple, the one building on the citadel mound that may deserve this title is one that was first identified as a *hammam* or hot-air bath, and later as the state granary (fig. 3.24). Initially excavated in the 1920s, the complete structure was reinvestigated by Sir Mortimer Wheeler in 1950 (fig. 3.25).[18] His imaginative reconstruction of this structure as a state granary was based on comparisons with Minoan Crete and Rome.

Located on the western edge of the mound at the southwest corner of the great bath, the foundation of this building appears to have been constructed before the great bath, whose exit drain cuts across the northeast corner of the foundation. Built on top of a tapered brick platform, this building had a solid brick foundation that extended for 50 meters east west and 27 meters north south. The foundation was divided into 27 square and rectangular blocks by narrow passageways, two running east west and eight running north south (one additional north south passageway was added at a later stage). Some of these blocks had square sockets for holding wooden beams or pillars. We think the entire super structure was made of timbers.

Wheeler identified a brick-paved staircase 4.5 meters wide that led from the southwestern edge of the structure to the plain level. A brick-lined well was located at the foot of the stairs, and a small bathing platform was found at the top of the stairs. To the north of the structure was a terraced platform with numerous sockets for wooden beams and an alcove that Wheeler interpreted as a loading dock. To the north of the terrace was a low courtyard or open area and two additional wells.

Since the entire structure was excavated without detailed recording of the types of artifacts found in the passageways or nearby rooms, we cannot accurately reconstruct the function of this structure. However, the earlier excavators did note the lack of charred grain and storage containers. Furthermore, the absence of sealings from bundles of goods and the unique nature of the structure all raise doubts as to the identification of this building as a state granary or storehouse.[19] A more appropriate name for this structure would be the great hall, since it was clearly a large and spacious building with wooden columns and many rooms.

At Harappa M. S. Vats identified a different type of building as a granary (figs. 3.26, 3.27). Located on Mound F, this structure is built on a massive mud-brick foundation that is over 50 meters north-south and 40 meters east-west. Two rows of six rooms that appear to be foundations are arranged along a central passageway that is about 7 meters wide and partly paved with baked bricks. Each room measures 15.2 by 6.1 meters and has three sleeper walls with air space between them. A wooden superstructure supported in some places by large columns would have been built on top of the brick foundations, with stairs leading up from the central passage area. Small triangular openings may have served as air ducts to allow the flow of fresh air beneath the hollow floors.

No special concentrations of burned grain or storage containers were discovered by the earlier excavators, who suggested that nearby circular brick platforms were used for husking grain (figs. 3.28, 3.29). During excavations in 1946, Wheeler found what he thought was a large wooden mortar placed in the center of one of these circular brick platforms. Wooden mortars are used in many parts of the world to remove the husks or crush grain. Even though these circular platforms were found near the granary, it is important to note that they were constructed inside smaller buildings and that they belong to many different building phases. In other words, there is little to suggest a connection between the circular platforms and the so-called granary. In fact, the main argument for suggesting that this structure was a granary is again based on comparisons with Roman buildings and not because of parallels with any building tradition in South Asia. Traditionally, grain in the northwestern subcontinent is stored in large mud plastered bins raised above the ground on bricks or wooden platforms.

Most scholars agree that there is little evidence for the construction of massive granaries at either Mohenjo-daro or Harappa and that these structures should only be seen as evidence for large public buildings. Rulers and state officials probably did meet in such large public buildings. Although many may have been used for specific religious functions; their precise function will likely remain a mystery.

Nevertheless, the size and complexity of these buildings demonstrate the ability of the Indus architects to construct imposing architecture. Instead of a single building within the city, the walled city as a whole may have stood as a symbol of total power. Towering high above the plain, with gleaming red-brick gateways and light gray mud-brick walls, the city would have been a landmark, visible for many kilometers. Inhabited continuously for over 700 years, these cities were home to effective and powerful rulers who were supported by generations of artisans, traders and farmers.

Fig. 3.24. The square blocks of the so-called granary of Mohenjo-daro are visible in the background, and the great bath is in the foreground.

Fig. 3.25. Plan of the granary at Mohenjo-daro, after Wheeler 1968, fig. 9.

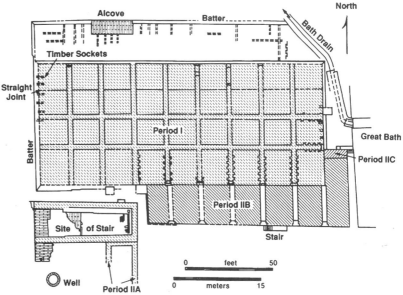

Fig. 3.26. The granary at Harappa is spread out over a larger area, but has approximately the same floor space as the building at Mohenjo-daro.

Fig. 3.27. Excavations of the granary at Harappa in 1926, with Mound AB clearly visible in the background.© Archaeological Survey of India,New Delhi.

Fig. 3.28. The early excavators found numerous circular platforms in the houses and small courtyards of Trench IV, which lies between the granary and Mound AB at Harappa. © Archaeological Survey of India,New Delhi.

Fig. 3.29. Reconstructed circular brick platforms in Trench IV, Mound F, Harappa.

Endnotes

1. Gregory L. Possehl, "Revolution in the Urban Revolution: The Emergence of Indus Urbanism," *Annual Review of Anthropology* 19 (1990): 261-82; M. Rafique Mughal, "The Consequences of River Changes for the Harappan Settlements in Cholistan," *Eastern Anthropologist* 45. 1-2 (1992): 105-16.

2. Walter A. Fairservis, Jr., "The Origin, Character and Decline of an Early Civilization," in *Ancient Cities of the Indus*, ed. Gregory L. Possehl (New Delhi: Vikas, 1979), 83.

3. J. Mark Kenoyer, "Early City-States in South Asia: Comparing the Harappan Phase and the Early Historic Period," in *The Archaeology of City-States: Cross Cultural Approaches*, ed. Deborah L. Nichols and Thomas H. Charlton (Washington, D.C.: Smithsonian Institution Press, 1997), in press.

4. Kenoyer, "Early City-States."

5. Ravindra Singh Bisht, "A New Model of the Harappan Town Planning as Revealed at Dholavira in Kutch: a surface study of its plan and architecture," in *History and Archaeology*, ed. B. Chatterjee (Delhi: Ramanand Vidhya Bhawan, 1989) 397-408.

6. Asko Parpola, *Deciphering the Indus Script* (Cambridge: Cambridge University Press, 1994), 204-6.

7. Parpola, *Deciphering the Indus Script*.

8. Michael Jansen, "City Planning in the Harappa Culture," in *Art and Archaeological Research Papers* no. 14, ed. Dalu Jones and George Michell (London: Art and Archaeology Research Papers, 1978), 69-74; Michael Jansen, "Settlement Patterns in the Harappa Culture," in *South Asian Archaeology, 1979*, ed. Herbert Härtel (Berlin: Dietrich Reimer, 1980), 251-69.

9. Parpola, *Deciphering the Indus Script*.

10. Bisht, "Harappan Town Planning."

11. Ravindra Singh Bisht, "Secrets of the Water Fort," *Down to Earth* May (May 1994): 25-31.

12. Bisht, "Secrets of the Water Fort."

13. J. Mark Kenoyer, "Ideology and Legitimation in the Indus State as Revealed through Public and Private Symbols," *Pakistan Archaeologists Forum* 4.1-2 (1995): 81-131.

14. Michael Jansen, "Preliminary Results on the "Forma Urbis" Research at Mohenjo-Daro," in *Interim Reports vol. 2: Reports on Field Work Carried out at Mohenjo-Daro, Pakistan 1983-84 by IsMEO-Aachen University Mission*, ed. Michael Jansen and Günter Urban (Aachen: IsMEO/ RWTH, 1987), 9-21.

15. Michael Jansen, "The Concept of Space in Harappan City Planning— Mohenjo-Daro," in *Concepts of Space: Ancient and Modern*, ed. Kapila Vatsyayan (New Delhi: Abhinav, 1991) 75-81.

16. Alexandra Ardeleanu-Jansen, Ute Franke and Michael Jansen, "An Approach Towards the Replacement of Artifacts into the Architectural Context of the Great Bath at Mohenjo-daro," *Forschungsprojekt DFG Mohenjo-Daro: Dokumentation in der Archéologie Techniken Methoden Analysen*, ed. Günter Urban and Michael Jansen (Aachen: RWTH, 1983), 43-70.

17. Ernest J. H. Mackay, *Further Excavations at Mohenjodaro* (New Delhi: Government of India, 1938), 17-19.

18. R. E. Mortimer Wheeler, *The Indus Civilization*, 3rd ed. (Cambridge: Cambridge University Press, 1968).

19. Marcia A. Fentress, "The Indus "Granaries": Illusion, Imagination and Archaeological Reconstruction, in *Studies in the Archaeology and Palaeoanthropology of South Asia*, ed. Kenneth A. R. Kennedy and Gregory L. Possehl (New Delhi: Oxford and IBH, 1984), 89-97.

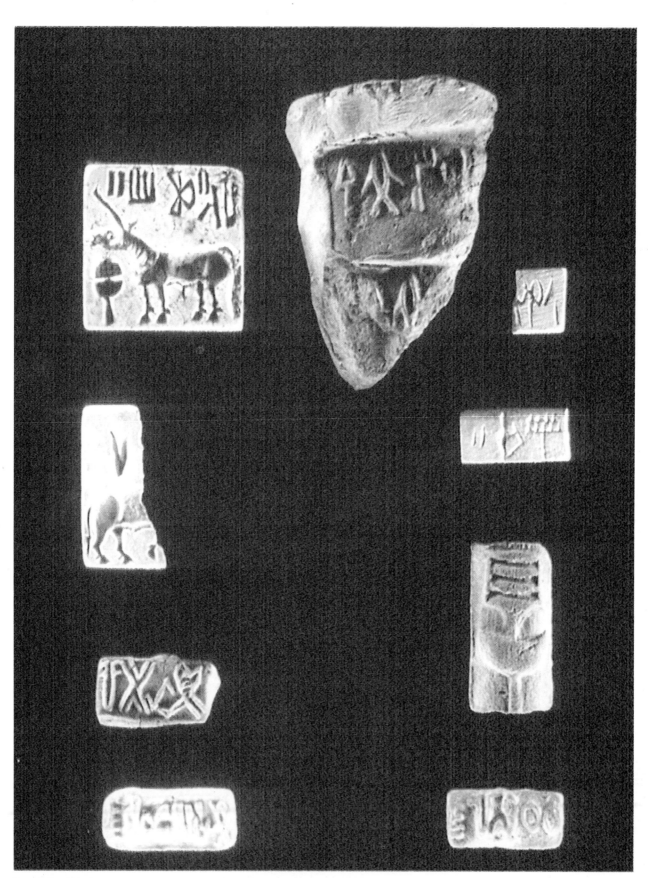

Fig. 4.1. Inscribed objects from Harappa, 2600-1900 B.C. Clockwise from top left, steatite seal, terracotta sealing, two incised steatite tablets, four different types of molded faience tablets, earliest Harappan seal fragment (Dales and Kenoyer 1991: fig. 13.44).

The Indus Script and Its Uses

The Origin of Writing

T he Indus script, invented around 2600 B.C. reflects the fundamental changes in social, political and ritual organization that accompanied the formation and consolidation of cities (fig. 4.1). When the first inscribed seals were used to stamp bundles of goods, they ushered in an era of economic and political hegemony that would last 700 years. Although archaeologists are still trying to find out where the script was invented and how to decipher it, they have begun to understand how the script was used and possibly why it disappeared.

The invention of a writing system is very different from the use of abstract symbols in rituals or for identification. Hundreds of years before the first writing appeared, Neolithic and Chalcolithic artisans painted and incised symbols on pottery and other material goods (fig. 4.2). Some symbols are simplified pictures of plants, animals or sacred mountains; others are abstract geometric shapes, lines, circles and triangles. Used for magical protection or simply to identify the owner of a vessel, these symbols reflect common cultural perceptions of the natural environment and sacred powers. These types of markings were probably woven into cloth or basketry, carved into wooden furniture, tools or containers, painted or tattooed on the body and used to arrange food items in ritual offerings. Because none

of these perishable materials remains in the archaeological record, we only see evidence for the use of symbols on pottery, stone or bone objects. The use of abstract symbols is common to all cultures, and signs similar to those used in the Indus Valley are found on pottery and other goods throughout the old world, from Egypt to China, without direct cultural connection.

On the basis of recent excavations of the Period 2 occupation levels at Harappa (2800-2600 B.C.), along with discoveries at other such early sites as Nausharo, it appears that there may have been one or more Early Indus scripts. At Harappa, we find increasing evidence for the use of multiple abstract symbols that were inscribed on pottery prior to or after firing (fig. 4.3). Some of these symbols are identical to characters used in the later Indus script and even occur in the same sequence, suggesting that they represented the same sounds or meanings (fig. 4.4).

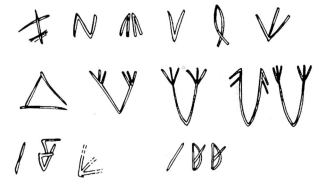
Fig. 4.3. Early Indus script from Harappa, ca. 3300-2600 B.C.

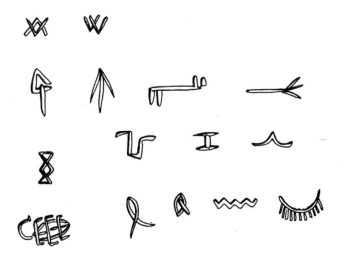
Fig. 4.2. Early potters' marks from Rehman Dheri, ca. 3500-2600 B.C., after Durrani et. al. 1995.

Fig. 4.4. Post firing graffiti on pottery from Harappa. On the left is an example of Early Indus script, ca. 2800 B.C., and on the right is the same sign used in the Indus script, ca. 2600 B.C.

The Early Indus script was probably distinct from the more widespread use of potters' marks, because such marks continued to be used even after the invention of the script. This pattern of use suggests that their function was different and, to some extent, independent of writing itself.

In Mesopotamia, writing was invented around 3300 B.C. to keep accounts and records of trade. Some scholars think the writing system of Egypt (3000 B.C.) developed in response to contacts with Mesopotamian traders or colonists who used writing. The Indus script (ca. 2600 B.C.) may have been inspired by contact with the southeastern corner of Mesopotamia (Elam in southwestern Iran), because some scholars believe it shows some similarities with the proto-Elamite script (3100-2900 B.C.) or some later form of this writing system.[1] However, all these regions had been in contact through overlapping trade networks for hundreds of years before the invention of writing. I would argue that the development of writing was much more complex.

Numerous writing systems may have been invented by individual spiritual leaders to record myths or by merchants to keep track of their goods, but none could have survived until a larger group of people, possibly even the community as a whole, developed the need for such a recording system. The invention, acceptance and eventual adoption of the Indus script by all of the regional settlements should be seen as a process stimulated primarily by local needs and fulfilled using a culturally meaningful set of signs. Numerous attempts have been made to relate the Indus script to other known scripts, but the only possible connection is with the proto-Elamite script of southwestern Iran. Even this connection is tenuous. On the basis of computer-aided comparative analysis of symbol sequences, Asko Parpola has concluded that the Indus script is not directly related to any known writing system.[2] In fact, none of the unique writing systems developed in Egypt, Mesopotamia and the Indus Valley reflects direct borrowing of ideas or techniques, but rather each represents different solutions to the unique needs of its own cultural and economic situation.

Writing in the Indus Valley is first found inscribed on pottery, but no single site has been identified as the place in which the writing system was invented. The earliest example of writing on a seal was recovered from Harappa, dating to around 2600 B.C. (fig. 4.5).[3] The bold, angular carving on the seal shows only a single sign and the rear end of a large animal, possibly a buffalo or a short-horned, humpless bull. This single example is not enough to determine that Harappa is the site where the script was first invented, but it does show that the style of writing and the techniques of seal carving changed over time. On later seals this sign is more rounded and symmetrical and the animal carving less angular.

Most examples (around 3,700) of Indus writing come from the excavations of Mohenjo-daro and Harappa, but some 60 different sites throughout the Indus Valley have contributed one or more objects with script.[4] Excavators before the 1940s did not record the stratigraphic context of each object systematically, thus making it impossible to sort out early and late examples of writing. Scholars have been forced to lump most inscriptions together as a single body of data. Clearly there are problems with this approach, and many statements about the script will undoubtedly be modified once the chronology of the seals and written objects is determined.

On the basis of the present evidence, the Indus script, as known from seals and other inscribed objects, emerged as a fully formed system of abstract signs, called graphemes (fig. 4.6). Over 4200 objects bearing the Indus script have been discovered so far, but most inscriptions are extremely short.[5] The average inscription contains five signs or graphemes; the longest series has twenty-six. After careful comparison of all the different signs, most scholars agree that there are between 400 and 450 different signs or graphemes. Because of handwriting differences or regional styles, graphemes were sometimes written in different ways, and researchers have dissimilar ideas about how to categorize these signs. Computerized studies have helped solve some problems by finding which ones occur most commonly next to other signs. Such computer-aided analysis makes it possible to identify signs that are basically the same but written slightly differently. Other complications arise when signs are actually joined together to form a compound character.

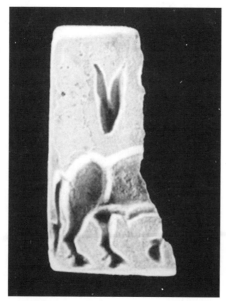

Fig. 4.5. Earliest steatite seal from Harappa, H90-1600.

Grapheme horned U, "fish"		idea (ideograph) hunting	
Allograph variants of a single sign		word (logograph) adze (phoneme) " A" syllable (morpheme) "yah"	
Circumgraph sound enclosed signs			
Ligature pipal leaf and box			

Fig. 4.6. The Indus script.

Many inscriptions consist of only one sign; in these cases, the grapheme must represent a word or an idea. The most common sign "⫟" is often used alone, but it also can be combined into other sign sequences. This sign may be a pictograph of a bull with horns, or a handled container, but it undoubtedly represents a very important word or idea. Another common sign is the symbol "⚹," which some believe may mean "fish" or "glittering star" or "god."[6] Some other ancient writing systems that have been deciphered begin by using pictographic symbols to represent an idea (ideograph) or a word (logograph), but over time, these same symbols come to represent a syllable or a single sound (phoneme). Along with these changes in meaning is usually a dramatic decrease in the number of signs needed to formulate meaningful communication. Early logographic scripts, such as archaic Sumerian had over 700 different signs, while later alphabetic scripts had fewer than fifty signs.

With 400 to 450 signs, the Indus script falls somewhere in the middle. Although it is generally agreed that the Indus script is not an alphabetic form of writing, it does not have enough different signs to be a logographic script. In between these two extremes is a type of writing system referred to as logosyllabic (morphemic) where a single sign can mean either a word, a syllable or a sound. Most scholars think the Indus inscriptions represent a logosyllabic writing system, where a sequence of two or more signs would represent either a complete word or a sentence of several words and grammatical indicators. However, some of the signs do look like pictographs, for example a fish, or a man holding a bow. When used individually, such signs may have represented ideas or words, or even entire stories. On some objects a single sign is found on one side while a series of signs is inscribed on the other. The use of graphemes in different linguistic contexts and combinations may indicate that the Indus script combined both logosyllabic and ideographic systems at the same time. This versatility may reflect the experimental nature of the script and its use by newly emerging elites.

Writing Styles and Uses

After the invention, adoption of the script may have taken several generations, but in archaeological terms this is seen as a rapid innovation. By 2600 B.C., specialized engravers made seals with the writing in reverse so that when stamped in clay it formed a raised positive message. Eventually, artisans used seals or wooden molds to produce numerous copies of inscriptions or narrative scenes on fired terracotta and glazed faience tablets. Potters used seals to impress the writing on pottery vessels, usually the disposable drinking cups (cat. nos. 193, 194). Molds for making large pottery vessels were incised on the exterior, possibly to identify the owner of the mold itself (fig. 4.7). On other molds the script was incised on the interior in reverse so that the base of the jar would have raised symbols. Artisans and workers, who may have been illiterate, produced these and other examples of the script, using or copying signs that they could not read.

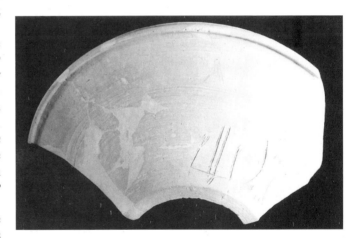

Fig. 4.7. Script incised prior to firing on the exterior of a terracotta mold from Nausharo used to make large globular jars. (10 cm height, NS III 87 (32) 153, Department of Archaeology, EBK 5996).

Many scholars would agree that the people who used these inscribed objects and read the messages encoded in the signs were the people who controlled the Indus cities. Some seals may have been used by religious leaders for special ceremonies, and others were used by landowners or traders. In all of the major settlements the literate elites, ritual specialists, merchants or landowners used writing in many different contexts in the home and at work: on personal ornaments and ritual objects as well as on trade goods. It appears to me that they were comfortable enough with the writing to scribble messages to each other on pottery vessels (fig. 4.8) and write names or protective charms onto wet clay vessels or sealings.

Some literate individuals who traveled to distant lands carrying their seals and writing had seals inscribed with words that appear to be foreign to the Indus language (see fig. 1.15), but so far, no seals or impressions with foreign writing have been found in the Indus Valley itself.

Only by carefully studying the different contexts in which the writing was used and the types of objects on which writing appears can we begin to understand the role it played in the Indus society. The Indus script was carved, incised, chiseled, inlaid, painted, molded, and embossed on terracotta and glazed ceramic, shell, bone and ivory, sandstone, steatite and gypsum, copper and bronze, silver and gold (fig. 4.9). We can also assume that the script was woven into fabrics and basketry, carved into wood, inscribed onto palm leaves, and possibly even painted on the human body, all perishable materials. The wide variety of materials and techniques involving the Indus script is unparalleled in the mid-third millennium B.C.

In most instances the script was written from right to left as is the practice in Semitic scripts such as Arabic or Hebrew. We can determine the direction of the writing system by the cramped lettering on the left edge of many inscriptions as well as the overlapping of letters scratched into pottery. However, many early writing systems allowed the signs to be written in either direction, and some Indus tablets show short texts written in opposite directions (fig. 4.10). Longer texts that comprised more than one line were sometimes written in alternating directions called boustrophedon, where the first line proceeds from right to left and the next line reads from left to right.[7] While this reversibility is confusing for archaeologists and linguists, it must have been quite normal for the people who were writing and using the script.

Fig. 4.8a. Black-slipped jar from Harappa with both pre-firing and post-firing inscriptions, cat. no. 177.

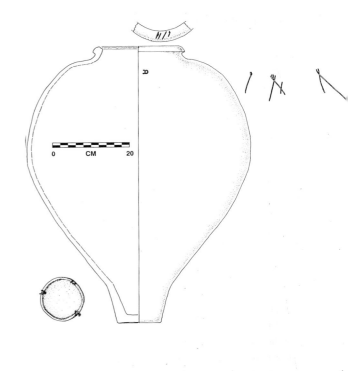

Fig. 4.8b. Line drawing of black-slipped jar, cat. no. 177.

Fig. 4.9. This silver seal with a unicorn motif is one of two found at Mohenjo-daro (Mackay 1938: vol. 2, Pl. XC, 1; XCVI, 520).

Seals and Their Uses

Square and rectangular seals made from fired steatite are the most extraordinary category of object with Indus script. The soft soapstone was carved, polished and then fired in a kiln to whiten and harden the surface. This hard outer surface is commonly refered to as a glaze, but it is not a glassy layer and results from a combination of surface preparation, possibly through the application of an alkaline solution, and firing.[8] Only after the outside had been hardened could this material be used to stamp wet clay repeatedly. Even then, repeated use of a seal on clay eventually wore down the corners and smoothed away the sharp edges of the script. Many worn seals have been found buried in the houses or in the streets of the major cities. Seals made of metal are extremely rare, but two finely made silver seals with unicorn motifs and script were found at Mohenjo-daro (see fig. 4.9), and two copper seals with less refined depictions of unicorn-like animals have been found at Lothal[9] and at the site of Ras al-Junayz in Oman.[10]

The square seals usually have a line of script along the top of the seal and a carved animal in the central portion. The animals depicted on the seals, usually males, include domestic and wild animals as well as mythical creatures such as the unicorn. A small feeding trough or mysterious offering stand is often placed below the head of the animal. Some seals contain more complex iconographic scenes that represent mythological or religious events. On the reverse side is a carved knob or boss, with a perforation for holding a thick cord (fig. 4.11). Large square seals with sharp corners and a boss at the back do not hang in a manner that would have been comfortable, and many of the largest seals may have been kept in a pouch. The smaller seals could have been hung from the waist or worn around the neck without much inconvenience, but due to minute cracks in manufacturing and the weakness of soapstone on the interior

of a seal, the seal often snapped off at the perforated knob or boss.

Many a surprised merchant must have reached for the seal to find a boss with no seal attached. A lost seal with the writing and animal motif intact could be used by anyone for any purpose, like a credit card today. In Mesopotamia, when a seal was lost, a herald announced its loss and the date so that any use of the seal after that announcement would be invalidated.[11] In Mesopotamia, there were severe punishments for people who used seals illegally. We do not know what the Indus people did when a seal was lost, but a change in seal design during the latter part of the Harappan Period suggests that they did change the design of the seals so they would not snap off so easily.

Long, rectangular seals had a hole drilled from the side across the middle of the seal (fig. 4.12). However, even this modified form occasionally broke in two pieces along the drill hole. A seal that was broken in two would have been useless, and most of the seals we have found in the streets of the cities may have been broken intentionally so that they could not be reused illegally. The complete seals we find in the streets almost always are missing the boss. In contrast, complete seals we find buried in the floor of a room or courtyard are often heavily worn and usually have the boss intact (fig. 4.11). This suggests that people occasionally lost their seals while walking or riding through the city, but that they usually broke the seals when they were no longer useful

Fig. 4.11. Heavily worn unicorn seal with boss still intact. This seal was found in disturbed floor levels of a house on Mound ET, Harappa, H95-2419/4609-1.

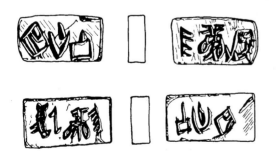

Fig. 4.10. Incised steatite tablets from Harappa, with writing in opposite directions (top, H95-2436; bottom, H95-2497).

Fig. 4.12. Long rectangular seal with writing from Mohenjo-daro, NMP 50.315.

or buried them in their homes for safekeeping. It is interesting to note that no seal has ever been found with a human burial in the Indus Valley, whereas in Egypt and Mesopotamia the person's seal was usually included with the burial offerings.

The long rectangular seals were less likely to fall off a cord, but the change in shape resulted in the elimination of the central animal motif. This type of seal is found with only abstract writing, which radically altered communication. Impressions made by the square seals carry two distinct messages, one is presented in the script that could only be understood by a literate person and the other in the animal motif, that even a child could comprehend. Illiterate workers loading or delivering bundles of goods stamped with animal motifs could very easily perceive who the owners were and which boats they should be taken to. The specific message in the written portion would verify to a literate merchant who the exact owner was. Rectangular seals on the other hand could only have been used to communicate with literate trading partners. Few sealings from long rectangular seals have been found; perhaps these seals were not used in everyday trade, but had a different function. These two types of seals may represent a chronological change in seal styles, but this has not yet been confirmed.

Incised and Molded Tablets

We see another common use of writing on miniature tablets made of incised steatite, molded terracotta or faience (see figs. 4.1, 4.10, 4.13). Occasionally these tablets have an animal motif on one side and writing on the other, but usually only writing, like the rectangular seals. Unlike the seals, however, these tablets were not used to make impressions, so the writing is not reversed. Most small tablets come from Harappa, and we think that many found at Mohenjo-daro, 570 kms to the south, may have originated in Harappa.

Numerous duplicates of the incised steatite tablets have been found, and many copies of the molded tablets were made from a single mold. The writing usually consists of a short inscription on one side and what we think are numerals on the opposite side. During excavations at Harappa in the 1920s many tablets and duplicates were found in excavations on Mound F. In one area two groups of identical incised steatite tablets (nine with one set of inscriptions and four with another set) were found along with seals, weights and pendants.[12] In area G, south of the recently discovered gateway on Mound ET (Chap. 3), Vats found a concentration of thirty-one identical cylindrical terracotta tablets of unknown use (fig. 4.13). Concentrations of tablets recovered through recent excavations at Harappa indicate that these tablets become popular during the late part of Period 3B and continued on into the final phase of the Harappan occupation (Period 3C).

Fig. 4.13. Cylindrical and twisted rectangular terracotta tablets from Harappa.

Tablets that do have numbers on one side may represent some accounting system. But whereas in Mesopotamia a scribe could immediately write down the accounts on a clay tablet, the Indus tablets made with a complex technological process involving lengthy manufacture (see Chap. 6) were not for on-the-spot accounting. The Indus tablets may have been used as tokens, made up in advance and distributed when goods were brought into the city as tribute or for sale.

These tablets appear to have been used exclusively in the large cities, because only one or two examples have been reported from each of the smaller settlements such as Lothal, Chanhudaro, Kalibangan and Rupar.[13] None of the actual seals or molds used to make the tablets have been found from any of these sites, but the main production center was probably at Harappa. Discovering the workshop where these tablets were made would be a major breakthrough and would help to interpret their function.

Copper Tablets

Rectangular copper tablets with incised writing and animal motifs are found almost exclusively at Mohenjo-daro (cat. no. 31, 32). The only eight inscribed copper tablets found at Harappa are made with raised script, using a different technique (fig. 4.14). The flat copper tablets from Mohenjo-daro have many duplicates, as do the steatite and faience tablets of Harappa, and the reverse side of the copper tablets usually has an animal or geometric motif. One tablet that has several copies shows a hunter with a bow wearing a horned headdress, similar to those on figurines and carved on some of the seals.

Unlike the tiny steatite or faience tablets, which may have only represented a value or a commodity, copper tablets have intrinsic value. They can be remelted and used to make other tablets or tools. Many copper tablets at Mohenjo-daro are approximately the same size and weight and may represent an attempt to create a standard currency or medium of exchange. The fact that these tablets are not found outside of Mohenjo-daro indicates that they were limited to interactions and communication at this site alone and not on a regional scale.

Fig. 4.14. Copper tablet from Harappa with raised script, H94-2198.

One of the least studied but potentially most informative contexts for writing is on pottery. Signs were molded on the base of a vessel or incised in the soft clay prior to firing. Such inscriptions were made by the potter or by a literate person who came to the workshop specifically to write on the unfired pottery. Seal impressions on pointed-base goblets were probably made by the potter, as these impressions were often made while the vessel was still on the wheel and the clay wet. Inscriptions made after firing, referred to as graffiti, could have been scratched on the vessel at any time.

Large black-slipped storage jars invariably have bold graffiti on the curving shoulder of the vessel, often written at an angle as if the writer did not care how it looked (see fig. 4.8). The inscriptions probably represent the owner's name, the vessel contents, or the destination. Parallel lines are often scratched onto the rims of jars of different sizes, but there is no correlation between the number of lines and

the size of the vessel. Perhaps they represent how many measures of grain, oil or beer were poured into the jar, or they may indicate the number of times a jar has been refilled and emptied into another container.

Inscriptions or graffiti scratched onto a vessel in use reflect the practical application of writing in the course of active transactions. The traders and consumers of these specific goods must have been able to read and write, or at least recognize specific symbols.

In addition to the commercial or economic applications of writing, this new invention is also attested on personal objects and ornaments used exclusively by wealthy and powerful individuals. Copper tools, gold ornaments and even tiny bone pins were inscribed with single or multiple signs that may have had some ritual significance or were the names of the owners.

At Harappa, tiny bone points that may have been used as hairpins or toothpicks have a miniature inscription at one end. The sign is too small to be visible at a distance and clearly was not a public communication; possibly these were personal identification marks or protective symbols.

One of the most exciting discoveries of the use of script resulted from the reexamination of gold ornaments excavated from Mohenjo-daro in the 1920s. A large collection of gold objects found together in a copper vessel included four ornaments with minute inscriptions that probably represent

Stoneware Bangles

Indus artisans, among the most highly skilled and creative artists in antiquity, transformed raw materials into totally new substances using complex technical processes and specialized furnaces or kilns. The oldest high-fired stoneware ceramics in the world were crafted by the Indus artisans into a standard ornament worn as a bangle or possibly carried as a ring of office (fig. 4.15). Each bangle bore a tiny inscription only visible on careful examination.

The process of manufacture must have been shrouded in mystery and preserved through complex rituals to enhance the value of the objects, because this technology disappeared at the end of the Indus cities and was not reproduced again in South Asia. After careful preparation the four or five bangles with tiny inscriptions were placed in a small canister that was stacked with other canisters and plastered with a mixture of clay and straw (fig. 4.16).[14] A single sign of the Indus script, possibly a sacred symbol to ensure a successful firing, was traced on the wet plaster. This stack of canisters was then placed inside a larger jar, covered

with clay and sealed with a square stamp seal. Each stage of manufacture and firing appears to have been accompanied by some use of the script, effectively controlling and protecting the production. The fact that this technology disappeared with the Indus elites is evidence for the total success of this strategy of secrecy and control. Even today, after almost ten years of experimentation, we have not been able to replicate these unique stoneware bangles perfectly.[15]

Fig. 4.15. Stoneware bangle (cat. no. 93) and inscribed bangle fragment from Mohenjo-daro.

Fig. 4.16. Diagram of canisters and containers for stoneware bangle firing, after Halim and Vidale 1984, fig. 63.

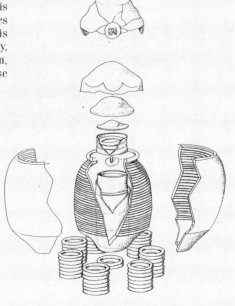

the names of the owners scratched on to the polished surface (fig. 4.17). It is possible that before this wealth was hidden away, the names of owners were incised on some of the gold jewelry. All inscriptions appear to have been made by the same sharp, pointed tool by the same hand. These inscriptions are extremely important because they are clearly different from the types of inscriptions found on the large copper celts and chisels which also have been found in large hoards (fig. 4.18).

Fig. 4.17a. Golden pendant with inscription from jewelry hoard at Mohenjo-daro, cat. no. 39.

Fig. 4.17b. Drawing of inscription that encircles the gold ornament.

Script on gold pendant.

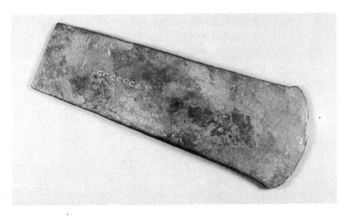

Fig. 4.18. Inscribed bronze ax from Mohenjo-daro, cat. no. 42.

On copper or bronze tools, the writing appears formal, carefully chiseled in a vertical line down the center of the ax or chisel. Other examples are oriented along the butt end of the celts, but in most instances the script would have been partially or totally obscured by hafting. One hoard found at Harappa contained fifty-six copper/bronze tools and weapons. Two of these objects, a dagger and an ax, both were inscribed with a sign that Parpola interprets as meaning "leader" or "king." Such inscriptions are uncommon and may represent the name of the owner or the deity to whom the valuable objects were dedicated.

Beyond the commercial and personal uses of writing, the Indus script appears to have had protective or magical powers. Single and multiple signs were carved or painted on objects that were a part of daily life: shell and terracotta bangles, beads, pottery and tools. The repetition of specific signs at many different sites suggests that some signs were probably not personal names, but may have had some ritual significance. Painted on the inside of a plate or the interior of a terracotta bangle (fig. 4.19), these signs may have blessed the food or protected the wearer.

Other ritual uses of the script occur in conjunction with narrative scenes of what are probably rituals involving deities and powerful spirits. Usually such scenes are preserved on molded terracotta tablets, more rarely on the carved steatite seals. Short inscriptions associated with these scenes may represent the names of deities, constellations or supernatural events. The script is also found carved on ivory and bone rods (fig 4.20), possibly used in divining the future or perhaps part of a ritual game.

Fig. 4.19. Painted Indus script on the inside of a bangle from Balakot, cat. no. 37.

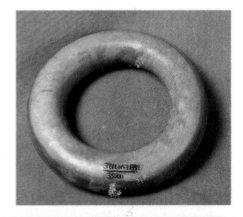

Fig. 4.20. Inscribed bone rod from Mohenjo-daro, cat. no. 38.

The Power of Writing

Inscribed objects are found in all sites, throughout the cities in the streets and houses. But this distribution does not mean that everyone used the writing or that the elites who used writing were living in all parts of the settlements. Many inscribed objects were inadvertently redeposited in secondary deposits in different parts of the city through the normal process of city growth. Broken seals, sealings and inscribed pottery would have accumulated with garbage on the streets or have been dumped into abandoned houses. Over hundreds of years, as new foundation platforms were constructed and filled with this same garbage, the inscribed objects were moved from the place where they originally were used or discarded (primary deposits) to foundation fill or secondary deposits at places in the city where literate people may not have lived or worked at all.

Many earlier excavators did not record the contexts in which seals were found, so we cannot assess whether they were in foundation fill (secondary deposits) or actual floor and street levels (primary deposits). Recent excavations at Harappa have defined these different contexts, and we can begin sorting out the complex problem of identifying where seals and inscribed objects were used in the city: the major streets leading into and out of city gateway, the craft workshop areas and near the houses in the high walled areas. Some houses have lots of seals and inscribed objects, and others have very few or none at all. In one pottery manufacturing area at the northwest edge of Mound E there are no seals or tablets, while in the bead and shellworking area of Mound ET there are a number of inscribed objects.

After reviewing the different ways in which the script was used, we see several patterns emerge. First, only certain people owned seals and few people were literate. Nevertheless, the script was generally used in a manner that was openly visible to the general public. For example seals were probably worn and used in public, and graffiti was openly visible on trade vessels. Writing was used in everyday contexts as well as for religious purposes, but the presence of script on gold jewelry, copper tools and stoneware bangles suggests that only the very rich and powerful wrote their names or attributions on personal objects. Objects with writing were scattered in all parts of the city, and almost every settlement of the Indus Valley has produced one or more seals or inscribed objects. A large signboard from Dholavira shows large writing, but most inscriptions are small or miniature. Perhaps the most important recent discovery is that the style of writing and carving of seals changed over time; small tablets without animal motifs but with script, come from the middle to late part of the Harappan Phase.

These patterns indicate that writing was not static but a dynamic invention that had permeated every aspect of urban life. Landowners, merchants, religious leaders, administrators and professional artisans were probably the only people who owned or used inscribed seals, but many of them may not have been able to read or write. Nevertheless, everyone in the society understood the power and authority reflected in writing, and its use throughout the Indus and Saraswati regions reveals a period of cultural and economic integration. The writing would have reinforced this integration and validated the power of the ruling classes. In combination with religious symbols and narratives the writing would have legitimized the power of the people who used it by associating them with supernatural powers. The writing on the seals is associated with symbolic animals representing clans or possibly trading communities. The most common animal, the unicorn, is mythical, and the other animals must have had some important symbolic meaning. On the small tablets, writing and occasional narrative scenes are on a miniature scale, but they probably illustrate public rituals or events that were viewed by the entire community or city. Some tablets may have functioned as ritual tokens or souvenirs, not unlike the molded or inscribed amulets available at the tombs of saints or at important shrines in Pakistan and India today. In all of the many ways in which writing was used, it is closely associated with cities, trade and ritual. Writing and seals remained important to the political and ritual elites as long as the trade networks and cities continued to exist.

Disappearance of the Script

The script disappeared when the elites who used this means of communication in trade and ritual were no longer dominant. More than any other fact, the rapid disappearance of the seals and writing by 1700 B.C. (based on recent dates from Harappa) demonstrates that writing was used exclusively by a small but powerful segment of the population and did not play a critical role in the lives of the common people. The seal carvers lost their jobs, and eventually, when new elites emerged, writing was not important. Molds used to make terracotta and faience tablets were destroyed or discarded when they no longer had economic or ritual significance. Traders no longer stamped bundles with seals or scribbled names and messages on storage jars. And although many of the crafts continued to be practiced, the artisans had no need to inscribe copper tools or pottery vessels with the script.

After the Indus script disappeared, between 1900 and 1700 B.C., there was no reason to invent a new script until the rise of new cities in the Ganges river valley around

300 B.C. During the intervening centuries, the villages and towns of the Indus and Ganga river valleys were controlled by Sanskrit-speaking Brahman priests, landowners and merchants who did write, but committed their sacred scriptures and sacrificial mantras to memory.

When Emperor Ashoka set up pillars and massive boulders inscribed with royal edicts around 250 B.C., he became the first ruler in ancient India to use writing to communicate to the masses. None of the awestruck peasants could actually read these edicts, but an imperial messenger probably stood by the monumental inscriptions and recited them from memory. The important thing was that these edicts, placed throughout the imperial realm, from Afghanistan to southern India, were not written in Sanskrit, the language of the Brahmanical elites, but were in the major local dialects.

Two new scripts were invented; Kharoshthi in the north-west was based on Aramaic, the language of the Achaemenid Persian Empire and was written from right to left; the Brahmi script in peninsular India was written from left to right and is thought to have been derived from a Western Semitic script. No one knows who invented these scripts, but they may have been commissioned by rulers and developed by Brahmans well versed in literature and phonetics. The recent discovery of Brahmi script on potsherds from Sri Lanka dates to around 500 B.C.,[16] but the use of both Kharoshthi and Brahmi on stone edicts in the peninsular subcontinent dates somewhat later, around 250 B.C. When they first appeared, these newly invented scripts represent fully developed writing systems with no direct connection to the earlier Indus script.[17]

Deciphering the Script

In order to decipher an ancient script it is necessary to establish certain parameters or assumptions. If the Indus script is logosyllabic, it cannot be deciphered as an alphabetic or syllabic script. A logosyllabic script can only be deciphered if the language that it represents is known. At present, no modern language can be directly traced to the Indus script, but most scholars agree that it belongs to the Dravidian language family. Over twenty-five Dravidian languages are presently spoken in the subcontinent, including Tamil, Telegu, Kannada and Malayalam. Most of these languages fall in the categories of central and southern Dravidian and are found in peninsular India and northern Sri Lanka, areas that were never part of the Indus culture. A branch of North Dravidian, called Brahui, is still spoken in Baluchistan and southern Afghanistan, a region at the western edge of the Indus Valley. Traces of Dravidian words are still found in the southern Indus Valley in the form of river names, and many Dravidian loan words are found in ancient Sanskrit, the Indo-Aryan language of the Rig Veda.

After the end of the Indus cities, Indo-Aryan languages must have spread throughout the regions once dominated by the Indus-Dravidian language.

Not all scholars agree with the Dravidian identification, but even if it does turn out to be correct, other languages may have been written using the Indus script. In Mesopotamia, Sumerian and Akkadian, two different languages were written with the same cuneiform writing system (as most modern European languages are written in the same script). Today, several different major languages are spoken in regions that were once under the influence of the Indus cities. Austro-Asiatic, Sino-Tibetan and Indo-Aryan are the most important language families, but there are also words belonging to the mysterious language "X" which cannot be associated with any modern linguistic family.[18] If individuals who spoke these other languages moved to the Indus cities and became established as merchants or landowners, their names and the names of their deities may have been written using the Indus script. In addition to the presence of different language families, there were undoubtedly many different dialects spoken throughout the Indus Valley. During the Early Historic period in South Asia many people spoke more than one dialect. For example Sanskrit was spoken in the ritual and administrative contexts whereas regional Prakrit dialects were spoken at home.[19] Although it is possible that the Indus script represents the formal language spoken by elites, some names and words could reflect local dialects that varied from region to region. Consequently, if the writing on the seals does represent more than one language or dialect, we cannot decipher it until a bilingual text or a dictionary has been discovered.

If proto-Dravidian is the major language component of the Indus script, we can take a second step by isolating root words that are shared by all of the various Dravidian languages. These root words represent a hypothetical language called proto-Dravidian, from which all of the various Dravidian languages evolved. Root words that refer to a concrete concept can be represented by a picture of that object, but abstract concepts must be communicated phonetically by using pictures of objects whose names could be combined to produce the intended word. This technique of communication is based on the rebus principle and the most common English example is the use of the symbol for "bee" and "leaf" to create the word "belief." The rebus principle, using symbols of concrete objects to create a word for an abstract concept, was commonly used in both Egyptian and Mesopotamian writing systems.

Proto-Dravidian root words were originally monosyllabic. Using the rebus approach, scholars have identified key words that may represent the general meaning of specific Indus signs. The most convincing example is the fish sign " ⚚ ". The Dravidian root for fish is "min" and the same word means "to glitter, flash or shine." The fish sign combined with six single strokes is very common in the Indus writing, and it could be translated as "aru min" or Six Stars, which would represent the constellation Pleiades. Another common occurrence is the fish sign with seven strokes ⚚ ⁞⁞⁞. In Dravidian this would translate as "elu-min" or Seven Stars, which is the name for the constellation of Seven Sages (Ursa Major or the Big Dipper).[20]

Although these interpretations sound convincing, the rebus approach can only be useful when there is some way to check and confirm the meaning or the grammatical sequence of the words. An example that illustrates some of the problems in trying to decipher language using this approach is "Eye-Heart-Apple." Most Americans would be able to interpret the symbols for Eye-Heart-Apple[👁 ♡ 🍎] as meaning I love the Big Apple (aka New York). Without knowing the proper sequence of the words or that "apple" should be read "BIG Apple" and that "Big Apple" is another name for "New York," the signs Eye-Heart-Apple could just as easily be read "I love apples," "Apples love eyes," "Eyes blood apples," or by using only the first letters of the words Eye - Heart - Apple, "EHA" and in reverse order, "AHE."

The discovery of longer texts, with many sentences would be the next best thing to finding a bilingual text. Grammatical structure and repeated sign sequences could be isolated and compared with the thousands of shorter inscriptions on seals and tablets. Unfortunately, no long texts have been found. If they were written on palm leaf manuscripts or parchment, they would not have been preserved in the humid climate of the Indus Valley. Over fifty different claims at decipherment have been published,[21] but none of them meets the stringent requirements of the general academic community. For the present we cannot check the proposed interpretations, and however logical or convincing they may be, they do not represent a decipherment.

Even though we may never know the specific meaning of the script or who could read and write, the script represents a shared set of symbols and beliefs that was spread out over an extremely large geographical area. These shared beliefs must have played an important role in the integration of the urban and rural populations and would have been reinforced by the exotic ritual items obtained through trade or created by new technologies.

Endnotes

1. Walter A. Fairservis, Jr., *Excavations at the Harappan Site of Allahdino: The Graffiti: A Model in the Decipherment of the Harappan Script, Papers of the Allahdino Expedition*, No. 1 (New York: American Museum of Natural History, 1977), 45; Walter A. Fairservis, Jr., "The Decipherment of Harappan Writing, Review of Tamil Civilization: Indus Script Special Issue, *The Quarterly Review of Archaeology 1986*, 4.3-4 (fall 1988): 10.

2. Asko Parpola, "Deciphering the Indus Script: A Summary Report," in *South Asian Archaeology, 1993*, ed. Asko Parpola and Petteri Koskikallio (Helsinki: Suomalainen Tiedeakatemia, 1994), 2:571-86.

3. J. Mark Kenoyer, "Urban Process in the Indus Tradition: A Preliminary Model from Harappa," in *Harappa Excavations 1986-1990*, ed. Richard H. Meadow (Madison, Wis.: Prehistory Press, 1991), 29-60.

4. Asko Parpola, *Deciphering the Indus Script* (Cambridge: Cambridge University Press, 1994); Asko Parpola, "Indus Script," in *The Encyclopedia of Languages and Linguistics*, ed. R. E. Asher and J. M. Y. Simpson (Oxford: Pergamon Press, 1994), 3: 1669-70.

5. Parpola, *Deciphering the Indus Script*; Parpola, "Indus Script."

6. Parpola, *Deciphering the Indus Script*.

7. Walter A. Fairservis, Jr., "The Script of the Indus Valley Civilization," *Scientific American* 248.3 (1983): 58-66; Asko Parpola, "The Indus Script: A Challenging Puzzle," *World Archaeology* 17.3 (1986): 399-419.

8. Ernest J. H. Mackay, *Further Excavations at Mohenjodaro* (New Delhi: Government of India, 1938), vol. 1, 346-7.

9. Shikarpur Raganatha Rao, *Lothal: A Harappan Port Town (1955-62)*, vol. 2 Memoirs of the Archaeological Survey of India, no. 78 (New Delhi: Archaeological Survey of India, 1985) CLIV,c, 314.

10. Serge Cleuziou, Gherardo Gnoli, Robin Christian and Maurizio Tosi, "Cachets Inscrits de la fin du IIIe millénaire avant notre ère á Ras' al-Junayz, Sultanat d'Oman," *Académie des Inscriptions & Belles-Lettres, Comptes rendus des séances de l'année 1994* (April-June 1994): 453-68.

11. J. Nicholas Postgate, *Early Mesopotamia: Society and Economic at the Dawn of History* (London: Routledge, 1992), 282.

12. Madho Sarup Vats, *Excavations at Harappa* (Delhi: Government of India Press, 1940), 58-59.

13. Jagat Pati Joshi and Asko Parpola, *Corpus of Indus Seals and Inscriptions. 1. Collections in India* (Helsinki: Suomalainen Tiedeakatemia, 1987).

14. Mohammad A. Halim and Massimo Vidale, "Kilns, Bangles and Coated Vessels: Ceramic Production in Closed Containers at Moenjodaro," *Interim Reports Vol. 1: Reports on Field Work Carried out at Mohenjo-Daro, Pakistan 1982-83 by IsMEO-Aachen University Mission*, ed. Michael Jansen and Günter Urban (Aachen: RWTH-IsMEO, 1984), 63-97.

15. J. Mark Kenoyer, "Experimental Studies of Indus Valley Technology at Harappa," in *South Asian Archaeology, 1993*, ed. Asko Parpola and Petteri Koskikallio (Helsinki: Suomalainen Tiedeakatemia, 1994), 1:245-62.

16. Frank Raymond Allchin, ed., *The Archaeology of Early Historic South Asia* (Cambridge: Cambridge University Press, 1995), 176-79.

17. Halim and Vidale, "Ceramic Production."

18. Walter A. Fairservis, Jr. and Franklin C. Southworth, "Linguistic Archaeology and the Indus Valley Culture," in *Old Problems and New Perspectives in the Archaeology of South Asia*, ed. J. Mark Kenoyer (Madison, Wis.: UW-Madison Department of Anthropology, 1989), 133-41.

19. A. K. Ramanujan, "Toward an Anthology of City Images," in *Urban India: Society, Space and Image*, ed. Richard G. Fox (Durham: Duke University, 1971), 224-44.

20. Parpola, *Deciphering the Indus Script*.

21. Parpola, "Indus Script: Summary Report."

Fig. 5.1. The so-called priest-king of Mohenjo-daro, cat. no. 118.

Rulers and Traders of the Indus Cities

Chapter 5

Ever since the discovery of the Indus Valley civilization, archaeologists have been looking for objects that would help to identify the rulers and political leaders of the cities (figs. 5.1). What they have found is quite unexpected, because it does not follow the general pattern seen in other early urban societies. The Indus rulers appear to have governed their cities through the control of trade and religion, rather than with military might. No monuments were erected to glorify their power, and no depictions of warfare or conquered enemies are found in the entire corpus of Indus art or sculpture. Instead, the rulers carried striking carved seals with animal symbols and writing (fig. 5.2) and wore ornaments made with secret technologies and rare materials. These symbols of wealth and power were what set the rulers apart from the common people, and they also reflect the many different social and economic levels that were controlled by the rulers.

In each large settlement, charismatic leaders supported by leading citizens from one or more powerful communities must have been responsible for the initial integration of different communities under a unified city government. These leaders would have been responsible for the establishment and maintenance of well-planned streets, housing, wells and drainage facilities. The identity of these rulers and the symbols of the clans to which they belonged are preserved on the carved stone seals; when the script is deciphered, we will be able to speak their names.

Using their political skills and backed by landlords and merchants, these early leaders created an urban society that was made up of many different social levels and organized in a way that had never before existed. Artisans and agricultural laborers, administrative elites and traders, ritual leaders and political rulers all lived together in walled cities divided into well-defined neighborhoods. Large buildings that may have been the houses or palaces of powerful leaders were not located in a single area of the city, but were scattered on all the different mounds. This living pattern was very different from Mesopotamian cities, where palaces and temples clearly marked the administrative and religious centers of the cities.

For over 700 years, the cities of the Indus Valley retained their position as centers of economic and political power. Thirty generations of rulers and traders came and went during this time, and all used a common set of symbols to represent their power. The square stone seals, with their undeciphered writing and carved animal motifs are the most important symbols of power wielded by the Indus rulers. On each seal was a name or title along with a totemic animal motif that may have represented a clan or political office. These distinctive seals first appeared with the rise of Indus cities and then totally disappeared with their demise. Other objects that were used or worn by the elites also emerge and disappear along with the seals, such as distinctive painted pottery, elaborate ornaments, metal tools and cubical stone weights that may have been used for taxation.

The continuity in many artifact styles and cultural symbols during this long time indicates a stability in trade and technology as well as religious beliefs. In the later Early Historic period around 300 B.C., the Mauryan kings were advised to promote four ideals in order to achieve a prosperous kingdom: *dharma* (right action), *artha* (wealth and trade), *kama* (the good life through peace and order) and *moksha* (spiritual release through the previous three objectives).[1] The first three concepts of urban rule appear to have been equally important to the Indus rulers, who promoted trade and increased the wealth of their cities without the extensive use of military coercion. The long stability of Indus religious symbols may indicate that religious order and right action were an important mechanism for integrating the cities and maintaining connections over a wide geographical area.

Nevertheless, there is clear evidence for the changing fortunes of political and economic power in the periodic

Fig. 5.2. Steatite seals from Mohenjo-daro, clockwise from top left, cat. nos. 11, 15, 16, and 17.

growth and decay of the cities. At Harappa, for example, the walls around Mound E were rebuilt at least three times between 2600 B.C. and 1900 B.C. The city gateways and drains that had become choked with garbage were cleared and repaired on numerous occasions. During periods of economic prosperity and political stability, the city almost doubled in size, as new suburbs with markets and craft areas were established to the east and north of the original walled mounds.

At each of the larger urban centers, similar major phases of rebuilding and growth can be taken to represent the rise of new rulers who had gained the support of powerful communities living in the city or its suburbs. Creating a city or building impressive monuments and temples is something that is traditionally associated with gods and kings. In South Asia new rulers often established new cities or renewed the old city, adding new markets to accommodate the merchants and building new temples to honor the gods and goddess that protected the kingdom. These publicly visible acts were an important first step in asserting economic, ritual and political authority over the city and the region in general.

However, unlike Mesopotamia and Egypt, where stone reliefs and sculptures showed the kings building or consecrating cities and temples,[2] in South Asia the representation of rulers in sculpture has never been a common tradition. More than 150 stone columns and carved stone edicts were set up by Ashoka Maurya (274-232 B.C.), the most powerful ruler of the Mauryan dynasty and the first emperor of the subcontinent. These monuments proclaimed the conquests of the king, his conversion to Buddhism and the new laws of the land, but not a single sculpture or portrait of the king ever accompanied the inscriptions.

Stone images of rulers appear briefly during the Kushana Period (100 B.C.-A.D. 230), when foreign conquerors from Central Asia established their control over the northern Indus and Gangetic river valleys. Influenced to some extent by Greek tradition, coins with images of the ruler also became common at this time, but these imperial visages disappeared with the rise of the indigenous Gupta rulers, who threw off the yoke of foreign conquerors. The Gupta era (A.D. 320-460) is known as the golden age of Hindu sculpture, during which thousands of stone and terracotta images of deities and mythological scenes were created, but no images of rulers have been identified.

Given this important historical pattern in later South Asia, it is not surprising that we do not find images of Indus rulers building temples or conquering human enemies. Only a few stone sculptures of what may have been rulers or elites of the Indus cities have been discovered. These images generally show a seated male with only a simple fillet tied around the forehead (fig. 5.1), and no weapons or symbols of authority are held in the hands. We will return to a more detailed discussion of these important images later, but they clearly do not characterize the exploits of rulers as was common in Mesopotamia and Egypt.

The narrative scenes that do show activities of leaders or priests are found only on tiny molded tablets of terracotta or faience. These tablets generally show ritual offerings to deities or battles with wild animals, but none of them depicts warfare or captive-taking. In fact, the entire corpus of Indus art yields only one example of humans fighting each other, and the object of conflict appears to be a woman and not military dominance over other communities (see fig. 6.32)

The absence of images depicting human conflict, however, cannot be taken to indicate a utopian society in which everyone worked together without warfare. We have to assume that there were periodic struggles for control and conflicts within a city as well as between cities. These battles and political confrontations may have been illustrated in other ways that are not preserved in the archaeological record. Painted cloth scrolls, carved wooden reliefs and narrative sculptures made from reeds and unfired clay are commonly produced in traditional India to represent important myths and legends that usually include battles.

Other ways of extolling the greatness of a ruler or leading community may have been through dramatic enactments or puppet shows. Terracotta masks and puppets have been found at both Mohenjo-daro and Harappa that include religious or mythological figures as well as the totemic animals similar to those found on seals (figs. 5.3, 5.4, 5.5). The connection between mythological and totemic symbols

Fig. 5.3. (Left) Horned deity represented on a terracotta finger-puppet mask or pendant, Mohenjo-daro, cat. no. 122.

Fig. 5.4. (Right) Enraged horned tiger-human deity on a terracotta finger-puppet mask or pendant, Harappa, cat. no. 123.

suggests that puppet shows and dramatic enactments covered both religious and possibly political themes.

In the rural areas of Pakistan and India, puppeteers and bards commonly reenact or recite the exploits of the gods along with famous kings and queens. The myths and legends passed down from generation to generation by memory have never been written down. These performers were traditionally supported by the ruling classes and traveled from city to village once or twice a year to proclaim the sacred myths and glorify the local rulers and their ancestors.

Some terracotta tablets depict processions of individuals carrying standards topped by totemic animals and ritual symbols that were probably made from carved wood or clay-plastered reeds (fig. 5.6). These processions represent important public ceremonies that would have been led by ritual and political leaders much as is done throughout the world today.

Fig. 5.5. Full-sized terracotta mask from Mohenjo-daro, cat. no. 124.

Fig. 5.6. Processional scene with totemic figures from a terracotta tablet, Mohenjo-daro, after Marshall 1931, Pl. CXVIII, 9.

Because of the diverse geographical areas that were integrated by the Indus rulers, they needed a versatile and mobile strategy for communicating with the rural settlements. Processions and dramatic presentations would have been an effective and economical way to reinforce and legitimize the power of the rulers and to demonstrate their support by the gods. These public displays could have taken place at annual events in the cities and traveled throughout the countryside during the nonagricultural season.

Another effective method for communicating to the common people was through the use of stamp seals that carried the image of totemic animals and the written names of the rulers. Worn openly by the elites or stamped onto trade goods, these symbols would have been everyday reminders of who was in control.

Stamp Seals, Ruling Communities and Traders

Seals for stamping a personal and official insignia onto goods or documents are employed in many societies throughout the world. In ancient Mesopotamia seals were used by people from all walks of life, and the same is true for modern Japan, where personal seals are commonly used to sign letters and commercial transactions. The seals of the Indus cities were probably used in much the same manner, and even though broken seals have been found scattered in the debris throughout the cities, they were probably used only by powerful landowners and merchants: wealthy individuals who owned commodities that could be traded in large quantities or over long distances.

Square stamp seals with animal motifs carried messages understandable to all the different communities living in the Indus cities. As a totemic symbol, the animal represented a specific clan or official, and additional traits, such as power, cunning, agility, strength, etc., may have been associated with each animal. At least ten clans or communities are represented by these totemic animals: unicorn, humped bull, elephant, rhinoceros, water buffalo, short-horned humpless bull, goat, antelope, crocodile and hare. Of these, the unicorn may represent the most numerous and widespread clan, and because of the sheer numbers of unicorn seals it is unlikely that they all represent rulers.

The name or title of the owner was carved along the top of the seal, and often a ritual offering stand or feeding trough was placed in front of the animal. The animals depicted are usually male, and most animals are carved facing left so that when impressed onto a clay tag, the animal would face to the right. There are several instances where identical inscriptions have been found on seals with different motifs.[3] Some of these seals are found at the same site or even in the same room, while others have been recovered at different sites. Since the animal motifs on these seals represent different messages, it is possible that a person may have held two separate affiliations. On the other hand when identical inscriptions are found at different sites, the explanation may be that individuals in two different clans had the same name or title.

Animal Seals

The majestic zebu bull, with its heavy dewlap and wide, curving horns is perhaps the most impressive motif found on the Indus seals (fig. 5.7, see fig. 1.2). Generally carved on large seals with relatively short inscriptions, the zebu motif is found almost exclusively at Mohenjo-daro and Harappa. One example has been recovered from the town Kalibangan, a site to the northeast of Harappa, and this may in fact have come from one of the larger centers, reflecting the strong economic and political links between big cities and regional towns.

The rarity of zebu seals is curious because the humped bull is a recurring theme in many of the ritual and decorative arts of the Indus region, appearing on painted pottery and as figurines long before the rise of cities and continuing on into later historical times. The zebu bull may symbolize the leader of the herd, whose strength and virility protects the herd and ensures the procreation of the species or it may stand for a sacrificial animal. When carved in stone, the zebu bull probably represents the most powerful clan or top officials of Mohenjo-daro and Harappa. Parpola, who noted that unique script sequences are found on the large zebu seals, suggests that they may represent royal titles.[4] Similar script signs have been found on some of the copper tools and weapons found at Harappa (see fig. 4.18).

The elephant is also an important symbol of power that in later historical periods came to be associated with royalty, wealth and the deity Ganesha, the remover of obstacles. Elephant seals fall in the medium-size range, and like the bull seals they are found primarily at the largest sites, Mohenjo-daro and Harappa (fig. 5.2). The few examples of elephant seals found at Kalibangan and Jhukar reinforce the links between these sites and the larger urban centers, but perhaps the most important evidence comes from numerous clay sealings from a single elephant seal that were recovered from a burned storehouse at the site of Lothal. These sealings were attached to goods that were being traded by a merchant or landowner who used an elephant seal, but the original seal has not been found.

Other animal motifs appearing on seals found primarily at the largest cities include dangerous wild animals like the rhinoceros, the water buffalo, the gharial (crocodile) and the tiger. All of these animals would have been familiar to people living at the edge of the thick jungles and swampy grasslands of the Indus plain; they were revered as totemic animals, closely associated with important myths and legends. These ritual associations probably extend back thousands of years, since many of these same animals are depicted in cave paintings of the Palaeolithic and Mesolithic periods in central India, dating from 20,000 to 8000 B.C.

The one-horned Indian rhinoceros was at one time quite common in the marshlands along the Indus river and its tributaries (fig. 5.8). Rhinoceros seals often show the animal feeding from a troughlike container, with script across the top of the seal. It is unlikely that the rhinoceros was ever

Fig. 5.7. Steatite bull seal from Harappa, H88-1201.

Fig. 5.8. Rhinoceros seal from Mohenjo-daro, cat. no. 15.

tamed, and most scholars interpret the feeding trough as a symbol of respect or ritual offering to the sacred animal. Similar feeding troughs are occasionally seen with the elephant motif and are quite common with the water buffalo and the short-horned, humpless bull.

When appearing alone on a seal, the water buffalo usually has its head held high as if testing the air with its flared nostrils (fig. 5.9). For both wild and domestic water buffalo, this posture is characteristic of a defensive stance when protecting the herd or when courting females. Like the bull motif, the male water buffalo may have represented fertility and protection. The wide, spreading horns with grooves or ridges are quite distinctive from those of the bull, and many of the headdresses seen on human or deity figures depict the water buffalo horns.

The short-horned, humpless bull is another important motif on the seals, but it is not clear if this figure represents a wild or a domestic animal (fig. 5.10). Short-horned and humpless species of cattle may have been introduced into the region, whereas humped zebu are probably indigenous to the Indus Valley and the Indian subcontinent.

Fig. 5.9. Water buffalo seal from Mohenjo-daro, cat. no. 17.

Fig. 5.10. Two-sided seal with short-horned bull and swastika motif, Mohenjo-daro, cat. no. 18.

Fig. 5.11. Three-sided molded terracotta tablet from Mohenjo-daro: a) boat, b) gharial motif, c) script, cat. no. 22.

Two varieties of crocodile are depicted on Indus seals; the gharial has a narrow snout and the crocodile has a wider mouth. The Indus crocodiles were probably associated with water deities or river goddesses as they were in later Hindu mythology. This motif is quite rare on the square stamp seals where the crocodile is depicted without any feeding trough or ritual object. However, depictions of the gharial are quite common on molded and carved tablets where it is often shown with a fish in its mouth (fig. 5.11b), or as part of a narrative scene (cat. no. 27).

Tiger seals, not very common, are found primarily at the largest cities with a few examples at the towns of Kalibangan and Lothal. The tiger, which is one of the most feared animals in the subcontinent, figures prominently in folk stories and legends. When appearing alone on the square stamp seals, the tiger is usually depicted in a formal pose; with a feeding trough or script symbol it is situated in front and head upraised. More commonly, the tiger figure is shown with other figures in different narrative scenes (see cat. nos. 26, 27), where it is generally associated with a human figure.

Other motifs associated with the highland regions bordering the Indus Valley are various species of mountain goat and sheep. One variety of wild goat, which has very distinctive backward-arching horns with short knobs, is often confused with the ibex. Another species known as the Markhor has twisted horns that spread to each side of the head. Although not found in great quantities, the goat seals have been discovered at both large and small sites. Antelope or gazelle with back-arching or front-arching horns (see cat. no. 19) are also an important motif on seals as well as on incised steatite tablets.

In addition to the animals mentioned above there is one example of a rabbit or hare used as a motif on a square stamp seal from Harappa. However, many other animals common in the region were not used on the seals. The hooded cobra, the peacock and other birds, monkey, squirrel, mongoose and onager (wild ass) are all seen in narratives or as terracotta figurines, but they were never used on the square stamp seals. Of the animals that are shown, most come from the alluvial plains and therefore may represent the local indigenous clans who founded the cities, but some animal motifs are clearly derived from the western highlands, such as the mountain goat and the short-horned, humpless bull. The combined sets of animals are an important reflection of the integration of local and regional elites into the economic and ritual structure of the city. Because no specific animal motif can be traced to a single site or region, it appears that the use of these symbols on seals was invented in the cities and not brought in from outside. Some seals may have been associated with a specific administrative office that only existed in the cities. For example the bull seals may have been for the highest ruler, while the elephant, bison and water buffalo seals may have been used by lesser administrative offices that would only be found in the largest cities or towns.

Ritual Offering Stands and Feeding Troughs

Seals carved with single animal motifs often have specific objects placed in front of the animal. The two most common objects are the so-called ritual offering stand and the feeding trough. Feeding troughs are depicted on seals in front of all varieties of animals except unicorns and may represent shallow basins that would have been filled with offerings of grain or water. These types of shallow basins with downward projecting rims have been recovered in excavations, but the object known as the ritual offering stand has never been found.

The ritual offering stand is made up of three parts, a tapering shaft or column which stands on the ground and pierces a hemispherical bowl-shaped container that is sometimes held on the shaft by a small pin. Projecting above the bowl, the shaft supports a square or dome-shaped object. This top component is usually cross hatched with a grid or zigzag lines, and the bowl portion is variously depicted with cross hatching or horizontal lines. The edges of the bowl often have tiny dots or radiating lines along the bottom edge and sometimes even along the top edge.

Sir John Marshall originally identified this object as an incense burner or sacred brazier,[5] but other scholars disagree. Mahadevan identifies this object as a filter for the preparation of a sacred intoxicating beverage called soma, which is used in later Vedic rituals.[6] The wavy lines and dots along the bottom of the bowl-shaped lower portion have been interpreted as liquid spilling out of the container, and the upper portion has been referred to as a filter. This apparatus may have been made of basketry and wood, and although no full-sized examples have been preserved, a miniature ivory replica was recovered in 1993 from excavations at Harappa (fig. 5.12). This object has a cylindrical top portion with diagonal cross hatching and a hemispherical lower basin with circles incised around the entire body. The

Fig. 5.12. Ritual offering stands on faience tablets (left, H90-1687, right, H93-2051) and carved in ivory (center, H93-2092), Harappa.

shaft extending from the base is broken.

This ritual offering stand was not only used on seals in conjunction with the unicorn but also was carried in processions with the unicorn standard (see fig. 5.6). It also is depicted without any associated unicorn symbol on molded faience tablets as well as on incised steatite tablets. After the end of the Indus cities, this object and the feeding trough disappear from the art and ritual iconography of later times, so it is unlikely that we will ever be able to understand their function fully. However, they do represent a unifying set of symbols that were depicted on seals and tablets throughout the Indus region and may have been associated with important seasonal rituals practiced by the ruling elites or religious leaders of the cities and towns.

The presence or absence of the ritual offering stand or feeding trough undoubtedly specifically affected the meaning of the animal motif on the seals. Unicorn seals always have the ritual offering stand, while the majestic bull is always depicted without any cult object. Elephant and rhinoceros are generally depicted on seals without any other object, but occasionally a feeding trough is placed before the animal. The short-horned and hump-less bulls almost always have a feeding trough, and the head is always lowered as if it is eating. Water buffalo are generally depicted on seals with a feeding trough, but the head is always raised, with one horn lying against the shoulder and the other raised in a dramatic curve above the head. Tiger figures are generally depicted with a feeding trough or without any object in front. Goats usually have their heads raised and a small branch or plant placed in front of them, but occasionally the area beneath the animal's head contains script. Multiple-headed animals and animals depicted in narrative scenes usually do not have a ritual offering stand or trough.

Fig. 5.13. Unicorn seal from Harappa, cat. no. 12.

Unicorn Seals

The most common motif on the seals is the unicorn (fig. 5.13), a mythical animal that Greek and Roman sources trace back to the Indian subcontinent.[7] Although no actual bones of a unicorn have been found, the Indus people did conceive of this animal as a concrete being and even made small clay figurines that could be set on a pole or placed in a shrine. Unicorn figurines found at Chanhudaro (fig. 5.14), Mohenjo-daro and Harappa are all slightly different and must reflect local artistic traditions (fig. 5.15). The unicorns on seals also show considerable stylistic variation in being carved with slightly different proportions and decorative embellishments. Even the ritual offering stands are carved in many different ways.

These figurines and the seal motifs demonstrate that the Indus people believed in this one-horned animal, and — even if it turns out to be only a mythical creature, — it was a very important symbol for their elites and traders. Perhaps this animal was like the mythical animals carved onto the Shang bronzes in early China that guided or protected the owner in the real world as well as in the spirit world.[8]

The unicorn motif is found at almost every site where seals have been recovered and even in Mesopotamian sites. At Mohenjo-daro, over 60 percent of the seals carry this motif, and at Harappa the unicorn is found on around 46 percent of the seals.[9] The predominance of the unicorn motif at the largest urban centers and its widespread distribution throughout the Indus Valley and beyond indicates that the people belonging to this clan or trading community were not only numerous, but were present in every major settlement and were involved in long-distance trade to areas outside of the Indus Valley.

Carved in many different styles, unicorn seals were probably made by local artisans at all of the major sites (cat. no. 14). Usually the head is upturned with the horn arching from the back of the skull; the flaring nostrils and wide eyes present a dynamic image. The unicorn is often shown with a collar around the throat and a decorated quilt or harness in the shape of a pipal leaf on the shoulders. The tufted tail and male genitalia are similar to those on the humped-bull motifs, but overall the unicorn has a delicate build similar to an antelope or gazelle.

On the basis of current evidence, we can assume that the unicorn clan probably represents the aristocracy or

Fig. 5.14. Painted terracotta figurine of a unicorn, Chanhudaro, cat. no. 132. Joint Expedition of the American School of Indic and Iranian Studies and the Museum of Fine Arts, 1935-1936. © 1997 Museum of Fine Arts, Boston.

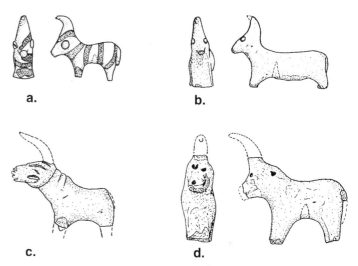

a.

b.

c.

d.

Fig. 5.15. Unicorn figurine styles from Chanhudaro (a, b), Mohenjo-daro (c) and Harappa (d).

merchants directly involved in governing the different settlements and supporting the political and economic power of the major cities. This does not mean that they were the most powerful clan or community, but that they implemented the laws and reinforced the religious practices and economic standards that united the Indus cities. The less widely distributed seals with the bull, elephant, rhinoceros and tiger motifs may have represented the most powerful and centralized communities which actually ruled the cities.

Combination Animal Seals

In addition to the square seals with single animal motifs, several seals have two or more different animals grouped together. On a famous seal from Mohenjo-daro, a figure seated in yogic position is surrounded by four animals (see Chap. 6), the elephant, the tiger, the rhinoceros and the water buffalo, while two antelope are seated below his throne. Another fragment of a similar seal was found at Mohenjo-daro, and both of these impressive seals may represent a ritual or perhaps a treaty between the main clans. The absence of the bull motif is interesting, but because the throne on which the deity sits has legs in the shape of bull's hooves, this animal is in fact represented in a central position.

Other seals simply combine the different animals and place them in the center of the seal. The unicorn and the short-horned bull are often grouped together as a two-headed animal, and sometimes are combined with an antelope to form a three-headed animal (cat. no. 29). This type of seal has been found at Mohenjo-daro and also at the small regional site of Amri, in Sindh.[10] At the site of Kalibangan a clay tag was found impressed by a seal that has an elephant with the horns of a bull.[11] Some seals show many different animals combined into a single fantastic figure (cat. no. 30). Made up of parts from each of the major animals, bull, tiger, elephant and goat, this creature has a human face and a tail from a hooded cobra. No ritual object is placed before this creature, but it is always accompanied by script. Although this combination animal may represent various attributes merged into one creature for some special ritual, it could also symbolize the joining together of several clans in a commercial or political treaty. One unique example of a two-sided seal from Mohenjo-daro has the standard unicorn motif on one face and the combined-animal motif on the opposite face.[12] Identical script symbols are found on both faces of this seal, possibly indicating that the owner sometimes functioned as a member of the unicorn clan and sometimes as the representative of the combined clans. Combination animal seals found at the largest sites and many regional centers all depict the same basic set of animals.

Geometric Button Seals

Generally, the geometric motifs found on glazed faience seals would not have been used for making impressions in clay (cat. no. 34), and therefore they are not usually considered when discussing the different clans or social divisions of the Indus society. The most common motifs are the swastika and stepped cross (cat. nos. 35, 36), but circle-and-dot motifs are also found. Clay sealings made with swastika motifs have been recovered from Lothal,[13] but since none of these seals has writing, it is possible that they were only used as a protective symbol or for good luck.

Seal Impressions

Impressions of seals on clay tags and on circular tokens show how the rulers and traders actually used their seals and provide insight into commercial procedures and the control of trade. Circular tokens with the impressions from square stamp seals on one or both sides were never attached to bundles of goods (fig. 5.16). In historical times such tokens bearing an official seal were used as passes to control road traffic[14]—much like a hauling permit in the modern context; in much the same way—the Indus tokens may have been issued to middlemen or transporters as certificates from a seal owner.

Lumps of clay were attached directly to the knots or binding on a bundle of goods (see fig. 4.1) and sealed to verify the contents and protect against pilfering en route, another technique for control. The unicorn is by far the most common motif found on such tags, a support for the idea that the unicorn seal owners were mostly involved in trade and commerce, but some other animals and even geometric

Fig. 5.16. Terracotta sealing from a unicorn seal, cat. no. 13.

designs such as the swastika motif have been found. That no impressions from the more complex narrative seals have been found on clay tags suggests that some seals were used exclusively for trade and commerce, while others were used in ritual contexts (see Chap. 6).

At the site of Lothal, over a hundred impressed clay tags were recovered near a large house that had burned down, thereby baking and preserving the normally unfired clay tags.[15] The most common impression is the unicorn motif, followed by the elephant motif and some swastikas. Many tags had stamps from more than one seal, and some had four different seal impressions. The animal motif of the previous sealing was usually obliterated by the subsequent impression, but in some cases the multiple sealings appear to belong to the unicorn group, as the tip of the horn is often still visible along with the writing.[16] These multiple sealings can be interpreted in two ways that have dissimilar implications for the organization of Indus trade. They may indicate that different owners were involved in a commercial transaction, but it is also possible that several officials or customs inspectors had to verify the contents of a bundle of goods before it could be shipped out or brought into the city.

The flow of goods along the trade networks was clearly controlled by the seal owners; these individuals were responsible for supplying the cities with essential food and finished goods, as well as raw materials for the craft workshops. These merchants would have been supported by landowners and state officials who financed and administered the trade between the cities and rural areas. The stability of the Indus political system was closely linked to a complex balance of power between the traders and administrators, consumers and producers.

Transport

The largest cities and towns of the Indus Valley are situated at strategic locations along major river systems and coastal areas where they could control the movements of goods and raw materials along the trade routes. Built on enormous mud-brick platforms high above the flood waters, the cities had a vantage point from which to view the surrounding plains. Towers rising above the city walls would have allowed watchmen to signal the approach of river boats and caravans bringing goods to the cities.

In this part of the subcontinent, the trading season usually begins after the monsoon rains are over and the flooded rivers have returned to their beds. During the monsoon rains, muddy roads and swollen rivers make any form of travel difficult, if not impossible. When the roads had dried and the mountain landslides were over, caravans

of pack animals, such as oxen, sheep and goat brought copper, precious stones, wool, fruit and nuts from the highland plateaus to the west. On the plains, long lines of carts pulled by humped zebu cattle carried heavy goods to the cities from the rural farmlands and nearby towns. Porters with wooden poles and suspended baskets hauled trade goods to the markets, returning home with grain and other commodities.

Living on the flat alluvial plains, the Indus people had developed several types of two-wheeled carts, some of which are preserved in the form of clay toys (fig. 5.17). Carts for transporting heavy goods were made in at least five different styles, which were possibly used by different ethnic communities or by different social classes. In Pakistan today, the carts made in different parts of the Indus Valley have distinctive designs, and each different community has its own style of decorating or carving. Some terracotta toy oxcarts have solid floors and side bars; others have hollow frames and holes for setting removable sidings. The ancient oxcarts would have been made from wood, with leather and sinew bindings for the harnesses. The heavy axle and solid wheel were probably joined together, rotating as a single unit like the traditional oxcarts still used in Sindh today. This simple construction is quite well adapted to the wide sandy plains, where wide turns are the norm and a squeaking axle does not bother anybody. The wheel span of the ancient carts were between 1.6 meters wide on the basis of cart tracks found preserved in the roadways and streets of ancient Harappa.[17]

Another type of two-wheeled cart is represented by bronze models found at both Harappa and Chanhudaro (cat. no. 46). The driver sits on a ledge at the front, and a small cabin with side bars provides a protected place for riders or perishable goods. Similar covered carts are used in Pakistan and India for long journeys or for special occasions such as weddings, when the bride travels in a covered cart to the home of her husband.

During most of the Harappan Phase there is no evidence for the use of the camel in long-distance transport, but the domesticated two-humped Bactrian camel was known in the highlands of Central Asia, and the one-humped dromedary camel was probably being used in the desert regions of Arabia. Towards the end of the Indus cities period there is evidence for the appearance of camels, which may have had some impact on the organization of inland trade.[18] The horse is another animal that was known in Central Asia during this time but never used nor depicted in the art of the Indus Valley until long after the decline of the Indus cities.

While oxcarts may have been the major form of overland transport, flat-bottomed river boats probably carried most of trade goods up and down the Indus Valley. Flotillas of boats carried trade goods down the river to the coast to meet up with the merchants bringing goods from Kutch and far away Oman. The trip up-river was probably aided by human porters pulling the boats from the river bank, but they also would have had long oars and sails made from mats or heavy cotton cloth. The ancient Indus boats depicted on seals (fig. 5.18) and molded tablets (see fig. 5.11a) have cabins, with ladders to the roof and a high-seated platform at the stern from which the large rudder could be manipulated. Modern river boats in Pakistan have these same basic features (fig. 5.19), because this type of boat is perfectly adapted to the shifting sandbars and slow-moving waters of the Indus and its tributaries.[19] Clay models of river boats have been found in recent excavations at Harappa, but no actual boat remains have been recovered yet.

Sea-going vessels would have differed from river boats and must have had sails as well as keels to withstand the ocean swells. A small model of a high-prowed sailboat was found at Lothal, but no other representations have been discovered. The seasonal trade by sea would have been determined entirely by the monsoon winds, which pick up in late May or June and subside in August. The last boats would have traveled back to the Indus Valley from Oman with the weak southwesterly winds at the beginning of the monsoon; after August the boats could begin the plying the coasts once again. Many Indus ships may have hopped along the Makran coast and then sailed on up the Persian Gulf to the port cities of Mesopotamia at the mouth of the Tigris and Euphrates rivers.

Fig. 5.17. Terracotta model oxcart from Nausharo, cat. no. 45.

Fig. 5.19. Traditional Sindhi houseboats on the Indus near Mohenjo-daro.

Fig. 5.18. Unfired steatite seal with a flat-bottomed boat incised on a steatite seal, Mohenjo-daro, cat. no. 21.

Exotic Goods and the Indus Traders

With efficient transport and well-protected trade networks, merchants were able to move exotic raw materials from distant resource areas to urban workshops where they were transformed into valuable status objects. Metal tools and weapons, painted ceramics, precious ornaments and decorative fabrics were used in ritual and social displays to reinforce the religious beliefs and maintain the social order within the cities. As is common today throughout the subcontinent, religious festivals at the large urban centers were probably combined with trade fairs attracting all of the surrounding rural communities as well as traders from distant towns and villages.

In the absence of strong military control, the cities were united with the surrounding regions primarily through economic and religious networks. Objects produced by highly specialized artisans living in the large urban centers were traded to the rural communities and smaller towns where they were used and worn by the local elites. In return, grain and other forms of produce would have flowed into the cities and then back to the distant resource areas for more raw materials.

Most of the Indus trade was focused on supplying the cities with food and the necessary raw materials for producing tools, status objects and trade goods. However, within the Indus Valley itself, there were limited resources for metals, stone and minerals, and many of the raw materials were obtained from nearby regions. Indus settlements gradually spread into Gujarat and parts of Baluchistan to exploit these resources, and more distant trading outposts or colonies were established in northern Afghanistan and along the Makran coast.

One important factor in the development and expansion of Indus trade networks is that many essential raw materials needed by the Indus cities were available in more than one locality. This unique distribution of raw materials appears to have stimulated economic competition and growth (fig. 5.20a-f).

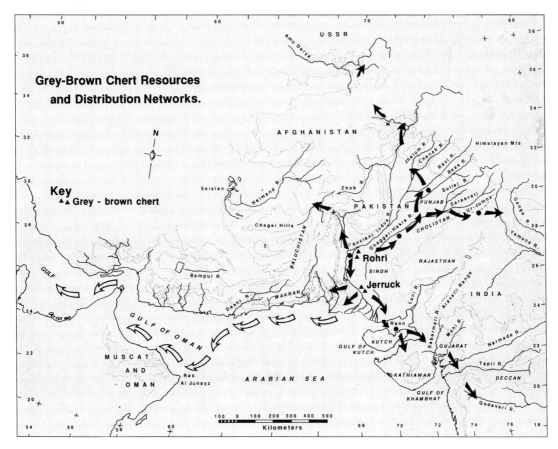

Fig. 5.20a. Gray-Brown Chert Resources and Distribution Networks.

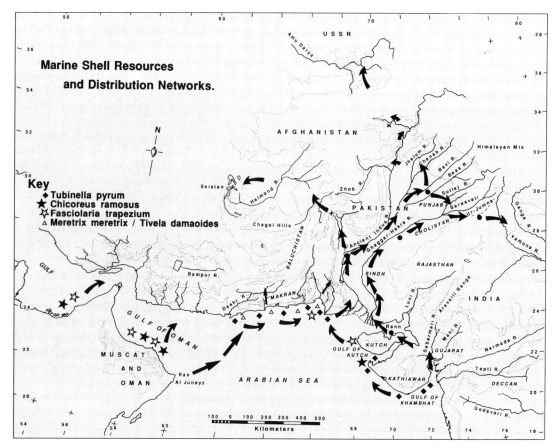

Fig. 5.20b. (Above) Marine Shell Resources and Distribution Networks.   Fig. 5.20c. (Below) Carnelian Resources and Distribution Networks.

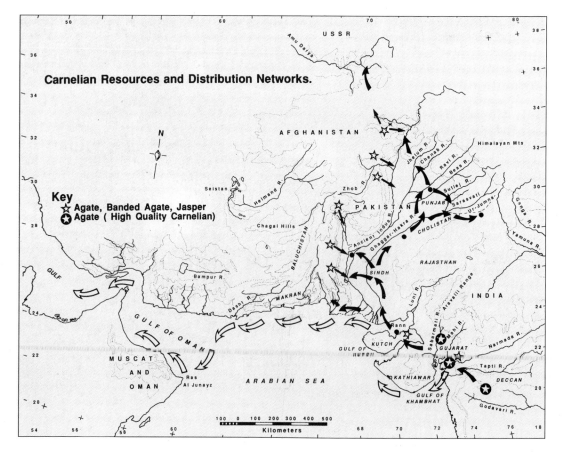

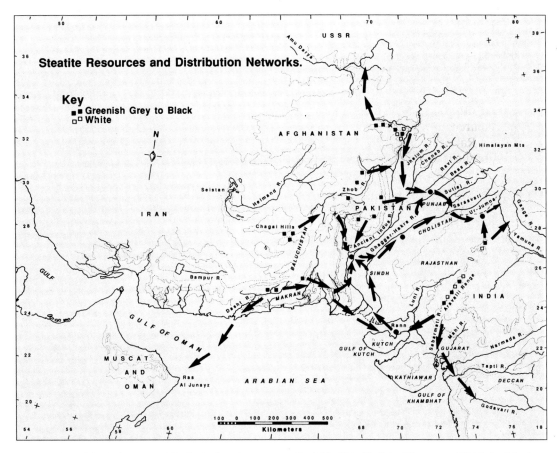

Fig. 5.20d. (Above) Steatite Resources and Distribution Networks.

Fig. 5.20e. (Below) Lapis lazuli Resources and Distribution Networks.

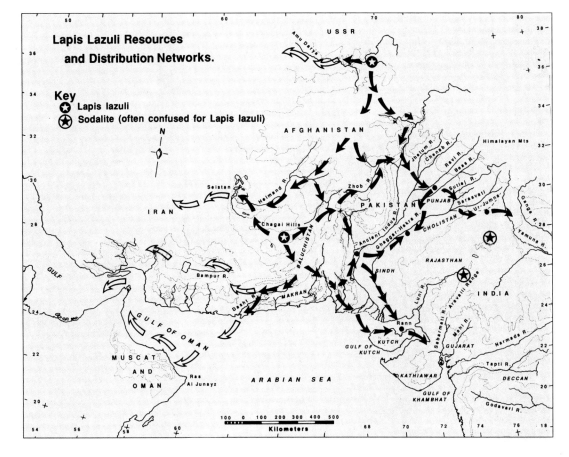

Copper ore was probably smelted near the mining sources and brought into the Indus Valley as bun-shaped ingots. Major copper sources are located to the west in Baluchistan, the east in Rajasthan and across the gulf in Oman (fig. 5.20f). Any of these areas could have produced enough copper to supply the entire Indus Valley civilization, but the Indus merchants were trading with all these areas. One can imagine traders shouting out the benefits of Oman copper, "It is a bit more expensive, but more pure than the slag from Baluchistan or Rajasthan." A merchant from Baluchistan would shout back, "Omani copper is soft like the meat of a date, while the highland copper is strong and hard like the pit."

Marine shell was also brought from three sources (fig. 5.20b). The Gulf of Kutch and Saurashtra to the east produced several species of shell that were used to make bangles, ladles and inlay (fig. 5.21). Similar species were obtained from the coast west of Karachi, and a third source

was the Omani coast. Complete shells as well as partly processed shell objects were traded from the coastal resource areas directly to the large cities, where they were finished according to local specifications. However, some coastal settlements produced their own finished goods and traded them to local consumers in competition with the products from the larger urban centers.

At the coastal site of Balakot, a local species of clam shell was used (fig. 5.22) to produce imitations of the elegant shell bangles that were made by sawing sections from large gastropods (fig. 5.23). The finished bangles were hardly distinguishable, but the process of manufacture was very different. From the heavy bodied bivalve *Tivela damaoides* bangles were made by a simple technique of chipping and grinding with locally available stone tools. The finished bangles from Balakot were traded to the local coastal and inland communities, while those made at the larger workshops were traded in the big cities and further inland settlements.

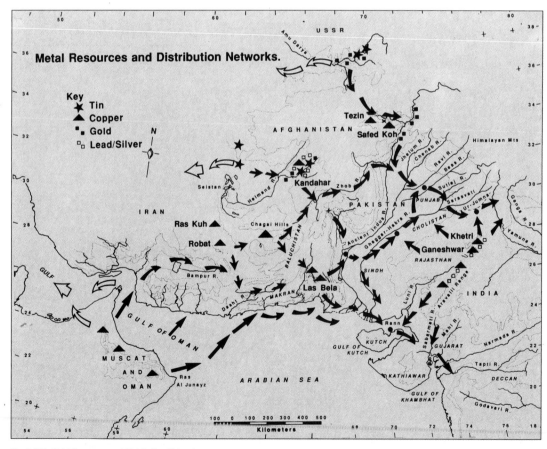

Fig. 5.20f. Metal Resources and Distribution Networks.

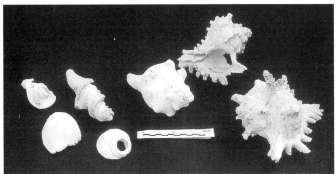

Fig. 5.21. The spiney murex, *Chicoreus ramosus* (a), knobbed whelk, *Fasciolaria trapezium* (b), and sawn fragments of the sacred conch, *Turbinella pyrum* (c).

Fig. 5.22. Shell bangles and manufacturing waste from Balakot, made from the clam shell *Tivela damaoides*.

Fig. 5.23. Shell bangle-manufacturing process for Turbinella pyrum. Preliminary chipping and removal of internal columella (a to f), sawing shell circlets (g to k), finishing the shell blank (l to n), and final incising (o).

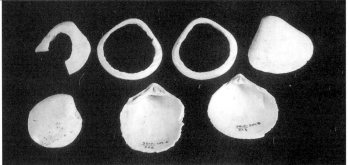

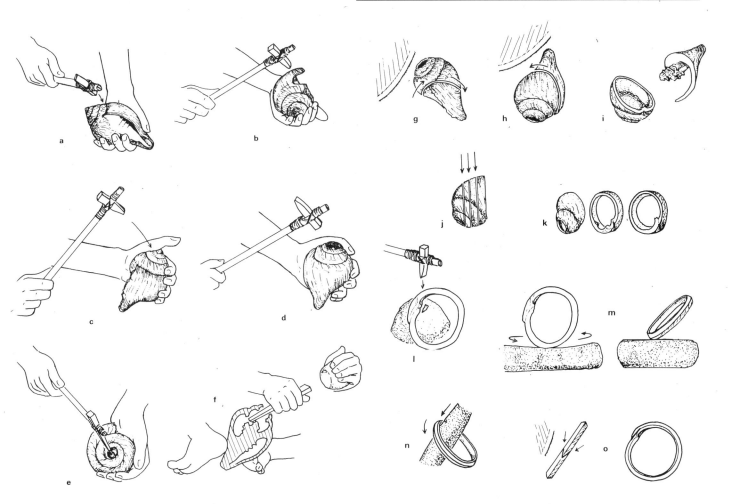

In contrast, the large gastropods *Turbinella pyrum* and *Chicoreus ramosus* were cut with a specialized bronze saw that would have been available only in the largest workshops. By studying the depth of each saw stroke on fragments of shell from the ancient workshops, we can reconstruct the basic shape of the saw. It had a very thin serrated edge that was long and curved, similar to the saws still used in shell banglemaking in modern Bengal. Even more astounding is the fact that the Indus bronze saw was able to cut the shell as efficiently as the modern steel saws, which suggests that the Indus bronze workers were able to produce a bronze that was as hard as steel.[20]

Fig. 5.24. Green stone (Fuchsite) tumbler from Mohenjo-daro, cat. no. 100.

ern Iran [21] and possibly other workshops in Baluchistan. These vessels were traded throughout the Near East and the Persian Gulf, and a few examples have been found at Mohenjo-daro.[22] These exotic containers may have been brought to the city by Indus traders living in southern Baluchistan along with copper and other highland raw materials.

One famous stone vessel found at Mohenjo-daro is a tall glass with concave sides that is similar in shape to ritual columns found in Baluchistan and Afghanistan (fig. 5.24). This green stone, called fuchsite, is rare, but it can occur with quartzite which is common throughout Baluchistan and Afghanistan. When this fuchsite vessel was

Precious stones of all varieties were highly valued in the Indus cities, and special designs and colors were sought after for making ornaments and utensils. Hard stones like agate and jasper that would hold a high luster polish appear to have been more popular than the softer varieties, such as lapis lazuli and turquoise, that would quickly wear away to a dull luster. Banded agate, variegated jasper and red-orange carnelian were among the most commonly used materials, obtained from distant sources in Kutch and Gujarat, as well as widely distributed sources throughout Baluchistan. Lapis lazuli was available from two sources, one in the Chagai hills of southern Baluchistan and the other in Badakhshan, northern Afghanistan (see fig. 5.20e). Turquoise also may have been obtained from southern Baluchistan or from the more distant regions of northern Iran, but neither of these stones was very popular with Indus city consumers. When worn as beads, these relatively soft stones become dull or change color. This may have stimulated the production of glazed faience beads that could be colored to look like turquoise or lapis lazuli (see Chap. 7).

Most stones came into the Indus workshops as raw materials, but there are rare examples of finished objects that were produced in the highlands to the west and brought to the cities by traders or visiting elites. Carved chlorite and green schist containers with distinctive woven mat designs were produced at sites such as Tepe Yahya in south-

first examined by a geologist in the 1930s, the only known source was in Mysore State, over 1600 km south of the Indus Valley.[23] Early scholars suggested that the stone was brought to the Indus cities from the south along with gold and ivory, but both of these important raw materials were actually available from nearby sources. Herds of elephants lived in the thick forests of Gujarat or the eastern Punjab, so ivory could have been obtained by Indus hunters themselves or traded from tribal communities living at the edge of the Indus plain. Gold was easily obtained from the sands of the upper Indus river where it is still panned by itinerant miners. Another source of gold was along the Oxus river valley in northern Afghanistan where a trading colony of the Indus cities has been discovered at Shortughai. Situated far from the Indus Valley itself, this settlement may have been established to obtain gold, copper, tin and lapis lazuli, as well as other exotic goods from Central Asia.[24]

Sea Trade

Because all of the basic raw materials needed by the Indus cities were available in the regions adjacent to the Indus Valley, there was no reason for Indus traders to travel to far off lands. But, lured by untapped markets and the rewards for bringing back exotic items, some adventurous Indus traders traveled across the sea to Oman and far up the Persian Gulf to the cities of Mesopotamia. Scholars have argued that the long distance trade was carried out by intermediary communities or middlemen,[25] but we have increasing evidence to suggest that at least a few Indus entrepreneurs traveled to these distant lands.[26] Most trade was probably carried on by sea, although we have some evidence for limited overland trade through southern Iran.

The trade with Oman was probably most heavy, although it was not critical to the Indus economy. Numerous Indus artifacts have been found in Oman and along southern coast of the Arabian Gulf,[27] and characteristic circular seals from the Gulf sites have been found in the Indus Valley (fig. 5.25).[28]

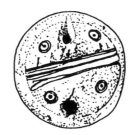

Fig. 5.25. Circular style Gulf seal from Lothal (after Rao, 1985, Pl. CLXI,b).

On the basis of archaeological finds, the major imports from Oman were copper, shell and possibly mother-of-pearl. In historical times the Arabian trade supplied the Indus Valley primarily with dates, pearls, incense, dried fruits and slaves. So far we have no archaeological evidence for slaves in the Indus Valley.

Exports to Oman would have included many perishable goods transported in large black-slipped storage jars (see fig. 4.8). Numerous jar fragments, often with Indus script on the shoulder, have been found at many different Gulf sites. These vessels may have conveyed indigo or liquid foods such as clarified butter, pickled vegetables or fruits, honey or wine. The narrow base may have been designed to allow the jars to be placed along the bottom of the ship's hold. At the site of Ras' al-Junayz in Oman, one of these large, black-slipped vessels with graffiti was found along with a bronze Indus stamp seal.[29]

Other exports may have included wood for boats, livestock, grain and fresh fruit, but the only preserved objects are Indus beads, cubical chert weights and ivory objects such as a comb.[30] These items may have been left in Oman by Indus traders or brought to the region by intermediaries. Current evidence suggests that most trade with Oman took place during the height of the Indus cities between 2200 and 2100 B.C.[31]

Further to the west in Mesopotamia, trade contacts with the Indus Valley are reflected in artifacts such as terracotta sealings from bundles of goods, as well as numerous texts that mention the goods that were being traded.[32] The earliest contacts, dating to between 2600 and 2500 B.C., are centered in southern Mesopotamia at the city of Ur. In the royal cemetery of Ur, kings and queens were buried with servants and livestock along with elaborate ornaments and personal objects. Lapis lazuli, shell and carnelian were combined with gold, silver and bronze to create exquisite ornaments, utensils and weapons. Among the beads found with the kings, queens and serving ladies, are distinctive long biconical carnelian beads and decorated carnelian beads that were produced by artisans from the Indus Valley.

Detailed studies of the drilling techniques and manufacturing processes confirm that many long biconical carnelian beads as well as the decorated carnelian and green amazonite beads were actually made in distant Indus workshops (figs. 5.26, 5.27). However, the long faceted carnelian beads may have been made by Indus artisans in Mesopotamia. These beads are drilled with the unique technique of the Indus Valley, yet the faceted shape is a style that was never produced in the Indus workshops. The pear-shaped decorated carnelian bead is also a shape that was never produced in the Indus, but it is made using a technology that has only been documented in the Indus cities (fig. 5.26) (see Chap. 7). These clues suggest that merchants or entrepreneurs from the Indus Valley may have set up shops in cities such as Ur to market their goods and also produce objects in local designs. If this can be confirmed through further studies, it would be the earliest evidence for a pattern that came to be the norm in later historical times, when craftsmen and merchants from the subcontinent extended their trade networks throughout West Asia as well as Southeast Asia.

Fig. 5.26. Carnelian bead decorated with white designs from the royal cemetery of Ur. Pear-shaped bead, UPM # 35-1-77, Field # U18880, PJ, Grave 57. String of decorated carnelian, lapis lazuli and gold beads, UPM # 30-12-573, PG 1422 (Courtesy of the University of Pennsylvania Museum).

Later textual references for Indus trade date to the period between 2300 and 1300 B.C., beginning with the reign of Sargon of Akkad (2334-2279 B.C.). This famous ruler boasts of ships from Dilmun, Magan and Meluhha that are docked at his capital city, Akkad. Most scholars agree that in these texts, Dilmun refers to the modern island of Bahrain, Magan refers to modern Makran and Oman, while Meluhha refers to the general region of the Indus Valley. Numerous texts describe the types of goods coming from Meluhha: hard woods, tin or lead, copper, gold, silver, carnelian, shell, pearls and ivory. Animals such as a red dog, a cat, peacocks or black partridges and monkeys are also mentioned. Many of these items would not be preserved in the archaeological record, but Indus weights, seals and seal impressions attest to the presence of merchants and bundles of trade goods. The discovery of carnelian beads, shell bangles, ivory and shell inlay in temples or burials indicates that most of the trade objects from the Indus Valley were destined for the gods and rulers of the Mesopotamian cities.

In contrast to the Mesopotamian evidence for Indus trade, no items produced in Mesopotamia proper have been found in the Indus region. Mesopotamian texts list such exports as wool, incense and gold, which are perishable or would have been transformed into new objects in the Indus cities. The absence of Mesopotamian cylinder seals and

sealings would indicate Mesopotamian traders were not directly involved with the Indus trade and that no bundles of goods sealed by Mesopotamian merchants were being sent to the Indus cities. There is not enough evidence at this time to argue for the exclusion of Mesopotamian traders from the Indus market, but the Indus cities were clearly involved in the import of raw materials and the export of finished goods. This extremely profitable trade strategy may have been another factor in the rapid growth and spread of the Indus settlements throughout the northwestern subcontinent.

Control of Trade

In order to benefit from the internal and external trade, the rulers of the Indus cities had to control the movement of goods and be able to profit from the commercial transactions. Most trade was probably conducted through a common barter system and reciprocal exchange of goods for services. Both systems are well documented in traditional economies throughout the subcontinent and in the absence of a monetary standard would have been essential for supporting the Indus urban centers. A third system of exchange is seen in the highly standardized system of cubical stone weights that is common at all Indus settlements (fig. 5.28, see cat no. 40). Most scholars have assumed that this standardized weight system was used primarily for market exchange, but these weights could have been also used for taxation.

The standardized Indus weights are unique in the ancient world and do not correspond to any of the numerous varieties of weights used in Mesopotamia or Egypt. However, the Indus weight system is identical to that used by the first kingdoms of the Gangetic plain around 300 B.C., and is still in use today in traditional markets throughout Pakistan and India.[33]

The cubical stone weights, made of banded chert or other patterned stone, are based on a complex system of measurement that is calculated by both binary and decimal increments. The base weight may have been a tiny black and red seed known as "gunja" (*Abrus precatorius*), which is still used by modern jewelers in Pakistan and India. However, it is possible that other grains such as barley or lentil seeds may have been used in the original calculation, because the "gunja" is equal to two mung bean seeds or two grains of barley. Scientific studies of the "gunja" seed show that the average weight is .109 grams, and eight "gunja" equal the smallest known Indus weight of 0.871 grams.

The first seven Indus weights double in size from 1 : 2 : 4 : 8 : 16 : 32 : 64, and the most common weight is the 16th ratio, which is approximately 13.7 grams. At this point the weight increments change to a decimal system where the next largest weights have a ratio of 160, 200, 320, and 640. The next jump goes to 1000, 3200, 6400, 8000, and 12,800. The largest weight found at the site of Mohenjo-daro weighs 10,865 grams (approximately 25 pounds) which is almost 100,000 times the weight of the "gunja" seed.[34]

Every excavated site of the Indus Valley has turned up

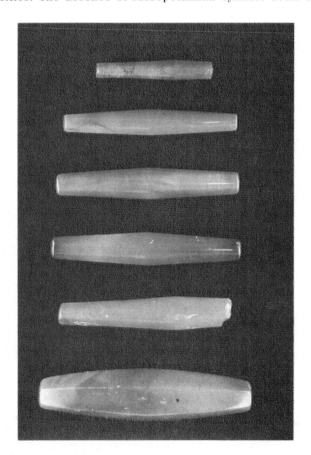

Fig. 5.27. Long carnelian beads from the royal cemetery at Ur. The long biconical form of all but the lowest bead is identical to beads found from workshops in the Indus Valley region. The lowest bead is faceted with six sides, a shape never found in the Indus workshops, UPM # B 16792, Field # U 8097, PG 57 (Courtesy of the University of Pennsylvania Museum).

such cubical chert weights, and all of the weights conform to the standard system established by the Indus rulers. Heavier weights have only been found at major trading centers such as Chanhudaro, or at the largest cities of Mohenjo-daro and Harappa, but complete sets of the smaller weights are found at most of the rural settlements. In addition to the common cubical weights many sites have truncated spherical weights that conform to the same weight system (fig. 5.29, cat. no. 41). Usually made from agate or colored jaspers, these weights may reflect a regional style of weight manufacture or perhaps a competing class of merchants.

In market exchange, the smaller weights may have been used for precious stones and metals, perfumes and valuable medicines. The larger weights would have been used for grain or large quantities of goods. This interpretation, however, does not fit well with the traditional trading practices of the subcontinent; there are not enough weights from the Indus sites for everyone to have been using them in commercial transactions.

A more plausible interpretation associates weights with taxation. In the recent excavations at Harappa, the highest concentration of weights has been found inside the city gateway, which is where goods coming into the city would have been weighed and taxed. Tax collectors or village elders in the smaller settlements would have needed only one or two sets of weights to collect tribute in precious commodities or produce. Finally, the large weights which are found only at the urban centers would have been well suited for weighing tribute coming from all of the surrounding villages and towns.

Rulers and Elites

The rulers who controlled the Indus cities appear to have maintained the standardized system of weights and kept the trade networks open for over 700 years without developing a standing army. While there may have been periods of conflict between competing settlements or feuding clans, there is a general lack of evidence for militarism. Coercion through trade and religion appears to have been the major form of control.

By building markets and promoting trade the rulers of the Indus cities increased the general wealth and prosperity of the entire city. To maintain order without resorting to physical coercion they constructed carefully laid-out cities surrounded by walls and gateways. The separate walled mounds with associated suburbs may represent the houses and workshops of competing merchant communities who were united in a single settlement by common language, culture and religion.

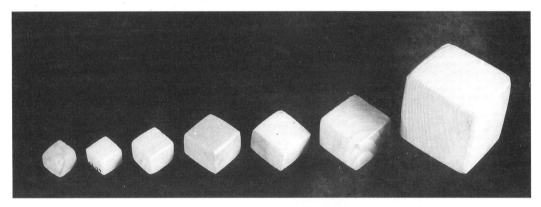

Fig. 5.28. Cubical chert weights from Allahdino.

Fig. 5.29. Truncated spherical weights from Mohenjo-daro.

The political organization of these cities was probably not a hereditary monarchy, where one would expect to see palaces and royal storehouses. On the contrary, numerous large buildings and public spaces in the lower town at Mohenjo-daro and on Mound F at Harappa support the interpretation that several distinct elite groups were living in the cities. An exception to this pattern is seen at smaller fortified sites on the periphery of the Indus Valley. For example, at Dholavira, in Kutch, the nested walled habitation area of the citadel does dominate the entire settlement and may represent the residences of a ruling family. However, the presence of unicorn seals and pottery identical to those found at Mohenjo-daro and Harappa indicate that this site and many other walled towns were probably colonies or regional capitals with governors appointed from one of the larger cities.

Due to the long distances between the four major cities, it is highly unlikely that a single ruler ever dominated the entire Indus Valley. Each of the largest cities may have been organized as an independent city-state, with different communities competing for control. At times a single charismatic leader may have ruled the city, but most of the time it was probably controlled by a small group of elites, comprised of merchants, landowners and ritual specialists. Alliances between the ruling elites at two or more of the largest sites would have stimulated extensive colonization of resource areas. On the other hand, competition between the cities may have resulted in the temporary breakdown of trade and the collapse of political power.

The famous stone sculptures found at Mohenjo-daro may represent the rise and fall of one such community of the ruling elite (see figs. 5.1, 5.30-5.32). These stone sculptures were found on the surface of the site or in the topmost levels, buried under the fallen walls of the latest Indus structures. Because all of these sculptures are broken, many scholars feel that they were intentionally vandalized. However, they are made from relatively soft stone, and some may have been damaged in the collapse of a building or through natural weathering.

Some sculptures appear to be unfinished, whereas others are carved with extreme detail and careful modeling. Overall they appear to represent a formal style of sculpture depicting a seated, bearded male with a cloak thrown over one shoulder and hands resting on the knees. One broken sculpture from the citadel mound may possibly represent a female because it has long unbound hair and no beard is discernible, but the nose and mouth have been badly eroded and any traces of the beard may have been obliterated.[35]

The almond-shaped eyes that would have been filled with shell or white stone inlay are portrayed in varying styles. Some eyelids are half-lowered, but usually they are rendered wide open and staring, much like the formal sculptures of elites found in Mesopotamia and Iran. The wide mouth with heavy lips is usually set in a firm line, contributing to the overall expression of calm authority and power.

At least four categories of hair styles can be identified, which many scholars have compared to similar hair styles on sculptures of Early Dynastic Mesopotamia and nearby Baluchistan.[36] Most figures have long hair tied in a bun on the back of the head and secured with a head band that is tied in a bow or hangs down the back of the neck in two strands. In some cases the hair is braided or wavy; in others it is combed back in straight lines or parted in the middle.

The head band probably represents a golden fillet similar to those recovered at Mohenjo-daro (see cat. no. 52), Harappa and Allahdino (see cat. no. 51). These golden fillets all have tiny holes at the ends for tying with a cord, which would have been secured as a bow or left free to hang down the back of the neck, as seen on these sculptures. The most famous "priest-king" sculpture has a disc-shaped ornament carved onto the fillet at the center of the forehead (see fig. 5.1). This disc may have been inlaid with red carnelian to create a spectacular eye-bead like those found in the excavations of Mohenjo-daro and Harappa (see cat. nos. 69-77). A matching arm ornament is carved on the upper right arm.

Similar golden fillets with central gold disc ornaments have been found in burials of both men and women at the royal cemetery of Ur, dating to the late Akkadian period,[37]

Fig. 5.30. Seated male figure with shell inlay in one eye, Mohenjo-daro, cat. no. 117.

which would correspond to the general date for the Mohenjo-daro sculptures. There may be no direct connection between these styles, but this period saw the introduction of many Indus elements into the artistic and economic sphere of southern Mesopotamia. The presence of Indus immigrants is clearly attested in the literature,[38] and the use of the water buffalo motif on cylinder seals becomes quite common.[39] The lack of definitive Mesopotamian styles or influences in the Indus cities at this time may indicate that the movement of styles was primarily from the Indus to Mesopotamia, undoubtedly carried by traders.

Most figures have short, combed beards, and some show the upper lip clearly shaved. The ears are usually depicted in a highly stylized kidney shape with double lines, and a hole drilled in the center to represent the auditory canal. This shape is much like that seen on the body of the unicorn pendant (see cat. no. 10) and is repeated in the design of some faience bangles (see cat. no. 92) and shell inlay (see cat. no. 110). The hole in the center of the ear may have had iconographic significance, but it also may have had a simple utilitarian function to secure some form of ear ornament or to support a horned headdress. Some of the sculptures have holes beneath the ears that may have been used to attach massive necklaces (see fig. 5.1).

Two of the sculptures definitely had some form of headdress attached to the top or back of the head. A small, shallow hole was drilled in the top of the head of one figure (fig. 5.32), and the back of the "priest-king's" head is cut at

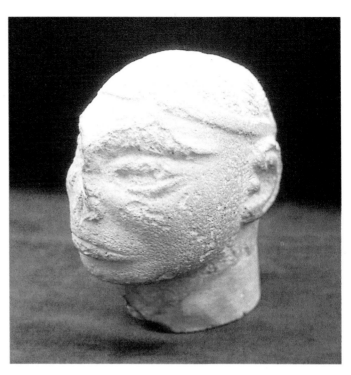
Fig. 5.32. Carved sandstone head, Mohenjo-daro, cat. no. 120.

Fig. 5.31. Seated limestone figure from Mohenjo-daro, cat. no. 119.

an angle, possibly to support a large horned headdress or the branch of the pipal tree as is seen on some of the seals (cat. nos. 24, 25).

With all of this elaborate ornamentation, it is likely that the sculptures were painted with bright colors. In two cases the garments were carved with special designs. On one fragmentary sculpture (HR 5785), the garment is covered with tiny drill holes that may have been filled with pigment to created a spotted cloak. In the cloak of the "priest-king," carefully drilled and hollowed out designs of circles, double circles and trefoils were originally filled with a red pigment. The rest of the garment may have been colored with other pigments, but no traces remain.

Many people have suggested that these designs represent block printing, but this is probably not the case because the design is not repeated identically over the entire garment. The cloak may have been made with embroidery, appliqué or decorated animal skin. In modern Pakistan, on festive occasions and particularly when cattle are marked for sacrifice, the white hide is often decorated with red spots made with henna. This practice has its roots in earlier traditions that may reach back to the Harappan Phase. The cloak of the "priest-king" was obviously a ceremonial garment and may have been decorated in a similar manner (see fig. 5.1).

In addition to the cloak, many figures show a lower garment that was tied around the waist and drawn through the legs to be tucked in the back like the traditional *dhoti* worn in many parts of the subcontinent. Some sculptures show the belly button.

Two seated positions are depicted in these sculptures, which can be compared to the seated positions of terracotta figurines (fig. 5.33) as well as to the anthropomorphic figures carved on seals (cat. nos. 24, 26). The basic posture has one knee bent to the ground and the other raised, so that one foot is forward, while the other is tucked beneath the buttocks. In some sculptures the right foot is forward and the right knee is raised (fig. 5.30), while in others the position is reversed (fig. 5.31). The raised knee is usually clasped by the corresponding arm while the other arm rests on the opposite knee or thigh. In all of the sculptures where the hands are visible, they rest directly on the knee or thigh and do not carry any form of symbolic object or weapon (fig. 5.31).

The partly kneeling position can be interpreted as supplication or subservience, but this is also a standard position for sitting in readiness for action. With one swift movement a person can stand up and move in any direction. In contrast, the yogic pose depicted on many of the seals (see cat. no. 23), heel to heel with widespread knees, is clearly a ritual posture that would require considerable effort to stand up.

Since most figures that can be identified as deities are shown standing with feet placed firmly on the ground or seated in the yogic posture, the stone sculptures from Mohenjo-daro are generally thought to represent clan leaders or ancestral figures. Comparisons have also been made with eight seated figures depicted on a silver vessel attributed to Bactria and generally contemporaneous with the late phase of the Indus cities.[40] Although these figures are seated in a broadly similar manner, their hair styles and the presence of hand-held objects represent an iconographic tradition different from that of the Indus sculptures.

A more appropriate comparison is with the three stone heads found in the Helmand basin in Baluchistan. These heads have been broken off of a larger figure, possibly seated, and have carved facial features and stylized ears similar to those of Mohenjo-daro.[41] The hair is tied back with a fillet that hangs in two strands down the back of the neck, but the hair is not tied in a bun. These heads appear to be contemporaneous with the Mohenjo-daro sculptures and possibly derive from a very similar sculptural tradition, but they were clearly made by different artisans in distinct workshops. The general similarities may reflect distant ethnic relations between a community of powerful merchants or landowners living at Mohenjo-daro and a group living in the Helmand basin. However, due to the long history of movement between the highlands and the Indus plain, we cannot use these sculptures to identify specific movements of elites in either direction. The general absence of Indus artifacts in the Helmand sites and the rarity of sherds from Baluchistan at Mohenjo-daro preclude any strong cultural interactions between these possibly related communities.

If the distribution of sculptures can be taken to indicate residence localities, then these communities were living on the citadel mound as well as in different neighborhoods of the lower city. Differences in hair style, garment decoration and seated posture may signify several generations of elders, whereas variations in carving style probably reflect several generations of stone carvers. It is likely that the individuals depicted in these sculptures were influential citizens or even rulers at Mohenjo-daro, but they probably did not have direct political control over other cities such as Harappa or Dholavira. Each of these large cities probably had its own powerful clans and rulers, but only at Mohenjo-daro do we see the carving of commemorative stone sculptures.

∎

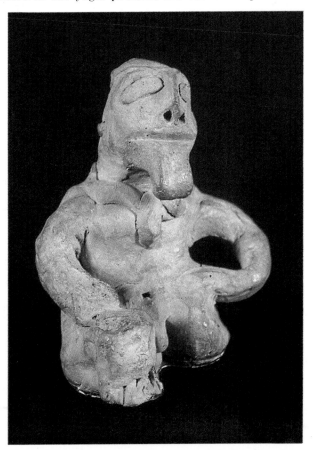

Fig. 5.33. Terracotta seated male figurine from Mohenjo-daro, NMP 50.563.

Endnotes

1. A. S. Altekar, *State and Government in Ancient India* (reprint of 3rd ed., 1958) (Delhi: Motilal Banarsidas, 1984); Hartmut Scharfe, *The State in Indian Tradition* (Leiden: Brill, 1989).

2. Mary W. Helms, *Craft and the Kingly Ideal: Art, Trade, and Power* (Austin: University of Texas Press, 1993), 77 ff.

3. Asko Parpola, *Deciphering the Indus Script* (Cambridge: Cambridge University Press, 1994), 114-17 and 248-54.

4. Parpola, *Deciphering the Indus Script*.

5. Sir John Marshall, *Mohenjo-daro and the Indus Civilization* (London: Probsthain, 1931), 69, 382, 369.

6. Iravatham Mahadevan, "The Sacred Filter Standard Facing the Unicorn: More Evidence," in *South Asian Archaeology, 1993*, ed. Asko Parpola and Petteri Koskikallio (Helsinki: Suomalainen Tiedeakatemia, 1994), 435-45.

7. Marshall, *Mohenjo-daro and the Indus Civilization*.

8. Kwang-chih Chang, *Art, Myth, and Ritual: The Path to Political Authority in Ancient China* (Cambridge, Mass.: Harvard University Press, 1983), 72-73.

9. Shereen Ratnagar, *Enquiries into the Political Organization of Harappan Society* (Pune: Ravish, 1991), 154.

10. Jean-Marie Casal, *Fouilles D'Amri* (Paris: Commission des Fouilles Archaeologiques, 1964); Syed G. M. Shah and Asko Parpola, *Corpus of Indus Seals and Inscriptions. 2. Collections in Pakistan* (Helsinki: Suomalainen Tiedeakatemia, 1991).

11. Jagat Pati Joshi and Asko Parpola, *Corpus of Indus Seals and Inscriptions. 1. Collections in India* (Helsinki: Suomalainen Tiedeakatemia, 1987), K-85, M 324.

12. Parpola, *Deciphering the Indus Script*; Joshi and Parpola, *Corpus of Indus Seals and Inscriptions. 1.*

13. Shikarpur Raganatha Rao, *Lothal: A Harappan Port Town* (1955-62), vol. 2, *Memoirs of the Archaeological Survey of India*, No. 78. (New Delhi: Archaeological Survey of India, 1985), 112-14.

14. Parpola, *Deciphering the Indus Script*.

15. Rao, *Lothal: A Harappan Port Town*.

16. Parpola, *Deciphering the Indus Script*.

17. R. E. Mortimer Wheeler, "Harappa 1946: The Defenses and Cemetery R-37," *Ancient India* 3 (1947), 85 and from current research at Harappa by the Harappa Archaeological Research Project.

18. Jim G. Shaffer, "One Hump or Two: The Impact of the Camel on Harappan Society, *Orientalia Iosephi Tucci Memoriae Dicata*, ed. Gherardo Gnoli and Lionello Lanciotti (Rome: IsMEO, 1988), 1315-28; Richard H. Meadow, "A Camel Skeleton from Mohenjo Daro," in *Frontiers of the Indus Civilization*, ed. B. B. Lal and S. P. Gupta (New Delhi: Books and Books, 1984), 137-40.

19. Basil Greenhill, *Boats and Boatmen of Pakistan* (New York: Great Albion Books, 1971).

20. J. Mark Kenoyer, "Shell Working Industries of the Indus Civilization: An Archaeological and Ethnographic Perspective," Ph.D. diss., University of California at Berkeley, 1983.

21. Clifford Charles Lamberg-Karlovsky, "Trade Mechanisms in Indus-Mesopotamian Interrelations," in *Ancient Cities of the Indus*, ed. Gregory L. Possehl (New Delhi: Vikas, 1979), 130-37; Philip L. Kohl, "The Balance of Trade in Southwestern Asia in the Mid-Third Millennium B.C.," *Current Anthropology* 19.3 (1978): 463-92.

22. Marshall, *Mohenjo-daro and the Indus Civilization*; Ernest J. H. Mackay, *Further Excavations at Mohenjodaro* (New Delhi: Government of India, 1938), 321;

23. Ernest J. H. Mackay, *Chanhu-Daro Excavations 1935-36* (New Haven, Conn.: American Oriental Society, 1943), 320-21.

24. Henri-Paul Francfort, *Fouilles de Shortugaï Recherches sur L'Asie Centrale Protohistorique* (Paris: Diffusion de Boccard, 1989); Tamara Stech and Vince C. Pigott, "The Metals Trade in Southwest Asia in the Third Millennium B.C.," *Iraq* 48 (1986): 39-64.

25. George F. Dales and Louis Flam, "On Tracking the Woolly Kullis and the Like," *Expedition* 12.1 (1969): 15-23; Gregory L. Possehl, *Kulli: An Exploration of an Ancient Civilization in South Asia* (Durham, N.C.: Carolina Academic Press, 1986).

26. Dilip K. Chakrabarti, *The External Trade of the Indus Civilization* (New Delhi: Munshiram Manoharlal, 1990).

27. Serge Cleuziou, "The Oman Peninsula and the Indus Civilization: A Reassessment," *Man and Environment* 17.2 (1992): 93-103; Elizabeth L. C. During-Caspers, "Harappan Trade in the Arabian Gulf in the Third Millennium B.C.," *Mesopotamia* 7 (1972): 167-91.

28. S. R. Rao, "A "Persian Gulf" Seal from Lothal," in *Ancient Cities of the Indus*, ed. Gregory L. Possehl (New Delhi: Vikas, 1979), 148-52.

29. Serge Cleuziou et al., "Cachets Inscrits de la fin du IIIe millénaire avant notre ère á Ras' al-Junayz, Sultanat d'Oman," *Académie des Inscriptions et Belles-Lettres, Comptes rendus des séances de l'année 1994.* (April-June 1994): 453-68; Cleuziou, Serge and Maurizio Tosi, "The Southeastern Frontier of the Ancient Near East," *South Asian Archaeology, 1985*, ed. Karen Frifelt and Per Sørensen (London: Curzon Press, 1989), 15-48.

30. Daniel T. Potts, "South and Central Asian Elements at Tell Abraq (Emirate of Umm al-Qaiwain, United Arab Emirates), c. 2200 BC - AD 400," in *South Asian Archaeology, 1993*, ed. Asko Parpola and Petteri Koskikallio (Helsinki: Suomalainen Tiedeakatemia, 1994) 2: 615-28.

31. Serge Cleuziou, "The Chronology of Protohistoric Oman as seen from Hili," *Oman Studies*, ed. P. M. Costa and M. Tosi (Rome: Serie Orientale, 1989), LXIII: 47-78.

32. Chakrabarti, *The External Trade of the Indus Civilization*.

33. V. B. Mainkar, "Metrology in the Indus Civilization," in *Frontiers of the Indus Civilization*, ed. B. B. Lal and S. P. Gupta (New Delhi: Books and Books, 1984), 141-51.

34. Marshall, *Mohenjo-daro and the Indus Civilization*; Mainkar, "Metrology in the Indus Civilization."

35. Alexandra Ardeleanu-Jansen, "Stone Sculptures from Mohenjo-Daro," in *Interim Reports Vol. 1: Reports on Field Work Carried out at Mohenjo-Daro, Pakistan 1982-83 by IsMEO-Aachen University Mission*, ed. Michael Jansen and Günter Urban (Aachen: IsMEO/RWTH, 1984), 144.

36. Ardeleanu-Jansen, "Stone Sculptures from Mohenjo-Daro"; George F. Dales, "Stone Sculpture from the Protohistoric Helmand Civilization," *Orientalia Iosephi Tucci Memoriae Dicata*, ed. G. Gnoli and L. Lanciotti (Rome: IsMEO, 1985), 219-24.

37. Sir Leonard Woolley, *Excavations at Ur* (London: Benn, 1955), 117.

38. Simo Parpola, Asko Parpola and Robert H. Brunswig, "The Meluhha Village: Evidence of Acculturation of Harappan Traders in Late Third Millennium Mesopotamia?" *Journal of the Economic and Social History of the Orient* 20.2 (1977): 9-165.

39. Parpola, *Deciphering the Indus Script*.

40. Pierre Amiet, "Antiquitiés de Bactriane," *La Revue du Louvre* 3 (1978): 153-64; Pierre Amiet, "Iconographie de la Bactriane Proto-Historique," *Anatolian Studies, The British Institute of Archaeology at Ankara* 33 (1983): 19-27; Alexandra Ardeleanu-Jansen, "The Sculptural Art of the Harappa Culture," in *Forgotten Cities on the Indus*, ed. Michael Jansen, Máire Mulloy and Günter Urban (Mainz, Germany: Von Zabern, 1991), 167-78.

Fig. 6.1. Steatite seal depicting a deity standing in a pipal tree looking down on worshipers and a giant ram, Mohenjo-daro, cat. no. 24.

Religious Art and Symbols

Chapter 6

Rising from the center of a circle of bricks, the wide, spreading branches of the pipal tree form a natural sanctuary, with a canopy of heart-shaped leaves that protect those who enter its shadows. In the absence of formal temples, sacred trees located in the heart of each neighborhood or along the roads leading to the city gates may have been the most important shrines of the Indus culture (fig. 6.1).

The worship of trees as sacred spaces and symbols probably has its origins at the dawn of human history, when trees were a place of refuge and sustenance. Deep in the jungle, the pipal tree still provides a natural sanctuary for animals. The red figs sprouting profusely from the trunk and branches attract deer and monkeys. Birds and honey bees live in the protective foliage, while snakes, rodents and a host of insects live in the hollows of its roots and trunk. Two related trees, the pipal (*Ficus religiosa*) with a heart-shaped leaf (fig. 6.2) and the banyan (*Ficus indica*) with a long oval leaf, are found throughout the Indus Valley. Seedlings of both

Fig. 6.2. A young pipal tree with heart-shaped leaves at the tomb of Baba Noor Shah, Harappa.

varieties often take root on old buildings, boulders or in the bole of another tree, but as they grow their roots gradually engulf the host tree or boulders. Even though many creatures benefit from the pipal tree, the powerful roots gradually strangle and kill the host tree or break apart the boulders that allowed the original seedling a footing.

Other trees may have also been held sacred (fig. 6.3), but for over 6000 years, different cultures of the region have used the pipal tree as an important symbol. Heart-shaped pipal leaves, often arranged in groups of three, were commonly painted on small jars (fig. 6.4) during the Early Harappan period before the rise of the Indus cities. We find elaborate paintings of the pipal tree and its wide, spreading branches on large storage jars as well as smaller domestic vessels from the Indus period. Depicted in the Indus script as well as on faience ornaments and shell inlay, the heart-shaped pipal leaf was reproduced in many contexts and styles throughout the Indus cities.

In narrative scenes molded on terracotta tablets, human figures with water jars bow before the tree. On other tablets and seals, deities emerge from the center of a pipal tree (fig. 6.1) or stand under an arch of pipal leaves (see fig. 6.5b). Many horned deities wear a distinctive headdress comprised of three heart-shaped pipal leaves, and even a well found at Mohenjo-daro was made in the shape of a pipal leaf. In the absence of written texts, the specific meaning of this symbol during the Indus period can only be inferred by examining its meaning in later cultures.

The pipal and banyan trees are quite common throughout Hindu mythology, where they serve as important symbols of fertility and protection and death. Phallic symbols dedicated to the god Shiva are often placed at the base of the pipal or banyan tree, and rituals to the goddess Savitri are performed with the tree to ensure many children and avoid widowhood. In contrast, the hanging roots which strangle the host tree are seen as the noose of Yama, the god of death, and water offerings are poured out at the base of the tree to appease Yama and assure fertility and long life.[1]

Two-thousand years after the foundation of the Indus cities, the Lord Buddha attained enlightenment seated under a banyan or bodhi tree, and he often instructed his disciples in the cool shade of its branches. Even in modern Pakistan, the tombs of Muslim saints are found under the protective branches of this magnificent tree, though there is no symbolic ritual connection between the tree and Islam.

The pipal tree is an important example of how a natural object, a tree, has been used as a symbol by many different cultures and religions for thousands of years. The general protective nature of the tree is recognized by each succeeding culture, but specific associations with fertility, long life and death have changed significantly over time. On the Indus seals, the protective and sacred power of the tree is clearly depicted, but other specific meanings cannot be confirmed. Many ritual objects and symbols created by the Indus people continued to be used in later times, but as with the banyan and pipal trees, the specific meanings may have changed. In the following discussion of Indus religious art and symbol, comparisons will be made with other contemporaneous cultures and later Hindu or Buddhist religions to understand the general meanings of the Indus symbols. The precise meanings will have to await the decipherment of the Indus script, which is the ultimate key to understanding Indus religious beliefs.

The use of the pipal tree as a religious symbol appears to have discrete regional variations. At Mohenjo-daro the deity is always shown standing in the midst of the tree, while at Harappa the deity is shown standing beneath an arch made of leaves.

In a famous seal from Mohenjo-daro (see fig. 6.1), the pipal tree is divided into two main branches, each with three leaves, and the deity wears a horned headdress with a curved branch emerging from the center. The face is shown in profile, and a long braid hangs to the back; both arms are covered with bangles. In front of the deity is a kneeling worshiper offering what appears to be a human head placed on a stool. The worshiper also wears a horned headdress with a branch that has three pipal leaves, which mirrors the triple leaves on each branch of the tree itself. Behind the figure is a giant ram and along the top is a series of script signs that may identify the ritual or the deity. In the lower register is a procession of seven robed figures with long braids, short curved head ornaments and arms covered with bangles. Some scholars identify the attendants as priestesses, but no specific gender is indicated, and lacking examples of female figurines with long braids and single plumed head ornaments, we cannot determine if the procession is comprised of male or female attendants. Although we may not be able to interpret the specific ritual represented in this narrative seal, it does confirm the idea that the pipal tree was considered the abode of a horned deity and that important religious activities involving numerous worshipers took place at the foot of the tree.

At Harappa, the use of garlands and arches created with pipal leaves further confirms the sacred nature of this tree. A recently discovered terracotta tablet from Mound ET at Harappa portrays a deity standing beneath a curved arch of thirteen pipal leaves (fig. 6.5b). Although this deity does not wear the horned headdress, a stylized branch that has three "leaves" projects from the center of the head and a long braid hangs at the back. Both arms are covered with bangles and held at the side in a formal pose. One other example from Harappa has an arch of thirteen leaves; three smaller tablets have seven- and eight-leafed arches. The number of leaves must be significant, especially the number thirteen, which is generally associated with exceptional power in the subcontinent. There are thirteen full moons in a year, and in the Vedic literature the thirteenth sacrifice is considered especially beneficial.[2] As is common in modern religious traditions, the number of leaves may have had many

Fig. 6.3. Growing from a low platform, this sinuous tree with short leaves may have been held sacred like the pipal tree. Terracotta tablet, Harappa, H95-2523.

Fig. 6.4. Jar with three pipal leaves, Nausharo, Period ID, 2600-2550 B.C., after Samzun 1992, fig. 29.4, no. 2.

Fig. 6.5. Square molded tablet from Harappa: a) unicorn sealing and script on one side and b) deity under pipal arch on the reverse, cat. no. 25.

different meanings, and for the present we must be satisfied knowing that they were important symbols of the religious beliefs that united different communities throughout the Indus Valley.

Public and Private Symbols

At the core of all religions are beliefs about how the world is ordered and who controls the universe. For the Indus culture, these beliefs are reflected in preserved symbols such as seals, figurines, painted pottery and even the layout of the cities. The use of these symbols in both public and private contexts reinforced the social order and religious traditions of the Indus cities and villages. Public symbols helped to integrate the many different ethnic communities under a single religion and culture. Monumental gateways and large public buildings were constant reminders of the power of Indus rulers; sacred symbols on seals and painted pottery linked religious beliefs to all facets of commercial and private life. Elaborate headdresses and different styles of ornaments were worn by the different communities as symbols of ethnic identity and status. In contrast to these more public symbols, personal identity and solidarity at the community level was reinforced by such private symbols as the shape of the hearth, household pottery styles and personal ornaments.[3]

Symbols that reflect ideology and social order have been used since the Palaeolithic period, but there was a dramatic increase in the production and use of symbolic objects in the context of early cities. Many objects or motifs, such as the pipal tree, had their origin long before the rise of cities, but other symbols, such as the unicorn, were newly created in the context of cities. In order to produce these symbolic objects, artisans developed many new technologies. Advanced metallurgy was needed to produce bronze sculptures; high-temperature kilns were invented to produce glazed ornaments, stoneware bangles and the all important Indus seals (see Chap. 8).

Many objects produced by these complex technologies became symbols of the beliefs that united Indus society, but other objects distinguished the different social classes on the basis of status and power. Clay figurines depicting a mother goddess may have been used by most people living in the cities, but bronze figurines were probably made only for the highest classes or wealthiest families. Rare stone beads with natural eye motifs were worn by powerful leaders, similar to those seen on the famous "priest-king" sculpture, but copies of these "eye" beads were made of painted terracotta or steatite for use by the common people.

Bangles, a unique symbol shared by all segments of Indus society, also differentiated social and economic classes. Worn on the wrist or upper arm, bangles are a simple ornament found in cultures throughout the world.

But no other early civilization used bangles to the extent we see in the Indus cities. As a visual example of encirclement, bangles often serve as a symbol of protection or control. In the tradition of South Asia, a warrior wears bangles to protect the wrist and arm in battle, while a woman wears bangles to protect her family and assure the long life of her husband.[4] Worn by both men and women of the Indus cities, bangles may have served as a form of public symbol or nonverbal communication, much as they are today in South Asia. The type of material and the style of bangle indicate the wearer's ethnic identity, social status and ritual power (figs. 6.6, 6.7). In the Indus cities, simple circlets of clay were probably worn by the common people, while shell, bronze and gold bangles may have been worn only by the more affluent. (see Chap. 7)

Fig. 6.6. Terracotta female figurine from Harappa wearing bangles painted white as if they were representing shell bangles.

Fig. 6.7. Burial of a woman from Harappa, with shell bangles on the left arm, Harappa, H87-49c.

Indus religious symbols include abstract diagrams, stylized representations of natural phenomena, images of plants and animals and fantastic combinations of human and animal forms. In many religions, the distinction between human and nonhuman is fluid, and symbolic representations combining humans with animals or plants are common. Although there are hundreds of variations in terracotta figurines and other symbolic artifacts, recurring groups of artifacts and narrative themes appear to represent the core beliefs that united the Indus communities. Some of these themes can be compared with early religions in Mesopotamia and Central Asia or with later belief systems of the subcontinent itself; others can only be understood in the context of the Indus cities.

Abstract Symbols

Purely abstract symbols were used in many contexts by the Indus people. Geometric designs, most commonly found on pottery and seals, also recur as carved decoration on tools, gaming pieces and even inlaid objects. Many designs and discrete symbols can be traced to earlier periods (see Chap. 2, fig. 2.21), but others were created specifically in the urban context. Some of these designs may have been symbols of the different facets of religious and social order that served to unite Indus culture.

The endless-knot motif found on copper tablets at Mohenjo-daro (fig. 6.8) may have been an important symbol of a specific cult or community. This identical motif does not appear on other objects, but related designs are found on tablets and seals, as well as on a copper celt from the site of Rojdi, Gujarat.[5] In Mesopotamia the endless-knot design and related forms are found on some seals, and in the subcontinent it continues to be used in later Buddhist and Hindu contexts (see fig. 6.13).[6] Traditional Hindu women throughout the subcontinent continue to paint similar ritual designs to protect and purify the home.

A more common and widespread symbol that appears to have gained considerable popularity among the Indus cities is the swastika motif. This symbol, which became infamous under the Nazis, is in fact an ancient symbol representing the order of the universe, which is divided into four sectors by the central cross. The bent arms define the direction in which the universe turns, to the right or left (fig. 6.9, see cat. no. 35). Left-turning and right-turning swastikas may indicate the presence of different cults or schools of philosophy. In later Hinduism and Buddhism the right- and left-turning swastikas represented the opposing forces of the universe. Other seals have stepped-cross motifs (fig. 6.9), which also may represent the structure of the world, a concept reflected in the north-south orientation of the Indus cities and houses.

Order is perhaps the most significant theme in the art and architecture of the Indus cities. Symmetry of design and style are inherent in most of the extant decorated objects. Carved designs on bone or ivory objects are divided into sectors and decorated with identical motifs. Pottery is divided into panels of painted geometric designs interspersed with naturalistic depictions of plants and animals. The intersecting circle, fish-scale design, hatched triangle, checker-board design and the circle-and-dot motif are among the more common geometric motifs on pottery (see cat. nos. 176, 186, 187). Many of these designs are repeated on seals, in shell inlay or carved on ivory gaming pieces and even on bath-tubs or tiles (see fig. 6.11). The geometric designs may represent a general abstract concept of order, while other

Fig. 6.8. Flat copper tablet with incised script on one side and the endless-knot motif on the reverse, Mohenjo-daro, cat. no. 33.

Fig. 6.9. Incised steatite seal with stepped-cross motif and four dots in the corners, Harappa, cat. no. 36; faience button seal with swastika design turning counterclockwise, Mohenjo-daro, cat. no. 34.

motifs could have links to more specific themes relating to fertility or protection.

We can propose general meanings for some motifs on the basis of later known associations. For example, painted globular storage jars that were probably used in rituals or as marriage gifts are often painted with the so-called fish-scale motif. This recurring pattern may have been a symbol for fish, which represent fertility in later Buddhist and Hindu iconography. Other

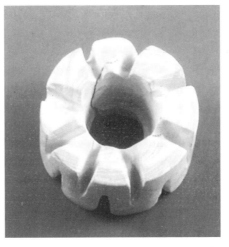

Fig. 6.10. Shell ring carved with alternating grooves to make a wavy design, Harappa, cat. no. 111.

symbols, such as the circle-and-dot motif (see cat. no. 115), could have had meanings ranging from the sun or moon to an eye or a navel; all may have played a significant role in one or more facets of Indus religion.

The circle is also a protective symbol that surrounds an object or the wearer with defense against evil powers (still used in the wedding band). Circles and wavy lines are commonly painted around pottery as part of the design, but they also may have had ritual significance as a protective bond. Some ancient pottery from Neolithic and Chalcolithic sites had single or double lines that often ended in the head of a snake. In later Indus pottery, snakes are never painted on the vessels, but single and multiple lines encircle pottery, often becoming the only design element (see cat. nos. 179, 180). Rings and wavy rings that were not used as body ornaments were made of stone, shell and clay. Many earlier scholars identified these objects as female fertility symbols, but they could have had varied uses and meanings. The shell wavy rings (fig. 6.10) probably decorated the handle of a staff or baton. Larger stone rings were used as column bases at the site of Dholavira (see Chap. 3, fig. 3.9), and numerous large ringstones have been found at Mohenjo-daro and

Harappa. The precise use of these massive stone rings probably differed from one generation to the next; the fact that many are broken and scattered over the sites may indicate that they were reused. At Harappa, excavators recently found wavy ringstone fragments near the main gateway at the southeastern corner of Mound E, possibly parts of massive pillars in the gateway area. Use as a pillar component does not diminish the symbolic significance of these objects, for in prominent contexts such as gateways, they would have been seen by everyone entering or leaving the city.

An intriguing geometric symbol is generally referred to as kidney or heart shaped (fig. 6.12), but the kidney and the Western heart-shaped design have never been used in the rituals of the subcontinent. The shape is very much like the section view of a shell bangle, which is traditionally associated with marriage, protection and fertility. An identical shape is found in traditional floor paintings in Bengal that represent the protective womb, and they are found carved onto rocks along the pilgrimage routes in northern Pakistan, again probably as protective symbols (fig. 6.13). In the Indus cities, this design is carved on seals appearing over the belly of the unicorn (see fig. 1.6, cat. no. 10). This symbol also is painted on pottery, sculpted in stone as the

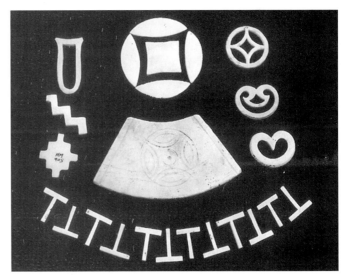

Fig. 6.12. Assorted shell inlaid objects with intersecting-circle and "womb" motif from Mohenjo-daro, cat. no. 110.

Fig. 6.11. Bathroom tile or base of large tub from Mohenjo-daro impressed with the intersecting-circle motif.

ears of the elite (see cat. no. 118) and even appears in the shape of faience bangles (see cat. no. 92). In each context the symbol may have had a slightly different meaning, but it is widespread throughout the Indus cities and continued to be used in later art traditions of the northwestern subcontinent and Central Asia (see Chap. 9).

Conical stone objects found in the early excavations at both Mohenjo-daro and Harappa have often been referred to as phallic symbols. In the past these objects were associated with the ringstones, which were thought to symbolize female reproductive organs. Yet many conical objects appear to have been used as pestles, and as discussed above, most ringstones can be associated with architectural features. Nevertheless, some conical stone pieces, both large and small, may in fact have been used as phallic symbols. Made from a variety of materials, most larger examples were made from white limestone or brown-and-yellow banded sandstone (fig. 6.14). Miniature conical pieces were made from shell, faience or even terracotta (fig. 6.15). While some may have been gaming pieces, others have a tiny hole in the base, as if they were to be attached or anchored to a base. Hemispherical bases of stone and terracotta with circular depression on the top have been found at both Mohenjo-daro and Harappa. Some scholars think these stands were used for supporting phallic stones or perhaps images, but so far none have been found in situ.

Fig. 6.13. The protective "womb" and the endless-knot designs are found with inscriptions dating from around 300 B.C. to A.D. 300, on the banks of the Indus river near Chilas, Pakistan.

Fig. 6.14. Large conical stone objects from Mohenjo-daro.

Fig. 6.15. Miniature terracotta conical objects or gaming pieces from Harappa.

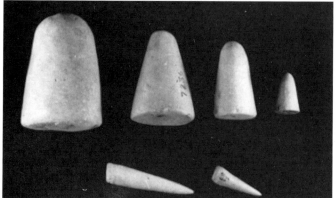

Male and Female Figurines

The act of procreation is a major theme in all ancient religions and is an important feature of modern religions as well. Because the fertility of the land and livestock is often linked to the worship of specific deities and natural powers, different objects may have been used in fertility rituals. Some of the abstract symbols discussed above may represent fertility and protection during childbirth, but male and female figurines of humans and some animals are more directly associated with the concept of fertility.

Male virility is represented in the nude male figurines, the male animal symbols on seals and stone phallic objects. We think female figurines with accentuated breasts and hips represent mother goddesses, and some objects may represent female reproductive organs. Terracotta tablets and inscribed objects show humans engaged in sexual intercourse, and others depict animals mating.[7] One of the most controversial seals from Chanhudaro [8] shows a short-horned bull engaged in what some think is sexual intercourse with a supine figure, presumably a female. These symbols together with the symbols discussed earlier, such as the fish and the pipal tree, imply that fertility cults to insure reproduction in people, plants and animals were an integral part of the Indus belief systems.

Female figurines identified as mother-goddess symbols are common in the larger sites of the Indus Valley and throughout Baluchistan, but they are less common in the Indus settlements of Gujarat and northern India. This variable distribution may reflect regional differences in beliefs or different perishable materials used in making figurines. In later Vedic rituals, figurines were often made of dough or unfired clay, while today many images are made of straw and paper.

Some female figurines portray a mother carrying a small infant in the left arm or suckling an infant at the left breast (cat. no. 134), a theme clearly associated with fertility and procreation. Other figurines portray a female with a short kilt about the waist and heavily ornamented with a belt, bangles, necklaces and elaborate headdresses (fig. 6.16). Many heavily ornamented figurines have cup-shaped headdresses that could have held oil, possibly as a votive lamp. The different styles of figurines may represent different cults or more likely the ethnic diversity of ornamentation and hairstyles.

Terracotta figurines were probably made by potters and then obtained by elites or the general population for use in domestic rituals beneath a sacred tree or in the courtyard of a home. After the ceremony the figurines were probably used as toys by children or discarded. None of these figurines has ever been found intentionally buried under structures or placed on a shrine, a common practice in the highlands to the west and in far-off Mesopotamia.

In traditional Hindu society, hand-modeled terracotta figurines are used for domestic rituals in which a woman seeks specific benefits: a child, good health and long life for her husband and family. These figurines are important during the actual ritual and offering, but after the ceremony is over, they often are left to the elements or used as toys by children. Eventually, the fragile objects are broken or forgotten and soon end up in the trash, much like the patterns we see from the Indus cities.

Male terracotta figurines are usually depicted nude, but wearing turbans or headdresses, neck ornaments and occasionally bangles (fig. 6.17). Many figurines stand with both feet firmly planted on the ground; others kneel with

Fig. 6.16. Female figurine heavily adorned with six graduated strands of chokers and pendant bead necklaces, Mohenjo-daro, cat. no. 135.

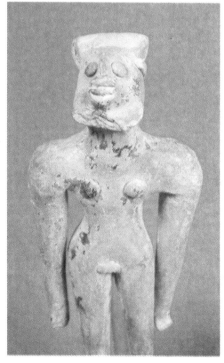

Fig. 6.17. Nude male figurine or deity with wide, spreading beard, wearing a broken headdress that may have had two curving horns, Mohenjo-daro, cat. no. 146.

one knee raised. Another pose common at Harappa is a seated figure with hands clasped around bent legs (see Chap. 8, cat. nos. 148, 149). This position is often interpreted as a praying or worshiping figure, but in later Buddhist and Hindu iconography a worshiper would never be depicted with the feet pointing towards a revered object or deity.

Similar postures are represented on seals and molded tablets, where male figures stand on the ground or in a tree. The standing figure is usually interpreted as a deity, the kneeling figure as a worshiper or priest. A unique posture found only on seals and molded tablets shows a male with horned headdress seated in a yogic position, with legs spread wide and heels pressed to the groin (figs. 6.18, 6.19). We trace the origins of this seated position and the horned deity itself to painted motifs on earlier pottery that present a horned deity and anthropomorphic plant motifs looking very much like the seated yogi figures. The tradition of yoga continues to the present throughout South Asia, and images of the Buddha and various Hindu deities, including Shiva, are often shown in the famous yogic posture called *padmasana*. The posture we see on the Indus seals can be correlated with a difficult position of highly advanced yoga called *mulabandhasana*.[9]

Bull-Tiger-Man-Plant

One of the most common motifs in Indus ritual art is the image of a bearded man wearing a headdress of wide, spreading bull or water-buffalo horns, which has a triple-leafed branch sprouting from the center. The eyes are usually long almond-shaped and sometimes the beard is spread out like the fur around a tiger's chin. This humanlike spirit combined with two of the most fearsome wild animals and the sacred pipal tree produces a complex image that appears for the first time in the Indus cities.

Horned images do appear on earlier painted pottery, and the pipal-leaf design as well as anthropomorphic plant shapes are not uncommon motifs prior to the rise of the Indus cities (Chap. 2). However, combined together with the tiger, this new motif must represent a synthesis of various beliefs or perhaps the culmination of a long process of religious development. On the basis of parallels with Mesopotamia and later South Asian iconography, we can say that human images wearing horned headdresses probably represent some form of deity or sacred power, while the plant motifs most likely relate to fertility or procreation.

We can identify from the Indus period two distinct horned deities found as terracotta figurines or carved onto seals. One figure has relatively short horns emerging from the top of the head like those depicted on the humped zebu; whereas the other has wide, curved horns spreading to the side, characteristic of the water buffalo. These two horned figures often have distinctive wide, spreading beards and shaggy or long hair. Some seated figures with horned headdresses appear to have additional faces carved at the side of the head, suggesting that this deity had three or even four heads if there was a face at the back of the head. It is tempting to associate this many-faced deity with later Hindu images of Shiva, but lacking textual corroboration we should see the multiple-headed Indus deity as a distinct and early phenomenon. A terracotta figurine from Mohenjo-daro has a double face, on front and back of the head,[10] but no figurines with three or four faces have been found. When carved on seals, the details of the faces and the difference between the two types of horns are often difficult to distinguish, except that the wide, curving horns usually occur with a central component made from a pipal branch with three leaves, often highly stylized and reduced to three projecting lines.

The human image with bull's horns is generally depicted with bull's tail and hoofed hind legs, but arms with human hands or tiger's claws.[11] On copper tablets from Mohenjo-daro this figure also has a tail and runs with a bow in one hand and arrows in the other.[12] This archer or hunter may represent a deity or simply the common practice of wearing camouflage while stalking game. However, such costumes may also have been worn in ritual dances or processions to represent natural or supernatural powers.

Small terracotta masks depict the bull-horned figure with a beard that is combed flat when the face is in a peaceful mode (see fig. 5.3, cat. no. 122), but when in an angry mode, the beard is spread wide and the fangs of a roaring tiger are visible (see fig. 5.4, cat. no. 123). These small masklike objects may have been used as finger puppets or worn as amulets. As puppets, they could have been used to reenact narrative scenes pictured on seals and tablets.

The second important horned deity wears a central branch as a headdress in addition to the wide, spreading horns of the water buffalo. The most famous representation of this image is on a seal from Mohenjo-daro that shows a male deity seated in yogic position with erect phallus (fig. 6.18).[13] The deity is heavily adorned with bangles on both

Fig. 6.18. Carved steatite seal with the so-called "proto-Shiva," Mohenjo-daro. National Museum of India, New Delhi, 5075/123; Joshi and Parpola 1987: M-304.

arms and a series of graduated necklaces reaching to his waist. He wears a massive headdress of wide, spreading water buffalo horns and a central fan-shaped element, possibly representing feathers or branches. Ferocious wild animals surround the deity: a rhinoceros, a water buffalo, an elephant and a tiger, while two gentle antelope are seen at the front of the dais. A single line of the undeciphered Indus script (in reverse) is carved along the top of the seal.

This seated figure has been referred to as "proto-Shiva" because of its similarity to later iconography of the deity Shiva from the Hindu pantheon. Whereas many later Hindu deities may have had their roots in earlier beliefs of the Indus Valley or other indigenous communities living in the subcontinent, we cannot confirm specific connections between the horned figure on the Indus seals and later Hindu deities. There are similarities in the iconography, but the meaning relayed may have been significantly different.

Along with the famous "proto-Shiva" seal two other seals with horned deities wearing bangles and seated in yogic position were found in the DK-G area of Mohenjo-daro. One is a relatively simple figure seated on a throne with legs carved in the shape of bovine hooves (fig. 6.19). The frontal visage is indistinct, but there appear to be additional faces on each side, making it a second example of the three-faced deity. The carving of the body shows well-defined pectoral muscles and stylized male genitalia. The headdress has three pipal leaves branching out of the center, and two curving horns on either side.

Not all seals or molded tablets picture this deity with three faces. On one example from Mohenjo-daro[14] the face is shown in profile with a massive braid of hair projecting to the back. A star is carved in the center of each curving horn, and the stylized branch with five leaves curls up from the center of the headdress. Both arms are covered with bangles; the deity is nude, seated with legs positioned in the standard yogic pose. Almost identical figures are found on other molded terracotta tablets from Mohenjo-daro as well as from Harappa. Two recently discovered tablets from Harappa

show this same deity seated on a throne, with a reed house or temple at one side (fig. 6.20). On other seals the seated deity is witness to the killing or sacrifice of a water buffalo (see fig. 6.24b). The various contexts and narrative motifs indicate that this deity or different deities depicted in similar manner were the focus of considerable worship and sacrifice.

Due to the fragile nature of the wide, spreading horns, most terracotta figurines of the deity are broken, but even these fragmentary pieces give a sense of the powerful beauty of the deity (fig. 6.21). Many examples of terracotta buffalo horns have been found with holes for attaching them to a headdress. Generally these horns are broken, but the complete horns may have been from 10 to 20 centimeters in length. Such terracotta horns may have been attached to actual headdresses worn by puppets or child performers. Full-sized headdresses may have used actual horns, as is still the practice among the Muria Gond communities in central India.[15] A unique aspect of this figurine is the goatlike beard that replaces the normal wide, spreading tiger beard. The goatlike beard may indicate a specific aspect of the deity that is correlated to a myth or cult associated with the wild goat, often depicted on seals (see fig. 6.1).

Fig. 6.20. Seated figure or deity with reed house or shrine at one side, Harappa, (left) H95-2524, (right) H95-2487.

Fig. 6.21. Male figurine or deity with goatlike beard, wearing a horned headdress (broken), Mohenjo-daro, cat. no. 147.

Fig. 6.19. Steatite seal depicting a male deity seated in yogic position, Mohenjo-daro, cat. no. 23.

Although most horned deities are bearded and therefore male, others are beardless and have a prominent breast that could represent either male pectoral muscles or female breasts. One seal from Mohenjo-daro shows a bull-horned deity with clawlike hands attacking a horned tiger.[16] The deity has the hindquarters and tail of a bull, but the torso is human, with a prominent pectoral muscle or breast in profile. If this does represent a female deity, it indicates that the horned deity had both male and female aspects, a concept that became articulated in later Hinduism as the power of the male principle—*shakta* and female principle—*shakti*.

Animal Myths

Most children of the subcontinent grow up hearing stories about tigers, either to frighten them into obedience or to instruct them on the improper use of power and the morals of right action. By its nature the ferocious tiger has the right to eat other animals, but when it abuses this right, it should be destroyed by whatever means necessary. The traditional Punjabi folk story about the "Tiger and the Hare" tells a how the hare coaxes the tiger to attack its own reflection in a well, thereby drowning the beast and ridding the jungle of a bloodthirsty tyrant.[17]

The thick jungles of the Indus Valley were full of tigers and leopards, so it is not surprising that the image of a ferocious feline is a recurring motif in ritual narratives on seals as well as on molded tablets. The most common scene shows a figure sitting on the branch of an acacia tree, gesturing to a tiger which is looking back at the figure over its shoulder (fig. 6.22). We cannot supply the narrative for this scene, but a seal from Mohenjo-daro shows a horned

deity attacking a horned tiger, meaning that this relationship was probably not very peaceful. The horned tiger is also shown on square seals (fig. 6.23) and is represented by terracotta masks (see fig. 5.4, cat. no. 123).

The struggle between wild animals and humans is even more graphically illustrated in a magnificent terracotta tablet discovered in 1995 from Mound ET at Harappa (fig. 6.24). On one side the tablet has a narrative motif showing a figure grasping two felines, probably tigers, and standing above an elephant. On the opposite side is a scene depicting the killing of a water buffalo.

The figure strangling the two tigers with bare hands may represent a female, as a pronounced breast can be seen in profile (fig. 6.24a). Earlier discoveries of this motif on seals from Mohenjo-daro definitely show a male figure, and most scholars have assumed some connection with the carved seals from Mesopotamia that illustrate episodes from the famous Gilgamesh epic.[18] The Mesopotamian motifs show lions being strangled by a hero, whereas the Indus narratives render tigers being strangled by a figure, sometimes clearly male, sometimes ambiguous or possibly female. This motif of a hero or heroine grappling with two wild animals could have been created independently for similar events that may have occurred in Mesopotamia as well as the Indus valley.

On the reverse of the same tablet (fig. 6.24b) is a narrative scene depicting the killing of a water buffalo. A person, possibly a man, with hair tied in a bun on the back of the head, impales a water buffalo with a barbed spear. The hunter's foot presses down the water buffalo's head as he thrusts the spear into its shoulder. In later Hindu rituals, the water buffalo sacrifice is associated with the worship of the goddess Durga, but on this seal the sacrifice takes place

Fig. 6.22. (Right) Steatite seal depicting a human figure in tree and a tiger looking back over its shoulder from below, Mohenjo-daro, cat. no. 26.

Fig. 6.23. (Right middle) Steatite seal with horned-tiger motif, Mohenjo-daro, cat. no. 28.

Fig. 6.24. Planoconvex molded tablet from Harappa, cat. no. 27:
a) (Far right) Obverse depicts a female deity battling two tigers and standing above an elephant,
b) (Right) reverse shows a hunter killing a water buffalo in front of a seated horned deity.

in the presence of a priest or deity seated in yogic position. The seated figure wears bangles and a horned and plumed headdress. Above the head of the hunter is a gharial, a small species of crocodile with a narrow snout that was once common in the Ravi and Indus rivers, but is now almost extinct. Similar scenes of an individual spearing a water buffalo have been found on other terracotta tablets from both Harappa and Mohenjo-daro, but none is associated with the figure strangling two tigers.[19]

We have found two other broken tablets at Harappa that appear to have been made from the same mold that was used to create the scene of a deity battling two tigers and standing above an elephant. One was found in a room located on the southern slope of Mound ET in 1996 and another example comes from excavations on Mound F in the 1930s.[20] However, the flat obverse of both of these broken tablets does not show the spearing of a buffalo, rather it depicts the more well-known scene showing a tiger looking back over its shoulder at a person sitting on the branch of a tree. Several other flat or twisted rectangular terracotta tablets found at Harappa combine these two narrative scenes of a figure strangling two tigers on one side of a tablet, and the tiger looking back over its shoulder at a figure in a tree on the other side.

One additional series of narrative scenes provides further insight into the stories of human conflicts with animals. We found this narrative sequence on molded faience tablets at Harappa; it consists of three different scenes and one line of text. Some tablets are two sided and only reveal one segment of the narrative and the text. Others tablets are three sided and reveal three scenes, or two of the scenes along with the text. But, several examples are four sided and have all three of the scenes along with the text. Due to various preservation factors, no single tablet has all scenes clearly represented, but we can obtain the details by examining all of the molded tablets.

In the first panel a human figure grapples with a short-horned bull, and a small plant with at least six branches is discernible behind the individual (fig. 6.25a). In the second panel a figure sits on a bed or throne in a yogic position, with arms resting on the knees (fig. 6.25b). Both arms are covered with bangles, and traces of a horned headdress and long hair are visible on some of the impressions. A second individual, also with long hair and wearing bangles, sits on a short stool to the proper left of the individual on the "throne." This figure reaches toward the seated deity or priest with the right hand and extends the left arm in the opposite direction. The third panel shows a deity wearing a horned headdress that has a curved branch with three projecting leaves (fig. 6.25c). Bangles visible on both arms are comparable to those seen on seated figures (figs. 6.18, 6.19, 6.20). The fourth panel is comprised entirely of script and has six characters, the first of which appears to be some form of animal (fig. 6.25d).

Although we cannot decode the exact meaning of these narrative scenes, we know that the stories or myths that they represent, in one form or another, are spread throughout the larger cities and the Indus region in general. Several terracotta tablets made from the same mold have been found in different parts of Harappa and other examples in Mohenjo-daro. More significantly, the same motifs or variations are found at both of the largest excavated sites as well as at many of the smaller regional towns and villages.

Although the rituals depicted on the seals and tablets may have been practiced by only the higher classes or priests, they appear to have been carried out in the open under a pipal tree. The purpose of public rituals is often to teach people the power of the deities and to legitimize the power of the rulers who worship the deities. People coming to the larger urban centers to trade and participate in seasonal festivals and rituals returned to their villages and

a.

b.

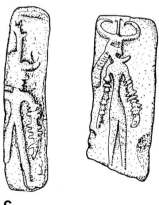

c.

d.

Fig. 6.25. Four narrative scenes depicted on a series of small tablets from Harappa: a) man fighting short-horned bull, b) seated figures, c) standing deity with horned headdress, d) script, H95-2519, H94-2263 and H97-3301.

towns carrying stories about the gods and rulers of the city along with trade goods. The narrative amulets and terracotta figurines may have been commemorative mementos of these events.

Human-Animal Spirits

In the Indus religion, the line between human and animal was indistinct, and many figurines as well as seals portray combined human and animal form. Some figures have human heads and animal bodies; others have animal heads and human bodies. A tiger with a man's bearded head (fig. 6.26) contrasts with a seated catlike animal with a woman's head (see cat. no. 127). Such images appear to have been serious ritual objects placed on shrines to appease the ferocious spirits or raised high above the house to ward off the evil powers.

Another category of human-animal figurines was probably used in puppet shows to amuse and teach the public. One of the most famous figures has a doglike head and a pot-bellied human body with holes for attaching moveable arms (fig. 6.27). A long penis was once attached under the bulging belly, and a broken tail can be seen at the back of the figure. A hole in the base indicates that it was attached to a stick, probably to allow a puppeteer to manipulate the figure while sitting behind a screen. Ithyphallic caricatures, common in most societies, usually attract and keep the crowd's attention in between more serious presentations. Another pot-bellied figurine has a long trumpetlike projection emerging from the mouth, with both hands covering the face as if in mock fear or laughter (see cat. no. 131). Whether this figure depicts a joker trying to sneak a kiss or a musician playing terrible music, it surely falls in the comic category along with the other pot-bellied figurines.

Multiple Animal and Human Images

More serious figurines that also may have been used as puppets or for special rituals combine several different forms of animals. The two examples of such figurines so far discovered come from the site of Naushare, Pakistan.[21] Three different animals are depicted, but not all are preserved on each of the broken figurines. The gray-colored example shows an elephant with a hollow trunk, as two horns from the missing head of a water buffalo or bull curve along the side of the elephant's face (fig. 6.28). We can see the bottom jaw of a feline with bared teeth at the back of the elephant's head. On the reddish brown example, the tiger's face is clear and the head of a water buffalo or bull is still attached, but the elephant face with hollow trunk is badly eroded (fig. 6.29). Because these figurines are broken, we do not know how they were held or used, but similar animals with multiple heads are carved on seals; perhaps the terracotta heads were attached to a body made of wood or reeds.

Although Naushare has the only terracotta figurines of multiple animals, multiple-headed animals are found on seals from most of the larger sites. One square seal from

Fig. 6.26. Feline figurine with male human face, Harappa, cat. no. 126.

Fig. 6.27. Animal-headed, pot-bellied, ithyphallic human figurine or puppet, Mohenjo-daro, cat. no. 130.

Fig. 6.28. Hollow three-headed animal figurine, Nausharo, cat. no. 128.

Fig. 6.29. Hollow three-headed animal figurine, Nausharo, cat. no. 129.

Mohenjo-daro shows a triple-headed combination of important totemic animals: the bull, the unicorn and the antelope (fig. 6.30). In another variation multiple creatures are combined into a single animal (fig. 6.31). The rounded human face has an elephant's trunk and a draping beard or tusk. A pair of inward curving ribbed horns rise above the head and a heavy mane like that on large Markhor goats hangs from the neck. The front hooves and genitalia are similar to those on bull and unicorn figures, but the back feet and haunches are that of a striped tiger. Finally, the tail is depicted as an upraised cobra. No ritual offering stand is pictured on this seal, but four script signs are written above the back of the creature.

One famous example of the combined animal-human forms is on a cylinder seal from the site of Kalibangan, India (fig. 6.32).[22] On this seal two men appear to be fighting over a woman, with long braided hair and bangles on each hand, who wears a long skirt. While trying to spear each other, the men grab the woman's hands, and their spears form an arch over her head. In the background what may be a female deity with the body of a tiger and the horns of a Markhor goat watches. The deity's arms are covered with numerous bangles, and she has long streaming hair. In front of the deity is a tree without leaves; behind her is a tree covered with leaves. A single sign of three strokes appears in front of the deity's face.

The theme of two men fighting over a woman is not unique to the Indus culture, but the human-tiger-Markhor deity watching the scene suggests a mythic dimension. Both men are dressed in the same manner, suggesting they are from the same ethnic group, so it is clearly not a battle to protect a woman from an outside raider. Perhaps the deity is protecting a queen or princess as the hero rescues her from a local opponent. The motif of the human-tiger-Markhor deity was discovered on another seal from Kalibangan,[23] and on a seal from the site of Nausharo,[24] but no examples have been discovered at the larger urban centers.

Fig. 6.30. (Above left) Steatite seal with multiple-headed animal motif, Mohenjo-daro, cat. no. 29.

Fig. 6.31. (Above right) Worn steatite seal with multiple creatures combined to make a single animal, Mohenjo-daro, cat. no. 30.

Fig. 6.32. (Left) Cylinder seal, and impression from Kalibangan, India.

The seals and figurines with combination figures probably reflect the synthesis of many local powers under a single set of deities. In the art of Bactria or Mesopotamia, such combination deities can be associated with known myths wherein the specific animals represent special powers. Since the Indus deities combine the most important totemic and plant motifs, they must be important symbols of Indus religious integration.

Animal Figurines

The abundance of animal figurines at the major urban centers suggests that they were commonly used in household and public rituals. All major domestic and wild animals are represented by terracotta figurines, but only a few animals were made in stone or faience. Two fragmentary stone sculptures of a seated ram were recovered from excavations at Mohenjo-daro.[25] The face of one figure was missing, but eventually was recovered many years later during surface surveys (fig. 6.33). This figure depicts a large male sheep with a massive bearded jowl and curled horns.

In contrast to the large stone sculptures, sheep figurines were also made in terracotta and faience. Miniature glazed faience figurines of seated rams have a perforation though the body so they could be worn as amulets (fig. 6.34). The white glazed surface is generally quite thick and well preserved, but it conceals the delicate modeling of the face. These figurines have been found at both Mohenjo-daro and Harappa, and one example of a tiny glazed ram was found at the site of Nausharo where it was originally identified as a horse-figurine head.[26]

Bull and water buffalo figurines made from terracotta are quite common at the larger urban centers and are found at many of the smaller settlements as well. The earlier figurines were hand modeled, but towards the end of the Indus period many were mass produced with molded heads attached to a hand-formed body (fig. 6.35). Some humped bull figurines are extremely large and quite elaborate. The body of this type of large figurine was hollow, and the molded head was carefully touched up with carving tools and appliqué (fig. 6.36). Figurines with moveable heads and holes for attaching wheels may have been used as toys, but others may have served as votive sacrifices.

Domestic and wild animals were probably sacrificed for specific Indus rituals, as indicated by narrative scenes on tablets, such as the killing of a water buffalo (see fig. 6.24b) or the scene of a man grappling with a short-horned and humpless bull (see fig. 6.25a). In later historical periods figurines made of flour or terracotta were often used for sacrificial purposes instead of the actual animals.

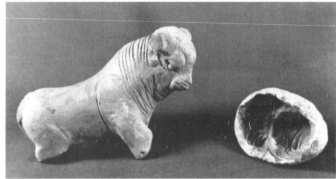

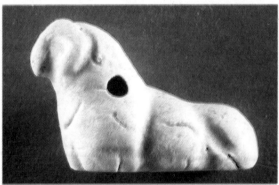

Fig. 6.33. (Top left) Stone sculpture of a seated ram, Mohenjo-daro, cat. no. 121.

Fig. 6.34. (Above left) Faience amulet of a seated ram, Harappa, cat. no. 172.

Fig. 6.35. (Top right) Humped-bull figurine with molded head twisted to the side, Mohenjo-daro, cat. no. 155, and terracotta mold for making bull figurine heads, Mohenjo-daro, cat. no. 156.

Fig. 6.36. (Above right) Large, hollow bull figurine with braided halter, Mohenjo-daro, cat. no. 157.

If animal figurines were used as votive offerings substituting for actual animal sacrifice, some human figurines may have served a similar function. Human sacrifice or the taking of heads may have been practiced by the Indus people, but we have only one possible depiction of this act: a human head placed as an offering in front of a deity (see fig. 6.1). Although the minute carving does not provide much detail, the hair appears to be tied in a double bun, as commonly shown on male figures. If this example does represent the offering of a male head, then some male figurines may have been used as votive sacrifices. We found one fragmentary male figurine in recent excavations at Harappa that appears to have his arms pressed to the back as if they had been bound. A more common type of figurine shows a seated male with legs together and hands clasped at the knees (cat. nos. 148-149). This type of figurine has been interpreted as a worshiper, but perhaps it represents a sacrificial victim with hands and feet tied together.

Ritual Utensils and Paraphernalia

Sacrifice of animals, plants and in some cases human beings is an integral part of all religions. These sacrifices can be symbolic or real, but they are crucial to the worship of the deities and the perpetuation of beliefs. Some sacrifices are carried out with simple tools in a specific sacred spot, but other sacrifices involve ritual paraphernalia. Carved seals and molded tablets illustrate many objects used in specific rituals. The most common object is the ritual offering stand that has been interpreted variously as a sacred filter for making an intoxicating drink called soma or an incense burner. Shallow basins or feeding troughs also may have had some ritual significance as a container for food offerings to totemic animals.

Ritual furniture includes the wide thrones on which the horned deities are seated. These thrones often have legs carved with the hooves of a bull (see fig. 6.18). Short stools were used by individuals sitting in front of the horned deity (see fig. 6.25b) and a short table displayed the human head offering (see fig. 6.1).

Elaborately crafted objects such as shell ladles (fig. 6.37) and libation vessels (fig. 6.38) may have been used for pouring sacred offerings of water, milk, oil or butter. Shell ladles were made from the spiney murex shell, *Chicoreus ramosus*, that was collected from the waters of Kutch or distant Oman. Coastal shellworkers cut and ground the shell to prepare a roughly shaped ladle. These unfinished pieces were then traded to larger sites such as Harappa and Mohenjo-daro, for the final grinding and polishing. Fragments of finished shell ladles have been found at most Indus settlements, but only rarely is a complete ladle recovered, usually buried in a room or as a funerary offering. At Harappa, we found a large ladle that had been repaired with a lead rivet in one of the burials along with some pottery (fig. 6.37).

Another ritual utensil is the libation vessel made from the conch shell *Turbinella pyrum*. Several examples of these distinctive vessels have been found at Mohenjo-daro (fig. 6.38) and one example made from another shell species, *Fasciolaria trapezium*, was found at the nearby site of Chanhudaro. The manufacture of this vessel from the conch shell was not an easy task, requiring hardened bronze chisels to break the strong central columella and interior whorls. After the interior was hollowed out, the exterior was ground smooth and incised with spiraling lines or circles that were filled with red pigment. Far to the west, the priests of Mesopotamian temples used similar vessels made from the *Lambis* sp. shell, for pouring oil in libation to the deities or for dispensing sacred unguents.[27] In later Hindu and Buddhist rituals, identical libation vessels made from *Turbinella pyrum* were used for anointing kings and for dispensing sacred water or milk. Even today, this type of libation vessel is used throughout the subcontinent for ritual libations and for dispensing medicinal preparations.[28]

Another ritual object made from the conch shell *Turbinella pyrum* is a trumpet that has a mouthpiece chipped at the apex of the shell (see cat. no. 104). This unique example of a conch-shell trumpet was found at the site of Harappa. Trumpets made from horn or shell are used in

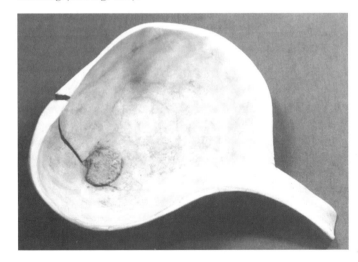

Fig. 6.37. Burial offering of a shell ladle made from the spiney murex shell, Harappa, cat. no. 102.

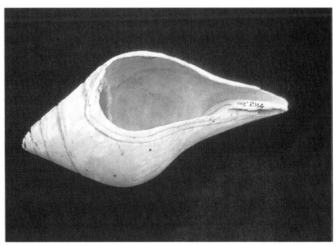

Fig. 6.38. Libation vessel from conch shell Turbinella pyrum, decorated with vermilion-filled incised lines, Mohenjo-daro, cat. no. 101.

many cultures throughout the Old World to call people together for rituals or for battle. In later Hindu and Buddhist rituals, the conch shell was sounded to call the deities to the sacrifice and purify the area in which the sacrifice was to take place. Since only one conch trumpet has been found, it is possible that this instrument was just beginning to be used when the cities began to decline. However, both the conch trumpet and the conch shell libation vessels continued to be used in later times and are still an essential component of Hindu and Buddhist rituals.

The spoon or ladle made from the murex shell was first created during the Indus period, but its use did not continue after the decline of the Indus cities. One explanation for these two trajectories is that the rituals involving the shell ladles became obsolete, while those involving the conch-shell trumpet and libation vessels continued into the period following the decline of the Indus cities (see Chap. 9 for further discussion).

An important category of ritual paraphernalia is pottery vessels for holding sacred water or offerings. Burial pottery probably held water and food for the dead, and other vessels may have been used for specific domestic rituals. The famous bronze sculptures of standing female figures both hold a small bowl in the right hand that may have held a food offering or oil for a lamp (see cat. no. 144). Another ceramic container that may have held special ritual offerings or liquids is the pointed-base goblet found most abundantly in the largest cities (see cat. nos. 193, 194). These goblets, made by the thousands, may have been used for everyday drinking or for special festivals commemorating a specific deity. Many pointed-base goblets have seal impressions, and sometimes numerous goblets were impressed with the same seal. These stamped goblets may have been produced for a specific individual or ritual, but most goblets were probably used as disposable drinking cups. They appear to have been discarded after use, rather than reused as were other containers.

Water and Ritual Purity

Water is essential for life, and all societies have a special reverence for the rains which water the fields and rivers or springs which emerge from the earth. Water motifs are commonly painted on Indus pottery, but no specific rituals associated with rain and rivers are recorded on narrative seals. Nevertheless, pure drinking water and the proper disposal of polluted water were important concerns for the Indus cities. At most sites, wells were dug to provide water for the inhabitants. The number of wells at Mohenjo-daro appears to exceed the normal needs of a large urban center (see Chap. 3). At Harappa, there are fewer wells, suggesting that there were other sources for water, but at both sites,

bathing platforms were found in every block of houses. When considered along with the massive construction known as the great bath at Mohenjo-daro, we assume that bathing and the purity of water may have had specific ritual significance in the Indus cities. This high regard for water and bathing is complemented by concern for the removal of polluted water and sewage. The Indus Valley civilization is not the only culture with concerns for the purity of water sources, but it is the first urban culture to develop specialized drainage technology throughout the entire urban settlement.

Games as ritual

In most cultures, ritual games are used for predicting the future or educating children about social and religious ideals. Gaming boards carved onto bricks or made of fired clay have been found at most Indus sites, but there is no standardized shape or form. Most boards have a large square divided by vertical, horizontal and sometimes diagonal lines (fig. 6.39) Many similar gaming boards are still used by children throughout the northern subcontinent to play strategy games, such as capturing the "tiger" with "elephants." Other game boards are used in fortune-telling and gambling, both favorite pastimes in cities and villages. Dice can be simple split reeds, cowrie shell, cubical dice or finely carved ivory rods with circles incised on each face. Traditional gaming pieces are usually made of wood or ivory in various conical or spherical shapes with distinctive designs or colors.

Many carved objects from the Indus cities are made of valuable materials such as shell or ivory, and may have been used in ritual games or the pastimes of wealthy city dwellers. Carved shell balls may have been rolled onto a square or depression (see cat. no. 112). Dice made from bone, shell, or terracotta were probably used in games of chance similar to those played throughout the subcontinent today (fig. 6.40, see cat. no. 113). Other bone and ivory counters with circles and lines, carved in ways that do not correspond to dice, may have been used for predicting the future (fig. 6.41).

Long bar-shaped dice (see cat. no. 113) are still used in Pakistan and India to play the game of pacheesi or chaupat, which may date as early as 1500 B.C. In this game, two to four players move pieces around the cross-shaped board, blocking and attacking each other until one player brings all his pieces safely "home." Cubical dice (fig. 6.40) are traditionally used to play the game of snakes and ladders, where ladders allow the player to climb to the heavens and snakes swallow the player and deposit him back in the world or underworld. Both games have important ritual significance but are usually played by children and adults for enjoyment or gambling. These complex gaming boards are traditionally made with painted or embroidered cloth, which would not be preserved for the archaeological record.

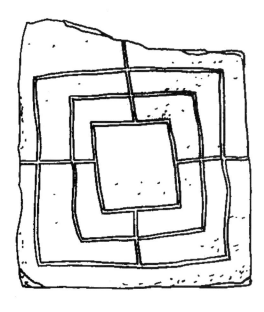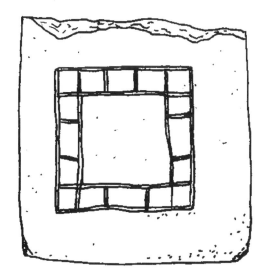

Fig. 6.39. Gaming board designs from Lothal (after Rao 1985, fig. 104) and Harappa (H94/5340-1).

Fig. 6.40. Cubical dice made of clay and stone, Harappa.

Fig. 6.41. Carved ivory counters, Mohenjo-daro: a) duck ornament, cat. no. 114, b) stylized figurine with triple-circle motifs, cat. no. 115, c) double duck-head ornament, cat. no. 116.

Burials and the Afterlife

The burials of the Indus people provide the most direct evidence for specific rituals and religious beliefs. Simple grave offerings of pottery suggest a belief in life after death, and the inclusion of modest personal ornaments may have served to identify the social and ritual status of the individual in the other world. No seals or inscribed objects have been found with burials, and presumably high-value objects such as copper tools and ornaments of gold and long carnelian beads are conspicuously absent. Some individuals were buried with great care and preparation, wrapped in a shroud and placed in a wooden coffin (fig. 6.42). But, in some instances, a corpse was thrown into an open pit filled with previously disturbed bones and broken pottery. The coffin burials may be the standard among elite communities, whereas interpretation of the casual disposal depends on the specific details of preservation and stratigraphy.

Scattered burials, as well as discrete cemeteries, have been found at sites in each of the major regions, but most cemeteries are small and do not represent all of local inhabitants. It is possible that only certain groups practiced burial while others were disposed of by other means. The lack of evidence for differential dietary stress among the individuals buried at Harappa[29] may indicate that the people were healthy and well fed, probably from among the upper classes. However, there are variations in the number of funerary offerings and ornaments with each burial, possibly indicating minor differences in social or ritual status.

At Harappa, the dead were usually buried in deep rectangular graves, sometimes lined with mud bricks. Pottery typical of that used in the home was placed at the bottom of the grave shaft (fig. 6.42). These vessels may have been filled with food and drink for use in the afterlife, but due to the poor preservation of organic material in the tropics, no traces have been preserved inside the vessels. At Harappa where many burials have been excavated, most graves show that the pottery was covered with a layer of soil and then the coffin was placed on top of this partially filled grave shaft.

Sir Mortimer Wheeler's excavations in 1946 recovered some fragments of wood from a coffin and shroud that were identified as rosewood (*Dalbergia latifolia*) and cedar (*Cedrus deodara*) respectively.[30] In more recent excavations coffins were visible as dark stains that could be measured, but no traces of wood remained. Most coffins were approximately 0.50 meters wide, 1.7 to 1.9 meters long and were made of boards that were 2 to 3 cm thick. Traces of a carbonized lid or shroud were found on one individual, and another corpse appeared to have been tightly wrapped with cloth, but no traces of the cloth or matting could be recovered.[31]

After the coffin had been interred, the entire pit was filled with earth, covering the burial and pottery offerings. We have found no traces of cenotaphs or grave markers, but the cemetery area may have been marked by wooden markers or low mounds of earth. Two mud-brick buildings in the cemetery at Harappa may have been used for rituals or bathing the body.

The cemetery at Harappa appears to have been used by a limited group, possibly all belonging to a single kinship group or clan. They were buried one on top of the other, and the later burials often cut through the graves of earlier individuals. This pattern suggests that the burial ground itself was possibly a sacred place and that all members of a single group wanted to be buried close together. The fact that many earlier burials were disturbed by later grave digging suggests that the grave diggers were of a different social class who were unconcerned about disturbing the earlier burials. In some instances, relatively fresh burials were disinterred and partly decomposed corpses were thrown into adjacent pits to make room for new burials. In several of the disturbed female burials, the shell bangles traditionally worn on the left arm of adult women were missing.

Fig. 6.42. Adult male buried in a coffin with personal ornaments and surrounded by burial pottery, Harappa, H88-196a.

People of the same kinship group would hardly rob or disturb the burials of their relatives or ancestors, but laborers of a different community might pilfer the disturbed tombs as they dug new ones. Unlike the grave robbers of ancient Egypt, who systematically robbed the gold-filled tombs of the wealthy, the meager grave goods in the Harappan burials did not leave the grave diggers much to steal.

Other than pottery vessels that would have been filled with food and drink, the Harappan burials contain very few grave offerings and few ornaments. Shell bangles worn on the left arm and anklets made of steatite disc beads were commonly buried with adult women (see fig. 6.7). A few beads of lapis lazuli, carnelian or copper have been found with both male and female burials, probably tied around the wrist or on a cord around the waist. Copper rings are found in many burial pits, and in one instance a ring was found in place on the left, "ring" finger of what was probably a female burial.[32] In South Asia today, ornaments and objects that pertain to marriage, initiations, or protection against magic or illness are seldom passed on to another person, but are broken, burned or buried with the dead. Based on modern analogies we can assume that the ornaments included with Harappan burials were symbolic objects that could not be passed on to the next generation.

A particular ornament found almost exclusively with adult females is a truncated cylindrical amulet that was worn at the throat. Usually these amulets were made of black stone (fig. 6.43), but other examples have been found in green serpentine (see cat. no. 88), steatite or faience. The association with adult women suggests that this ornament identified married women or adult women who belonged to a specific cult. A flattened conical ornament with a groove running along the perimeter (see cat. no. 89) may have been a variant of this type of amulet, and one example from Mohenjo-daro was set in a copper frame or pendant.[33]

While one or two stone beads cannot be considered elaborate grave offerings, several adult female burials at Harappa were accompanied by a copper/bronze mirror. Because metal mirrors can be recycled and have intrinsic market value, their inclusion with pottery and personal amulets must have some specific ritual significance. The elaborate headdresses and hair ornaments depicted on the terracotta figurines probably needed repeated inspections, and mirrors would have been an essential toiletry item during a woman's life. If the household pottery with food offerings indicates a belief in an afterlife, then it is not surprising to find mirrors which also would have been necessary for everyday grooming in the next life. However, it is also possible that mirrors were used in magical rituals and were buried for superstitious reasons. Whatever the explanation, these copper/bronze mirrors were not passed on to the next generation and were not recycled.

Male burials have modest funerary offerings, but two adult men at Harappa were buried with valuable personal ornaments. One older man was wrapped in a shroud and entombed in a coffin surrounded by pottery offerings (fig. 6.42). He was wearing a long necklace of 340 graduated steatite beads and three separate pendant beads made of natural stone and three gold beads (fig. 6.44). A single copper bead was found at his waist. The fact that the stone beads were polished and rounded from long use suggests that they may have been worn for a very long time, possibly as amulets. The most prominent pendant bead is made of a

Fig. 6.43. Truncated cylindrical stone amulets from Harappa, 0.65 cm to 2.5 cm height.

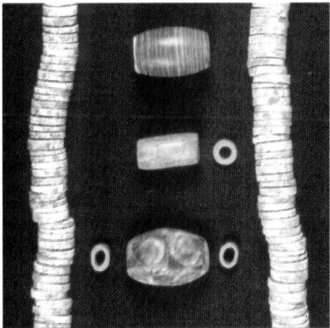

Fig. 6.44. Steatite disc bead necklace and three stone beads from adult male burial, Harappa, cat. nos. 65-68.

rare variety of onyx with natural eye designs in alternating shades of red, white, tan and green. Gold beads framed this important ornament. The other two stone beads were made of banded jasper and turquoise, with a single gold bead at one end of the turquoise bead. Even though these ornaments may have had some commercial value, they were buried with the owner and not passed on to another individual.

The other important adult male was also entombed in a coffin with more than a dozen vessels arranged at the head of the pit and additional vessels along the side. A broken shell bangle was found on his left wrist and near the right hand was a single carnelian bead. An unusual hair ornament was found along the right side at the back of his head, where we would expect to find long hair tied into a double bun like those on the stone sculptures and seals. This ornament was made out of numerous strands of tiny steatite microbeads twisted together in circlets or bunches, with two or three shell rings and a jasper bead (fig. 6.45). The value of such an ornament can only be appreciated when the techniques of manufacture are considered. Each of the thousands of tiny steatite beads is approximately one millimeter in diameter and one millimeter in length. Some scholars suggest that the beads were made individually by delicate drilling and grinding, while others propose that they were made from a steatite paste that was extruded like a hollow noodle and then cut into short segments.[34] Even today, it is difficult to make glass beads of this size, and no one has been able to replicate convincingly the techniques used by the ancient Harappans.

Although this microbead hair ornament may have been worn as a crown or ritual headdress during life, it evidently could not be passed on to a surviving relative or clan leader. In contrast to the terracotta figurines and seals, which depict heavily ornamented men and women, the Harappan burials reflect a very practical attitude towards material wealth and symbols. Precious metals, gold and valuable stone beads were generally kept in circulation among the living, while only the most essential personal objects were buried with the dead: shell bangles, beads with eye designs, steatite disc beads and mirrors. As a whole, the Harappan burial customs further reinforce the importance of ornaments and public symbols to define social and ritual status among the living.

■

Fig. 6.45. Hair ornament made from tiny steatite microbeads, a tan jasper bead and two or three shell rings, Harappa, cat. no. 04.

Endnotes

1. Asko Parpola, *Deciphering the Indus Script* (Cambridge: Cambridge University Press, 1994), 240 ff.

2. Dr. Hans Hock, University of Illinois, Champagne-Urbana, personal communication, 1995.

3. J. Mark Kenoyer, "Ideology and Legitimation in the Indus State as Revealed through Public and Private Symbols," *Pakistan Archaeologists Forum* 4.1-2 (1995): 81-131.

4. J. Mark Kenoyer, "Shell Working Industries of the Indus Civilization: An Archaeological and Ethnographic Perspective," Ph.D. diss., University of California at Berkeley, 1983.

5. Gregory L. Possehl and M. H. Raval, *Harappan Civilization and Rojdi* (New Delhi: Oxford and IBH and AIIS, 1989), 162, fig. 77.

6. Parpola, *Deciphering the Indus Script*, 56-57.

7. Parpola, *Deciphering the Indus Script*, 218-24.

8. Frank Raymond Allchin, "The Interpretation of a Seal from Chanhu-daro and Its Significance for the Religion of the Indus Civilization," in *South Asian Archaeology, 1983*, ed. Janine Schotsmans and Maurizio Taddei (Naples: Istituto Universitario Orientale, 1985), 369-84.

9. Yan Y. Dhyansky, "The Indus Valley Origin of a Yoga Practice," *Artibus Asiae* 48.1/2 (1988): 89-108.

10. Ernest J. H. Mackay, *Further Excavations at Mohenjodaro* (New Delhi: Government of India, 1938), Pl. LXXVI, 8.

11. Mackay, *Further Excavations at Mohenjodaro*, Pl. CXI, 356.

12. Sir John Marshall, *Mohenjo-daro and the Indus Civilization* (London: Probsthain, 1931), Pl. CXVII, 16; Mackay, *Further Excavations at Mohenjodaro*, Pl. XCIII, 14.

13. Mackay, *Further Excavations at Mohenjodaro*, Pl. XCIV, 420.

14. Mackay, *Further Excavations at Mohenjodaro*, 1938), Pl. LXXXVII, 235.

15. Steven Fuchs, *The Gonds and Bhumia of Eastern Mandla* (New York: Asia, 1960).

16. Marshall, *Mohenjo-daro and the Indus Civilization*, Pl. CXI, 357.

17. Charles Swynnerton, *Folk Tales from the Upper Indus* (reprint, Islamabad: Institute of Folk Heritage, 1978), 4-6.

18. Parpola, *Deciphering the Indus Script*, 247.

19. J. Mark Kenoyer and Richard H. Meadow, "New Inscribed Objects From Harappa," *Lahore Museum Bulletin*, in press.

20. Madho Sarup Vats, *Excavations at Harappa* (Delhi: Government of India Press, 1940), 59, Pl XCII, 308, Trench IV, Mound F; Jagat Pati Joshi and Asko Parpola, *Corpus of Indus Seals and Inscriptions. 1. Collections in India* (Helsinki: Suomalainen Tiedeakatemia, 1987), H-181, 209.

21. Catherine Jarrige, "Une tête d'éléphant en terre cuite de Naushuro (Pakistan)," *Arts Asiatiques* 47 (1992): 132-35.

22. Joshi and Parpola, *Corpus of Indus Seals and Inscriptions. 1. India*, K-65.

23. Joshi and Parpola, *Corpus of Indus Seals and Inscriptions. 1. India*, K-50.

24. Jean-François Jarrige, "Excavation at Mehrgarh-Naushuro 1987-88," *Pakistan Archaeology* 24 (1989): 21-67, Pl. XIV, B.

25. Alexandra Ardeleanu-Jansen, "The Theriomorphic Stone Sculpture from Mohenjo-Daro Reconsidered," in *Interim Reports, vol. 2: Reports on Field Work Carried out at Mohenjo-Daro, Pakistan 1983-84 by IsMEO-Aachen University Mission*, ed. Michael Jansen and Günter Urban (Aachen: IsMEO/RWTH, 1987), 59-68.

26. Jean-François Jarrige, "Excavations at Naushuro." *Pakistan Archaeology* 23 (1988): 149-203.

27. Thomas R. Gensheimer, "The Role of Shell in Mesopotamia: Evidence for Trade Exchange with Oman and the Indus Valley," *Paléorient* 10.1 (1984): 65-73.

28. Kenoyer, "Shell Working Industries of the Indus Civilization."

29. Nancy C. Lovell and Kenneth A. R. Kennedy, "Society and Disease in Prehistoric South Asia," in *Old Problems and New Perspectives in the Archaeology of South Asia*, ed. J. Mark Kenoyer (Madison, Wis.: UW-Madison Department of Anthropology, 1989), 89-92; Kenneth A. R. Kennedy, "Biological Anthropology of Human Skeletons from Harappa: 1928-1988," *Eastern Anthropologist* 45.1-2 (1992): 55-86; Kenneth A. R. Kennedy, "Trauma and Disease in the Ancient Harappans," in *Frontiers of the Indus Civilization*, ed. B. B. Lal and S. P. Gupta (New Delhi: Books and Books, 1984), 417-24.

30. K. A. Chowdhury and S. S. Ghosh, "Plant Remains from Harappa 1946," *Ancient India* 7 (1947): 3-19.

31. George F. Dales and J. Mark Kenoyer, "Excavation at Harappa—1988," *Pakistan Archaeology* 24 (1989): 68-176.

32. Dales and Kenoyer, "Excavation at Harappa—1988."

33. Stefano Pracchia and Massimo Vidale, "The Archaeological Context for Stoneware Firing at Mohenjo-Daro," *East and West* 43.1-4 (1993): 23-68, fig. 34, 2.

34. K. T. M. Hegde, R. V. Karanth and S. P. Sychanthavong, "On the Composition and Technology of Harappan Microbeads," in *Harappan Civilization*, ed. Gregory L. Possehl (New Delhi: Oxford and IBH, 1982), 239-44.

Fig. 7.1. Terracotta figurines from Harappa reveal the diversity of ornaments and hairstyles popular in the ancient city, thus suggesting diverse ethnic groups and social classes.

People and Profession

Chapter 7

Living in the City

In the busy marketplace of modern Harappa City, people from the surrounding countryside mix with the city dwellers, while merchants and traders hawk their wares. Leading a buffalo to market, a sunburned farm girl wearing heavy ornaments brushes past an elegantly dressed city lady wearing delicate glass bangles. A camel herder haggles with a merchant over the price of brass bells. In the background a carpet maker calls out the designs to nimble fingered apprentices as they tie woolen knots. Dusty children playing in the streets fill the air with laughter, and a mother cradles her suckling infant in the shadow of a doorway. As a meeting place for people of many different occupations and ethnic groups, modern Harappa City is probably not much different from the ancient towns and villages of the Indus civilization (fig. 7.1). However one important difference is that many large villages, towns and large cities exist within 20 kilometers of modern Harappa (fig. 7.2), while at 2600 B.C. the population density was much less. Some small Indus period sites have been discovered in the countryside near the ancient mounds of Harappa, but the nearest large cities would have been at Ganweriwala (280 km) and Rakhigarhi (350 km) (fig. 7.3).

In contrast to the sparsely populated countryside, the ancient Indus cities must have been very colorful and lively places. The rush of traffic streaming in through the city gates (fig. 7.4) each morning would have brought together merchants and nomads from distant regions with local fisherfolk, hunters and farmers. In addition to the rulers and traders, the city would have hosted administrators, shopkeepers and workshop owners, different classes of artisans and other professionals. Although the Indus writing has not been deciphered, we can determine much about the people living in the cities from their artifacts. Most of the communities represented in the archaeological record can be directly correlated to the types of communities found in the Early Historic cities (third century B.C.) and enumerated in the later texts.[1]

Administrative and service classes of the Indus cities would have included state officials and their attendants under the control of the ruling elites (see Chap. 5). Small rooms near the gateways at Harappa and Dholavira housed gatekeepers and probably tax-collectors as well. Sweepers and garbage collectors worked along the streets and neighborhoods of the city, filling baskets with refuse to throw over the city walls, or loading cartloads of waste to be dumped at the edge of the roads leading from the city.

Fig. 7.2. Trinket vendors, food stalls and carnival stands line the road to Harappa during the annual Sang pilgrimage. Thousands of villagers from nearby settlements throng to the city for the one-day festival. Women who desire children, especially sons, bring offerings for the pilgrims who will convey their prayers to the tomb of the saint Sakhi Sarvar in Baluchistan.

Fig. 7.3. A young girl carrying water from a nearby well passes a farmer bringing milk into the modern city of Rakhigarhi, India, which is built on top of an ancient city contemporaneous with Harappa. In the background a man balances on his head a cloth filled with chopped fodder for his cattle.

Fig. 7.4. Modern reconstruction of the floor plan of the ancient southern gateway to Mound E, Harappa. Only one oxcart at a time could have passed through this gateway, but inside the city the main streets allowed two-way traffic.

Some farmers may have lived within the city, walking to the fields each morning and herding livestock to nearby grazing grounds. From the numerous terracotta net weights and arrow points found in both Mohenjo-daro and Harappa, we can deduce that fisherfolk and hunters also lived inside the city.

Texts from the later Early Historical cities period identify a host of independent professionals who lived or worked in the cities, including merchants and shopkeepers, physicians, barbers, washerfolk and astrologers. Stockpiles of jewelry (fig. 7.5) and bronze weapons, as well as actual workshops and public structures indicate the presence of merchants and shopkeepers at most Indus towns and cities; bathing platforms near a large well at Harappa may have been a public washing area, possibly for washerfolk. Bronze razors, pins and pincers must have been the tools of a barber or a physician, two frequently overlapping professions. Ritual specialists must have worked with healing herbs and incantations, but such materials are not preserved in the archaeological record.

Much of the textile work may have been carried out in the villages surrounding the city, as is common throughout the subcontinent today, but some domestic and high-quality commercial weaving may have taken place in the city itself (fig. 7.6). Although we do not know the color of Indus fabrics, we can determine the high quality of weaving and the use of wool and cotton from fabric impressions in faience or clay and from cloth fragments preserved on silver or copper objects. It is not unlikely that the technique for block printing on fabric was practiced, but excavations have produced no concrete evidence.

Carpetmaking was probably developed by nomadic communities long before the rise of the Indus cities, but it may have been practiced in the ancient urban centers. All major Indus settlements have examples of small, curved copper blades that have been called razors, but actually may have been specialized tools for cutting the tied threads on pile carpets (fig. 7.7).

Fig. 7.5. (Left) A hoard or stockpile of jewelry at Mohenjo-daro contained this valuable necklace made up of gold beads combined with beads of agate, jasper, steatite and green stone (lizardite or grossular garnet), cat. no. 55.

Fig. 7.6. (Below) In the VS area of Mohenjo-daro, a room with specially prepared brick basins, a water-tight floor and corner drain may have been a workshop for starching or dying cloth. A brick dust bin for garbage and a square sump pit connected to a drain are visible across the street.

Fig. 7.7. (Right) Barbers and/or carpet makers may have used this type of curved copper knife from Harappa. Finely woven cloth has been wrapped around one end, possibly to make a handle.

Basketmaking and mat-weaving, which may have been domestic crafts, are well represented through impressions on hard-packed clay floors and fired clay lumps. Coiled baskets and woven mats were made from reeds and grasses, possibly using polished bone awls and spatulas. In addition to woven materials, various types of twisted cord were made from hemp or other vegetable fibers, for tying bundles of goods and supporting greenware pottery as it dried.

Well diggers, architects and brick masons were needed to keep the water sources cleared and maintain the massive city walls, gateways, drains and domestic buildings. Large wooden houses and columned verandahs were built on top of baked brick foundations by specialized carpenters (see Chap. 3, fig. 3.9). Huge doors would have been needed for the city gates, and smaller carved doors and lattice-work windows were made for brick houses (see fig. 3.13). On the basis of terracotta replicas and depictions on seals, we know that furniture produced in the cities included thrones with legs carved to imitate cattle hooves, beds with woven cording and other types of furniture inlaid with shell and stone. Furniture makers may also have made musical instruments such as drums. A different group of carpenters probably specialized in making wooden boats and oxcarts that were needed to carry out trade between the cities.

Much debris from kilns and ceramic manufacturing attests to the presence of potters, faience workers and stoneware banglemakers living in residential neighborhoods or at the edge of the city. Copper and bronze workers also had their workshops inside the city, even though the smoke and fumes from metalworking must have been quite unbearable in the hot summers. Evidence for gold and silver working has been found in various parts of Harappa and on Mound ET it is associated with numerous such other crafts as steatite and agate beadmaking, shellworking and ivory carving.[2]

Stone carvers produced both large and small objects of utilitarian and symbolic function. Grinding-stones, pestles and loom weights were made for everyday use; massive ringstones and conical objects were produced for public buildings or ritual functions. Exclusive sculptural schools may have flourished in the big cities such as Mohenjo-daro where seated animal (see cat. no. 121) and human sculptures were carved in sandstone and steatite (see cat. nos. 117-120). After the "priest-king" the most famous stone sculpture of the Indus civilization is the small male torso from Harappa (fig. 7.8).[3] This figurine is a masterpiece carved from a fine-grained red sandstone, a material that was never used by later sculptors. Holes drilled in the torso attached separately carved arms and head, while the nipples and some form of shoulder ornament would have been inlaid. The technique of manufacture and general modeling conform to Harappan styles that are well represented on another male sculpture from Harappa itself (see fig. 7.9), and numerous faience animal figurines from both Harappa and Mohenjo-daro (see cat. nos. 172-175).

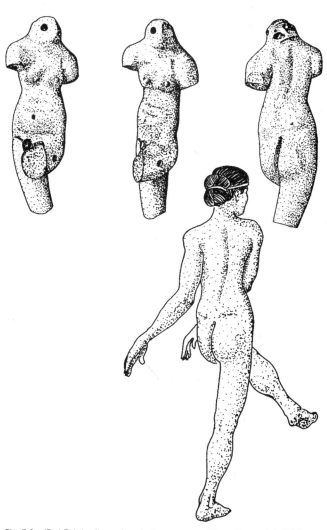

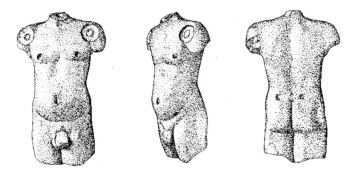

Fig. 7.8. Male torso, red sandstone, Harappa, height 8.5 cm.

Fig. 7.9a. (Top) Twisting figure of a male dancer, gray sandstone, Harappa, height 8.5 cm.

Fig. 7.9b. (Above) Conjectural sketch of dancer from Harappa, after Marshall 1931, fig. 1.

In addition to crafts that are directly reflected in the archaeological record, other specialists living in the cities would have included perfumers, liquor and oil manufacturers, leather workers, garland makers and many other smaller scale crafts. Tiny faience bottles may have been used to hold precious perfumes and scented oils, while perforated pottery (see cat. no. 192) may indicate the preparation of brewed beverages. Each specialized craft would have been practiced by a separate group of artisans, and although related craft communities may have overlapped, recent excavations at Harappa indicate that many specialists lived or worked together in distinct neighborhoods in particular parts of the city (see Chap. 8).

A major factor in the well being of any city is the presence of amusement classes: singers, dancers, actors, musicians and prostitutes, people who provide distraction from the humdrum existence of cleaning drains, chipping agate beads or building houses. While we can not identify singers, the line of seven figures on a seal from Mohenjo-daro (see cat. no. 24) may represent a line dance or ritual procession; we think some figurines represent dancers, such as a fragmentary stone sculpture from Harappa of a male torso twisted in a classical dance pose, with one leg raised across the body and the arms outstretched (fig. 7.9a and b).[4] Carved from gray stone, the torso has tiny dowel holes to attach the head and arms, which may have been movable.

Actors and musicians were probably quite common in the big cities, but their costumes and musical instruments have not been preserved for posterity. A terracotta mask from Mohenjo-daro (see fig. 5.5) was probably used in ritual dramas, while various terracotta puppets (see fig. 6.27 and cat. no. 132) may have been used by street performers to entertain the public during special ritual holidays or festivals. We have recovered no evidence for stringed instruments, and our only representation of a musician is on a tablet from Harappa, where a drummer is shown playing before a tiger deity.[5] The drum is a long cylinder with membranes at either end, much like the *dholak* or *pakawaj* style drum still played in the Punjab today. Other instruments

that may have been used for ritual as well as everyday enjoyment include the conch-shell trumpet, terracotta whistles and painted rattles (fig. 7.10, see cat. nos. 104-108). While relatively simple, these instruments effectively establish rhythm and tonal background sound.

Performances with humans may have been important for ritual and aesthetic reasons, but as is common throughout the Indus Valley today, animal races and bear-baiting become the focus of attention after the harvest is done. Terracotta toys found at most Indus settlements provide a glimpse of the pastimes that might have involved trained animals. Terracotta oxcarts with movable parts (see cat. nos. 45, 46) pulled by movable-headed oxen (see cat. no. 162) are perhaps the most common. Throughout the Indus Valley people still race oxcarts, especially in the regions around Mohenjo-daro, where on-track betting ends with large sums of money or land changing hands.

Dog figurines (fig. 7.11) and bear figurines with collars suggest that animal fights may have been another common form of entertainment. Itinerant performers who engage in dog and bear fights today often use trained animals that do not actually kill each other but simply put on a good show. The fighting dogs were also probably used in tracking and hunting down elusive game along the river's flood plain. Our information about dogs used by the Indus people comes from bones and from the figurines, which depict short-haired, small-bodied dogs that may have been bred from wild red dogs and wolves that used to inhabit parts of the Indus Valley. Some dogs were also trained to show off, such as the

Fig. 7.10. Painted terracotta rattles from Nausharo.

Fig. 7.11. Fighting dog with a projecting collar, Mohenjo-daro, cat. no. 163.

terracotta figurine of a begging dog from Harappa that is wearing a beaded collar (fig. 7.12). Given the range of activities from hunting and fighting to performing, perhaps several types of dogs were bred in the urban centers.

Pet monkeys were also probably a common sight in the bazaars or neighborhood markets. Figurines of monkeys were made of terracotta or glazed faience (fig. 7.13), depicting one or more monkeys in various amorous or acrobatic poses (see cat. no. 175). All the monkey figurines are of the short-tailed rhesus or macaque species, but the long-tailed langurs would have been known to the Indus people living in Gujarat and the northern Punjab, because this species is quite common throughout these regions today. The fact that they did not make any figures of the long-tailed monkeys is quite intriguing, and it is also odd that no monkeys are illustrated on the seals or narrative tablets. The Harappan bias against depicting monkeys in glyptic art is one of the important differences with later Hindu art, where monkeys are a common motif and the long-tailed langur is directly associated with the deity Hanuman.

The one performance tradition that is popular in modern South Asia but is not represented on any of the Indus seals or tablets is snake-charming. Only a few individual snakes are depicted on terracotta molded tablets, and the snake motif is included with some of the multiple animal figures, but none of these representations shows a snake-charmer interacting with the snake.

Except for a few examples, such as snake-charmers, most of the occupational specialists and professional classes that were present in the Early Historic cities have parallels in the first cities of the Indus region. However, we have no indication that during the Harappan Phase occupational specialists were organized into rigid social categories called *jati* or caste, a feature that became common only much later. The social hierarchy and stratification of different classes in the Indus cities may have been somewhat flexible, especially for individuals who wanted to change professions, exploit new resources or develop new technologies.

Images of the people who lived in ancient Mohenjo-daro and Harappa can be seen in the ritual figurines and toys made from clay and bronze. Actual ornaments and utensils found in the excavations show the range of materials and styles that were used to differentiate the social classes. Burials from sites such as Harappa allow a detailed look at the physical characteristics and health of the city dwellers. Together, these different kinds of information provide a glimpse of the life of Indus people from childhood through adulthood, to old age and death.

Fig. 7.12. Begging dog with beaded collar, Harappa, cat. no. 164.

Fig. 7.13. Faience monkey figurine or amulet, Mohenjo-daro, cat. no. 174.

Childbirth and Childhood

Numerous fertility symbols and ritual objects attest to the desire for children, but our most direct evidence is from tiny terracotta figurines of infants or young children. These figurines, common at most Indus sites, may have been votive offerings to pray for children or to protect them from illness. Childbirth in the Indus cities must have been joyful, but also filled with apprehension and fear for the safety and health of the child and for the mother. A sad reminder that many children and mothers must have died in childbirth is found in the burial of a mother and infant at Harappa.[6]

Most figurines of infants and children are male, possibly demonstrating a cultural bias towards the desire for male children and for their protection, a pattern that continues in many parts of the world even today. Individual votive figurines of infants may have been placed on household shrines. Many female votive figurines carry a suckling infant on the left hip, a characteristic pose among village women throughout Pakistan and India today (fig. 7.14). When held with the right arm free, a woman can continue her household work

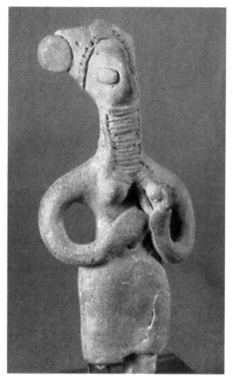

Fig. 7.14. Female figurine holding an infant to her left breast, Mohenjo-daro, cat. no. 134.

while nursing her child. No female figurines have been found showing an infant carried in a sling at the back or side, a position that is common among some communities in the subcontinent.

Other figurines depict children playing with toys that are similar to objects found in the excavations of the cities. A tiny clay figurine of a child holding a small disc (fig. 7.15) may provide a clue to the many pottery discs found in the Indus cities. We found groups of three to seven discs in the recent excavations at Harappa (fig 7.16) that we think were used in a game similar to one that is still played by children in villages and towns throughout northern India and Pakistan. In the modern version of this game, called *pittu*, one player throws a ball to knock down a stack of pottery discs (fig. 7.17). The defender of the stack must quickly pile them in the graduated sequence as the rest of the children scatter in a raucous game of tag. Rules vary from region to region, but the popular game appears to have kept children amused for at least 4500 years.

Other toys used to amuse the many children living in the cities include hollow animal figurines with wheels, such as the moveable toy ram figurine from Chanhudaro (see cat.

Fig. 7.15. (Above left) Child figurine wearing a turban and a necklace, Mohenjo-daro, cat. no. 150; child figurine with turban, holding a disc-shaped object, Mohenjo-daro, cat. no. 151.

Fig. 7.16. (Left) Chipped pottery discs made in graduated sizes have been found in recent excavations at Harappa.

Fig. 7.17. (Above) Young boys at Harappa, playing *pittu* with pottery discs.

no. 161). Terracotta tops (fig. 7.18) and clay marbles are found on the floors of courtyards and kitchen areas, where children could play under the watchful eye of the mother. Some tops are made of shell (see cat. no. 109) or have a copper tip to cause a much longer spin than the terracotta tip, whereas others have a shallow depression. Tops with depressions on the tip may have been spun on top of a thin rod as jugglers and magicians commonly do today.

Some toys may have been simply for amusement, others to teach and socialize children to their role as adults. Miniature cooking vessels made in the same design as larger cooking vessels (see cat. no. 195) would teach a child its important symbolism and prepare girls for running households. Other miniature household objects, such as toy beds (see cat. no. 152), provide a glimpse of the everyday items that were important for children.

Musical instruments were also made for children. Terracotta rattles (see fig. 7.10) and whistles shaped like a small partridge or dove (7.19) have been found at most sites in the core regions of the Indus civilization. In traditional communities in Pakistan today, rattles are often used by

jugglers to make noise while performing, and bird whistles are often used to coax pet birds to call.

Itinerant performers probably entertained children and also helped in the socialization of children as they still do in traditional towns and villages today. Traveling from city to the countryside, these performers would have served as communication channels to the villages and distant resource areas. Masks and puppets made of clay or wood would have been used to teach children the religious myths and the powers of the gods and goddesses. Once children had learned these important stories, they would be ready to move into adult life as householders, farmers or other occupations.

Womanhood

The position of women in the cities of the Indus Valley may have been different from the role women play in modern cities of the subcontinent. Terracotta figurines of women predominate in most sites (fig. 7.20), and powerful female deities are depicted on the seals along with male deities (see cat. no. 27). These indirect indicators suggest that some women of the cities may have had important social and ritual positions and that female deities played an important role in the legitimation of beliefs and political power.

At Harappa, scholars have used genetic trait analysis to try to understand the relationships between the people buried in the same general cemetery. Initial studies suggested that many of the women may have been related to each other by descent, while the men were not strongly related.[7] In other words, a woman was buried near her mother and grandmother, and a man was buried near his wife's ancestors rather than with his own. Further samples and more reliable statistical results are needed to confirm this initial hypothesis; however, if this pattern of matri-local burial can

Fig. 7.18. The technique for spinning the ancient terracotta tops from Harappa.

Fig. 7.19. Hollow egg-shaped and bird figurine whistles from Nausharo.

Fig. 7.20. Female figurines with different headdress styles, Harappa, from right to left, cat. nos. 136, 138, 139, 137 and another figure on the far left.

be confirmed by further studies, it would indicate the powerful position of certain women in the social order of Harappan society.

Even without such studies, however, the importance of females as symbols of religious power is supported by the fact that figurines of women or mother goddesses are more common than male figurines. The wide variety of headdresses and ornament styles depicted on the figurines may reflect the ethnic diversity of the city as well as the continuously changing styles. Many of the ornaments depicted on the figurines, both male and female, can be correlated to actual ornaments, belts, fillets, necklaces, bangles and other categories.

Hairdressing was an essential part of urban life, and many of the elaborate and oftentimes massive hair styles that we see on the figurines would have required the hands of a skilled hairdresser. We see some of these hair styles from all major Indus cities; others are peculiar to specific sites and probably reflect different ethnic communities. The rolled hair lifted high above the head and the fan-shaped headdress are styles common to both Harappa and Mohenjo-daro (fig. 7.20), but Harappa had a distinctive variation with four flowers arranged on the front of the headdress (see fig. 1.7, cat. no. 133). At the side of the headdress are cup-shaped ornaments or lamps with a braided edging. These figurines are heavily adorned with multiple chokers, necklaces and belts. Such figurines with the cup-shaped projections at the side of the head used as oil lamps may represent the mother goddess. The fan-shaped headdress on the figurines originally was painted black and probably represents hair draped over a frame. The stylized flowers arranged over the forehead may represent actual flowers or flower-shaped ornaments similar to those of shell, ivory, faience and semi-precious stones. The necklaces probably represent beaded ornaments of gold, bronze, carnelian and agate. The wide belt, probably made of long carnelian beads and bronze medallions, was worn over a short skirt of finely woven cotton or woolen cloth (see Chap. 8, cat. nos. 47, 48). Such figurines were probably originally painted with red, yellow, white and black pigments as we see at Nausharo (see cat. no. 2).

In the recent excavations on Mound ET at Harappa, we found a broken figurine of a woman with the large fan-shaped headdress lying on a bed with the end of the headdress draped over the end to avoid messing it up. The care needed to maintain such hairdressing would have been beyond the means of many women, but we also see less complex, more practical styles. One female figurine has braided or curled locks of hair hanging down the side and back (see cat. no. 137). She wears a choker with pendant beads and two projecting ear ornaments, similar to those found on other figurines. A single knobbed ornament hanging at the middle of the forehead may represent a type of conical gold ornament found in the jewelry hoards discussed later in this chapter.

Another style features hair rolled into a bun on the side of the head (see cat. no. 138), but some women did not show their hair, covering their heads with a turban decorated with minute punch marks, possibly representing beads (see cat. no. 139). Some turbaned figurines are quite fat and heavily ornamented with bangles on both wrists and upper arms, ankle bracelets and a choker (fig. 7.21). The right hand is held to the mouth and the left hand clutches the heart, an expression of amazement still typical in the subcontinent today. These turbaned figurines are common at many larger sites; the fat figurines may represent portly matrons or pregnant women.

Many figurines show women standing in a formal pose, but less highly modeled figures show women at work, preparing food and grinding grain (fig. 7.22), which continue to be a time-consuming aspect of a woman's daily routine in South Asia even today. The precise use of these figurines is uncertain, but if they were made by different communities for household rituals or children's toys, it is possible that they reflect the styles of ornaments and headdresses popular with different ethnic communities living in the cities. Bangles and necklaces are the most common types of ornaments, but the specific style and quantity of necklaces worn by a single figurine is variable.

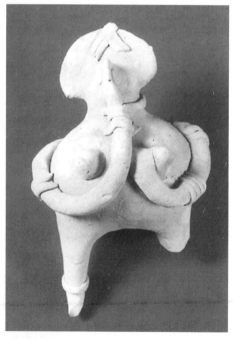

Fig. 7.21. Fat woman figurine with turbanlike headdress, Nausharo, cat. no. 142.

Figurines with elaborate headdresses and numerous layers of necklaces are usually somewhat larger than the more simple terracotta figurines. A figurine with three sets of chokers and necklaces—one of the largest found at Harappa (fig. 7.23)—has the common fan-shaped headdress with cups on both sides of the head. Although much of the headdress is missing, traces of black pigment or soot inside the cups suggest that they were filled with oil for use as a sacred lamp. It is also possible, however, that a sooty black pigment may have been

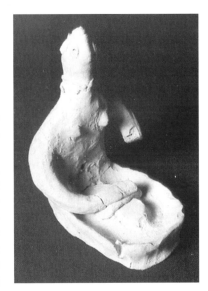

Fig. 7.22. Seated woman grinding grain, Nausharo, cat. no. 143.

used to depict black hair. The forward projecting face is made separately and attached to the body after all the ornaments had been applied. Large, heavily ornamented figurines also have been found at Mohenjo-daro (see cat. no. 135), and both sites have produced hoards of jewelry containing ornaments identical to those on these figurines.

Although most figurines were made of terracotta, excavators have recovered a few bronze sculptures that render women wearing ornaments and holding an object similar to a bowl in the left hand. In one example from Mohenjo-daro, the hair is tied in a horizontal bun hanging low on the back of the neck and traces of long-almond shaped eyes are visible (fig. 7.24). Many bangles adorn the upper left arm and a few bangles are indicated above the right elbow. Because these bronze figurines are not copies of terracotta figurines, they may have been made for a specific ethnic community or perhaps used in special rituals that required bronze votive statues. But, unlike terracotta figurines that break and are discarded, bronze can be melted and recycled for other objects. The few bronze sculptures recovered reflect a high level of skill in modeling and lost-wax casting, a well-established in the first cities that continues to the present throughout the subcontinent.

Fig. 7.23. Large terracotta figurine of a heavily adorned woman, Harappa, cat. no. 141.

Fig. 7.24. Bronze figurine of a woman wearing bangles and holding a small bowl in her right hand, Mohenjo-daro, cat. no. 144.

Manhood

Figurines of Indus men are not as varied as those of the women but do reflect several different styles of personal ornaments and hairstyles. Some terracotta figurines have turbans or headbands, but they are usually bare headed (fig. 7.25). In contrast, the carved stone sculptures (see cat. nos. 117, 118, 120) show elaborate styles of braids and finely combed hair that was often tied into a double bun or twisted bun at the back of the head. Some men may have worn additional ornaments in their hair, and one burial of an adult male at Harappa had a delicate hair ornament at the back of the head, where the bun of hair might have been (see fig. 6.45). Composed of tiny steatite beads, shell rings and a jasper bead, this ornament may have been braided with the hair and tied into a bun.

We also see the bun hair style on a miniature bronze sculpture of a male spear-thrower or dancer (fig. 7.26). Traces of eyes and nose are present. The hair is arranged in a bun on the back of the head, with a turban or long hair wrapped around the head. The twisting posture and upraised arm suggest a spear held in the right arm.

On some of the terracotta tablets (see cat. nos. 24, 25, 27) male figures have a long braid or matted hair hanging from the back of the head, similar to that seen on the stone sculpture of a seated figure from Mohenjo-daro (see cat. no. 119). However, this type of braid was also worn by women and is seen on female figures in narrative scenes on tablets and seals (see fig. 6.32).

Most male figurines have beards, but different styles were illustrated (fig. 7.27). A narrow beard like a goatee is seen on some figurines (see fig. 6.21); others have a closely combed and possibly waxed beard, as on a terracotta mask

Fig. 7.25. (Above) Seated male figurines, Harappa, cat. nos. 148-149.

Fig. 7.26. (Above right) Bronze figurine of a male spear-thrower or dancer, Chanhudaro, cat. no. 145. Joint Expedition of the American School of Indic and Iranian Studies and the Museum of Fine Arts, 1935-1936. © 1997 Museum of Fine Arts, Boston.

Fig. 7.27. (Right) Assorted male figurines from Harappa, showing different hair and beard styles.

(see cat. no. 122) and on the "priest-king" sculpture (see cat. no. 118). The most common form of beard is combed out and spread wide (see cat. no. 146), a style popular throughout the subcontinent until about a hundred years ago. Modeled with scented oils or beeswax these wide spreading beards are reminiscent of the projecting fur at the edge of a tiger's jowl. Many horned deities wear this kind of beard, which is clearly associated with a tiger on a terracotta mask from Harappa (see cat. no. 123).

The styles reflected in the figurines and sculptures indicate that some hair styles of men and women overlapped, but others were quite distinct. The occasional overlap of gender ornamentation is also true. Figurines of little boys and men wear necklaces with numerous pendant beads worn at the throat like a choker, a style also worn by most female figurines. Most male figurines, however, do not wear numerous graduated necklaces as do females, but exceptions include one terracotta male figurine wearing four graduated necklaces,[8] and an adult male was buried at Harappa with a long string of disc beads and three graduated strands, each with a stone bead or a combination of stone and gold beads (see fig. 6.44).

Both men and women wear bangles. Although bangles are rarely found on male terracotta figurines, they are shown on seated or standing male figures on seals and narrative tablets (see cat. nos. 23, 24). Other examples of men with bangles include a male buried at Harappa who had a broken shell bangle at his left wrist[9] and the "priest-king" sculpture which wears an armband on the left upper arm. The overlapping use of ornaments may be confusing in carvings, but in reality, bangles worn by men and women were probably made of different materials or specific styles.

Clothing worn by men is difficult to reconstruct from terracotta figurines, because unlike the female figurines shown wearing short skirts, most male figurines are nude. This probably does not indicate that men wore no clothes, since these figurines may have been used for fertility rituals, but it does suggest different standards for male and female modesty. In contrast to the terracotta figurines, stone sculptures show men wearing a variety of garments. Usually, a long cloak or shawl was draped over the edge of the left shoulder, covering the folded legs and lower body, but leaving the right shoulder and chest bare. On the stone sculptures a lower garment is worn around the waist and drawn through the legs to be tucked in the back like the traditional *dhoti*. These garments were probably made of finely woven cotton or wool, bleached white or colored with locally available dyes, such as those traditionally used in the subcontinent: indigo (blue), madder (red), turmeric (yellow) or onion skin (brown).

Male and female hairstyles, ornamentation and dress are generally distinct, though there are areas in which the gender is not well defined. Overlapping or androgynous styles may reflect a fluidity of styles or cross-dressing, a practice common in most societies. Today in Pakistan and India, men often take the role of women for specific social and ritual purposes. A figurine from Nausharo portrays a male figurine wearing a feminine type of headdress and holding an infant to his left side (see cat. no. 4) mimicking the style of the more common female figurines (see fig. 7.14). Some illustrations on seals or in figurines may reflect men dressed as women or vice versa. One terracotta male figurine from Harappa has a beard and small nipples (common on male figurines) but wears a long skirt decorated with cone-shaped ornaments.[10] Most Western scholars have associated the long skirt with females, and an example from Kalibangan shows two spear throwers (men?) fighting over a smaller skirted figure (woman?) (see fig. 6.32). However, in many Asian traditions, men wear long skirtlike garments, so we cannot define the long skirt as an exclusively feminine style. A procession of seven figures wearing long braids and long skirts is usually described as seven female figures, but unlike most depictions of females, no breasts are indicated (see cat. no. 24). In the context of the Indus cities, long braids, bangles, and skirts appear to have been worn by both men or women, and where no specific gender is depicted, such figures may represent androgynous figures.

Figurines and carvings reflect a vibrant urban society of children, women and men who wore different styles of ornaments and dress to distinguish themselves from each other and also to signal their affiliation with the Indus culture. The common use of bangles and beads can be seen as a sign of cultural and religious integration, though the specific styles and materials from which these ornaments were made distinguished people according to economic and socio-ritual status.

Stone beads were made from various valuable colored stones, some of which are still classified as semiprecious or precious gemstones. Beads were generally strung end to end, making a long necklace with special gems hung as pendants at the center of the necklace. This style of ornament is depicted on many terracotta and bronze female figurines and on some of the male figurines.

One jewelry hoard found in the HR area at Mohenjodaro contained necklaces and chokers that reveal the diversity of ornaments worn by some of the wealthiest Indus elite. Several necklaces that were reconstructed by the early excavators based on how the beads were found indicate a range of necklace styles. One style has pendant beads made from blue green faience, turquoise, bleached agate and gold (fig. 7.33). Another style uses a combination of paper-thin, flat gold disc beads, interspersed with beads of onyx, amazonite (microcline), turquoise and banded agate (fig. 7.34). Some beads have gold finials with additional small

spherical gold beads used as spacers. A gold-beaded choker necklace has six rows of beads with divider bars and half moon-shaped terminal (see fig. 7.31, cat. no. 57). Another multistrand necklace has five strands of tiny gold, faience and steatite beads (see fig. 7.31, cat. no. 58).

A separate hoard located in another part of the city contained different styles, reflecting the desire for unique designs and highlighting the creative abilities of the Indus artisans. One necklace has hollow biconical gold beads and barrel-shaped green stone (lizardite or grossular garnet) beads with large jasper and agate pendant beads (see fig. 7.5). The pendant agate and jasper beads are attached with thick gold wire.

A variety of gold ear ornaments has been found in some of the hoards, usually in pairs. One example is dome-shaped with a circular depression in the center for inlay (cat. no. 59). The ribbed edging is made of chiseled wire and soldered onto the body of the ornament. The hollow post is joined

Fig. 7.33. (Above) Necklace with pendant beads made from blue green faience, turquoise, bleached agate and gold, cat. no. 54.

Fig. 7.34. (Above Right) Necklace made up of paper-thin flat gold disc beads, interspersed with beads of onyx, amazonite (microcline), turquoise and banded agate, cat. no. 56.

Fig. 7.35. (Right) Faience ear studs or buttons, and grooved faience ornament, Harappa, cat. nos. 85, 86, 87.

with mastic and may have had a cotton plug to keep the stud from falling off of the ear. Faience ear ornaments were made with a wide knob on the back to hold them firmly in the ear lobe (fig. 7.35).

The most elaborate examples of inlay decorating gold ornaments was composed of tiny steatite, faience and gold beads; this was found at Harappa. Two identical spiral ornaments along with a kidney-shaped piece that may have been attached to a headband or a belt as brooches were found on Mound F.[14] Although much of the inlay has fallen out, the double-spiral brooch (fig. 7.36) has a design made with two lines of blue black glazed steatite and gold bead inlay. These pieces are set with mastic, in a frame made from a sheet of gold or electrum with three gold bands used as dividers. The use of inlaid components to form complex ornaments further demonstrates the creativity of the Indus artisans.

Other types of inlaid ornaments used single pieces, such as the ribbed faience disc from Harappa (see cat. no. 87),

that may have been set into a copper ornament or sewn onto clothing. Another form of inlay used flat, polished pieces of carnelian set in gold to accentuate the translucent qualities of the stone. Numerous inlaid shapes, such as droplets or circles, have been found at both Mohenjo-daro and Harappa, but we did not know how these were incorporated into ornaments until we discovered a complete pendant at Harappa in 1987 (fig. 7.37). The flat, drop-shaped carnelian inlay is held by a gold frame that has a deep channel on the exterior. Traces of black mastic present in the channel suggest that it once contained inlay, possibly tiny beads of steatite, faience, or even lapis lazuli. This ornament may have been worn on a necklace or possibly in the middle of the forehead, recalling the red vermilion that was used to decorate the part of the hair in earlier figurines (see Chap. 1, cat. no. 2). This carnelian pendant may represent the first use of an attachable red ornament on the forehead, a practice common among Hindu women who wear a colored gemstone or plastic dot (*tika*) on their forehead today.

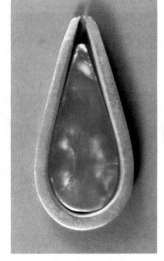

Fig. 7.36. Double spiral brooch with steatite and gold inlay, Harappa, cat. no. 59.

Fig. 7.37. Carnelian and gold pendant or hair ornament, Harappa, cat. no. 63.

The use of forehead ornaments is clearly represented in the many terracotta female figurines, but usually these were conical shaped and were probably made of gold or silver, like the large cone-shaped gold ornament found in one of the hoards from Harappa.[15] This conical ornament has a tiny loop on the inside that could be threaded with a strand of hair or attached to a headband. Fifty-four smaller gold caps were found in the same hoard (see fig. 7.38) that may have been sewn onto clothing or a belt. One famous terracotta figurine of a bearded male is shown wearing a skirt or wide belt covered with conical projections that may have been just this type of golden cap.[17]

Complete ornaments from the Indus culture are spectacular, but each individual bead used in these ornaments is itself a work of art and probably also had special ritual significance. Throughout Asia the red orange carnelian is a symbol of blood, power and fertility, while blue green turquoise and stones with natural eye designs are commonly used to ward off the evil powers, especially the evil-eye. Indus beadmakers developed special techniques to heat carnelian to deepen the red color, and they were skilled at bringing out the natural designs of banded agate. Beads with horizontal banding and vertical banding were skillfully prepared from natural agates, and occasionally imitations were made by laminating different colors of shell and stone. Because spotted or banded stones with designs resembling an eye were especially popular, artisans took great care to bring out unique patterns of eye designs (see fig. 7.39).

The most highly valued eye beads were red with white lines (fig. 7.40), a color combination also used for the circular designs on the cloak of the "priest-king" sculpture (see cat. no. 118). Variegated jasper with spherical structures and some varieties of onyx found in Gujarat and Baluchistan are the only natural stones that produce such eye patterns. Because these natural stones were extremely rare, the Indus artisans developed techniques to make imitation red-and-white eye beads. Permanent white designs were bleached onto carnelian beads by painting the design with a solution of calcium carbonate, then heating the beads in a kiln. However, the whitening process weakens the surface of the bead,

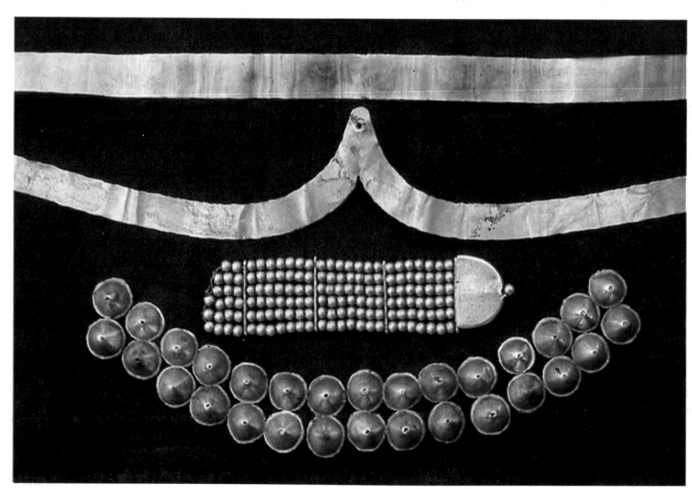

Fig. 7.38. Straight and curved gold fillets, cat. nos. 52, 53, beaded choker, cat no. 57, and thirty hollow cap-shaped gold ornaments with tiny hoops on the inside of the tip, cat no. 61.

and depending on the soil conditions, it can weather away after several thousand years. Early scholars often referred to such beads as etched carnelian, because the eroded design surface appeared to have been etched (fig. 7.41).

Artisans created many variations of these permanent white designs and painted them on various bead shapes. Some lenticular (shaped like a biconvex lens) beads had single eye designs on both faces (see cat. nos. 69, 70) while others had double eye designs (see cat. no. 71). Spherical beads often had three eye-motifs painted with concentric circles around the perimeter of the bead (see cat. no. 72). At Harappa an imitation eye bead was made from white and red brown faience (see cat. no. 73). This unique bead is the only example of red brown colored faience in the Indus Valley.

Whereas the bleached carnelian and faience beads were probably made for the wealthier classes, imitation eye beads were made of terracotta or fired soapstone with red-and-white paint, materials more affordable for the common classes. Some examples imitate the lenticular single eye beads (see cat. no. 74), and others imitate the rare orbicular jasper that has a red matrix and white circles (see cat. no. 75). Others were made with transverse spiraling bands to imitate natural banded agate (see cat. no. 76). The reproduction of identical shapes and styles using different raw materials helps to unify people within a single culture and belief system, even though not everyone enjoys the same wealth or status. Even today many people wear imitation gemstones as symbols of beauty or wealth, but only the affluent wear real gems.

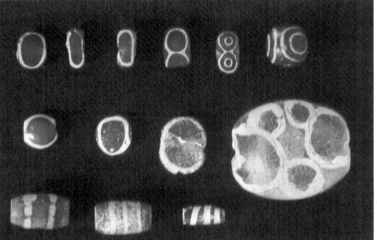

Fig. 7.39. (Left) Agate, jasper, green serpentine beads made in different shapes and designs, cat. no. 62.

Fig. 7.40. (Above) Red-and-white decorated beads made from carnelian, painted steatite and faience, Harappa, cat. nos. 69-76.

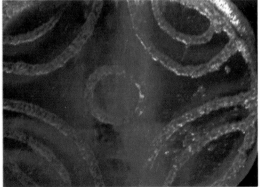

Fig. 7.41. After 4500 years, the original white bleached design on this carnelian bead from Balakot has weathered away, leaving the appearance of an etched design.

Bangle Styles

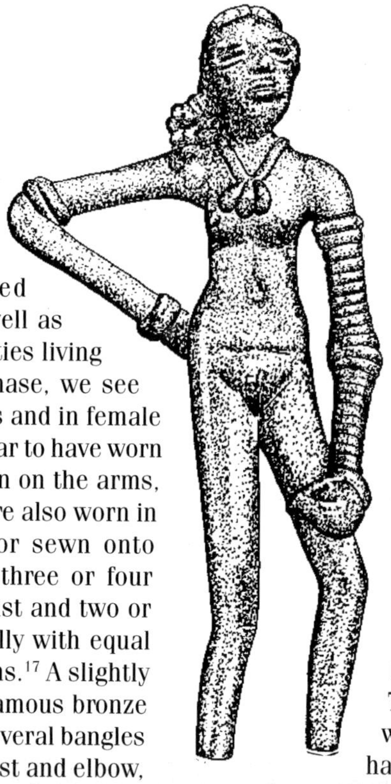

Bangle styles also demonstrate how the Indus artisans produced ornaments that served to unite as well as to differentiate the various communities living in the cities. From the Harappan Phase, we see bangles primarily on female figurines and in female burials, although some males do appear to have worn bangles. Bangles were generally worn on the arms, but circlets that look like bangles were also worn in the hair, on belts, on the ankles or sewn onto clothing. When worn on the arms, three or four bangles were often placed on the wrist and two or more bangles above the elbow, usually with equal numbers of bangles worn on both arms.[17] A slightly modified pattern is depicted on the famous bronze figurines from Mohenjo-daro, where several bangles were worn on the right arm at the wrist and elbow, but the left arm was filled with bangles from wrist to shoulder (see fig. 7.42).[18]

Although figurines and seals show how bangles were worn, they do not permit identification of the types of bangles or the combinations of design and color. The only bangles found in the cemetery excavations at Harappa are white shell bangles that were worn on the left arms of middle-aged adult women (ages 35-55). Sometimes they were worn on the lower arm or wrist, and in two cases bangles were worn both above and below the elbow. The bangles in the earliest burials, around 2600 B.C. (fig. 7.43) are slightly wider than those found in later burials, about 2400 B.C., and the thinnest bangles are found in the latest burials around 2000 B.C.

The decreasing width of shell bangles worn by women buried in the cemetery at Harappa may indicate that over several generations these women became less and less involved in heavy manual labor.[19] Thin-shell bangles are easily broken when chopping wood or loading oxcarts, whereas wide, heavy shell ornaments stand up to repeated battering. At Harappa and many other Indus sites, wide shell bangles have been found in various neighborhoods, but never in the burials (fig. 7.44). These wide shell bangles are also incised with the standard Indus chevron, but they may have been worn by women who were involved in heavy labor, as is common among nomads or farmers today. However, even though the width of the bangles changed, all were incised with the same style of chevron motif oriented in the same direction. There is only one example of a middle-aged adult male with a broken shell bangle that appears to have been worn on the left wrist.[20] None of the individuals buried at Harappa or any other reported site has been found wearing terracotta, faience, copper or stoneware bangles. Such ornaments may have been removed or broken at death, a practice that is common in later Hindu rituals.

Fig. 7.42. (Above center) Bronze statuette of a woman wearing bangles and holding a small bowl in her left hand, Mohenjo-daro, National Museum, New Delhi.

Fig. 7.43. (Above) Shell bangles from burial of an elderly woman from Harappa, cat. no. 90.

Fig. 7.44. (Right) Wide bangle made from a single conch shell and carved with a chevron motif, Harappa, cat. no. 91.

Shell bangles appear to have been used as a symbol that expressed an overarching unity as well as gender and possibly ethnic distinctions. The distinctive style of shell bangles with incised chevron design are found at most settlements of the Harappan Phase, but the limited quantity of such bangles indicates that they were not available to all members of the Indus society.

The extensive manufacture and use of other types of bangles in contexts outside of burials is also quite significant. Glazed faience bangles were made in a variety of styles and widths. Wide, white glazed faience bangles with a single chevron incised on the exterior imitated shell bangles. A more common style is the blue green glazed bangle decorated with multiple chevron and herring-bone designs repeated around the entire circlet. The finest design of faience bangle is a kidney or womb-shaped circlet, imitating the shape of some shell bangles with the exterior decorated by deeply carved cogs or ribbing (fig. 7.45).

Terracotta bangles are both the most common and the most varied. Thousands of bangle fragments have been recovered from the recent excavations at Harappa, and thousands more are scattered over the surface of the mounds. Many terracotta circles were setters for firing pottery, distinguished from bangles by crude shape. As with the shell and faience ornaments, terracotta bangles range from wide to narrow and plain to highly decorated (fig. 7.46). The surfaces were sometimes modified by pinching, incising or painting. Red or black pigment was commonly used to make diagonal lines or a single wide band on the exterior of the bangle (see cat. no. 95).

Most terracotta bangles were formed by hand, but those made on a potter's wheel are perfectly circular and have graduated diameters to fit different sizes of hands (see cat. no. 94). However, one style of bangle was always made the same size, between 5.5 and 6 cm interior diameter with a highly burnished surface fired to a red or a gray black color. Generally referred to as stoneware bangles because they were fired at very high temperatures, these standardized ornaments were almost always inscribed on the outside edge with minute signs of the Indus script (fig. 7.47). Relatively few stoneware bangles were made, probably to be worn as a badge of office or ritual ornament. Since they were made

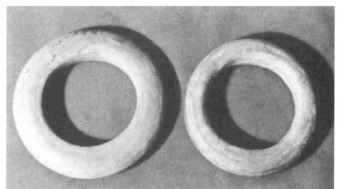

Fig. 7.45. (Above) Faience bangle made in the shape of a shell bangle or the stylized "womb" motif, Harappa, cat. no. 92.

Fig. 7.46. (Above right) Fine terracotta bangles, Harappa, cat. nos. 94, 95.

Fig. 7.47. (Right) Stoneware bangle with highly burnished surface, Mohenjo-daro, cat. no. 93 on right.

in standardized sizes that would not have fit a large hand, it is possible that they were attached to a necklace or worn in the hair instead.

While ceramic and shell bangles were invariably made as circlets in order to improve their strength, metal bangles usually had an open edge to slip over any size of wrist. Copper or bronze bangles were generally made as solid bars curved to fit the shape of the wrist (fig. 7.48), but some examples are hollow, making a lighter and yet equally impressive ornament. Gold bangles always had a hollow core to be easily twisted open and shut to fit over the wrist or ankle (fig. 7.49).

From terracotta to stoneware and gold, bangles made from various raw materials were worn by men, women and children in all of the far-flung settlements of the Indus region. Some styles were only found at the largest cities, and specific styles may have changed over time, but once the tradition of wearing bangles was established during the Neolithic period, about 6500 B.C., it remained an important form of symbolic ornamentation throughout the subcontinent.

Today, throughout India and Pakistan, children wear specific types of bangles as amulets for health and to enhance beauty. A young woman wears bangles during courtship, and at marriage these bangles are replaced by different types of bangles to symbolize her changed status. Throughout a woman's life, bangles are worn as ornaments and also to protect and preserve her family's well being. These bangles are removed or broken at the death of her husband, and all valuable ornaments are passed on to subsequent generations. Men often wear bangles for physical protection in battle, for amuletic purposes, for defining status and ethnic affiliation and simply as ornaments.

In the Indus cities, ornaments such as bangles and beads would have been accessible to all members of the society, thereby reinforcing important belief systems and the social order. Although these ornaments were made from different raw materials, many would be indistinguishable when viewed from a distance and would communicate similar symbolic messages. Close examination, however, could distinguish the precise nature of the ornament, its relative value and presumably the economic and socio-ritual status of the wearer. Ranking or stratification within the society as a whole would be reinforced by the relative value of the raw materials themselves. The manufacture of similar styles of bangles and beads from different raw materials is not unique to the Indus civilization, but only in the Indus cities do we find such a complex hierarchy of materials combined with unifying symbols.

During the period of the Indus cities (2600-1900 B.C.), the need for unique and appealing objects for ritual and political status resulted in the invention of many new technologies, such as the coloring of carnelian beads and stoneware bangle making, while old technologies were taken to new levels of complexity. Faience technology became more refined and ceramic production saw the introduction of new techniques and styles of production. Copper and bronze metallurgy became highly specialized for the production of tools, ornaments and utensils. The new products and imitations resulting from these developments were distributed far and wide throughout the Indus region, but the actual developments in technology were probably taking place in the largest cities, such as Harappa and Mohenjo-daro.

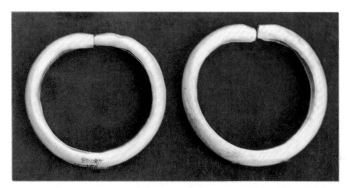

Fig. 7.48. Bronze bangles from Mohenjo-daro and Harappa, cat. nos. 96, 97.

Fig. 7.49. Hollow bangles of hammered sheet gold, Mohenjo-daro, cat. nos. 98, 99.

Endnotes

1. Kameshwar Prasad, "Urban Occupations and Crafts in the Kusana Period," in *Essays in Ancient Indian Economic History*, ed. Brajadulal Chattopadhyaya (New Delhi: Munshiram Manoharlal, 1987), 111-20.

2. Richard H. Meadow and J. Mark Kenoyer, "Excavations at Harappa 1993: The City Walls and Inscribed Materials," in *South Asian Archaeology. 1993*, èd. Asko Parpola and Petteri Koskikallio (Helsinki: Suomalainen Tiedeakatemia, 1994), 2:451-70.

3. Madho Sarup Vats, *Excavations at Harappa* (Delhi: Government of India Press, 1940), 74-75, Pl. LXXX.

4. Vats, *Excavations at Harappa*, 22, Pl. LXXXI, a-d.

5. Meadow and Kenoyer, "Excavations at Harappa 1993": Vats, *Excavations at Harappa*, Pl. XCIII, 306

6. George F. Dales and J. Mark Kenoyer, "Excavation at Harappa—1988," *Pakistan Archaeology* 24 (1989): 68-176.

7. Brian E. Hemphill, John R. Lukacs and Kenneth A. R. Kennedy, "Biological Adaptations and Affinities of Bronze Age Harappans," in *Harappa Excavations 1986-1990*, ed. Richard H. Meadow (Madison: Prehistory Press, 1991), 137-82.

8. Vats, *Excavations at Harappa*, Pl. LXXVI, 12.

9. Dales and Kenoyer, "Excavation at Harappa—1988."

10. Vats, *Excavations at Harappa*, Pl. LXXVI, 12.

11. Walter A. Fairservis, Jr., "Cattle and the Harappan Chiefdoms of the Indus Valley," *Expedition* 28.2 (1986): 43-50.

12. Peter R. S. Moorey, *Materials and Manufacture in Ancient Mesopotamia: The Evidence of Archaeology and Art* (Oxford: BAR International Series, 1985), S237.

13. Alfred Lucas, *Ancient Egyptian Materials and Industries* 4th ed., ed. J. R. Harris (London: Arnold, 1962).

14. Vats, *Excavations at Harappa*, Pl. CXXXVII, 8, 15.

15. Vats, *Excavations at Harappa*, Pl. CXXXVII, 2.

16. Vats, *Excavations at Harappa*, Pl. LXXVI, 12.

17. Ernest J. H. Mackay, *Further Excavations at Mohenjodaro* (New Delhi: Government of India, 1938), Pl. LXXXV, 5, 10.

18. Mackay, *Further Excavations at Mohenjodaro*, Pl. LXXII, 10 and Pl. C.

19. J. Mark Kenoyer, "Ornament Styles of the Indus Tradition: Evidence from recent excavations at Harappa, Pakistan." *Paléorient* 17.2 - 1991 (1992): 79-98.

20. Dales and Kenoyer, "Excavation at Harappa—1988."

Fig. 8.1. Burial pottery from Harappa shows distinctive regional shapes and painted motifs, cat. nos. 186, 187.

Technology and Crafts

Chapter 8

With the rise of cities, around 2600 B.C., technology and crafts became essential mechanisms for creating unique objects to distinguish high officials and rulers from other elites and the common people. Although there may have been some form of military power to reinforce social and political order, artisans of the Indus cities played a significant role by inventing new and more complex technologies that required special knowledge and manufacturing processes. These technologies could be controlled by the rulers and merchants to create symbolic objects that would help to unite the different communities living in the cities. They could also create different qualities of objects that would help to differentiate the various economic and social classes. The contrasting patterns of cultural unity and social stratification are essential for the effective organization of many different communities in a large city, and crafts of the Indus cities provide a key to understanding the complexity of Indus social and economic organization.

Craft specialization that began during the preceding period (3500 to 2600 B.C.) became more complex as the urban workshops developed new technological processes using new varieties and combinations of raw materials. New styles of objects were produced to reflect the synthesis of many different regional cultures, but even though there is considerable uniformity in style throughout the greater Indus region, specific ornaments and ceramic types reveal important regional variations. Harappa and Mohenjo-daro have distinct regional styles of ceramics, which can be contrasted with local styles in Baluchistan, Gujarat and the Gangetic region (fig. 8.1). The larger urban centers and some smaller regional settlements become primary manufacturing centers, thereby creating and controlling access to items that were essential for everyday activities as well as for ritual purposes and social status.

Ceramic production, stone tool manufacture and metallurgy are found in most settlements because pottery vessels were necessary for the everyday activities of food storage, preparation and serving, whereas tools and weapons were needed for farming, hunting and self-defense. The preliminary stages of other crafts were practiced predominantly at settlements near the source of specific raw materials. Shell was processed on the coast; copper was mined and smelted in the remote regions near copper ores. Partly processed raw materials such as shell, agate, steatite and copper were transported to the large urban centers where they were then manufactured into ornaments, tools or ritual objects.

By bringing partly processed raw materials to the urban workshops, the rulers and merchants of the Indus cities were able to control the production of specific items that were used in important rituals or to define status. In this way, it was possible to maintain the status quo through a control of economics and technology, rather than through overt military action. The control of specialized crafts became an important strategy in supporting the state and maintaining the social and ritual order.

Control was exercised both directly and indirectly through restrictions on raw materials, on technological knowledge, on labor, on distribution of finished goods, through taxation or outright prohibition.[1] Crafts that could be easily managed were obviously more beneficial to the rulers than those which were logistically and economically difficult to control. Some crafts could be regulated because the raw materials were difficult to obtain, others because the technology was complex. By considering these two variables, technology and raw materials, we can distinguish four major categories of crafts that were practiced in the large Indus cities (figs. 8.2-8.5):

1) Crafts processing locally available materials using relatively simple technologies include woodworking, basketmaking, simple weaving, terracotta ceramic production, and house-building.

2) Crafts using imported materials with relatively simple technologies include stone-shaping for domestic purposes and chipped stone tool-making.

3) Crafts using local materials and complex technologies and production processes include stoneware bangle manufacture, elaborate painted and specialized ceramic production, complex weaving and carpetmaking, inlaid woodwork production and construction of decorative architecture.

4) Crafts using imported materials and highly complex technologies include agate bead manufacture, seal production, copper/bronze metalworking, stone-carving, precious metalworking, shellworking and faience manufacture.[2]

Each craft was important for the proper functioning of the Indus cities, but some had more value in maintaining socio-economic and ritual order. Such crafts as stoneware banglemaking, seal production and chert weight manufacture may have been directly controlled in segregated workshops by the rulers or the state to limit access to these important symbols of power. These crafts and the objects they produced required standardized form, size or decoration. Other crafts such as ceramic production, metallurgy and faience making were probably grouped together to share resources, labor or raw materials. In contrast to the state-controlled crafts, pottery and ornaments may have been standardized through other mechanisms. For example, if a daughter learns to make pottery from her mother or aunt, painting styles and techniques are gradually standardized over several generations. These standardized technologies and decorative styles spread to new settlements as artisan families spread out to new markets or an apprentice leaves the master's workshop to open up his own shop in a new town. Crafts using local materials and simple technologies are the most varied throughout the Indus Valley, while crafts using nonlocal materials and highly complex technologies

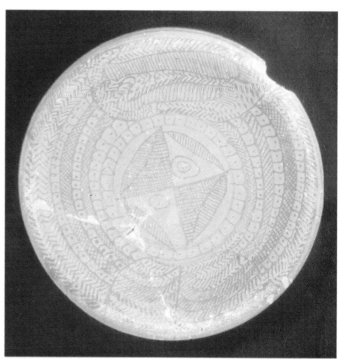

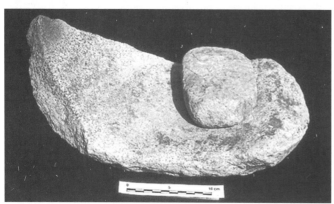

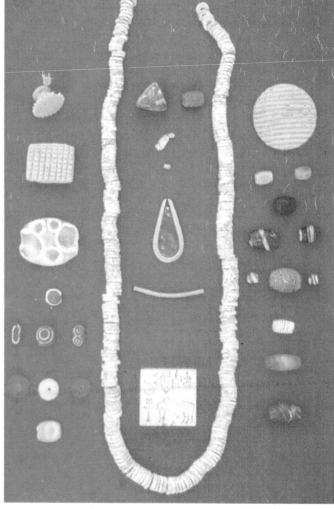

Fig. 8.2. (Top left) Terracotta nodules and various shapes of terracotta cakes from Harappa were formed of local clay and fired at low temperatures. These nodules and cakes had multiple uses, such as heat insulation in the mouths of kilns and ovens. They were also crushed up and reused as gravel in house wall foundations.

Fig. 8.3. (Above) Sandstone quern and muller from Harappa are made with simple techniques, but imported materials.

Fig. 8.4. (Top right) Painted dish made with local clay and imported pigments, using complex technology of wheel-throwing and kiln-firing, Harappa, cat. no 188.

Fig. 8.5. (Right) Assorted ornaments from Harappa made from exotic materials and complex technologies.

are the most standardized. Those crafts which combine local raw materials and highly complex technologies, such as stoneware banglemaking or painted pottery, also show considerable standardization depending on the social or ritual importance of the finished objects.

Ceramic Technology

Ceramic technologies of the Indus cities range from relatively simple fired bricks and plain pottery to finely made wares with highly sophisticated painted designs, fired in specialized kilns. Some of the ceramic goods, such as cooking pots and storage vessels, were important for everyday food preparation, but ornaments and ritual objects were important status symbols. Ceramic technology played an integral role in many aspects of Indus urban society. Fired bricks were used in wells, drains and architecture, along with terracotta tiles, pipes and channel spouts. Aside from the architectural uses, ceramic technologies include low-fired plain or painted terracotta pottery and figurines, high-fired stoneware bangles, refractory ceramics used in crucibles and kilns and glazed faience ornaments and miniature vessels.

Since most settlements of the Indus civilization were located on the alluvial plains, clay was locally available; with simple pit kilns or updraft kilns, almost anyone could have made nodules and terracotta cakes (fig. 8.2), simple plain pottery or figurines. Platters, shallow bowls and small pots were built by hand, but most Indus pottery was formed on a wheel that was turned at both low and high speeds (fig. 8.6). The potter's wheel had been in use for well over one thousand years before the rise of the Indus cities, but its full potential for rapid mass production was not realized until the urban period. When the potter's wheel is turned at high speeds, centrifugal force is harnessed to shape the clay rapidly. Indus potters used the fast wheel to produce rapidly small vessels that were thrown off a large hump of clay. After the shape was formed and smoothed, a string was used to cut the base, and the vessel was removed while the wheel was still turning. The process was repeated again and again until the hump of clay had been used up, thereby conserving time and effort required in repeatedly centering a lump of clay for each vessel. These rapidly produced vessels generally were left undecorated and untrimmed and may have

Fig. 8.6. (left) Mohammad Nawaz, master potter from Harappa uses the wheel in different ways to make a replica of an ancient storage jar. The base is started in a mold and the lower body thrown using the fast wheel, while the upper body and rim are added in large slabs as the wheel is turned slowly by an assistant.

Fig. 8.7. (above) Plain pottery styles from Harappa, pedestaled jar with flaring rim (center, cat. no. 179), small cylindrical jar with flaring rim and ledge shoulder (left, cat. no. 184), small jar with flaring cylindrical shape (right, cat. no. 185).

been used as disposable containers (fig. 8.7, cat. no. 185).

Other vessels were made first on the wheel and then trimmed by hand and burnished to produce more elegant forms and more refined surfaces (fig. 8.7, see cat. nos. 179, 184). Many vessels were trimmed on a slow-turning wheel, leaving the chatter-marks of the trimming tool visible on the vessel surface (see cat. no. 182). Some of the larger vessels were made in several sequential stages with the base formed in a mold or chuck and the upper body and rim added in one or more additional stages.[3] In recent experimental studies we have shown that medium and large-sized jars were produced with significantly different manufacturing stages, requiring different allocations of production time and work space. Both types of vessels may have been made in the same workshops, but probably only the most skilled potters were able to throw and build the very large storage jars (fig. 8.6).[4]

Although pottery production was a specialized craft, the absence of sealings or graffiti indicates that it was not directly controlled by the ruling elites of the larger cities. Pottery kilns have been found scattered throughout various mounds at Mohenjo-daro, Harappa, Chanhudaro and Nausharo, and in many instances the kilns had been made in old, abandoned buildings.[5] Although some potterymaking took place in widely dispersed localities, a series of pottery kilns on the northwestern corner of Mound E at Harappa demonstrates that pottery was made in a segregated area of the city.[6] Beginning in the late Kot Diji Phase (around 2800 B.C.) and continuing through the Harappan Phase (2600-1900 B.C.) these potters' workshops remained in the same locality for hundreds of years (see fig. 2.17, figs. 8.8, 8.9).

Potters could have been hereditary specialists living in the same location as their ancestors; potterymaking could have been organized as a cottage industry involving men and women potters, with children as assistants. In modern South Asia, the potter's wheel is usually associated male potters and mass production, but potterymaking is still organized along family lines, where women play an important role in clay preparation, the manufacture of molded and hand-formed pottery, as well as the painting and decoration of vessels. Children also contribute to the production as apprentices, making simple pottery shapes such as cups and lids, or modeling clay figurines.

All technological processes used to produce plain pottery were also necessary to prepare painted pottery. Most painted pottery of the Indus cities was covered with a red

Fig. 8.8. Large updraft kiln of the Harappan period (ca. 2400 B.C.) found during excavations on Mound E, Harappa, 1989.

Fig. 8.9. A full-scale reconstruction of the ancient Harappan kiln, first built in 1989, is repaired and reused each year for experimental pottery production at the Harappa Archaeological Research Facility. In 1996 a large storage jar was fired along with other types of pottery and figurine replicas.

slip and then painted with black designs, but some large storage vessels were covered on both the exterior and interior with a black slip (cat. nos. 177, 178). The red color was made from red ochre (iron oxide); the black color was made from a combination of dark red-brown iron oxide and black manganese. Around 2600 B.C. the style of painted designs included floral and geometric motifs arranged in panels beginning at the rim and extending to the lower body of the vessel (see fig. 1.1, cat. no. 176). Many of these painted designs, such as the pipal leaf, the fish-scale design and intersecting-circle motifs have roots in earlier regional cultures (3300-2600 B.C.) (see fig. 2.23 and cat. no. 204), but the combination of various motifs and the style of decoration reflects a new synthesis characteristic of the Indus cities (fig. 8.10).

Polychrome painting with white, green or yellow is found in some regional cultures prior to the Indus cities, and although this technique is found at Harappa and Mohenjo-daro, it is not common in the Indus ceramic repertoire. Most polychrome paints were applied after firing, using organic or fugitive mineral pigments; their poor preservation may explain the rarity of polychrome decorative pottery.

Recent studies of painted pottery from Harappa[7] and the smaller regional site of Nausharo[8] show that painted designs and styles of pottery changed significantly during the Harappan Phase. These changes were not uniform throughout the Indus Valley but reflect regional patterns of cultural development that took place at different times during the 700 years of the Indus cities. The most striking illustrations are on the cemetery pottery from Harappa, where hundreds of burial vessels have been recovered.[9] The pottery from the earliest burials, which may date from 2600 to 2400 B.C., have painted designs comprised of plant and geometric motifs (fig. 8.11). These painted designs are similar to the elaborately painted pottery found in the habitation areas of the mound. In the middle levels of the cemetery, we found the same general shapes, but they were much larger and painted with only geometric designs (see cat. nos. 176, 177) or simple horizontal bands (figs. 8.12, 8.13). In the latest levels, which probably date to around 2000 B.C., the burial pottery was primarily unpainted and unslipped, a trend also seen in the dominance of unpainted pottery in the living areas of the city.

Because painted pottery takes longer to produce and the painted designs have specific social and ritual symbolism, the transition from highly decorated to less decorated pottery probably reflects important changes in economic, social and ritual organization of the Indus cities. We see a

Fig. 8.10. Intersecting-circle motif variations on pottery from Mohenjo-daro.

Fig. 8.11. Changes in painted motifs are clearly demonstrated in the burial pottery from early levels (smaller vessels) and the middle levels (larger) of the cemetery at Harappa (cat. nos. 186, 187).

striking example of this change in some highly decorated burial pottery that was intentionally covered with a plain red slip to obscure the painted design (fig. 8.14, cat. nos. 186, 187). Several examples of this intentional overslipping have been found in the Harappan cemetery, but the trend toward unpainted burial vessels appears to be a short-term pattern that was eventually abandoned (see Chap. 9).

Household Ceramic and Metal Containers

Although ceramic decorative styles change significantly, many basic shapes stayed the same throughout the Harappan Phase, with each household having a similar array of pottery vessels. The large storage jars without painted designs probably held water or grain, whereas the elaborately painted vessels may have been wedding gifts or used for ritual purposes. Many smaller drinking vessels with flat bases may have been used in the home for drinking water, milk, buttermilk, fruit juices and alcoholic beverages (fig.

8.15). Shallow bowls probably contained cooked foods or bread; the larger plates may have been used for eating (fig. 8.15, cat. no. 189). The Indus potters created elegant pedestaled dishes or bowls, commonly referred to as dish-on-stand and bowl-on-stand. Some are decorated with incised circles and covered with red slip and simple black bands (fig. 8.15, cat. no. 190), others with elaborate floral and geometric designs (see cat. no. 188). These vessels, which come in many different styles and decorative patterns, were probably used for serving food to guests or for presenting ritual offering.

Another distinctive vessel associated with the Indus cities is the perforated cylindrical jar that may have been wrapped in cloth and used as a strainer for the preparation of fermented beverages (fig. 8.16). These vessels have been found with burial offerings in the Harappan cemetery, where they are placed vertically inside large open-mouthed vessels (fig. 8.17) that may have been filled with fermenting mash, probably barley. With the cloth on the outside, the numerous perforations would allow the liquor to strain through and collect in the central hollow area and be removed with a dipper or by long straws. Studies of the sediments inside these perforated vessels have not revealed the nature of the beverage being brewed, but ongoing research of the porous pottery itself may recover some traces of organic materials to help identify the vessel's contents.

Over time there was a gradual change in the shape of drinking vessels used in the cities. Earlier flat-bottomed forms became more globular and were scored with multiple grooves (fig. 8.18). In the latest phase of the Indus cities (ca. 2000-1900 B.C.) the distinctive pointed-base goblets

Fig. 8.12. (Above) The burial of a woman and her infant at Harappa contained thirty-three vessels, most of which are unpainted, cat. nos. 180-185.

Fig. 8.13. (Right) Pedestaled jar, with red slip and painted black bands, Harappa, cat. no. 180.

Fig. 8.14. (Far right) Painted designs on some burial pottery at Harappa were covered with a red slip and refired to produce "plain" pottery. In most cases the slip is not well fused and it was removed on part of this vessel to reveal the underlying design, cat. no. 186.

Fig. 8.15. Flat dish with short bilaterally projecting rim, cat. no. 189, and dish-on-stand with incised concentric lines at the center of the plate, Harappa, cat. no. 190.

were made by the thousands, using the fast wheel for rapid mass production. Simple grooves were incised on the exterior, possibly to keep them from slipping out of the hand. We do not know what beverages were dispensed in these goblets, probably water, buttermilk and some form of liquor. Immense quantities of broken goblets found in the streets and garbage dumps indicate that many city dwellers used these goblets and threw them away after a single drink.

In traditional South Asian cities, disposable pottery is used for dispensing food and drink to the general public during ritual events or for feeding travelers who are not carrying their own drinking and eating containers. Religious rules of ritual purity require Hindus and many other communities to avoid eating or drinking from used pottery vessels, especially if they have been used by someone of a lower caste or social level. Such religious restrictions may have originated from practical considerations of hygiene, since deadly bacteria can grow on tiny food particles caught in porous terracotta pottery. The only exception to this rule is vessels in which food is prepared by cooking or fermenting.

Throughout northern India and Pakistan, yogurt is traditionally prepared in wide open bowls used over and over. The milk fats seal the pores, and bacteria used to culture the yogurt is not harmful. Cooking vessels used to heat milk or cook large quantities of food for feasts are also used repeatedly. Any harmful bacteria are killed by cooking, and after each use the carbonized oils and food coat the inside surface, making the pot less porous. Because no one ever eats directly from the vessels in which food is prepared, such vessels do not become polluted unless an outsider touches them. In traditional homes, women carefully clean and maintain the purity of the kitchen and food preparation vessels, and outsiders are usually not allowed to touch the cooking vessels or the hearth areas.

The distinctive cooking pots of the Harappan Phase evolved from earlier Amrian and Kot Dijian styles and gradually spread to all of the Indus settlements. Cooking pots were made in sizes that range from miniatures used as toys (see cat. no. 195) to extremely large vessels that may have been used for cooking community feasts. Although there

Fig. 8.16. Perforated jar, Harappa, cat. no. 192.

Fig. 8.17. Deep bowl with wide mouth and flaring rim, cat. no. 191 and perforated jar found inside, Harappa, cat. no. 192.

Fig. 8.18. Earlier (left) and later forms of scored goblets from Harappa. The pointed-base goblet on the left must be supported to stand upright.

are some regional variations, most vessels have either a red- or black-slipped rim, with one or two ridges (fig. 8.19). The highly functional form has a rounded bottom to provide even distribution of heat and a low center of gravity to keep it from tipping over when filled with boiling liquid. On the lower body, the vessel was usually plastered with a thick slurry of clay mixed with ground pottery or grog. This thermal insulation protected the vessel from direct flame so it would not crack during repeated heating. Another important feature of the Indus cooking pot is the strong, outward projecting rim, which makes it is easy to lift the hot cooking pot with two sticks or even with the bare hands. This optimal form of cooking pot remained in used throughout the northern subcontinent long after the decline of the Indus cities and is still found in most traditional households (fig. 8.20).

Whereas most Indus people used terracotta vessels, some copper alloy or bronze containers have been recovered, often buried with bronze tools and weapons or jewelry hoards. Copper and bronze vessels, which would have been used only by the most wealthy and powerful classes, were usually made in the same style as terracotta vessels (fig. 8.21), except where the differences in raw material made it impractical. For example, wide plates of bronze usually had

vertical sides with simple rims (fig. 8.22), rather than the bilaterally projecting rim found on terracotta plates (see cat. no. 189).

Metal containers were much more durable than terracotta and may have been passed on from one generation to the next as objects of wealth, but because they could be recycled into other objects, relatively few have been recovered. Many copper/bronze containers were probably melted down to make ornaments or tools; this pattern of recycling could explain the rarity of vessels made of more precious metals such as gold and silver. Even the most valuable metal containers, such as the silver jars with lids from Mohenjo-daro, are made in the same style as tall ceramic vessels with flaring rims.[10] In cases such as this, where function does not appear to have been a factor, the pervasive use of a specific shape demonstrates the important cultural symbolism that the shape of vessels conveyed.

Although no gold vessels have been discovered, the overall ranking of raw materials from undecorated pottery to precious metals indicates that cooking and serving vessels may have been used to define social and economic status in much the same way as ornaments (see Chap. 6). The similarities in shape and style of pottery and metal vessels

Fig. 8.19. (Above) Ledge-shouldered cooking pots from Nausharo, cat. no. 196 on left.

Fig. 8.20. (Above right) Modern aluminum cooking pots retain many of the features of the ancient Harappan cooking pots.

Fig. 8.21. (Right) Bronze cooking vessel with high neck and flaring rim. This vessel contained a hoard of copper tools, Harappa, cat. no. 197.

Fig. 8.22. (Far right) Bronze plate with vertical sides, Mohenjo-daro, cat. no. 198.

may demonstrate the vertical integration of different classes within a larger cultural system, whereas the differences in raw materials help to reinforce the social and economic hierarchies. Small variations in rim shape and decorative colors on terracotta vessels may have signaled differences between ethnic groups or occupational specialists, a pattern that is well documented in historic South Asia.[11] These differences would be displayed as potters sold their wares or as women carried vessels to and from the home. While walking to the market, women from wealthy families would have been very visible as they carried vessels made of polished copper, bronze or precious metal. But, in contrast to publicly displayed ornaments, cooking and serving vessels were primarily used in the relative privacy of the home, where they continued to reinforce the identity of the family and its place in society.

Stoneware and Faience Technology

Although the production of low-fired ceramics may have been decentralized in the Indus cities, the production of high-fired ceramics, such as stoneware bangles and glazed faience objects, was more directly controlled. Stoneware bangles as important symbols of power were inscribed with the names or titles of elites and used by the elites in only the largest urban centers (see Chap. 4 Box). Glazed faience also may have been a valuable material that was produced in specialized workshops, but unlike stoneware, it was available to a wider public and was traded throughout the Indus region.

Indus faience is a glassy, or vitreous, paste produced from quartz and colored with various minerals. Some aspects of Indus faience technology are broadly similar to Mesopotamian faienceworking, where powdered rock quartz was combined with a colorant, an adhesive and a flux of plant ash to produce simple glazed beads or pendants. The

Indus artisans took this process further by first melting the rock quartz in high temperature kilns (over 1000° C) to produce a glassy frit mixed with the colorant. After regrinding on smooth stones the powder was once again mixed with a powdered flux and moistened with water. This faience paste, which had the texture of talcum powder and a grain size of less than 30 microns, was then formed into delicate objects. The soluble salts in the flux would accumulate or effloresce on the surface of the object as it dried. When fired at around 920° C, the concentration of the flux on the exterior would result in a thin glaze, while the interior of the object was fused into a compact glassy mass.[12]

Finely carved wooden molds were probably used to make ornaments and pendants in the shape of squirrels or monkeys (fig. 8.23). Tiny perfume or unguent jars were made by forming the fine paste over a fabric core (fig. 8.29). A variety of ornaments (see cat. nos. 85, 86, 87) and beads were made by hand modeling, with different colors to imitate natural turquoise (fig. 7.36, cat. no. 54), bleached carnelian (see cat. no. 73) or banded agate (see cat. no 76).

Because of the fine paste and resulting compact glassy matrix, Indus faience was strong enough to be made into bangles that were incised or carved with various designs (see cat. no. 92). Although many cultures produced faience ornaments, only Indus faience was strong enough to produce

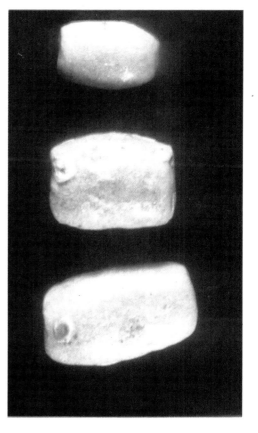

Fig. 8.23. Molded faience amulets of a palm squirrel, three monkeys in embrace, and a seated monkey, from right to left, cat. nos. 173, 175, 174.

Fig. 8.24. Glazed faience beads from Harappa look like highly polished turquoise.

thin bangles that would not break with normal jostling on the wrist. When we consider the importance of bangles and the fact that both stoneware and faience bangles were symbols of status in the Indus cities, we might conclude that the desire to produce bangles made of unique materials stimulated the development of these two complex technologies. The secrets of stoneware technology were lost at the end of the Indus cities, but compact glassy faience bangles continued to be made in later times and may have been the foundation for the glass technology that appeared first during the Late Harappan period (see Chap. 9, cat. no. 205) and became quite common during the Early Historic period.[13]

Copper Metallurgy

Unlike ceramic technology, which uses locally available clay and fuel, copper and bronze metallurgy depends on materials that originate far from the alluvial plains and the Indus cities. Smelting of copper ore took place in the distant highland mining regions of Baluchistan, the mountains of Rajasthan, or even far-off Oman. Traders or nomads would have brought the distinctive bun-shaped ingots of smelted copper, along with tin, lead and other metals to the skilled metalworkers in the city workshops. Given the fumes, smoke and fire associated with metal processing, many of the metal workshops were probably located along the edges of the settlement or in separate craft villages such as Chanhudaro, where copperworking and lapidary arts were practiced alongside ceramic production, shellworking and possibly even sealmaking.[14]

Crude copper (derived directly from smelting and rich in sulfur) or refined copper was used to make a variety of tools and ornaments used in the cities, while copper alloyed with arsenic or tin was produced for specific objects. Arsenical copper makes extremely hard-edge tools, such as saws or chisels, but the edges were slightly more brittle than those of tin bronzes. By measuring the depth of saw cuts on shell manufacturing waste from Mohenjo-daro and Harappa, we can determine that hardened bronze saws were as effective as the traditional steel saws still used by shellworkers in Bengal.[15]

Although the addition of tin can be used to make copper harder, the main objective may have been for producing distinctive colors. Slight amounts produce a golden hue, while larger amounts lend a silver tint. Relatively few metal objects have been subjected to compositional analyses, but these initial studies suggest that the Indus metalsmiths did not maintain a uniform standard for alloying. However, it is also possible that part of the variation in alloy percentages may result from indiscriminate recycling, where objects with different percentages of tin or arsenic alloy were combined to make a new object.[16]

In the urban metal workshops, apprentices would have fabricated tools or weapons (fig. 8.25) by hammering and grinding or casting the molten copper in molds to create figurines (fig. 8.26), all under the watchful eye of the master. Because of the presumed high value of metal tools and

ornaments, it is likely that the production and distribution of metal objects was closely monitored by the ruling elite and merchants. This could have been accomplished most effectively by dividing the labor into distinct stages that could be organized and controlled by a single merchant or head artisan. For example, figurines made by the lost-wax process (fig. 8.26, cat. no. 145) may have been cast by one group of artisans and finished or fabricated by another group in a separate workshop. Incised copper tablets were probably fabricated by assistants and then inscribed by a master artisan (see cat. nos. 31-33). Ornaments such as beads and spacers (see cat. no. 47) may have been cast and fabricated in a metal workshop, but polished and strung with carnelian beads in a merchant's showroom.

Finished metal objects were important symbols of wealth and power in the Indus cities, and monitoring their production would have been needed to avoid pilfering of raw materials or theft of the finished objects. Merchants often hid their stocks of raw materials and finished objects by burying them under the floor. The best-preserved metal objects found in the Indus cities have come from such hoards, buried in the house of a merchant or wealthy citizen who never returned to collect the treasure. One such hoard from Harappa consisted of a large cooking pot (see cat. no. 197)

Fig. 8.25. Copper/bronze weapons from Mohenjo-daro and Harappa, cat. nos. 43, 44.

Fig. 8.26. Copper/bronze ram figurine from a large pin, Mohenjo-daro, cat. no. 160.

covered by a bronze plate. Inside the pot were numerous copper weapons and tools; four axes with straight edges, eight shouldered axes, eight long and narrow blade axes, two unfinished double axes, two daggers with long tangs and tips curved back, seven tapered daggers (see cat. no. 44), one marble mace head, thirteen spear heads, ten chisels, two thick bars, two saws, one arrowhead, one double-edged dagger, one lance head, one semi-oval chopper and one small bowl.[17] Careful examination of the tools indicates that some of them were brand new and unused, others old and worn out from repeated sharpening.

This hoard of copper objects may represent the hidden stock of a large-scale centralized workshop in one area of the site, but the distribution of waste products from copperworking in other parts of the site suggests that small-scale workshops may have been scattered throughout the city, catering to the needs of specific neighborhoods. The contrast between centralized, large-scale production and dispersed, small-scale production illustrates the complex forces at work within the Indus cities. On the one hand the rulers and merchants may have tried to control the production and distribution of specific types of metal objects, but total control was not possible due to the fact that metal can be recycled and modified using relatively simple processes, such as hammering and grinding.

Textiles

Production of cotton and fine woolen fabrics, carpets and embroidery may have been important crafts of the Indus cities, but we have little archaeological evidence for this. The numerous Indus figurines shown with skirts and cloaks tell us that local people wore woven fabrics. Mesopotamian texts speak of the cotton imported from Meluhha. South Asia has historically been an important producer of high-quality fabrics for export to the west. Even though there was little direct control of production, the sale of fabrics and carpets has been an extremely important source of income for the state. Most weaving and carpetmaking were traditionally done in the home as a cottage industry (figs. 8.27, 8.28), and state control was exercised indirectly by taxing the sale of raw materials and finished goods.

Recent excavations at Harappa have recovered numerous examples of plain-weave fabric impressions on the interior of faience vessels (fig. 8.29) and inadvertently pressed onto pottery containers. The uniform thickness of threads in a single piece of fabric and the tight weave reflected by these impressions indicate the use of spinning wheels. Hand-spun thread usually is quite irregular; spinning wheels allow more uniform tension and twisting, which results in standardized threads.

The high quality of these threads is confirmed by the rare examples of thread preserved by metal salts. Traces of cotton fabric were identified at Mohenjo-daro, where they were preserved by contact with a corroding silver jar.[18] Many examples of cotton thread and fabric were identified on copper tools.[19] At Harappa possible cotton threads were found wrapped around the handle of a small copper mirror from a female burial and also around the handle of a curved copper razor (see fig. 7.7).

We have discovered no depictions of Indus looms, but various sized grooved bricks and stones were probably loom weights, presumably for upright frame looms. Backstrap looms, which are still common in the villages and nomadic camps throughout Pakistan, may also have been used to produce narrow strips of fabric that would have been sewn together to form wide cloaks or blankets. Indirect evidence for the production of carpets has been found in the Indus cities in distinctive curved copper/bronze knives that are functionally very similar to the curved blades used today for cutting the knotted threads of pile carpets. Flat-weave carpets and pile carpets are commonly produced both in households and large-scale workshops throughout Pakistan and western India. Weaving and carpetmaking were undoubtedly important household or cottage industries throughout the Indus Valley and may have contributed to the exports traded to Mesopotamia and neighboring regions.

Fig. 8.27. Fine home-spun cotton thread is still prepared with a hand-turned spinning wheel in a village near Harappa.

Fig. 8.28. Weaving home-spun thread on a traditional loom at the town of Shorkot, Pakistan.

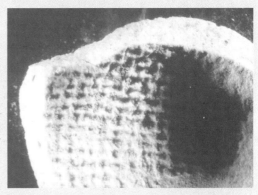

Fig. 8.29. Finely spun thread and tightly woven fabric is clearly visible in this impression from the interior of a faience vessel from Harappa.

Beadmaking

Beadmaking is one of the oldest known crafts of the Indus Valley. Hundreds of years before the invention of pottery at Mehrgarh, lovely beaded ornaments were made from precious stones, shell and even copper.[20] Most tools and raw materials needed for making beads are well preserved in the archaeological record, so we can reconstruct how beads were shaped and perforated (fig. 8.30). For several thousand years before the rise of the Indus cities, beads were made with simple techniques using stone or copper tools to cut, shape and perforate relatively soft raw materials. Shell, bone and ivory were common materials along with soft stones such as limestone, steatite, turquoise and lapis lazuli. Such hard stones as agate, carnelian and jasper were used, but because they were perforated with a chipping technique only very short beads could be produced (fig. 8.31). Most drilling was done with hardened copper drills or tapered cylindrical stone drills made from chert or jasper.[21] These beadmaking techniques were common throughout the Indus region and Baluchistan, and almost every excavated site shows some evidence for beadmaking.[22]

With the rise of the Indus cities beadmaking became highly specialized in order to meet the needs of urban elites and traders. Stone beads continued to be produced at many sites using the earlier techniques, but in some larger towns and cities, specialized workshops began to manufacture unique styles of beads using new raw materials and new techniques of manufacture (fig. 8.30). A new type of constricted cylindrical drill was made from a rare form of metamorphic rock, which may have been further modified by artificial heating.[23] These drills have been found at most of the larger sites such as Mohenjo-daro, Harappa, Dholavira and Chanhudaro, where they were used to perforate beads made from hard agate, carnelian and jasper (fig. 8.32). Important discoveries in drilling beads made it possible to

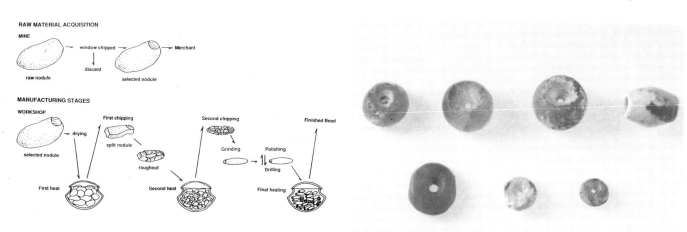

Fig. 8.30. (Above) Stages of bead manufacture.

Fig. 8.31. (Above right) Short-barrel beads of carnelian with chipped perforation (except for top right hand bead), Harappa. (See cat. no. 78)

Fig. 8.32. (Right) Experimental replicas of "Ernestite" stone drills in different sizes for drilling long biconical carnelian beads. (See cat. no. 79)

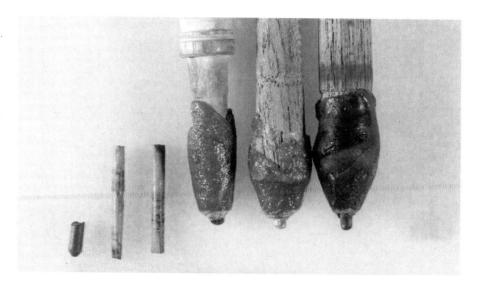

produce long slender beads of hard agate and carnelian. New techniques were invented to decorate stone beads with permanent designs and to make imitation turquoise, agate or carnelian beads from artificial materials such as faience and fired steatite (see fig. 8.24).

The manufacture of long carnelian beads may have taken place at some of the larger cities, but so far, the only confirmed workshop is at the site of Chanhudaro in Sindh.[24] Ernest Mackay was excited by the discovery of the Chanhudaro workshop because of his familiarity with the striking beaded belts found at Mohenjo-daro (see cat. no. 47) and Harappa, as well as the Indus carnelian trade beads found in far-off Mesopotamia (see fig. 5.27). He carefully excavated and collected all stages of bead manufacture along with the associated tools, providing later scholars with a unique window on an important Indus craft.

Detailed studies of the manufacturing waste and finished beads from Chanhudaro, supplemented by ethnographic and experimental studies among modern agate beadmakers in Khambhat, India, have made it possible to reconstruct the basic processes of manufacture.[25] First, long nodules of carnelian were brought to Chanhudaro from far-off mines in Gujarat. After drying in the sun for several months these nodules were heated in shallow ovens to make the agate more flakable and easier to saw. Larger nodules were sawn lengthwise to produce two or more segments that were then chipped to make bead roughouts. These roughouts may have been reheated to deepen the red color, which also made the hard agate easier to flake and grind. Using a copper-tipped stake and a soft antler or horn hammer, the worker shaped the bead blank by indirect percussion (see Chap. 2) and sometimes by pressure flaking with a copper or antler point. These delicately shaped bead blanks were then partially ground on grooved sandstone or quartzite grinding stones (see cat. no. 83).

Indus beadmakers have the distinction of producing the longest and most slender beads of carnelian in the world, prior to the advent of diamond drilling. They were able to accomplish this feat by using a special constricted cylindrical drill made from a rare form of fine-grained metamorphic rock that is a mottled gray-and-tan color (fig. 8.33). By heating this rock they changed the original crystalline structure to create an artificial material composed primarily of quartz, sillimanite, mullite, hematite and titanium-oxide phases. This extremely hard and durable material is referred to as "Ernestite" in honor of Ernest J. H. Mackay, who was the first to discover and recognize the importance of these drills.[26] Due to the hardness of "Ernestite," it may have taken a full day of heating, chipping and grinding to make a single drill, and as many as six different sizes of drills were used to perforate a single bead (not counting broken drills).

The drilling was probably accomplished by using a hand held bow drill, with the bead held firmly in a wooden vise. Because of the intense heat produced, the whole process of drilling may have been done under water or with water continuously dripping onto the drill hole. Drilling experiments indicate that "Ernestite" drills could perforate carnelian at a rate of 2.5 mm per hour, which was more than twice as effective as jasper or copper drills used with hard corundum (ruby) powder. Even then, it would have taken more than twenty-four hours, or three eight-hour working days of steady drilling, to perforate a 6 cm long bead. The beads on the belts from Allahdino and Mohenjo-daro, ranging from 6 to 13 cm in length, would have required between three and eight days of steady drilling to perforate. Most modern bead drillers in Gujarat take long breaks after every few hours of work due to the strenuous nature of the drilling process. Considerable time is also taken in the preparation and repair of drill bits.

Many beads found in the Indus workshops were broken during the drilling, but those that survived were carefully ground and polished to complete the elegant biconical shape. Based on experimental observations and average working times, when all of the different stages of manufacture are calculated, from initial heating to final polishing, it would have taken one worker more than 480 working days to complete a belt of 36 beads like the one found at Allahdino. Even with several workers participating in the production,

Fig. 8.33. Different stages of manufacture for producing long biconical carnelian beads, Chanhudaro cat. no. 81. Expedition of the American School of Indic and Iranian Studies and the Museum of Fine Arts, 1935-1936. © 1997 Museum of Fine Arts, Boston.

it is unlikely that a complete belt could have been fashioned within one year. The high humidity of the monsoon rainy season would restrict manufacturing processes such as heating and drying the nodules. Furthermore, long carnelian nodules are relatively rare in the agate deposits of Gujarat, and the good quality nodules used in the Indus workshops were probably collected over several years. Given these factors, a single belt was probably made over two or three years by a group of artisans under the close supervision of the workshop owner. These belts have been found at Mohenjo-daro, Harappa, and Allahdino, and individual beads were traded throughout the Indus Valley and adjacent regions.

Many of the long carnelian beads were traded as far as Mesopotamia, where they have been found in the burials of the royal cemetery at Ur. Detailed studies of these beads indicate that some of them were made in the Indus Valley, whereas other examples, made with Indus drilling technology and Indus raw materials may have been produced in Mesopotamian styles for Mesopotamian elites. It is possible that these beads were made by migrant Indus artisans residing in Mesopotamia, members of the so-called Meluhhan minority that are documented in Mesopotamian texts.[27]

The importance of long carnelian beads to Indus ornament styles can only be fully appreciated when compared with the imitations that were made in terracotta (fig. 8.34). Painted with red pigment to look like carnelian, these long terracotta beads, made into long necklaces or chokers, are found in all of the Indus settlements. When worn as a belt or necklace, terracotta beads strike against one another to make a delicate clinking sound, not unlike that produced by the real carnelian beads. In modern Pakistan and India, the sound of ornaments is often referred to in poetry to evoke sensual beauty, and the sound of beads

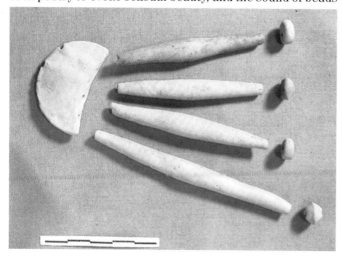

Fig. 8.34. Terracotta imitations of long carnelian beads, Harappa.

and bangles clinking against one another may have been just as important as the visual symbolism evoked by Indus ornaments.

By looking closely at all aspects of Indus crafts, we can gain a fuller understanding of the people who made and used these otherwise mute objects. The urban centers were a totally new context for interaction and display, and the Indus artisans met the challenge by creating a wide variety of utilitarian and ornamental objects. Each different craft contributed in some way to the overall structure of the Indus cities, by linking some communities and distinguishing others. Complex technologies and rare materials allowed the creation of valuable objects that served to differentiate the ruling elites from the common people. At the same time, symbols of Indus religion and culture were incorporated into pottery, ornaments and everyday tools in a way that helped to unite people within the urban centers and link them with distant rural communities.

Feeding the Cities

As populations within the cities became larger and more diverse, new and more reliable patterns of food production were necessary to ensure the steady flow of foodstuffs to the city markets. For thousands of years, farming and animal husbandry, supplemented by hunting, fishing and the gathering of wild plant foods had been organized to support relatively small communities living in villages or small towns. These subsistence strategies remained basically unchanged until the emergence of cities.

During the initial stages of urbanism the changes in the Indus subsistence economy are not seen in advanced farming techniques or new species of animals, but rather in the establishment of trade networks that would facilitate the flow of subsistence resources to major cities and regional centers. Unlike a small village that could be abandoned during a drought year while the inhabitants dispersed to surrounding regions, the abandonment of a city or its regional centers would have had devastating consequences in terms of political and economic stability. The geographic and climatic diversity of the Indus Valley was a kind of safety net, because if the crops failed in the hinterland around one city, surplus production in other regions could have been brought in to feed the general population.[28]

Many plants and animals used by the Indus people can be identified through the motifs on pottery, seals, tablets and terracotta figurines. We find other sources of information in the animal bones and plant remains preserved in the city streets and garbage dumps or the floors of houses. In addition to these ancient sources, we can observe modern farming and herding techniques to help reconstruct specific practices such as the seasonally of certain crops or herd management.

Fig. 8.35. Winter wheat has been harvested, and the fields are being prepared for the summer rice crop in the upland valley of Swat.

Two major grain crops could have been raised in most regions of the Indus Valley provided there was adequate and timely rainfall. The *rabi* or spring-harvested crop is planted in the fall and watered by winter rains, while the *kharif* is planted in the summer, during or after the monsoon, and harvested in the fall. The *rabi* crops were more important in the alluvial plains and piedmont regions; the *kharif* crops appear to have been dominant in the region of Gujarat and possibly the northern Gangetic plain.

Throughout the Indus Valley and along the Baluchistan piedmont, the predominant grain crops of wheat and barley would have been planted in the fall and harvested in the spring or early summer (fig. 8.35). With sufficient winter rain these *rabi*, or spring crops, would not have needed irrigation. Other supplementary crops would have included pulses (fig. 8.36), sesamum, peas, vegetables and possibly perennial cotton. The *kharif* crops, including cotton, mustard, sesamum, dates, melon (fig. 8.37) and peas would have been planted on higher ground during the monsoon or in drained land at the end of the monsoon flooding. Rice, sorghum and various millets (*Setaria, Panicum, and Eleusine* spp.) may have been cultivated as monsoon crops in Gujarat at the beginning of the Harappan Phase, around 2600 B.C.,[29] but they were not grown in the main Indus Valley until much later.

The specific tools used to prepare the fields for agriculture probably varied according to the types of soils and topography. A plow pulled by draft oxen may have been used throughout the alluvial plains; this is confirmed by the discovery of a plowed field at Kalibangan,[30] as well as a toy terracotta plow from the site of Banawali.[31] In the rocky piedmont soils people may have turned the soil with hoes or digging sticks, and they probably cast out seed freely along the receding banks of rivers or oxbow lakes.[32]

Given the Harappan expertise in building drains within the cities, it is not surprising that several methods were used to control water for agriculture. Water-diversion channels and dams for trapping soil and moisture are well documented along the piedmont zone, whereas irrigation canals were used in the highlands of Afghanistan[33] and possibly in the deserts of Rajasthan and Haryana.[34] Wells may have been used for irrigating near small settlements such as at Allahdino[35] or for watering gardens within the city. At the site of Lothal people built a large water tank as a reservoir for the city,[36] and a similar tank may have been constructed in the center of ancient Harappa.

Fig. 8.36. (Left) Winter-grown pulses (lentils) in Gujarat.

Fig. 8.37. (Above) A roadside fruit vendor in Swat uses fresh spring water to cool summer fruits from the hot plains – mango, melon, banana and guava – and plums from mountain valleys.

Fragmentary bones of the one-horned rhinoceros (*Rhinoceros unicornis*) that are found at Mohenjo-daro, Harappa and Nausharo indicate that the Indus hunters killed or trapped these dangerous and unpredictable beasts. Numerous terracotta figurines (fig. 8.43) and the accurate depictions carved on seals (cat. no. 15) demonstrate an intimate familiarity with the character and temperament of this animal. Although this species is now extinct in the Indus Valley and is only found in Nepal and eastern India, it was relatively common in the marshlands around Mohenjo-daro and Harappa during the Harappan Phase. The Indus people probably ate rhinoceros meat and may have prized the heavy bones for making tools and weapons, using the hide for making shields. The rhinoceros horn, which is so precious today as an aphrodisiac, may have been collected as well, but because of its organic composition no horn fragments are preserved in the archaeological record.

In the Indus Valley, the Indian elephant (*Elaphas maximus*) may have lived in the same general habitat as the rhinoceros, and both animals were probably hunted with poisoned arrows and spears, or by large pit traps. Recent studies of spindlelike bone points and barbed arrowheads at Harappa suggest that the Harappans used detachable link-shafts with copper tips that may have been poisoned. Similar detachable points coated with poison were made in ancient Egypt and until recently were used in Ethiopia for hunting large game and for war.[44] Based on modern observations, once the animal has been shot, the arrow shaft falls loose, but the poisoned barbs of the tip remain lodged under the skin, allowing the poison to take effect. The hunters will then track the animal until it falls dead, and after cutting away the poisoned area, return to the settlement with the remaining meat and hide.

During the Indus period, the elephant was probably hunted as much for its meat and hide as for the precious ivory that was used for ornaments, inlay and gaming pieces. We have no depictions of people riding elephants, but one painted elephant figurine may indicate occasional use of tame elephants in the Indus cities (fig. 8.44). In traditional South Asia, tame elephants are used for heavy labor and hauling logs out of the jungles, but they have other roles in warfare or as symbols of power in religious and political processions. A common practice is to paint the face of the elephant with red-and-white pigments to accentuate the eyes and forehead (fig. 8.45). The painted figurine from Harappa, with red-and-white bands painted across the face, may have

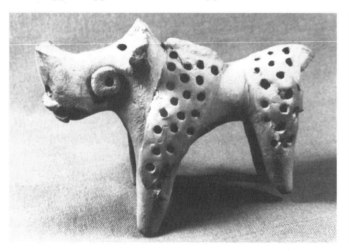

Fig. 8.43. (Above) Rhinoceros figurine, Harappa, cat. no. 165.

Fig. 8.44. (Above right) Painted elephant head with stylized wide spread ears, Harappa, cat. no. 166.

Fig. 8.45. (Right) Elephants returning from a temple ritual in Gujarat with traces of red and white pigment on their faces.

been used as a toy or puppet to show a tame elephant or sacrificial elephant.

The most dangerous animals living in the vicinity of the Indus cities and villages were tigers and leopards (fig. 8.46). The tiger, which figures prominently in figurines and on the seals, is distinguished by its wide, spreading beard. The leopard is rarely depicted, but some figurines have spotted faces that may indicate the distinctive markings of this elusive cat. Both of these large predators would have been a serious threat to human life and domestic animals. Before the introduction of firearms, these animals were usually killed in traps or with poisoned arrows. Among some Naga communities of eastern India, the tiger is a totemic animal and the meat is never eaten by members of the tiger clan. Other communities do eat the meat, but it is considered to be very "hot," stimulating a fiery and ferocious temper. While such a temperament is undesirable for some individuals, it is needed for hunters and warriors and may explain the symbolic meaning of the tiger-bearded male figurines from Harappa and Mohenjo-daro (see cat. nos. 123, 146).

One other wild animal that was rarely depicted in figurines of the Indus is the onager (*Equus hemionus*) (fig. 8.47), a species of wild ass that was common along the desert fringes of the Indus Valley and is still found in parts of Gujarat and Sindh. While this animal may have been hunted, it was not tamed for use in transport or farming. We have no evidence for the use of domestic horse (*Equus caballus*), donkey (*Equus asinus*) and Bactrian two-humped camel (*Camelus bactrianus*) by the Indus people even though they were used in Central Asia and parts of Afghanistan.[45] Nomadic communities or traders may have occasionally brought such exotic animals to the hot plains, but they were not adopted for transport until after the decline of the Indus cities.

Fig. 8.46. (Left) Tiger or leopard figurine with incised facial features, Harappa, cat. no. 167.

Fig. 8.47. (Above) Onager (*Equus hemionus*) figurine, Nausharo, cat. no. 168.

in medicines and cooking. Cloves, cardamom, nutmeg and various types of black pepper are found primarily in South India, but we do not know if they were available in the north during the Harappan Phase, though they are mentioned in the later Vedic texts as important ingredients in food preparations.[49]

Given the wide array of foods and spices available to the Indus cities, food preparation using expensive spices, dried fruits and nuts was probably as important in defining status as wearing ornaments or seals. Most of the population probably survived on a relatively simple diet of wheat or barley, with a few vegetables, and occasionally some meat or fish. In rice- or millet-producing areas, these grains may have been the staple, but each of these major grains represents different cultural patterns of farming and food preparation. Merchants or artisans who had moved to the cities from the highlands or the coasts may have preferred to eat foods that related to their home regions. In contrast to these more conservative communities, cosmopolitan urban elites may have distinguished themselves with exotic foods carried in by traders and hunters. As with the crafts and architecture, the diversity and hierarchies of food in the early Indus cities would have been important for reinforcing social differences as well as unifying communities through feasts and ritual sacrifices.

■

Endnotes

1. J. Mark Kenoyer, "Harappan Craft Specialization and the Question of Urban Segregation and Stratification," *Eastern Anthropologist* 45.1-2 (1992): 39-54.

2. Kenoyer, "Harappan Craft Specialization."

3. George F. Dales and J. Mark Kenoyer, *Excavations at Mohenjo Daro, Pakistan: The Pottery* (Philadelphia: University Museum Press, 1986); also see Rita P. Wright, "The Indus Valley and Mesopotamian Civilizations: A Comparative View of Ceramic Technology," in *Old Problems and New Perspectives in the Archaeology of South Asia*, ed. J. Mark Kenoyer (Madison, Wis.: UW-Madison Department of Anthropology, 1989), 145-56.

4. J. Mark Kenoyer, "Experimental Studies of Indus Valley Technology at Harappa," in *South Asian Archaeology, 1993*, ed. Asko Parpola and Petteri Koskikallio (Helsinki: Suomalainen Tiedeakatemia, 1994), 1:245-62.

5. Kuldeep K. Bhan, Massimo Vidale and J. Mark Kenoyer, "Harappan Technology: Methodological and Theoretical Issues," *Man and Environment* 19.1-2 (1994): 141-57; Catherine Jarrige, "The Mature Indus Phase at Naushara as Seen from a Block of Period III," in *South Asian Archaeology, 1993*, ed. Asko Parpola and Petteri Koskikallio (Helsinki: Suomalainen Tiedeakatemia, 1994), 1:281-94; Stefano Pracchia, Maurizio Tosi, and Massimo Vidale, "On the Type, Distribution and Extent of Craft Industries at Mohenjo-daro," in *South Asian Archaeology, 1983*, ed. Janine Schotsmans and Maurizio Taddei (Naples: Istituto Universitario Orientale, 1985), 207-47.

6. George F. Dales and J. Mark Kenoyer, "Excavation at Harappa–1989," *Pakistan Archaeology* 25 (1990): 241-80.

7. Paul C. Jenkins, "Continuity and Change in the Ceramic Sequence at Harappa," in *South Asian Archaeology, 1993*, ed. Asko Parpola and Petteri Koskikallio (Helsinki: Suomalainen Tiedeakatemia, 1994), 1:315-28.

8. Gonzaque Quivron, "The Pottery Sequence from 2700-2400 BC at Naushara, Baluchistan," in *South Asian Archaeology, 1993*, ed. Asko Parpola and Petteri Koskikallio (Helsinki: Suomalainen Tiedeakatemia, 1994), 2:629-44.

9. George F. Dales, "Some Specialized Ceramic Studies at Harappa," in *Harappa Excavations 1986-1990*, ed. Richard H. Meadow (Madison, Wis.: Prehistory Press, 1991), 61-70.

10. Sir John Marshall, *Mohenjo-daro and the Indus Civilization* (London: Probsthain, 1931), Pl. CXL, 1-3, and 585-586.

11. Dales and Kenoyer, *Excavations at Mohenjo Daro, Pakistan: The Pottery*.

12. Blythe McCarthy and Pamela B. Vandiver, "Ancient High-strength Ceramics: Fritted Faience Bangle Manufacture at Harappa (Pakistan), ca. 2300-1800 B.C.," in *Materials Issues in Art and Archaeology*, vol. 2, no. 185. ed. Pamela B. Vandiver, James R. Druzik and George S. Wheeler (Pittsburgh: Materials Research Society, 1990), 495-510.

13. J. Mark. Kenoyer, "Faience from the Indus Valley Civilization," *Ornament* 17.3 (1994): 36-39, 95.

14. Massimo Vidale, "Specialized Producers and Urban Elites: On the Role of Craft Industries in Mature Harappan Urban Contexts," in *Old Problems and New Perspectives in the Archaeology of South Asia*, ed. J. Mark Kenoyer (Madison, Wis.: UW-Madison Department of Anthropology, 1989), 171-82.

15. J. Mark Kenoyer, "Shell Working Industries of the Indus Civilization: A Summary," *Paléorient* 10.1 (1984): 49-63.

16. J. Mark Kenoyer and Heather M.-L. Miller, "Metal Technologies of the Indus Valley Tradition in Pakistan and Western India," in *The Emergence and Development of Metallurgy*, ed Vincent C Pigott. University Monographs No. 89 (Philadelphia: University Museum, 1997).

17. Madho Sarup Vats, *Excavations at Harappa* (Delhi: Government of India Press, 1940), 85, 384.

18. Marshall, *Mohenjo-daro and the Indus Civilization*; A. N. Gulati and A. J. Turner, *A Note on the Early History of Cotton*. Bulletin 17, Technological Series 12 (Bombay: Indian Central Cotton Committee, 1928).

19. Ernest J. H. Mackay, *Further Excavations at Mohenjodaro* (New Delhi: Government of India, 1938), 440.

20. Jean-François Jarrige and Richard H. Meadow, "The Antecedents of Civilization in the Indus Valley," *Scientific American* 243.2 (1980): 122-33.

21. J. Mark Kenoyer and Massimo Vidale, "A New Look at Stone Drills of the Indus Valley Tradition," in *Materials Issues in Art and Archaeology*, III, No. 267, ed. Pamela B. Vandiver, James R. Druzick, George S. Wheeler and Ian Freestone. (Pittsburgh: Materials Research Society, 1992), 495-518.

22. Bhan, Vidale and Kenoyer, "Harappan Technology: Methodological and Theoretical Issues."

23. Kenoyer and Vidale, "A New Look at Stone Drills of the Indus Valley Tradition."

24. Ernest J. H. Mackay, *Chanhu-Daro Excavations 1935-36* (New Haven, Conn.: American Oriental Society, 1943).

25. J. Mark Kenoyer, Massimo Vidale and Kuldeep K. Bhan, "Contemporary Stone Bead Making in Khambhat India: Patterns of Craft Specialization and Organization of Production as Reflected in the Archaeological Record," *World Archaeology* 23.1 (1991): 44-63; J. Mark Kenoyer, Massimo Vidale and Kuldeep K. Bhan, "Carnelian Bead Production in Khambhat India: An Ethnoarchaeological Study,"in *Living Traditions: Studies in the Ethnoarchaeology of South Asia*, ed. Bridget Allchin (New Delhi: Oxford and IBH, 1994), 281-306.

26. Kenoyer and Vidale, "A New Look at Stone Drills of the Indus Valley Tradition."

27. Simo Parpola, Asko Parpola and Robert H. Brunswig, "The Meluhha Village: Evidence of Acculturation of Harappan Traders in Late Third Millennium Mesopotamia?" *Journal of the Economic and Social History of the Orient* 20.2 (1977): 9-165.

28. Richard H. Meadow, "Continuity and Change in the Agriculture of the Greater Indus Valley: The Palaeoethnobotanical and Zooarchaeological Evidence," in *Old Problems and New Perspectives in the Archaeology of South Asia*, ed. J. Mark Kenoyer (Madison, Wis.: UW-Madison Department of Anthropology, 1989), 61-74.

29. Gregory L. Possehl, "African Millets in South Asian Prehistory," in *Studies in the Archaeology of India and Pakistan*, ed. Jerome Jacobson (New Delhi: Oxford and IBH and AIIS, 1987), 237-56; Steven A. Weber, "South Asian Archaeobotanical Variability," in *South Asian Archaeology, 1989*, ed. Catherine Jarrige (Madison, Wis.: Prehistory Press, 1992), 283-90.

30. B. K. Thapar, "New Traits of the Indus Civilization at Kalibangan: An Appraisal," in *South Asian Archaeology*," ed. Norman Hammond (London: Duckworth, 1973), 85-104.

31. Ravindra Singh Bisht, "Excavations at Banawali, 1974-77," *Harappan Civilization: A Contemporary Perspective*, ed. G. L. Possehl (New Delhi: Oxford and IBH, 1982), 113-24.

32. Seetha N. Reddy, "On the Banks of the River: Opportunistic Cultivation in South India," *Expedition* 33.3 (1991): 18-26, 76-77.

33. Henri-Paul Francfort, *Fouilles de Shortugaï Recherches sur L'Asie Centrale Protohistorique* (Paris: Diffusion de Boccard, 1989).

34. Pierre Gentelle, "Landscapes, Environments and Irrigation: Hypotheses for the Study of the 3rd and 2nd Millenniums," *Man and Environment* 10 (1986): 101-10.

35. Walter A. Fairservis, Jr., "Allahdino: An Excavation of a Small Harappan Site," in *Harappan Civilization*, ed. Gregory L. Possehl (New Delhi: Oxford and IBH/ AIIS, 1982), 107-12.

36. Lawrence S. Leshnik, "The Harappan "Port" at Lothal: Another View," in *Ancient Cities of the Indus*, ed. Gregory L. Possehl (New Delhi: Vikas, 1979), 203-11.

37. Richard H. Meadow, "The Origins and Spread of Agriculture and Pastoralism in South Asia," in *The Origins and Spread of Agriculture and Pastoralism in Eurasia*, ed. David R. Harris (Washington, D.C.: Smithsonian Institution Press, 1996), 390-412.

38. Jim G. Shaffer, "One Hump or Two: The Impact of the Camel on Harappan Society," in *Orientalia Iosephi Tucci Memoriae Dicata*, ed. Gherardo Gnoli and Lionello Lanciotti (Rome: IsMEO, 1988), 1315-28.

39. Meadow, "The Origins and Spread of Agriculture and Pastoralism in South Asia."

40. Shaffer, "One Hump or Two: The Impact of the Camel on Harappan Society."

41. E. Sollberger, "The Problem of Magan and Meluhha," *Bulletin of the London Institute of Archaeology* 8-9 (1970): 247-50; Dilip K. Chakrabarti, *The External Trade of the Indus Civilization* (New Delhi: Munshiram Manoharlal, 1990), 146.

42. Bisht, "Excavations at Banawali, 1974-77."

43. Meadow, "The Origins and Spread of Agriculture and Pastoralism in South Asia."

44. J. Desmond Clark, "Interpretations of Prehistoric Technology from Ancient Egyptian and Other Sources—Part II," *Paléorient* 3 (1974): 127-50.

45. Meadow, "The Origins and Spread of Agriculture and Pastoralism in South Asia."

46. William R. Belcher, "Riverine Fisheries and Habitat Exploitation of the Indus Valley Tradition: An Example from Harappa," in *South Asian Archaeology, 1993*, ed. Asko Parpola and Petteri Koskikallio (Helsinki: Suomalainen Tiedeakatemia, 1994) 1: 71-80.

47. Richard H. Meadow, "Prehistoric Subsistence at Balakot: Initial Considerations of the Faunal Remains," in *South Asian Archaeology, 1977*, ed. Maurizio Taddei (Naples: Istituto Universitario Orientale, 1979), 275-315.

48. K. T. Achaya, *Indian Food: A Historical Companion* (Delhi: Oxford University Press, 1994), 31-37.

49. Achaya, *Indian Food: A Historical Companion.*

Fig. 9.1. Large cremation urn from the later levels of Cemetery H, ca. 1700 B.C., Harappa, cat. no. 201.

Decline and Legacy of the Indus Cities

Chapter 9

Sprouting amidst tangled roots that mark the furthest growth of the parent tree, a new pipal sapling struggles to spread its own roots into fertile soil. Over time the sapling grows to dominate the jungle with rich foliage and fruit, and imperceptibly what was once the edge of the old tree becomes the center of the new. In much the same way, the first urban civilization of the subcontinent gradually faded into the background as new cultures emerged at the eastern and northern edges of the Indus Valley region (fig. 9.1). It took over one-thousand years for the political and cultural center of the northern subcontinent to shift from the Indus Valley to the middle Ganga region (fig. 9.2). Because the process of change was gradual, it is unlikely that anyone living during the period between the decline of the Indus cities (1900 to 1300 B.C.) and the rise of the Early Historic cities (800 to 300 B.C.) would have been aware of the shift.

Factors that played a role in the decline of the Indus cities are as diverse as those which stimulated their growth. In the core regions of the Indus and Ghaggar-Hakra valley, the wide extension of trade networks and political alliances was highly vulnerable to relatively minor changes in the environment and agricultural base. Due to sedimentation and tectonic movement, some water that would normally have flowed into the ancient Saraswati river system was captured by two adjacent rivers, the Sutlej river of the Indus system to the west and the Yamuna river of the Gangetic system to the east.[1] With the increase in water flow, the Indus itself began to swing east, flooding many settlements and burying them with silt.[2] The mounds of Mohenjo-daro survived because they were on slightly higher land and were protected by massive mud-brick walls and platforms, but many smaller sites were destroyed. Extensive and repeated flooding, combined with shifting rivers,

had a devastating effect on the agricultural foundation and economic structure of the Indus cities. Although sites such as Harappa continued to be inhabited, the economic infrastructure for long-distance trade to the south was irreparably damaged as many less fortunate settlements along the dry bed of the ancient Saraswati river were abandoned. The refugees were forced to develop new subsistence strategies or move to more stable agricultural regions.

The cultivation of summer crops, such as rice, millet and sorghum, made it possible to expand into the monsoon-dominated regions of the Ganga-Yamuna Doab and Gujarat that were previously underdeveloped. During this period of change, animals that had been in use in the western highlands were adapted for transport and communications on the plains. Horse and donkey as well as the Bactrian camel were gradually integrated into the economic sphere and in the symbolic and decorative arts. Terracotta animal figurines and painted pottery styles reflecting these new developments were incorporated into the previously existent technologies, many of which continued to be practiced.

Excavations at sites such as Mehrgarh, Naushauro and Pirak provide a complete sequence of the gradual transformation that was going on in the Kachi Plain,[3] and

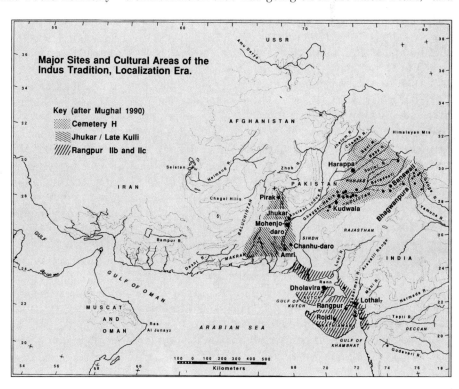

Fig. 9.2. Major sites and cultural areas of the Indus Tradition, Localization Era.

excavations in Swat Valley to the north provide a complementary perspective.[4] Additional information on the nature of cultural developments outside the Indus Valley come from recent work in Central Asia at sites belonging to the Bactria-Margiana Archaeological Complex.[5] To the east, in the Ganga-Yamuna Doab[6] and Gujarat numerous surveys and excavations[7] have radically altered models for the decline of the Indus cities and the emergence of new cities of the Indo-Gangetic Tradition (see Chap. 1).[8]

Prior to these relatively recent discoveries, most scholars thought the introduction of new pottery styles, plants and animals, as well as "foreign" artifacts represented the intrusion of new peoples. The discovery of unburied skeletons among the latest levels of the Harappan occupation at Mohenjo-daro combined with uncritical and inaccurate readings of the Vedic texts led some scholars to claim that the decline of the Indus civilization was the result of "invasions" or "migrations" of Indo-Aryan speaking Vedic/ Aryan tribes.[9] The invasion and/or migration models assumed that the Indo-Aryan-speaking Vedic communities destroyed the Indus cities and replaced the complex urban civilization with their new rituals, language and culture. Many scholars have tried to correct this absurd theory, by pointing out misinterpreted basic facts, inappropriate models and an uncritical reading of Vedic texts.[10] However, until recently, these scientific and well-reasoned arguments were unsuccessful in rooting out the misinterpretations entrenched in the popular literature.[11]

Current theories on the role of Indo-Aryan-speaking peoples are beyond the scope of this book, but there is no archaeological or biological evidence for invasions or mass migrations into the Indus Valley between the end of the Harappan Phase, about 1900 B.C. and the beginning of the Early Historic period around 600 B.C. In Central Asia and Afghanistan the Bactria-Margiana Archaeological Complex (BMAC), dating from around 1900 to 1700 B.C., represents a complex mixture of nomadic and settled communities; some of these may have spoken Indo-Aryan dialects and practiced Indo-Aryan religion.[12] These communities and their ritual objects were distributed from the desert oases in Turkmenistan to southern Baluchistan and from the edges of the Indus Valley to Iran. As nomadic herders and traders moved from the highlands to the lowlands in their annual migration, they would have traded goods and arranged marriages as well as other less formal associations resulting in the exchange of genes between the highland and lowland communities.

Recent biological studies of human skeletal remains from the northern subcontinent and Central Asia have uncovered no evidence for new populations in the northern subcontinent during this time. Yet, these two regions were not isolated from one another. A limited degree of interaction is clearly demonstrated by overlapping genetic traits that would normally occur between adjacent populations.[13] This pattern is not surprising because the highlands of Afghanistan and Central Asia had intermittent contact with the Indus Valley for thousands of years prior to and during the Harappan Phase. There is no major change in this relationship during the decline of the Indus cities.[14]

In the absence of direct external forces, we can attribute the decline of the Indus cities to internal factors that over time undermined the economic and political power of the ruling elites. Overextended networks of trade and political control were easily disrupted by changes in river patterns, flooding and crop failure. Refugees and overcrowded cities would have caused a legitimacy crisis for the ritual leaders and political rulers that ended with the emergence of new elites and localized polities around 1900 B.C. The previously integrated regions of the Indus Valley and Gujarat broke up into three major localized cultures that can be defined by new painted motifs and ceramic styles, seals with geometric designs and new burial customs (fig. 9.1). For 600 years, until around 1300 B.C. the Localization Era (commonly referred to as the Late Harappan period) was an interlude during which a new social order was being established as new technologies and agricultural practices spread up and down the Indus Valley, east into the Ganga-Yamuna Valley and into the peninsular subcontinent.[15]

The three cultural phases of the Localization Era were named after the important sites where specific pottery styles were first discovered or the geographical region in which their cites and towns are found. The Punjab Phase refers to the northern regional culture that includes the large site of Harappa and sites further to the east in northern India. In the southern Indus Valley the Jhukar Phase is named after a site near Mohenjo-daro and incorporates all sites in Sindh, as well as parts of Baluchistan. The Rangpur Phase refers to the entire region of Kutch, Saurashtra and mainland Gujarat.

At the site of Harappa the Punjab Phase is represented by elaborately painted ceramics that are referred to as the Cemetery H culture, because they were first discovered in a large cemetery filled with painted burial urns and some extended inhumations. In contrast to the use of plain pottery in burials during the final Harappan Phase, the reemergence of heavily decorated burial pottery reflects a major change in ritual practices and ideology. New painted motifs include ritual symbols that combine animal, plant and human themes in a manner unknown on the earlier Harappan phase painted ceramics (fig. 9.1). In addition to fairly normal illustrations of humped bull, gazelle, blackbuck, flying peacocks, unique combination figures include double serpents with a horned headdress that has two pipal leafs sprouting from the center;

humped bulls with three pipal leaves sprouting from the middle of the forehead and flying peacocks with antelope horns or a five-pronged tail made of pipal leaves. One spectacular form combines a bull's body, antelope horns and a human head and torso, with hands resting on the hips and arms covered with bangles (fig. 9.3).[16] Although the style of these motifs is unique, the use of the trefoil and pipal leaf headdresses along with horned figures strongly argues for the incorporation of some Indus beliefs with the new rituals.

Recent research at Harappa has shown that the transition from the Harappan to the Punjab Phase (Cemetery H culture) was gradual, thus confirming what was found in the excavations of cemetery H in the 1930s. The earlier burials in this cemetery were laid out much like Harappan coffin burials, with pottery arranged at the head and feet. Painted jars with high flaring rims are a new style that can be associated with highland cultures to the west, but the large jars with ledge rims and the heavy dish-on-stands have strong links with earlier Harappan styles. Decorative plates or lids and votive offerings in small pottery vessels (fig. 9.4) were placed in the burials. A new variation of the dish-on-

stand has ridges on the base and a hole in center that may have been used in preparing some form of distilled drink (fig. 9.5). In the later burials, adults were cremated, but children were placed inside large urns, then covered with a second pot. These large burial urns are heavily decorated with painted motifs described above (fig. 9.3).

Cemetery H pottery and related ceramics of the Punjab Phase have been found throughout northern Pakistan, even as far north as Swat,[17] where they mix with distinctive local traditions. In the east, numerous sites in the Ganga-Yamuna Doab provide evidence for the gradual expansion of settlements into this heavily forested region.[18] Although the Punjab Phase encompassed a relatively large area, the trade connections with the western highlands began to break down as did the trade with the coast. Lapis lazuli and turquoise beads are rarely found in the Punjab Phase settlements, and marine shell for ornaments and ritual objects gradually disappeared. On the other hand the technology of faience manufacture becomes more refined, possibly in order to compensate for the lack of raw materials such as shell, faience and possibly even carnelian.

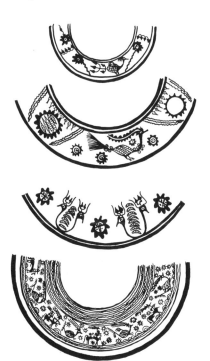

Fig. 9.3. (Above) Cemetery H pottery motifs from Harappa, after Vats 1940, Plate LXII.

Fig. 9.4. (Above right) Small painted globular pot associated with cremation urns, ca. 1700 B.C., Cemetery H, cat. no. 202, and painted dish or lid from the early levels of Cemetery H, Harappa, ca. 1900 B.C., cat. no. 200.

Fig. 9.5. (Right) Dish-on-stand from the lower levels of Cemetery H, Harappa, ca. 1900 B.C., cat. no. 199.

Fig. 9.6. Bead pot showing top most layer of beads, Harappa, cat. no. 205.

In 1996, excavations at Harappa uncovered a small pot (fig. 9.6) in a room dating to approximately 1730 B.C. during the Punjab Phase (Corresponding to Periods 4 and 5 in the Harappa chronological sequence). This pot was filled with 133 beads and other small objects, many of which had been collected from the eroding layers of earlier occupations at the site (fig. 9.7). However, a large number of the beads that cannot be associated with the earlier periods of the site must reflect the technological changes that were occurring at Harappa during the Punjab Phase.

Some faience beads of this period reflect a change in style that includes new colors and shapes, some of which are delicately carved and glazed. For the first time a deep azure faience (fig. 9.8) is made that may represent an imitation of lapis lazuli. Even more significant is a red-brown glass bead (fig. 9.8) that is the earliest glass bead from the Indus Valley and represents the beginning of local glass production. This same color of glass bead becomes more common in the Early Historical period (600-300 B.C.) and is found at sites throughout northern India and Pakistan.

Another significant discovery in this pot is beads that have been drilled with a tubular copper drill using an abrasive (fig. 9.9). This drilling technique was known during the previous Harappan Phase and was used for making perforations in large ringstones, but it was never used on small beads because they were perforated using the specialized "Ernestite" drills. During the Punjab Phase, it appears that the access to "Ernestite" was cut off and a new application was created for an already existing technology. Some of these beads are made of black-and-white banded agate (fig. 9.7) that we

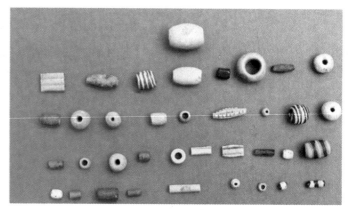

Fig. 9.7. (Above) Contents of the bead pot cat. no. 205.

Fig. 9.8. (Above right) Deep azure faience and carved turquoise colored faience beads from the bead pot date to the Punjab Phase (Late Harappan Period), ca. 1900-1700 B.C. The red brown glass bead in the top row, fourth from the right, is the earliest glass bead found from the Indus Valley.

Fig. 9.9. (Right) Tubular drilling technique used to perforate ringstones and tiny beads.

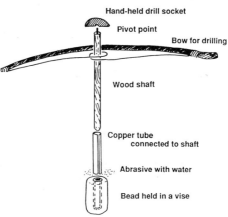

TUBULAR DRILLING TECHNIQUE

think originates in the Vindhyan or Chota Nagpur plateaus far to the east. We have not discovered the actual source of this stone, possibly because its immense popularity during the Early Historic period may have depleted the accessible geological deposits.

Copper objects continue to be manufactured, but we cannot determine if tin from the western highlands was used to produce bronze. The general pattern seen during the Punjab Phase is one of eastern expansion into the Ganga-Yamuna Doab accompanied by rural dispersal and the localization of interaction networks to the exclusion of southern resources and western resources.

In the southern Indus Valley, the Jhukar and subsequent Pirak phases represent a similar process of gradual change during which a new group of elites emerges with different ceramic styles once again employing circular seals with geometric designs. The Jhukar Phase overlaps the Harappan Phase, but continues much later at sites such as Jhukar, Chanhudaro, Mohenjo-daro and Amri[19] and has stylistic links to the site of Pirak on the Kachi plain.[20] The continued occupation of these relatively large regional centers argues for a strong localized culture. Many of the technological features of the pottery and other objects show a strong continuity with the preceding Harappan phase. The major differences we see are in the pottery designs, the absence of script and Harappan-style animals on seals and the increased use of circular seals with geometric designs. The Jhukar Phase begins with the final phase of the Indus cities, around 2000 B.C. to 1900 B.C., and ends with the Pirak Phase which dates from around 1800 B.C. to 800 B.C.[21]

The site of Pirak, located on the Kachi plain to the northwest of Jhukar, has strong cultural connections to other sites on the Kachi plain and settlements in the highlands to the west.[22] The continued interaction between the plains and the hills may explain the appearance of terracotta figurines of horses and camels with riders (figs. 9.10, 9.11). These figurines are conclusive evidence for the introduction of these important animals to the Indus region, and in the later levels of Pirak (Period II) the horse figurines are painted with elaborate trappings and have attached wheels to be used as movable toys. Human figurines are made with pinched features and appliqué hairstyles and ornaments similar to figurines of third millennium Mehrgarh (see cat. no. 1) and Shahr-i-Sokhta.

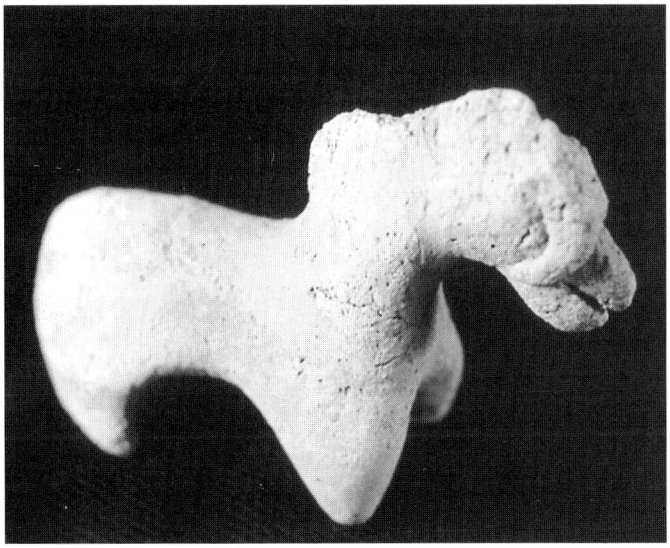

Fig. 9.10. Terracotta figurine of a horse from Pirak, Baluchistan, Period Ib, ca. 1600 B.C.

Fig. 9.11. Terracotta figurine of a camel from Pirak, Baluchistan, Period IIb, ca. 1400 B.C.

Important artifacts are seals made of terracotta and bronze that are totally different from those of the Indus cities. These compartmented seals–square and circular with geometric forms (fig. 9.12)–are similar to the circular Jhukar seals that can be traced back even earlier to seals made at Mehrgarh some two-thousand years earlier during Period V (3300 B.C.) to Period VII (2800 B.C.) (see Chap. 2, fig. 2.21). Painted ceramic styles at Pirak also have links to earlier polychrome geometric designs and seem to indicate the reemergence of local designs after a period of Harappan hegemony (fig. 9.13). New developments in pottery shapes include the large globular water vessel, handled cups and heavier forms of cooking pots. We can link such modifications to important developments in food preparation and storage.[23]

Unlike the Punjab Phase settlements, those of the Pirak Phase continued to have contacts with the lapis lazuli and copper sources in Baluchistan as well as the shell collectors along the nearby coasts. Extensive use of rice, a monsoon crop, is well documented at Pirak, as well as the newly introduced sorghum and millets, which would have been necessary to provide fodder for animals not adapted to the arid Kachi plain (horse and possibly some cattle).[24]

In the southern regions of the Indus Valley, the period following the decline of the Indus cities is not one of abandonment and desolation, as portrayed in much of the earlier literature, but rather a continued dynamic relationship between agriculturalists and pastoralists who exploited both the plains and the highlands to the west.

Jarrige argues that the intensification of subsistence practices, multicropping and the adoption of new forms of transportation (camel and horse) were made by the indigenous inhabitants of this region and not by new people streaming into the region.[25]

Further southeast in the islands of Kutch and mainland Gujarat, a different but related process of change was going on. Refugees from the dried-up regions of the ancient Saraswati river may have moved to the vast plains of north Gujarat where, during this time there is a dramatic increase in the number of settlements.[26] The gradual siltation of the shallow Rann of Kutch caused the reorganization of shipping routes and a breakdown of connections to the core regions of the Indus Valley. Most diagnostic Harappan Phase artifacts such as inscribed seals and weights, perforated vessels, terracotta cakes and the famous Indus goblet disappear, indicating the breakdown of earlier ritual and social hierarchies. As the characteristic Harappan painted pottery decreases, local pottery shapes and decorative styles begin to dominate. The use of writing continues in the form of graffiti on pottery, even after the disappearance of square stamp seals. Other important traditions begun during the Harappan Phase also continue, such as the manufacture of shell bangles and the production of faience beads and ornaments. However, none of these objects was traded to the northern regions, indicating a major break in trade networks that continued until around 600 B.C., with the rise of Early Historic city-states.[27]

Fig. 9.12. Geometric seals in terracotta and bronze, Pirak, Baluchistan, Period IIIb, ca. 1000 B.C.

Fig. 9.13. Polychrome pottery from Pirak, Baluchistan, Periods II and III, 1600-800 B.C.

Changing Social Order

Although the Localization Era covers the decline of the Indus cities, it is also a time of regional development leading up to the rise of new cities in the larger geographical area encompassed by the Indo-Gangetic tradition.[28] In each major region of the Indus Valley, even as the Indus cities decline, small city-states or chiefdoms began to reorganize the social life and consolidate regional power.[29] These regional polities destroyed the integration achieved by the Harappan Phase cities and established new peripheral polities in Afghanistan and Central Asia and to the east in the Ganga-Yamuna Doab.[30] In both regions the rise of new polities is clearly an indigenous process and not the result of outside invaders.

In the Gangetic region from 1200 to 800 B.C., the gradual spread of communities using a distinctive form of pottery known as Painted Gray Ware can be related to the Indo-Aryan communities of the later Vedic texts and the Mahabharata Epic.[31] The Northern Black-polished Ware culture (500-300 B.C.) is the term given to the next major cultural development, but both the Painted Gray Ware and the early Northern Black-polished Ware culture can be grouped together as the formative phases that precede the development of urban states in the Indo-Gangetic region.[32]

This was a time of social and religious change, as Indo-Aryan languages, religion and culture gained dominance first in the Punjab and Gangetic regions and then down the Indus Valley and across the Malwa plateau into Gujarat. For the first time in South Asia, archaeological evidence for these transformations is supplemented by oral traditions that later came to be codified in ritual texts such as the Rig Veda, the Ramayana and the Mahabharata. During this period religious traditions such as Brahmanical Hinduism, Buddhism and Jainism emerged.

The change of focus from the Indus to the Gangetic plains is a pattern that can be best explained through core-periphery models of political development.[33] A new social hierarchy based on different belief systems, ritual practices and language could not have developed within the Indus Valley, where towns and cities of the Localization Era still existed. The peripheral regions of the Ganga-Yamuna and eventually the Middle to Lower Ganga provided the necessary setting for the establishment of a new religious elite and a new urban process. The Early Historic city-states reflect the development of a sociopolitical system that reached a completely different level of integration during the Indo-Gangetic tradition than was possible in the preceding Indus Valley tradition (fig. 9.14). By 300 B.C. the smaller city-states established throughout the Indo-Gangetic region were integrated through the newly created military power of the Mauryan Empire, supported by cavalry, horse-drawn chariots, iron weapons and a highly developed political infrastructure.[34]

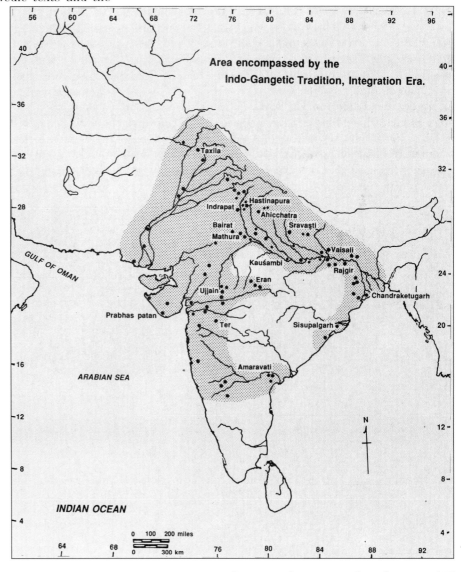

Fig. 9.14. Area encompassed by the Indo-Gangetic Tradition, Integration Era.

The Legacy of the Indus Valley Civilization

Since the discovery of the Indus cities, scholars have made comparisons and contrasts between the Indus cities and later urban cultures of the subcontinent. Current studies of the transition between the two early urban civilizations claim that there was no significant break or hiatus. All of the major subsistence items and grains that became important during the Early Historic period had already been cultivated in some region of the Indus Valley during the Harappan Phase or the subsequent Localization Era. Nevertheless, a more complex process of seasonal agriculture and multicropping using the recently exploited summer crops of sorghum, millet, rice allowed the production of considerable surplus that was needed to support the new cities and their armies.[35]

Newly established trade networks linked the rapidly developing urban areas to distant resource areas and rural producers. These networks add to, and build from, the earlier interaction networks of the Indus Valley tradition. As such, they undoubtedly incorporated many of the remnant polities, economic and technological features of the Indus Localization Era.

Copper metallurgy of the Early Historic period built on the earlier technical expertise of Indus artisans and their descendants who may have formed specialized occupational communities that continued to smelt and process copper ores. Copper workers may have invented iron production which appeared in the northern subcontinent around 1200 B.C.

Earlier scholars proposed that iron technology was brought to the subcontinent by invading Aryan tribes, but a careful reading of the early Vedic texts indicates that there was no invasion and in fact, the earliest Indo-Aryan speaking communities of the northwestern subcontinent did not know of or use iron.[36]

The earliest ironworks (1200 B.C.) were located in the northern Aravalli hills, close to the important sites of Mathura, Noh, Bairat and Indrapat (Delhi), which lie in the core area of the Indo-Gangetic tradition (fig. 9.14). Later, during the early Northern Black-polished Ware period, a second iron source area was exploited far to the east, in the Chota Nagpur plateau, adjacent to the most important sites of the middle and lower Ganga plain, i.e. Rajgrha, Pataliputra, and Champa.[37] The control of iron production and trade may have been a critical factor in determining the location and eventual dominance of the major cities and capitals of the Early Historic states.

Other resources that came to be exploited by the early cities include agate and other semiprecious stones. Agate beadmaking was not unique to the Indus cities, but the techniques for drilling long beads with constricted cylindrical drills was exclusively an Indus phenomenon. Beadmakers in same regional settlements continued to use both tapered cylindrical and constricted cylindrical stone drills long after the decline of the Indus cities, but these were replaced with diamond-tipped drills by the beginning of the Early Historic period, about the fifth century B.C.[38] New techniques for coloring and bleaching beads with white on black designs were developed, again building on the technique for making

Fig. 9.15. (left) Sindhi farmer with carnelian prayer-bead necklace and pipal leaf-shaped pendants.

Fig. 9.16. (above) A Gujarati woman wearing glass bangles and a seed bead choker buys gold colored glass beads to make wedding ornaments.

white designs on red carnelian invented by the Indus artisans. New styles of beads and a different repertoire of designs were introduced, reflecting the changes in beliefs and social organization. The use of red on white versus black on white designs may indicate different beliefs or ritual meaning, as does red-slipped and black-slipped pottery in modern South Asia. The basic technologies of heating stones to make them flakable or to change their color must be credited to the Indus artisans, but the new technique of faceting of stone beads to reflect light and create a new sense of aesthetics begins with the Early Historic period. Rock quartz and amethyst were the first stones to be faceted, setting the stage for later developments in faceted gemstones. Even with all of these developments however, the tradition of wearing carnelian beads or using them in prayer beads continues today (fig. 9.15).

Artisans continued to manufacture faience, but alongside this technique a vigorous glass technology developed for the production of multicolored bangles, beads, ear discs, seals and containers.[39] Glass technology appears to have developed indigenously in the northern subcontinent around 1700 B.C., and this technology may derive from the compact faience technology invented during the Indus period.[40] The knowledge of glassmaking rapidly spread, and glass beads and bangles were produced at many sites throughout the subcontinent during the first millennium B.C.[41]

Glass ornaments and vessels were not used in rituals, but were primarily for domestic consumption and trade (fig. 9.16). Foreign authors such as Pliny the Elder from faraway Rome, writing around 75-77 A.D., remarked on the high quality of Indian glass which he supposed was made from pounded rock crystal.[42]

Although glass was not often used for glazing terracotta tiles or architectural components, some flat, glazed tiles decorated with azure, black, white and yellow glazes were found in association with the later levels of the Dharmarajika Stupa in Taxila Valley, dating to the fourth to fifth centuries A.D.[43] Glazed tiles, rarely used in Buddhist and Hindu architecture, did not become important for architectural decoration until after the introduction of Islam in the seventh century A.D. With the new religion came new architectural traditions and new styles of decoration which incorporated predominantly blue-and-green glazed tiles, with black, white and yellow for details or in mosaic tile work. Glazed tiles were commonly used in mosques and the tombs of saints or important leaders, and the manufacture of glazed tiles became focused in large cities or near the tombs of famous saints (fig. 9.17). The rapid adoption of glazed tile production in the subcontinent and its gradual acceptance into later Hindu and Jain architectural traditions can be attributed, in part, to the presence of a strong history of faience and glass production, with roots reaching back to the first Indus cities.

Fig. 9.17. Tile work produced by Mohammed Sajid Ansari of Multan, using techniques introduced from Iran and Afghanistan, but adapted to the materials of the Indus Valley itself. On the left, a more modern rendering by his young son.

Endnotes

1. Virendra N. Misra, "Indus Civilization and the Rgvedic Saraswati," in *South Asian Archaeology, 1993*, ed. Asko Parpola and Petteri Koskikallio (Helsinki: Suomalainen Tiedeakatemia, 1994), 2: 511-26.

2. Louis Flam, "Fluvial Geomorphology of the Lower Indus Basin (Sindh, Pakistan) and the Indus Civilization," in *Himalayas to the Sea: Geology, Geomorphology and the Quaternary*, ed. John F. Shroder, Jr. (London: Routledge, 1991), 265-87.

3. Jean-François Jarrige, "The Final Phase of the Indus Occupation at Naushāro and Its Connection with the Following Cultural Complex of Mehrgarh VIII," in *South Asian Archaeology, 1993*, ed. Asko Parpola and Petteri Koskikallio (Helsinki: Suomalainen Tiedeakatemia, 1994), 1:295-314; Jean-François Jarrige, "Continuity and Change in the North Kachi Plain (Baluchistan, Pakistan) at the Beginning of the Second Millennium B.C.," in *South Asian Archaeology, 1983*, ed. Janine Schotsmans and Maurizio Taddei (Naples: Istituto Universitario Orientale, 1985), 35-68.

4. Giorgio Stacul, "Swat, Pirak, and Connected Problems (Mid-2nd Millennium B.C.)," in *South Asian Archaeology, 1989*, ed. Catherine Jarrige (Madison, Wis.: Prehistory Press, 1992), 267-70; Giorgio Stacul, "Continuity and Change in the Swat Valley (18th-15th Centuries B.C.)," in *Old Problems and New Perspectives in the Archaeology of South Asia*, ed. J. Mark Kenoyer (Madison, Wis.: UW-Madison Department of Anthropology, 1989), 249-52.

5. Fredrik T. Hiebert, "Production Evidence for the Origins of the Oxus Civilization," *Antiquity* 68 (1994): 372-87; Victor Sarianidi, "Recent Archaeological Discoveries and the Aryan Problem," in *South Asian Archaeology, 1991*, ed. Adalbert J. Gail and Gerd J. R. Mevissen. (Stuttgart: Steiner, 1993), 252-63.

6. Ravinder Singh Bisht, "Further Excavations at Banawali: 1983-84," in *Archaeology and History*, ed. B. M. Pande and B. D. Chattopadhyaya (Delhi: Agam Kala Prakashan, 1987), 135-56; K. N. Dikshit, "The Legacy of Indus Civilization in North India," *Puratattva* 21 (1991): 17-20; Jagat Pati Joshi, "Interlocking of Late Harappan Culture and Painted Grey Ware Culture in the Light of Recent Excavations," *Man and Environment* 2 (1978): 98-101; Jim G. Shaffer, "Reurbanization: The Eastern Punjab and Beyond," in *Urban Form and Meaning in South Asia: The Shaping of Cities from Prehistoric to Precolonial Times*, ed. Howard Spodek and Doris Meth Srinivasan (Washington, D.C.: National Gallery of Art, 1993), 53-67.

7. Kuldeep K. Bhan, "Late Harappan Gujarat," *Eastern Anthropologist* 45.1-2 (1992): 173-92; Gregory L. Possehl, "The Harappan Civilization in Gujarat: The Sorath and Sindhi Harappans," *Eastern Anthropologist* 45.1-2 (1992): 117-54; Gregory L. Possehl, "The Harappan Cultural Mosaic: Ecology Revisited," in *South Asian Archaeology, 1989*, ed. Catherine Jarrige (Madison, Wis.: Prehistory Press, 1992), 237-44.

8. J. Mark Kenoyer, "Interaction Systems, Specialized Crafts and Culture Change: The Indus Valley Tradition and the Indo-Gangetic Tradition in South Asia," in *The Indo-Aryans of Ancient South Asia: Language, Material Culture and Ethnicity*, ed. George Erdosy (Berlin: de Gruyter, 1995), 213-57; Jim G. Shaffer and Diane A. Lichtenstein, "The Cultural Tradition and Palaeoethnicity in South Asian Archaeology," in *The Indo-Aryans of Ancient South Asia: Language, Material Culture and Ethnicity*, ed. George Erdosy (Berlin: de Gruyter, 1995), 126-154.

9. R. E. Mortimer Wheeler, *The Indus Civilization*, 3rd ed. *Cambridge History of India* (Cambridge: Cambridge University Press, 1968).

10. Jarrige, "Continuity and Change in the North Kachi Plain"; Shaffer, "Reurbanization: The Eastern Punjab and Beyond."

11. Dale M. Brown, ed. *Ancient India: Land of Mystery* (Alexandria, Va.: Time-Life Books, 1994).

12. Hiebert, "Production evidence for the origins of the Oxus Civilization"; Fredrik T. Hiebert, "South Asia from a Central Asian Perspective," in *The Indo-Aryans of Ancient South Asia: Language, Material Culture and Ethnicity*, ed. George Erdosy (Berlin: de Gruyter, 1995), 192-205.

13. Brian E. Hemphill, John R. Lukacs and Kenneth A. R. Kennedy, "Biological Adaptations and Affinities of Bronze Age Harappans," *Harappa Excavations 1986-1990*, ed. Richard H. Meadow (Madison, Wis.: Prehistory Press, 1991), 137-82; Brian E. Hemphill and John R. Lukacs, "Hegelian Logic and the Harappan Civilization: An Investigation of Harappan Biological Affinities in Light of Recent Biological and Archaeological Research," in *South Asian Archaeology, 1991*, ed. Adalbert J. Gail and Gerd J. R. Mevissen (Stuttgart: Steiner, 1993); Kenneth A. R. Kennedy, "Have Aryans Been Identified in the Prehistoric Skeletal Record from South Asia?" *The Indo-Aryans of Ancient South Asia: Language, Material Culture and Ethnicity*, ed. George Erdosy (Berlin: de Gruyter, 1995), 32-66.

14. Jarrige, "The Final Phase of the Indus Occupation at Naushāro."

15. Jim G. Shaffer, "The Indus Valley, Baluchistan and Helmand Traditions: Neolithic Through Bronze Age," in *Chronologies in Old World Archaeology*, ed. R. Ehrich, 3rd ed. (Chicago: University of Chicago Press, 1992), 441-64.

16. Madho Sarup Vats, *Excavations at Harappa* (Delhi: Government of India Press, 1940), Pl. LXII, 13.

17. Giorgio Stacul, "Harappan Post Urban Evidence in the Swat Valley," in *Frontiers of the Indus Civilization*, ed. B. B. Lal and S. P. Gupta (New Delhi: Books and Books, 1984), 271-76.

18. Dikshit, "The Legacy of Indus Civilization in North India."

19. M. Rafique Mughal, "Jhukar and the Late Harappan Cultural Mosaic of the Greater Indus Valley," in *South Asian Archaeology, 1989*, ed. Catherine Jarrige (Madison, Wis.: Prehistory Press, 1992), 213-22.

20. Gregory L. Possehl and M. H. Raval, *Harappan Civilization and Rojdi* (New Delhi: Oxford and IBH and AIIS, 1989).

21. J. Mark Kenoyer, "Early City-States in South Asia: Comparing the Harappan Phase and the Early Historic Period," in *The Archaeology of City-States: Cross Cultural Approaches*, ed. Deborah L. Nichols and Thomas H. Charlton (Washinton D.C.: Smithsonian Institution Press, 1997), in press.

22. Jean-Marie Casal, "Recent Excavations at Pirak," *Archaeology* (October 1970): 343-44; Jean-François Jarrige and Marielle Santoni, *Fouilles de Pirak* (Paris: Diffusion de Boccard, 1979).

23. Jarrige, "Continuity and Change in the North Kachi Plain."

24. Jarrige, "Continuity and Change in the North Kachi Plain."

25. Jarrige, "The Final Phase of the Indus Occupation at Naushāro."

26. Bhan, "Late Harappan Gujarat"; Possehl, "The Harappan Civilization in Gujarat: The Sorath and Sindhi Harappans"; Possehl and Raval, *Harappan*

Civilization and Rojdi.

27. Kenoyer, "Early City-States in South Asia."

28. Kenoyer, "Interaction Systems, Specialized Crafts and Culture Change"; Shaffer and Lichtenstein, "Cultural Tradition and Palaeoethnicity in South Asian Archaeology."

29. Kenoyer, "Interaction Systems, Specialized Crafts and Culture Change"; Kenoyer, "Early City-States in South Asia."

30. Jarrige, "The Final Phase of the Indus Occupation at Nausharo."

31. Braj Basi Lal, "The Two Indian Epics vis-a-vis Archaeology," *Antiquity* 55 (1981): 27-34.

32. Shaffer, "Reurbanization: The Eastern Punjab and Beyond," 53-67; Jim G. Shaffer and Diane A. Lichtenstein, "Ethnicity and Change in the Indus Valley Cultural Tradition," in *Old Problems and New Perspectives in the Archaeology of South Asia*, ed. J. Mark Kenoyer (Madison, Wis.: UW-Madison Department of Anthropology, 1989), 117-26; George Erdosy, "The Prelude to Urbanization: Ethnicity and the Rise of late Vedic Chiefdoms," in *The Archaeology of Early Historic South Asia*, ed. Frank Raymond Allchin (Cambridge: Cambridge University Press, 1995), 73-98.

33. Kenoyer, "Early City-States in South Asia."

34. George Erdosy, "City States of North India and Pakistan at the Time of the Buddha," in *The Archaeology of Early Historic South Asia*, ed. Frank Raymond Allchin (Cambridge: Cambridge University Press, 1995), 99-122; Frank Raymond Allchin, ed., *The Archaeology of Early Historic South Asia* (Cambridge: Cambridge University Press, 1995).

35. Steven A. Weber, *Plants and Harappan Subsistence: An Example of Stability and Change from Rojdi* (New Delhi: Oxford and IBH, 1991); Steven A. Weber, "South Asian Archaeobotanical Variability," in *South Asian Archaeology, 1989*, ed. Catherine Jarrige (Madison, Wis.: Prehistory Press, 1992), 283-90.

36. Dilip K. Chakrabarti, "Distribution of Iron Ores and the Archaeological Evidence of Early Iron in India," *Journal of the Social and Economic History of the Orient* 20.2 (1977): 166-84.

37. Chakrabarti, "Distribution of Iron Ores and the Archaeological Evidence"; Dilip K. Chakrabarti, "Iron and Urbanization: An Examination of the Indian Context," *Puratattva* 15 (1984-85): 68-74; Dilip K. Chakrabarti, "The Beginning of Iron in India," *Antiquity* 50 (1976): 114-24, 150.

38. J. Mark Kenoyer, Massimo Vidale and Kuldeep K. Bhan, "Carnelian Bead Production in Khambhat India: An Ethnoarchaeological Study," in *Living Traditions: Studies in the Ethnoarchaeology of South Asia*, ed. Bridget Allchin (New Delhi: Oxford and IBH, 1994), 281-306.

39. Ravindra N. Singh, *Ancient Indian Glass: Archaeology and Technology* (Delhi: Parimal, 1989).

40. J. Mark Kenoyer, "Faience from the Indus Valley Civilization," *Ornament* 17.3 (1994): 36-39, 95.

41. Samarendra Nath Sen and Mamata Chaudhuri, *Ancient Glass and India* (New Delhi: Indian National Science Academy, 1985), 6-82.

42. Sen and Chaudhuri, *Ancient Glass and India*, 6-82.

43. Sen and Chaudhuri, *Ancient Glass and India*, 6-82.

44. J. Mark Kenoyer, "Shell Working Industries of the Indus Civilization: An Archaeological and Ethnographic Perspective," Ph.D. diss., University of California at Berkeley, 1983.

45. V. B. Mainkar, "Metrology in the Indus Civilization," in *Frontiers of the Indus Civilization*, ed. B. B. Lal and S. P. Gupta (New Delhi: Books and Books, 1984), 141-51; Saradha Srinivasan, *Mensuration in Ancient India* (Delhi: Ajanta, 1979).

46. Purushottam Singh, "The Narhan Hoard of Punch Marked Coins (A Preliminary Report)," in *The 10th International Congress of Numismatics in London*, ed. I. A. Carradice (London: International Association of Professional Numismatics, 1986), 465-69; Kameshwar Prasad, *Cities, Crafts and Commerce under the Kusanas* (Delhi: Agam Kala Prakashan, 1984); Kunwar Deo Prasad, *Taxation in Ancient India: From the Earliest Times up to the Guptas* (Delhi: Mittal, 1987).

47. Michael Witzel, "Rgvedic History: Poets, Chieftans and Polities," in *The Indo-Aryans of Ancient South Asia: Language, Material Culture and Ethnicity*, ed. George Erdosy (Berlin: de Gruyter, 1995), 307-352.

48. Braj Basi Lal and K. N. Dikshit, "The Giant Tank of Shringaverapura," in *The Illustrated London News* (January 1982): 59.

Catalogue

Cat. no. 1. (also text figure 2.7)

Female figurine with elaborate coiffure and ornaments. The arms are tucked beneath the breasts, and the body is bent at the knees. Layers of graduated necklaces adorn the neck and breasts. The hair is piled up in two massive bunches on either side of the head. No traces of pigment remain on this example, but other figurines from Mehrgarh have hair painted with black or red (henna?) and the ornaments often are painted red and yellow, possibly representing carnelian and gold or polished bronze. The eyes are punctated and the ornaments and hair are all appliqué. Mehrgarh, Period VI, ca. 3000 B.C.

Material: terracotta
Dimensions: 9.48 cm height, 3.08 cm width
Mehrgarh, MRF 9c, 4 76-93
Islamabad Museum, EB 1005
Jarrige, C. 1988: 65-70

Cat. no. 2. (also text figure 2.19)

Female figurine with arms tucked beneath the breast and body bent as if seated. The hair is painted black and parted in the middle of the forehead, with traces of red pigment in the part. This form of ornamentation may be the origin of the later Hindu tradition where a married woman wears a streak of vermilion or powdered cinnabar (sindur) in the part of her hair.

The choker and pendant necklace are also painted with red pigment, possibly representing carnelian beads. Other figurines of similar design have yellow pigment on the disc-shaped ornaments at the shoulder, possibly representing gold or polished bronze brooches. The eyes are punctated and the ornaments and hair are all appliqué. This figurine comes from Nausharo, Period IB, but it is identical to many figurines from Mehrgarh Period VII, dating between 2800 and 2600 B.C.

Material: terracotta
Dimensions: 11.6 cm height, 30.9 cm width
Nausharo, NS 91.01.32.01
Department of Archaeology, Karachi, EBK 7416
Jarrige 1988: 87, fig. 41

Cat. no. 1. (also text figure 2.7)

Cat. no. 2. (also text figure 2.19)

Cat. no. 3.

Standing male figurine with turban and long hair. Long almond-shaped eyes with punctated pupils are lined with black pigment, simulating kohl or eyeliner. Stylized chest and nipples are applied to the core of the body, and the separate legs are joined at the waist. A narrow belt at the waist may be holding up trousers that are gathered at the calf. The red brown painted hat or turban wraps to the back and hangs down on one side. Reddish brown pigment covers the face, hair and arms, while the trousers and feet are painted a darker red brown. Black smudges on the hair may be remains of pigment or the result of burning. This figurine was found with seven others in a burned room of Nausharo, Period ID, dating between 2600 and 2500 B.C.

Material: terracotta
Dimensions: 12.84 cm height, 5.72 cm width, 2.17 cm thickness
Nausharo, I 87 15 i
Department of Archaeology, Karachi, EBK 5779
Jarrige, C. in Jarrige 1988: 193-95, fig. XXIV, b6; Samzun 1992: 245-52, fig. 29.5, 1

Cat. no. 3.

Cat. no. 4. (also text figure 2.20)

Male figurine wearing an elaborate headdress and carrying a male infant. The headdress is bordered by large disc-shaped ornaments similar to many female headdresses of the same time period. The headband is painted red; the hair and face are painted red brown. Long almond-shaped eyes are lined with black pigment. The chest and small nipples are applied to the core of the body. This figure wears trousers gathered at the calf. The infant wears a turban or cap similar to the larger male figurine in cat. no. 3. Eyebrows and long almond-shaped eyes are painted black. This figurine was found with seven others in a burned room of Nausharo, Period ID, dating between 2600 and 2500 B.C.

Material: terracotta
Dimensions: 12.42 cm height, 5.09 cm width, 2.14 cm thickness
Nausharo, NS 87
Islamabad Museum, EBK 5784
Jarrige, C. in Jarrige 1988: 193-95, fig. XXIV, b1; Samzun 1992: 245-52, fig. 29.5, 5

Cat. no. 5.

Young boy figurine dressed and painted in a manner almost identical to the larger male figurine of cat. no. 3. The turban or cap is painted black; the eyes and eye brows are heavily outlined with black paint. Long black hair hangs down to the shoulder, and a yellow-colored slip covers the shoulder and upper body. This figurine is part of the group from a burned room of Nausharo, Period ID, dating between 2600 and 2500 B.C.

Material: terracotta
Dimensions: 8.5 cm height, 4.23 cm width, 1.41 cm thickness
Nausharo, NS 87.15-178
Department of Archaeology, Karachi, EBK 5782
Jarrige, C. in Jarrige 1988: 193-95, fig. XXIV, b8; Samzun 1992: 245-52, fig. 29.5, 3

Cat. no. 6. (also text figure 2.1)

Tall, flaring jar with discrete horizontal panels of geometric polychrome designs painted on a buff background. The horizontal lines and basic design shapes are painted with brown pigment and filled with white, red and brown black pigment. This style of pottery is generally referred to as the Kechi Beg style after the site where it was first encountered in the highlands of Baluchistan to the west. At Mehrgarh, this type of pottery is found during Period IV, ca. 3300 B.C.

Material: terracotta
Dimensions: 39 cm height, 23 cm dia.
Mehrgarh, MR.1. 10I/j CCXXXIV, 82.115.11
National Museum, Karachi, NMP 3879
Jarrige and Meadow 1980; Jarrige 1988: 103

Cat. no. 6. (also text figure 2.1)

Cat. no. .7. (also text figure 2.12)

Shallow bowl with swirling fish motif arranged in two panels. Three fish circle counterclockwise in the outer panel, and two fish circle in the same direction in the center panel. Water plants fill in the empty spaces, and a wavy line around the rim suggests that the whole scene is under water. Fired to a light gray color with gray black paint, this style of pottery is called Faiz Mohammed Gray Ware. Although this pottery is named after a site in Baluchistan to the west, it was actually produced in Mehrgarh and traded throughout the region during Period VII, ca. 2800-2600 B.C.

Material: terracotta
Dimensions: 3.7 cm height, 23.2 cm dia., 10 cm base dia.
Mehrgarh, MRK 3D, CXXXIX(3), 77-39
Islamabad Museum, EBK 2442
Jarrige et al. 1995:185, fig. 3.13a, 3.14b.

Cat. no. 4. (also text figure 2.20)

Cat. no. 5.

Cat. no. 7. (also text figure 2.12)

Cat. no. 8. (also text figure 2.18)

Large, painted storage jar with a humped bull tied to a pipal or sacred fig tree. A bird, possibly the egret, is sitting on the bull's back. Further along in the panel a wild goat is tied to a tree with ball-shaped leaves or fruit. The goat has alternating hatching to fill the body, while the humped bull is painted solid black. A geometric panel just below the rim has parallels to earlier pottery in this region and from the highlands of Baluchistan to the west. From shape and painted style, however, the vessel was clearly made at Nausharo. The designs were painted in a gray black pigment on top of a buff colored background. Found in burned rooms of Period ID (2600-2500 B.C.) along with several other jars that were painted with similar style and motifs.

Material: terracotta
Dimensions: 46 cm height, 35 cm maximum dia., 10 cm base dia.
Nausharo, NS I G.88.11
Quetta Museum, EBK 6430
Samzun 1992:248, fig. 29.3, no. 3.

Cat. no. 9. (also text figure 1.2)

Large square seal with humped-bull motif and Indus script. The humped-bull seals are generally quite large and carved with great detail. Six signs of the Indus script appear along the top of the seal, but no ritual offering stand is depicted. What appears to be a braided collar hangs from the back of the neck to the bottom of the dewlap. Magnificent curving horns grace the expressively carved face, and the heavy dewlap balances the powerful body. The two horns are shown as if viewed from the front, although the head and body of the bull are viewed from the side. The detail with which the muscles, genitalia, hooves and tail are carved attest to many hours of careful observation and a highly developed sense of style.

The curved edge of the seal may have been designed to accommodate stamping on the concave neck of large storage jars. Or the seal carver may have made a mistake and recarved

Cat. no. 8. (also text figure 2.18)

the head of the bull after scraping away the edge of the seal. This seal has not been fully fired or hardened and may represent an unfinished object. The boss on the back is broken.

Material: unfired tan steatite
Dimensions: 3.75 x 3.9 cm
Mohenjo-daro, B 588
Islamabad Museum, 50.236
Marshall 1931: pl. CXI, 337

Cat. no. 10. (also text figure 1.6)

Pendant or medallion pictures the unicorn combined with many sacred symbols of the Indus religion. The body of the figure has a kidney or womb-shaped symbol in its belly, the same motif is elaborated to form the frame for the pendant, which is also a common design for shell inlay (see cat. no. 110). Two leaf shapes of the sacred fig or pipal tree are depicted at the animal's shoulder and rump. A ritual offering stand is placed in front of the image. The deeply incised frame and the symbols on the unicorn would have been set with inlay.

Material: unfired tan steatite
Dimensions: 6.3 x 6.8 cm
Mohenjo-daro, DK 8063
National Museum, Karachi, 50.125
Mackay 1938: 546, pl. CXL, 59

Cat. no. 9. (also text figure 1.2)

Cat. no. 10. (also text figure 1.6)

Cat. no. 11. (also text figure 5.2)

Cat. no. 12. (also text figure 5.13)

Cat. no. 11. (also text figure 5.2)

Large square unicorn seal with perforated boss on the back. A relatively long inscription of eight symbols runs along the top of the seal. The elongated body and slender arching neck is typical of unicorn figurines, as are the tail with bushy end and the bovine hooves. This figure has three incised lines depicting a pipal leaf-shaped blanket or halter, while most unicorn figures have only a double incised line. The arching horn is shown as if spiraling or ribbed, and the jowl is incised with multiple folds. A collar or additional folds encircle the throat. In front of the unicorn is a ritual offering stand with droplets of water or sacred liquid along the bottom of the bowl. The top portion of the stand renders a square grid or sieve that actually may have been a circular cylinder.

Material: fired white, hardened steatite
Dimensions: 5.08 x 5.08 cm
Mohenjo-daro, HR 743
National Museum, Karachi, NMP 50.192
Marshall 1931: pl. CIII, 8

Cat. no. 12. (also text figure 5.13)

Medium-sized square unicorn seal with perforated boss on the back. The face of the unicorn is deeply carved, and the head is not raised as high as on some examples. The double line of the halter or blanket is also clearly depicted, as is the bushy end of the tail. A ritual offering stand is situated in front of the unicorn, and five signs of the Indus script are carved above it. The right-hand sign shows a rare figure with square ankle bracelets on each leg.

Material: fired white, hardened steatite
Dimensions: 2.6 x 2.5 cm, 0.71 cm thickness
Harappa, Lot 14-01
Islamabad Museum, H87-262
Dales and Kenoyer 1989: fig. 59.2

Cat. no. 13. (also text figure 5.16)

Sealing or token with impression made from a unicorn seal with script. The back is smooth and rounded, suggesting that this object was a certificate or pass representing the seal owner and not something attached to a bundle of goods. Three script signs appear above a unicorn which stands facing right, with a ritual object or offering stand placed under the head.

Material: terracotta
Dimensions: 2.45 cm length, 2.14 cm width, 0.78 cm thickness
Mohenjo-daro, DK 12257
Mohenjo-daro Museum, MM 481, 50.409
Mackay 1938: pl. XCI, 22

Cat. no. 13. (also text figure 5.16)

Cat. no. 14.

Unfinished seal with unicorn outline lightly engraved. Traces of script outlines are visible above the animal motif. This unfinished piece came from a workshop area at Mohenjo-daro where many other partly finished seals were discovered.

Material: unfired gray steatite
Dimensions: 2.7 x 2.95 cm
Mohenjo-daro
National Museum, Karachi, NMP 1995.246
Sharif 1990: 16, pl. IA

Cat. no. 14.

Cat. no. 15. (also text figures 5.2 and 5.8)

Square seal with rhinoceros motif and script. A feeding trough or ritual object is sometimes shown in front of this wild animal but not on this seal. The back has a perforated boss.

Material: fired white, hardened steatite
Dimensions: 3.8 x 3.8 cm, 0.8 cm thickness
Mohenjo-daro, DK 7462
National Museum, Karachi, NMP 50.273
Mackay 1938: 330-1, pl. XCIX, 651

Cat. no. 15. (also text figures 5.2 and 5.8)

Cat. no. 16. (also text figure 5.2)

Square seal with elephant motif and script. A feeding trough is sometimes depicted in front of this wild animal but not on this seal. The back has a perforated boss.

Material: fired white, hardened steatite
Dimensions: 2.58 x 2.63 cm, 0.77 to 0.9 cm thickness
Mohenjo-daro, DK 5848
Mohenjo-daro Museum, 50.264, MD 151
Mackay 1938: 329, pl. XCVII, 590

Cat. no. 16. (also text figure 5.2)

Cat. no. 17. (also text figures 5.2 and 5.9)

Seal with water buffalo, standing with upraised head and both horns clearly visible. This posture is typical of all water buffalo seals except when they are depicted attacking or being sacrificed (cat. no. 27). A feeding trough is placed in front of the animal, and a double row of script fills the entire space above it. The horns are incised to show the natural growth lines on water buffalo horns.

Material: unfired gray steatite
Dimensions: 2.79 x 2.79 cm, 0.5 cm thickness
Mohenjo-daro, SD 2697
National Museum, Karachi, MM 50.279
Mackay 1938: 330, pl. LXXXII, 696

Cat. no. 18. (also text figure 5.10)

Flat square double-sided seal. On one side, four script signs are inscribed in reverse, above a short-horned bull with head lowered to the feeding trough. A swastika motif turning counterclockwise is shown on the reverse. The seal is perforated from the side along the axis of the animal motif.

Material: unfired gray brown steatite
Dimensions: 2.04 x 2.04 cm, 0.74 cm thickness
Mohenjo-daro, HR 4503
Mohenjo-daro Museum, 50.258, MM 487
Marshall 1931: pl. CX, 311

Cat. no. 19.

Square seal with antelope motif and two signs of script. The forward-arching horns are not known to occur on any South Asian antelope or gazelle. A ritual offering stand is placed in front of the figure.

Material: fired white, hardened steatite
Dimensions: 2.3 x 2.3 cm, 1.27 cm thickness
Chanhudaro, 1269
Museum of Fine Arts, Boston, MFA 36.971
Mackay 1943: pl. LI, 21

Cat. no. 17. (also text figures 5.2 and 5.9)

Cat. no. 18. (also text figure 5.10)

Cat. no. 19. Joint Expedition of the American School of Indic and Iranian Studies and the Museum of fine Arts, 1935-1936. © 1997 Museum of Fine Arts, Boston.

Cat. no. 20.

Cat. no. 20.

Long, rectangular seal with seven signs of Indus script. The back of this seal is convex, and it is perforated from the side. The central sign, which may represent a house or temple, is often repeated on seals with horned deities seated in yogic position. (See text figure 6.20)

Material: fired white, hardened steatite
Dimensions: ca. 3.74 cm length, 1.47 cm wide
Mohenjo-daro, DK 5567
National Museum, Karachi, NMP 50.315
Shah and Parpola 1991: M-1271

Cat. no. 21. (also text figure 5.18)

Seal depicting a high-prowed, flat-bottomed boat with central cabin and large double rudder. The back is broken along the lateral perforation but has an incised grid design on the remaining surface. This seal is unfired and may have been discarded due to cracks or breakage during the drilling process.

Material: unfired gray steatite
Dimensions: 3.33 cm length, 1.64 cm width, 8.5 cm thickness
Mohenjo-daro, DK 10355
Mohenjo-daro Museum, MM 489
Mackay 1938: pl. LXXXIII, 30

Cat. no. 22. (also text figure 5.11)

Three-sided molded tablet, with boat, gharial and script. One side is a flat-bottomed boat with a central hut that has leafy fronds at the top of two poles. Two birds sit on the deck, and a large double rudder extends from the rear of the boat. On the second side is a snout-nosed gharial with a fish in its mouth. The third side has eight signs of the Indus script.

Material: terracotta
Dimensions: 4.6 cm length, 1.2 x 1.5 cm width
Mohenjo-daro, MD 602
Islamabad Museum, NMP 1384
Dales 1965a: 147, 1968: 39

Cat. no. 21. (also text figure 5.18)

Cat. no. 23. (also text figure 6.19)

Square seal depicting a nude male deity with three faces, seated in yogic position on a throne, wearing bangles on both arms and an elaborate headdress. Five signs of the Indus script appear on either side of the headdress, which is made of two outward projecting buffalo style curved horns, with two upward projecting points. A single branch with three pipal leaves rises from the middle of the headdress. The figure wears seven bangles on the left arm and six on the right, with the hands resting on the knees. The heels are pressed together under the groin, and the feet project beyond the edge of the throne. The feet of the throne are carved with the hoof of a bovine as on the bull and unicorn seals. The seal may not have been fired, but the stone is very hard. A grooved and perforated boss is present on the back of the seal.

Material: unfired? tan steatite
Dimensions: 2.65 x 2.7 cm, 0.83 to 0.86 thickness
Mohenjo-daro, DK 12050
Islamabad Museum, NMP 50.296
Mackay 1938: 335, pl. LXXXVII, 222

Cat. no. 22. (also text figure 5.11)

Cat. no. 23. (also text figure 6.19)

Cat. no. 24. (also text figure 6.1)

Seal depicting a deity with horned headdress and bangles on both arms, standing in a pipal (sacred fig) tree and looking down on a kneeling worshiper. A human head rests on a small stool. A giant ram and seven figures in procession complete the narrative. The figures wear a single plumed headdress, bangles on both arms and long skirts. Several script signs are interspersed with the figures along the top of the seal, and a single sign is placed at the base of the tree. This scene may represent a special ritual sacrifice to a deity with seven figures in procession. The seal has a grooved and perforated boss, and the edges are worn and rounded from repeated use.

Material: fired tan steatite with traces of glaze
Dimensions: 4.06 x 3.95 cm, 0.8 cm thickness.
Mohenjo-daro DK 6847
Islamabad Museum, NMP 50.295
Mackay 1938: pl. XCIV, 430; pl. XCIX, 686a.

Cat. no. 24. (also text figure 6.1)

Cat. no. 25. (also text figure 6.5)

Square molded tablet with impressions on both faces. The obverse sealing has five script signs and shows a finely carved unicorn facing a ritual offering stand. On the reverse a deity stands under a curving arch that has thirteen pipal leaves. Each end of the arch terminates in a tight swirl. The figure wears bangles on both arms and hair in a long braid. A branch with three prongs or leaves rises from the top of the head.

Material: terracotta
Dimensions: 2.0 x 1.89 cm, 0.51 cm thickness
Harappa, Lot 5719-02
Harappa Museum, H95-2485
Meadow and Kenoyer 1997

Cat. no. 25. (also text figure 6.5)

Cat. no. 26. (also text figure 6.22)

Cat. no. 26. (also text figure 6.22)

Square seal depicting a human figure in tree and a tiger looking back over its shoulder from below. The figure has hair tied in a double bun on the back of the head and sits on a branch with one knee raised. One hand securely holds the tree as the other gestures towards the tiger. A partial script sign is visible at the broken edge of the seal. A grooved and perforated boss is present on the back of the seal.

Material: unfired gray steatite
Dimensions: 1.93 x 1.97 cm, 0.55 to 0.65 thickness
Mohenjo-daro, D392
National Museum, Karachi, 50.282
Marshall 1931: 387-8, pl. CXI, 353

Cat. no. 27. (also text figure 6.24)

Planoconvex molded tablet shows female deity battling two tigers and standing above an elephant. A single Indus script sign depicting a spoked wheel is above the head of the deity. On the reverse is an individual spearing a water buffalo with one foot pressing the head down and one arm holding the tip of a horn. A gharial is pictured above the sacrifice scene; a figure seated in yogic position wearing a horned headdress looks on. The horned headdress has a branch with three prongs or leaves emerging from the center.

Material: terracotta
Dimensions: 3.91 length, 1.5 to 1.62 cm width
Harappa, Lot 4651-01
Harappa Museum, H95-2486
Meadow and Kenoyer 1997

Cat. no. 28. (also text figure 6.23)

Square seal with horned tiger motif. No ritual offering stand is shown with this figure, but two signs of script are carved above the back of the tiger, which has its head raised. The curved horns are like those on the bull figures (cat. no. 9) and correspond to the short, incurving horns depicted on the miniature terracotta masks (cat. nos. 122, 123).

Material: fired tan steatite with traces of glaze
Dimensions: 2.5 x 2.4 cm, 0.6 cm thickness
Mohenjo-daro, DK 12897
National Museum, Karachi, NMP 50.293
Mackay 1938: pl. LXXXIX, 360

Cat. no. 29. (also text figure 6.30)

Square seal with animal whose multiple-heads include three important totemic animals: the bull, the unicorn and the antelope. All three animals appear individually on other seals along with script, but this seal has no script. The perforated boss on the back is plain, without the groove found on most seals. It is possible that this is a specific style of boss similar to the small seal from Miri Qalat (cat. no. 35).

Material: unfired gray brown steatite
Dimensions: 2.4 x 2.4 cm, 0.53 cm thickness
Mohenjo-daro, DK 7734
Islamabad Museum, NMP 50.289
Mackay 1938: pl. XCVI, 494

Cat. no. 30. (also text figure 6.31)

Square seal with multiple creatures combined to make a single animal. The rounded human face has an elephant's trunk and a draping beard or tusk. A pair of inward curving, ribbed horns rises above the head, and a heavy mane like we see on the large Markhor goats hangs from the neck. The front hooves and genitalia are similar to those on bull and unicorn figures, but the back feet and haunches are those of a striped tiger. Finally, the tail is depicted as an upraised cobra. There is no ritual offering stand, but four script signs are incised above the back of the creature.

Material: fired white, black steatite
Dimensions: 1.3 x 1.3 cm, 1.4 thickness with knob
Mohenjo-daro, DK 6658
Lahore Museum, L. P-1727
Shah and Parpola 1991: M-1177

Cat. no. 27. (also text figure 6.24)

Cat. no. 28. (also text figure 6.23)

Cat. no. 29. (also text figure 6.30)

Cat. no. 30. (also text figure 6.31)

Cat. no. 31.

Flat rectangular tablet with incised script on one side and a two-headed animal design on the other. The animal heads have two short horns; the long necks show many folds and the front haunches are spotted. The only short-horned animal with this build is a large antelope known as a nilgai or "blue bull." It is possible that this figure depicts two superimposed animals standing head to tail in a watchful stance.

Material: copper
Dimensions: 3.4 x 2.2 cm, 0.25 cm thickness
Mohenjo-daro, VS 983
Mohenjo-daro Museum, MM 546
Marshall 1931: 399, pl. CXVII, 3
Shah and Parpola 1991: M-1534

Cat. no. 31.

Cat. no. 32.

Flat rectangular tablet with script incised on one side and a long-necked animal on the other. This animal resembles a dromedary or one-humped camel, but no bones or figurines of this type of camel have been recovered from sites of the Indus Valley. Perhaps this drawing was made by someone who had seen dromedary camels in the Arabian Gulf.

Material: copper
Dimensions: 3.2 x 2.2 cm, 0.25 cm thickness
Mohenjo-daro
Mohenjo-daro Museum, MM 538
Shah and Parpola 1991: M-1532

Cat. no. 32.

Cat. no. 33. (also text figure 6.8)

Flat square tablet with incised script on one side and the endless-knot motif on the reverse. The endless-knot motif is found on several rectangular tablets, and other versions of this design appear on clay sealings and tablets.

Material: copper
Dimensions: 2.84 x 2.67 cm, 0.3 cm thickness
Mohenjo-daro, DK 3696
Mohenjo-daro Museum, MD 50.420, MM 554
Mackay 1938: 364, pl. XCIII, 4
Shah and Parpola 1991: M-1457

Cat. no. 33. (also text figure 6.8)

Cat. no. 34. (also text figure 6.9)

Square button seal with swastika design turning counterclockwise. Because it was originally covered with a glaze that would have flattened the surface and provided little or no relief, this seal may not have been used for stamping but simply as an ornament or button. The back has a perforated boss.

Material: yellow faience
Dimensions: 1.78 x 1.62 cm
Mohenjo-daro
National Museum, Karachi, NMP 1985.302

Cat. no. 35.

Square seal with incised swastika motif. The swastika is turning clockwise but when impressed would be turning counterclockwise. A simple perforated boss is carved on the back.

Material: fired white, hardened steatite
Dimensions: 1.2 x 1.2 cm, 0.31 cm thickness
Miri Qalat, Baluchistan
Department of Archaeology, Karachi, EBK 1/92/I 59.636
Besenval 1994: 89

Cat. no. 36.

Square seal with incised stepped-cross motif and four dots in the corners. A simple perforated boss is carved on the back.

Material: steatite
Dimensions: 1.6 x 1.6 cm, 0.4 cm thickness
Harappa, 13797
National Museum, Karachi, NMP 52.3015
Shah and Parpola 1991: H-631

Cat. no. 34. (also text figure 6.9)

Cat. no. 35.

Cat. no. 36.

Cat. no. 37. (also text figure 4.19)

Finely made bangle with red script painted on interior. The wide brushstrokes used to paint the two script signs reflect the skill of someone who habitually used a brush. A single wide band of black paint runs around the exterior edge of the bangle. Both the red script and the black band were applied prior to firing.

Material: terracotta
Dimensions: 8.57 cm dia., 3.53 cm thickness
Balakot, 3 BLK-189/326
Department of Archaeology, Karachi, EBK 1344

Cat. no. 38. (also text figure 4.20)

Inscribed rod with double bands of hatching at each end. The seven script signs inscribed from right to left were not used for making an impression. Traces of vermilion pigment fill all the incised lines.

Material: bone
Dimensions: 7.25 cm length, 0.7 - 0.8 cm dia
Mohenjo-daro
National Museum, Karachi, MM 412
Dales 1967: 38

Cat. no. 39. (also text figure 4.17)

Needlelike pendant, with script incised around the tapered cylindrical body. Scholars originally interpreted the faint incising as teeth marks and thought the object was used as a needle. Two other examples, one with a different series of incised signs, were found together. The pendant is made from a hollow cylinder with soldered ends and perforated point. Hoard No. 2, DK Area, Room 1, House 1, Trench E.

Material: gold
Dimensions: 4.16 cm length, 0.66 cm base dia., 0.13 cm hole dia.
Mohenjo-daro E 2044 b
Mohenjo-daro Museum, MM 1374, 50.271
Marshall 1931:521, pl. CLI, B 3

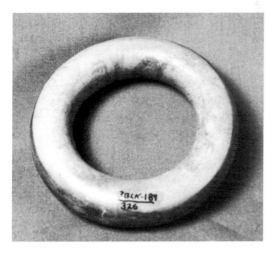

Cat. no. 37. (also text figure 4.19)

Cat. no. 38. (also text figure 4.20)

Cat. no. 39. (also text figure 4.17)

Cat. no. 40.

Cubical weights in graduated sizes. These weights conform to the standard Harappan binary weight system that was used in all of the settlements. The smallest weight in this series is 0.856 grams; the most common weight is approximately 13.7 grams, which is the 16th ratio. In the large weights the system becomes a decimal increase where the largest weight is 100 times the weight of the 16th ratio in the binary system. At Chanhudaro the largest cubical weight is 1330.68 grams, which is 40 grams short of the official standard. Obviously someone was losing out when using this weight.

Material: chert, agate
Dimensions: maximum widths - 36.2297, 0.7 cm; 36.2299, 1.0 cm; 36.2305, 1.12 cm; 36.2308, 1.5 cm; 36.2316, 1.9 cm; 36.2307, 1.6 cm; 36.2322, 2.4 cm; 36.2274, 8.6 cm.
Chanhudaro, various contexts
Museum of Fine Arts, Boston, MFA 36.2274, 36.2297, 36.2299, 36.2305, 36.2308, 36.2316, 36.2322, 36.2325, 36.2328, 36.3000.
Mackay 1943: 239-46, pl. XCI 29-32

Cat. no. 40. Joint Expedition of the American School of Indic and Iranian Studies and the Museum of fine Arts, 1935-1936.
© 1997 Museum of Fine Arts, Boston.

Cat. no. 41.

Truncated spherical weights and barrel-shaped weights. Although made in a different shape, these weights also conform to the standard Indus system. In this collection the small agate weight is 27.36 grams, which is the 32nd ratio. The two larger weights are 273.59 grams (320th ratio) and 544.77 grams (640th ratio) respectively.

Material: porphyry, agate, sandstone
Dimensions: dia. x height - 36.2337, 2.9 x 1.8 cm; 36.2336, 2.8 x 1.8 cm; 36.2276, 4.5 x 32 cm; 36.277, 7.2 x 6.1 cm
Chanhudaro, various contexts
Museum of Fine Arts, Boston, MFA 36.2337, 36.2336, 36.2276, 36.2277
Mackay 1943: 239-46, pl. LXXXIX, 10; XCI, 27, 28

Cat. no. 41. Joint Expedition of the American School of Indic and Iranian Studies and the Museum of fine Arts, 1935-1936. © 1997 Museum of Fine Arts, Boston.

Cat. no. 42. (also text figure 4.18)

Cat. no. 42. (also text figure 4.18)

Ax with inscription. This large ax may never have been intended for use and possibly was made for ritual presentation. It could have been hafted vertically as an ax or transversely as an adze. Similar tools have been found at most Indus sites and reflect a unique style of cutting tool.

Material: copper/bronze
Dimensions: 28.3 cm, 7.2 to 10.3 cm width
Mohenjo-daro, DK 7535
National Museum, Karachi, NMP 50.990
Mackay 1938: 454, pl. CXXVI, 5

Cat. no. 43. (also text figure 8.25)

Spear point with flat blade and tang, with no central rib. Most spears of the Indus culture were made without pronounced central thickening to support the blade on impact. Without a central rib, the blades would buckle on impact; this feature has led to the assumption that they were not specialized offensive weapons.

Material: copper/bronze
Dimensions: 18.6 cm length, 5.9 cm width
Mohenjo-daro?
National Museum, Karachi, NMP 51.987
Mackay 1938: 459-460

Cat. no. 44. (also text figure 8.25)

Dagger with tapering blade and long tang. Sharpened along one edge and both edges at the tip, this weapon also has no pronounced thickening as would daggers used in battle. This dagger was found inside a bronze cooking pot (cat. no. 197) along with many other weapons and tools, thought to be the hoard of a copper merchant.

Material: copper/bronze
Dimensions: 17.9 cm length, 4.5 cm width
Harappa 277 f/2
National Museum, Karachi, NMP 54.271
Vats 1940: 87, pl. CXXIII, 30.

Cat. no. 44. (also text figure 8.25)   Cat. no. 43. (also text figure 8.25)

Cat. no. 45. (also text figure 5.17)

Toy cart with wheels. Holes along the length of the cart held wooden side bars, and at the center of the cart two wooden side bars could be extended below the frame to hold the axle. A long stick inserted into the holes at the end of the cart would have been used to support a yoke. The two wheels were found lying next to the cart frame. The wood fittings are modern. Period III, Harappan, 2300-2200 B.C.

Material: terracotta
Dimensions: cart, 17 cm length, 8 cm width, 1.2 cm thickness; wheel, 7 cm dia., 1.2 cm thickness
Nausharo, NS/88/IV
Department of Archaeology, Karachi, EBK 6916
Jarrige 1989: XVa

Cat. no. 46.

Cart with roof and side panels. A short ledge in front serves as a seat for the driver. Probably made by lost-wax casting. A second cart with driver was found at Chanhudaro, and similar carts have been recovered from Harappa.

Material: copper/bronze
Dimensions: 4.3 cm length, 6.1 cm height, 2.8 cm width
Chanhudaro, 2291
Museum of Fine Arts, Boston, MFA 36.2237
Mackay 1943: pl. LVIII. 2

Cat. no. 46. Joint Expedition of the American School of Indic and Iranian Studies and the Museum of fine Arts, 1935-1936. © 1997 Museum of Fine Arts, Boston.

Cat. no. 45.
(also text figure 5.17)

Cat. no. 47. (also text figure 1.5)

Carnelian and copper/bronze necklace or belt. The metal has not been analyzed and some of the components may be copper, while other pieces may be bronze. This ornament has 42 long biconical carnelian beads, 72 spherical bronze beads, 6 bronze spacer beads, 2 half moon-shaped bronze terminals, and 2 hollow cylindrical bronze terminals. Hoard No. 2, DK Area, Room 1, House 1, Trench E.

Material: carnelian, copper/bronze
Dimensions: carnelian beads range from 8.22 cm to 12.4 cm length, 0.9 cm maximum dia.; bronze beads ca. 86 cm length, .85 cm dia.; bronze spacer beads 0.2 cm length, 0.63 cm width, 6.2 cm height; bronze moon-shaped terminal 3.9 cm length, 0.8 cm thickness, 6.1 cm height; bronze hollow terminal, 2.39 cm length, 1.0 cm maximum dia.

Mohenjo-daro
Mohenjo-daro Museum, MM 1121
Marshall 1931: 520, pl. CLI, B 10

Cat. no. 47b.

Marshall 1931, vol. 3, pl. CLI. Gold and carnelian ornaments from Mohenjo-daro, cat. no. 47; gold pendant, cat. no. 39 (on right) and ear ornament, cat. no. 59 (on left).

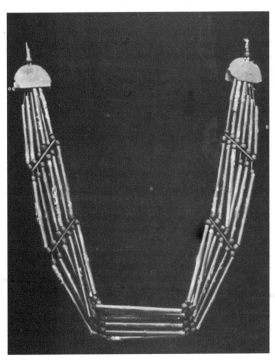

Cat. no. 47a. (also text figure 1.5)

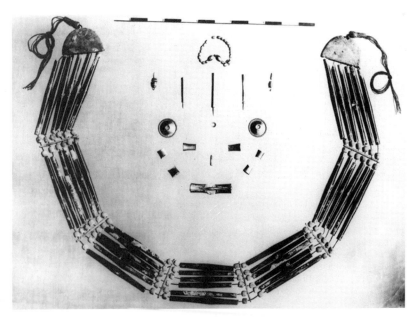

Cat. no. 47b.

Cat. no. 48. (also text figure 7.30)

Necklace or belt of carnelian and copper/bronze beads; 36 long bicone carnelian beads; original bronze beads and terminals are badly corroded. This belt was found in a small terracotta jar along with silver necklaces (cat. no. 49), silver rings (cat. no. 50), agate beads and gold ornaments (cat. no. 51).

Material: carnelian
Dimensions: carnelian beds range from 6.5 to 10 cm length, 0.9 cm maximum dia.
Allahdino
Department of Archaeology, Karachi, EBK 2076 to 2081,2090(B)

Cat. no. 49. (also text figure 7.30)

Necklace made of 8 silver discs and triple strands of silver beads with 3-holed spacer beads. The central component or possibly the clasp is a moon-shaped piece with two hollow terminals.

Material: silver
Dimensions: discs, 3.8 x 3.9 cm; moon-shaped piece, 5.1 cm length, beads range from 1 cm to 2 cm in length; spacer beads 0.25 length, 0.96 width
Allahdino
Department of Archaeology, Karachi, EBK 2069, 2070, 2071, 2072, 2073, 2109, 2110, 2100(A-N)

Cat. no. 50. (also text figure 7.30)

Coiled silver wire toe rings or finger rings made of between 14 and 16 spirals of wire.
Material: silver
Dimensions: ca. 1.5 cm dia., wire is 0.1 to 0.13 cm thickness
Allahdino
Department of Archaeology, Karachi, EBK 2101, 2102, 2103, 2104, 2105

Cat. no. 51. (also text figure 7.30)

Crumpled gold fillets and various pieces of gold ornaments in different stages of recycling. Paper-thin hollow beads or ear ornaments have been folded into little triangular pieces, lumps of melted or hammered gold are the result of melting such pieces.

Material: gold
Dimensions: various measurements
Allahdino
Department of Archaeology, Karachi, EBK 2107

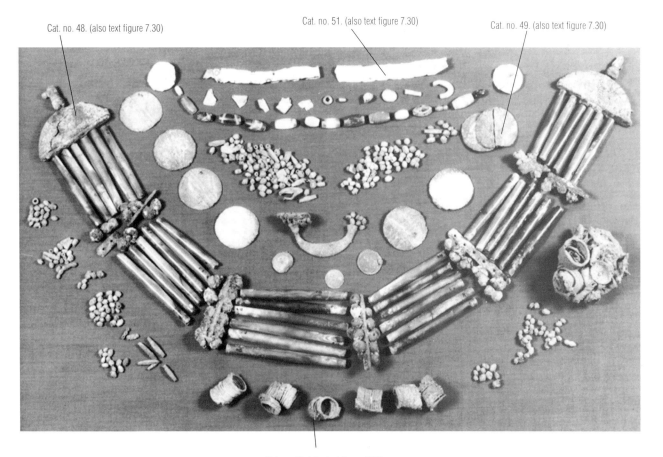

Cat. no. 48. (also text figure 7.30)

Cat. no. 51. (also text figure 7.30)

Cat. no. 49. (also text figure 7.30)

Cat. no. 50. (also text figure 7.30)

Cat. no. 52. (also text figures 7.31 and 7.32)

Straight gold fillet or headband with holes at both ends for holding a cord. Each end of the fillet is decorated with a punctated design depicting the ritual offering stand that is common on the unicorn seals. Finely burnished gold with no traces of hammer marks.

Material: gold
Dimensions: 42 cm length, 1.4 cm width
Mohenjo-daro, VS 3091
Mohenjo-daro Museum, MM 1366
Marshall 1931: 220, 527, pl. CXVIII, 14 (for punctated design)

Cat. no. 53. (also text figure 7.38)

Curved gold fillet with holes at center and ends for holding a cord. This ornament was probably worn with the center point at the top of the forehead and the sides curving down over the eyebrows. Finely burnished gold with no traces of hammer marks. Hoard No. 3, HR Area, Room 8, House VIII, Block 2, Section B.

Material: gold
Dimensions: 27.8 cm length, 1.0 cm wide, gold sheet is 0.016 cm thickness
Mohenjo-daro, HR 4212 a (q)
Mohenjo-daro Museum, MM 1364, 50.28/8
Marshall 1931: pl. CLI, A 6

Cat. no. 54. (also text figure 7.33)

Necklace with pendant beads made from blue green faience, turquoise, bleached agate and gold. This necklace fragment is only half of the original ornament which was divided between India and Pakistan in 1947. Hoard No. 3, HR Area, Room 8, House VIII, Block 2, Section B.

Material: gold, agate, turquoise, faience
Dimensions: 8.23 cm length
Mohenjo-daro, HR 4212 a (f)
Mohenjo-daro Museum, MM 1375
Marshall 1931: pl. CXLIX, 4 (complete necklace)

Cat. no. 54b.

Marshall 1931: pl. CXLIX. Complete ornaments from Mohenjo-daro as reconstructed after excavation; cat. no. 57 (top), cat. no. 54 (second from top), cat. no. 58 (fourth from top), cat no. 56 (bottom).

Cat. no. 52. (also text figures 7.31 and 7.32)

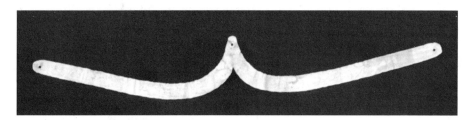

Cat. no. 53. (also text figure 7.38)

Cat. no. 54. (also text figure 7.33)

Cat. no. 54b.

Cat. no. 55. (also text figure 7.5)

Necklace made from gold, agate, jasper, steatite and green stone (lizardite or grossular garnet). The gold beads are hollow, and the pendant agate and jasper beads are attached with thick gold wire. Steatite beads with gold caps separate each of the pendant beads. This necklace fragment is only half of the original ornament, which was divided between India and Pakistan in 1947. Hoard No. 1, found in a silver vessel in DK Area, Room 2, eastern end of Block 16, Section B and C.

Material: gold, green stone (lizardite or grossular garnet, originally reported as jade)
Dimensions: green stone beads: 2.0 cm length, 1.0 cm dia., gold beads 0.44 cm length, 1.0 cm dia.
Mohenjo-daro DK 1541
Mohenjo-daro Museum, MM 1367
Marshall 1931: pl. CXLVIII, A 6

Cat. no. 55b.

Marshall 1931: pl. CXLVIII. Complete necklace from Mohenjo-daro, cat. no. 55, as reconstructed after excavation.

Cat. no. 56. (also text figure 7.34)

Necklace made up of paper-thin flat gold disc beads, interspersed with beads of onyx, amazonite (microcline), turquoise and banded agate. Some beads have gold finials, and additional small spherical gold beads are used as spacers. This necklace fragment is only half of the original ornament, which was divided between India and Pakistan in 1947. Hoard No. 3, HR Area, Room 8, House VIII, Block 2, Section B.

Material: gold, onyx, amazonite (microcline), turquoise, banded agate
Dimensions: gold disc beads - 1.49 cm length, 1.42 cm width
Mohenjo-daro, HR 4212 a (d)
Mohenjo-daro Museum, MM 1369
Marshall 1931: pl. CXLIX, 7 (complete necklace)

Cat. no. 57. (also text figure 7.31)

Beaded choker necklace with six rows of beads with divider bars and half moon-shaped terminal. This fragment is only half of the original ornament, which was divided between India and Pakistan in 1947. Hoard No. 3, HR Area, Room 8, House VIII, Block 2, Section B.

Material: gold
Dimensions: 6.68 cm length, 0.26 thickness, gold beads - 0.3 cm length, 0.27 cm dia.
Mohenjo-daro, HR 4212 a (e)
Mohenjo-daro Museum, MM 1383, 50.28/2
Marshall 1931: 522, pl. CXLIX, 3 (complete necklace)

Cat. no. 55. (also text figure 7.5)

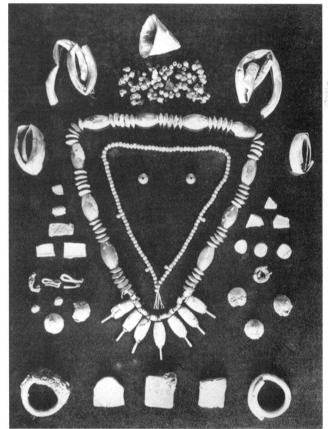

Cat. no. 55b.

Cat. no. 56. (also text figure 7.35)

Cat. no. 57. (also text figure 7.31)

Cat. no. 58. (also text figure 7.31)

Necklace made with five strands of tiny beads of gold, faience and steatite. The strands are separated by divider bars and pulled together in semicircular terminals. Hoard No. 3, HR Area, Room 8, House VIII, Block 2, Section B.

Material: gold, faience, fired steatite
Dimensions: ca. 23 cm length
Mohenjo-daro, HR 4212a (I)
Mohenjo-daro Museum, MM 1370, 50.28/1
Marshall 1931: 523, pl. CXLIX, 6

Cat. no. 59. (also text figure 7.37)

Double spiral brooch with steatite and gold inlay. The spiral design is made with two lines of blue black glazed steatite and gold bead inlay. These pieces are set with mastic in a frame made from a sheet of gold or electrum and three soldered gold bands.

Material: gold, dark glazed steatite
Dimensions: 6.6 cm length, 3.25 cm width, 0.31 cm thickness
Harappa, 8060 e
Mohenjo-daro Museum, MM 1376, 50.22/2
Vats, 1940: 64, similar to pl. CXXXVII, 15

Cat. no. 60. (also text figure 7.36)

Ear ornament (one of pair), dome-shaped with circular depression in center for inlay. The ribbed edging is made of chiseled wire and soldered onto the body of the ornament. The hollow post is tightly fitted and joined with mastic. Hoard No. 2, DK Area, Room 1, House 1, Trench E.

Material: gold
Dimensions: 2.87 cm dia., 0.64 height, post is 1.3 cm long and 0.57 cm dia.
Mohenjo-daro DK 2044
Mohenjo-daro Museum, MM 1378
Marshall 1931: 253, 521, pl. CLI, B 7

Cat. no. 61. (also text figure 7.38)

Hollow gold cap-shaped ornaments with tiny loops on the inside of the tip. The loops could be used to attach the ornament to clothing or as a hair ornament. At Harappa, 54 small gold caps were found in a hoard of gold jewelry from Mound F, Trench IV, House 2. A much larger gold cap was also discovered that may have been worn as a conical forehead ornament as shown on many terracotta figurines.

Material: gold
Dimensions: 1.17 cm dia., 0.64 cm height
Mohenjo-daro?, DK(i) 270 (possibly from Harappa as no such gold objects have been reported from Mohenjo-daro DK area)
Mohenjo-daro Museum, MM 1368
see Vats 1940: 64, pl. CXXXVII, 6 and 20

Cat. no. 61b.

Vats 1940: pl. CXXXVII. Gold and agate ornaments from Harappa, cat. no. 61 (bottom left and right).

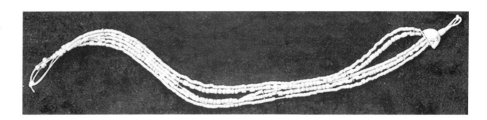

Cat. no. 58. (also text figure 7.34)

Cat. no. 59. (also text figure 7.36)   Cat. no. 60. (also text figure 7.37)

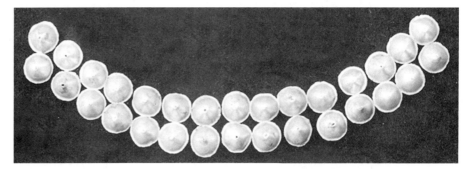

Cat. no. 61. (also text figure 7.38)

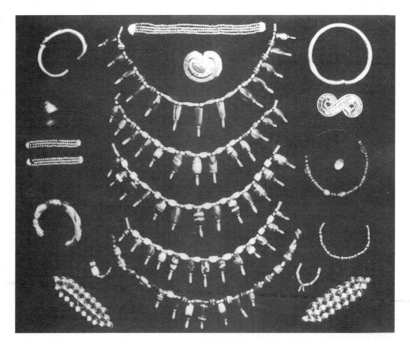

Cat. no. 61b. (also text figure 7.34)

Cat. no. 62. (also text figure 7.39)

Beads made in different shapes and designs to accentuate natural colors and banding. Small short bicone is a composite bead made of laminated shell and stone to imitate natural banded agate.

Material: agate, jasper, green serpentine
Dimensions: lengths range from 1.23 cm to 2.9 cm
Mohenjo-daro, various contexts
Mohenjo-daro Museum, MM 1119
Marshall 1931: pl. CL

Cat. no. 63. (also text figure 7.37)

Pendant or hair ornament made of carnelian and gold. The flat, drop-shaped carnelian inlay is held by a gold frame that has a deep channel on the exterior. Traces of black mastic present in the channel suggest that it once contained inlay, possibly tiny beads of steatite or faience.

Material: gold, carnelian
Dimensions: gold frame, 3.1 cm length, carnelian 2.37 cm length
Harappa, Lot 03-21
Harappa Museum, H87-203
Dales and Kenoyer 1989

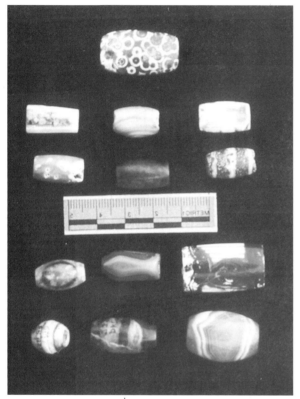

Cat. no. 62. (also text figure 7.39)

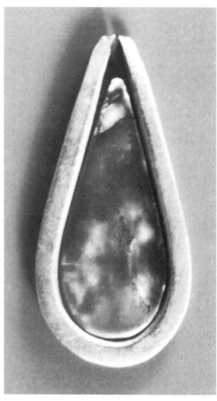

Cat. no. 63. (also text figure 7.37)

Cat. no. 64. (also text figure 6.45)

Hair ornament made from tiny steatite micro-beads, a tan jasper bead and two or three shell rings. This ornament was found beneath the skull of a male buried in the Harappan cemetery.

Material: steatite
Dimensions: each bead is less than .01 cm long and less than .01 cm dia.
Harappa, Lot 136-04
Harappa Museum, H87-664
Dales and Kenoyer 1989: 89-91, fig. 33

Cat. no. 64. (also text figure 6.45)

Cat. no. 65. (also text figure 6.44)

Necklace made up of 340 wafer-thin disc beads. This necklace was found with an adult male burial (196a) and encircled six other beads that were found on the chest at different distances from the neck (cat. nos. 66, 67, 68). The three gold beads comprise the only gold ornaments ever found in a burial of the Harappan period. The individual may have been wrapped in a shroud and was buried in a rectangular wooden coffin.

Material: fired white, hardened steatite
Dimensions: 0.59 to 0.75 cm dia.; 0.09 to 0.2 cm thickness
Harappa, Lot 194-1 to 340
Harappa Museum, H88-1091
Dales and Kenoyer 1989: 92-3, figs. 34, 35

Cat. no. 66. (also text figure 6.44)

Barrel-shaped banded jasper bead from burial 196a.

Material: jasper
Dimensions: 1.34 cm length
Harappa, Lot 194-01
Harappa Museum, H88-860
Dales and Kenoyer 1989: 92-3, figs. 34, 35

Cat. no. 67. (also text figure 6.44)

Long cylindrical turquoise bead with a single gold bead on one side. Found with burial 196a.

Material: turquoise, gold
Dimensions: 1.5 cm length
Harappa. Lot 196-342, 343
Harappa Museum, H88-862
Dales and Kenoyer 1989: 92-3, figs. 34, 35

Cat. no. 68. (also text figure 6.44)

Lenticular barrel-shaped onyx bead with green, white and tan eye design. Two gold beads fit against the edges of the central bead. Found with burial 196a.

Material: onyx, gold
Dimensions: 1.92 cm length
Harappa, Lot 196- 344, 345, 346
Harappa Museum, H88-861
Dales and Kenoyer 1989: 92-3, figs. 34, 35

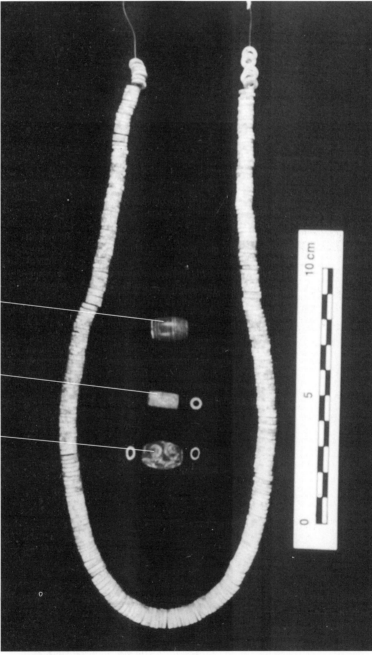

Cat. no. 66. (also text figure 6.44)

Cat. no. 67. (also text figure 6.44)

Cat. no. 68. (also text figure 6.44)

Cat. no. 65 - 68. (also text figure 6.44)

Cat. no. 69. (also text figure 7.40)

Decorated carnelian bead with white, bleached elliptical design on both faces. Short lenticular barrel shape.

Material: carnelian
Dimensions: 0.62 cm length, 0.75 cm width, 0.35 cm thickness
Harappa, Lot 2020-02
Harappa Museum, H89-1484

Cat. no. 70. (also text figure 7.40)

Decorated carnelian bead with white, bleached elliptical design on both faces. Short lenticular barrel shape.

Material: carnelian
Dimensions: 0.39 cm length, 0.91 cm width, 0.47 cm thickness
Harappa, Lot 3072-22
Harappa Museum, H89-1826

Cat. no. 71. (also text figure 7.40)

Decorated carnelian bead with white, bleached double-eye design on both faces. Short lenticular barrel. Surfaces are highly polished and edges are worn and rounded.

Material: carnelian
Dimensions: 0.53 cm length, 0.97 cm width, 0.39 cm thickness
Harappa, Lot 1152-42
Harappa Museum, H90-1886

Cat. no. 72. (also text figure 7.40)

Spherical, carnelian bead with triple-eye motif bleached onto the surface.

Material: decorated carnelian
Dimensions: 0.89 length, 0.99 dia.
Harappa, Lot 348-11
Harappa Museum, H88-1146
Dales and Kenoyer 1990

Cat. no. 73. (also text figure 7.40)

Circular eye bead with red-and-white design imitating bleached carnelian eye beads. This unique bead is the only example of red brown colored faience in the Indus Valley.

Material: red brown and white-glazed faience
Dimensions: 1 cm x 1 cm
Harappa, 3000-26
Harappa Museum, H93-2010

Cat. no. 74. (also text figure 7.40)

Steatite bead with red slip and white, bleached elliptical design on both faces. Short lenticular barrel shape. This single eye motif on steatite is a direct copy of beads made from bleached carnelian.

Material: fired steatite
Dimensions: 1.06 cm length, 1.28 cm width, 0.32 cm thickness
Harappa, Lot 3091-03
Harappa Museum, H89-1827

Cat. no. 75. (also text figure 7.40)

Steatite bead with red slip and white, bleached design. The white design is made to imitate rare orbicular jasper that has red matrix and white circles as in the bead from Mohenjodaro (cat. no. 62). Long lenticular barrel shape.

Material: steatite
Dimensions: 2.8 cm length, 2.26 cm width, 0.65 cm thickness
Harappa, Lot 3047-01
Harappa Museum, H90-1825

Cat. no. 76. (also text figure 7.40)

Steatite bead with red slip and white, bleached bands. Long barrel shape and transverse bands imitate natural banded agate.

Material: fired steatite
Dimensions: 1.34 cm length, 0.81 dia.
Harappa
Harappa Museum, H88-1646
Dales and Kenoyer 1989

Cat. no. 69.   Cat. no. 70.   Cat. no. 71.   Cat. no. 72.

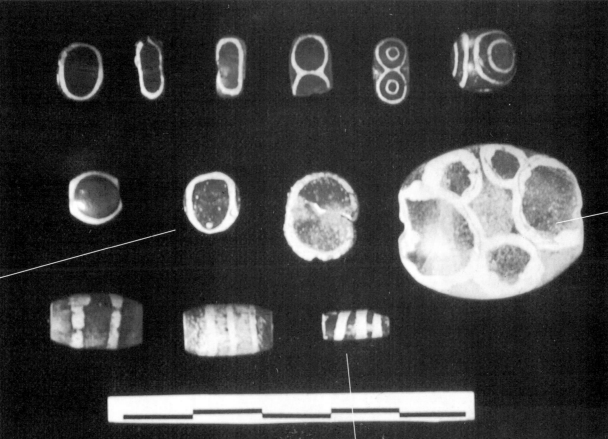

Cat. no. 73.
Cat. no. 74.
Cat. no. 75.

Cat. no. 69 - 76. (also text figure 7.40)   Cat. no. 76.

Cat. no. 77.

Carnelian beads with bleached designs; lenticular ellipse with single white circle or eye design, lenticular ellipse with double-eye design, standard cylinder with three eye designs, lenticular barrel with herringbone pattern.

Material: carnelian
Dimensions: 1.4 x 1.0 x 0.4 cm, 1.0 x 0.5 x 0.4 cm, 0.5 x 0.5 cm, 1.5 x 0.8 x 0.4
Chanhudaro
Museum of Fine Arts, Boston, MFA 36.1073, 36.1080, 36.1078, 36.1082

Cat. no. 78. (also text figure 8.31)

Short barrel beads of carnelian, perforated by a chipping from both ends, resulting in a rough biconical hole that is very narrow at the center and wide at the exterior of the bead. The sharp edges of the drill hole would have cut through any cord used, which may explain why so many of these types of beads are found scattered around Harappan sites.

Material: carnelian
Dimensions: 4.2 to 6.5 cm length, 8.2 to 9.5 cm dia.
Chanhudaro
Museum of Fine Arts, Boston, MFA 36.1122
Mackay 1948: LXXXVI, a 1

Cat. no. 79. (also text figure 8.32)

"Ernestite" stone drills in different stages of manufacture and use. The drills are chipped from a very hard stone that was modified by heating (36.1597, 36.1646, 36.2708). After chipping, the artisan made the constricted cylindrical shape by grinding on a very hard sandstone (cat. no. 80). Drills were made in different lengths and different diameters in order to perforate half of the bead in two or three stages (36.1647, 36.1648, 36.1654). Then the bead was turned over and the opposite side was perforated, meeting in the middle of the bead. The stone, made of various minerals including sillimanite, iron and titanium oxide, has been called "Ernestite" after Ernest J. H. Mackay, the excavator who first discovered these drills.

Material: "Ernestite"
Dimensions: unfinished drills, 2.18 to 4.38 cm length; finished drills, 2.31 to 3.25 cm length. tip dia., 0.26 to 0.34 cm
Chanhudaro, various contexts
Museum of Fine Arts, Boston, MFA 36.1597, 36.1646, 36.2708, 36.1647, 36.1648, 36.1654
Mackay 1948: LXXXVI, b 8; Kenoyer and Vidale 1992

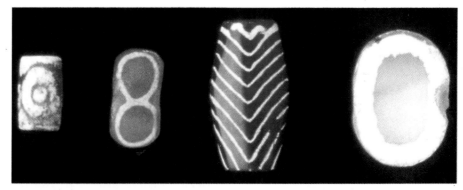

Cat. no. 77. Joint Expedition of the American School of Indic and Iranian Studies and the Museum of fine Arts, 1935-1936. © 1997 Museum of Fine Arts, Boston.

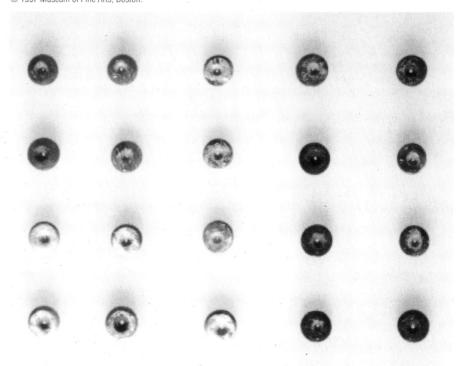

Cat. no. 78. (also text figure 8.31) Joint Expedition of the American School of Indic and Iranian Studies and the Museum of fine Arts, 1935-1936. © 1997 Museum of Fine Arts, Boston.

Cat. no. 79. (also text figure 8.32) Joint Expedition of the American School of Indic and Iranian Studies and the Museum of fine Arts, 1935-1936. © 1997 Museum of Fine Arts, Boston.

Cat. no. 80.

Drill grinding stone with many parallel grinding marks from preparing the tiny "Ernestite" drills.

Material: sandstone
Dimensions: 9.4 cm length, 3.9 cm maximum width, 3.1 cm maximum thickness
Chanhudaro
Museum of Fine Arts, Boston, MFA, CD 5044
Mackay 1943: pl. XCIII, 10

Cat. no. 81. (also text figure 8.33)

Different stages of manufacture for producing long biconical carnelian beads. The first stage after heating a long agate nodule is to saw and chip a roughout (36.1555, 36.1556, 36.1676, 36.1506). More refined chipping and grinding gradually transforms the roughout into a bead blank (36.1498, 36.1502). The final bead shape is achieved after time consuming drilling and polishing (36.1061, 36.1057, 36.1059). The red color of the carnelian is obtained by repeated heating. At any stage in the process the bead may be broken and discarded.

Material: carnelian
Dimensions: roughouts, 7.8 to 9.1 cm length; blanks, 6.4 to 6.6 cm length; beads, 5.4 to 6.8 cm length
Chanhudaro, 2290, 2866, 3853, 4010, 3627, 4008
Museum of Fine Arts, Boston, MFA 36.1061, 36.1057, 36.1059, 36.1498, 36.1502, 36.1555, 36.1556, 36.1676, 36.1506
Mackay 1943: pl. XCIII, 14

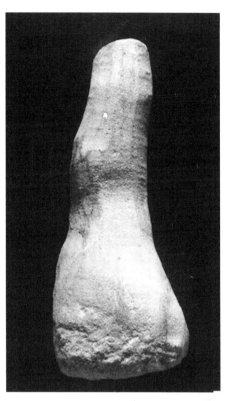

Cat. no. 80. Joint Expedition of the American School of Indic and Iranian Studies and the Museum of fine Arts, 1935-1936. © 1997 Museum of Fine Arts, Boston.

Cat. no. 81. (also text figure 8.33) Joint Expedition of the American School of Indic and Iranian Studies and the Museum of fine Arts, 1935-1936. © 1997 Museum of Fine Arts, Boston.

Cat. no. 82.

Unfinished short carnelian and agate beads showing how the artisans chipped and shaped the beads to bring out the natural lines and eye designs. At this stage of manufacture the agates have only been heated slightly to facilitate chipping. After repeated heating, the yellow gray colored agate will turn deep red orange to become carnelian.

Material: agate/carnelian, 36.1514, 36.2673, 36.2676, 36.2681, 36.1516; steatite, 36.2683
Dimensions: 36.1516, 1.76 cm length; 36.1514, 2.8 cm length; 36.2673, 2.12 cm length; 36.2681, 1.5 cm length; 36.2676, 2.81 cm length; 36.2683, 2.15 cm length.
Chanhudaro
Museum of Fine Arts, Boston, MFA 36.1514, 36.2681, 36.2673, 36.1516, 36.2683, 36.2676
Mackay 1940: pl. LXXIII, 57
Wis.: Prehistory Press, 1991), 61-70.

Cat. no. 82. Joint Expedition of the American School of Indic and Iranian Studies and the Museum of fine Arts, 1935-1936. © 1997 Museum of Fine Arts, Boston.

Cat. no. 83.
Bead-grinding stone with grooves resulting from repeated grinding. Sandstone and quartzite of different grain size were used for different stages of grinding and polishing.

Material: quartzite
Dimensions: 18 cm length, 8.5 cm width, 4 cm thickness
Chanhudaro
Museum of Fine Arts, Boston, MFA, 36.4338
Mackay 1943: similar to pl. XCI, 31

Cat. no. 84.
Bead-grinding stone with grooves resulting from repeated grinding. This fine-grained quartzite block has been used extensively for fine grinding and polishing.

Material: quartzite
Dimensions: 22 cm length, 14 cm width, 2.4 cm thickness
Chanhudaro
Museum of Fine Arts, Boston, MFA, 36.4786
Mackay 1943: similar to pl. XCI, 31

Cat. no. 85. (also text figure 7.35)
Ear ornament made of blue green glazed faience. The outer portion is a convex disc with serrated or cogged edges, and the post is plain.

Material: faience
Dimensions: 1.7 cm dia., 1.2 cm length
Harappa, Lot 11-19
Harappa Museum, H87-193

Cat. no. 86. (also text figure 7.35)
Ear ornament made of blue green glazed faience. The outer convex disc is plain with no decorative carving and is only slightly larger than the inner knob.

Material: faience
Dimensions: 1.13 cm dia., 1.17 cm length
Harappa, Lot 1112-01
Harappa Museum, H89-1531

Cat. no. 87. (also text figure 7.35)
Disc-shaped ornament of blue green faience. Parallel ribbing of light blue green alternates with white paste in the bottom of each groove.

This unique ornament may have been sewn onto cloth or inlaid onto a metal ornament.

Material: blue green and white faience
Dimensions: 3.2 cm dia., 0.8 cm thickness
Harappa, Lot 3000-27
Harappa Museum, H90-2011

Cat. no. 88.
Truncated cylindrical amulet with an incised line at the top for holding a cord or wire. Very finely shaped and smoothed and usually made in very small sizes. This type of amulet is common at all Harappa sites and associated with female burials, suggesting it was worn primarily by women.

Material: serpentine
Dimensions: 1.29 cm height, 0.7 cm base dia., 0.49 cm top dia.
Harappa, Lot 182-14
Harappa Museum, H88-788
Dales and Kenoyer 1989: 89-91; 1991:195

Cat. no. 83. Joint Expedition of the American School of Indic and Iranian Studies and the Museum of fine Arts, 1935-1936. © 1997 Museum of Fine Arts, Boston.

Cat. no. 84. Joint Expedition of the American School of Indic and Iranian Studies and the Museum of fine Arts, 1935-1936. © 1997 Museum of Fine Arts, Boston.

Cat. no. 88.

Cat. no. 85 (left), 86 (right), 87 (center). (also text figure 7.35)

Cat. no. 89.

Flattened conical amulet with groove along outer edge for fastening with cord or copper wire. Possibly attached to an arm band or head ornament as on sculptures (cat. no. 118) and figurines (cat. no. 134) .

Material: basalt
Dimensions: 1.8 cm dia., 1.02 cm height
Mohenjo-daro, MD 215
Department of Archaeology, Karachi

Cat. no. 90. (also text figure 7.43)

Seven shell bangles from burial of an elderly woman (Burial 114). All of these bangles were worn on the left arm; the chevron motif carved at the suture was pointed to the left edge of the arm. Three bangles were worn on the upper arm and four on the forearm. These bangles had been worn for many years and were rubbed smooth where they touched each other.

Material: marine shell, *Turbinella pyrum*

Cat. no. 89.

Cat. no. 91. (also text figure 7.44)

Dimensions: graduated sizes from 6.3 x 5.7 cm to 8 x 9 cm exterior measurements
Harappa, Lot 114
Harappa Museum, H87-635,-636,-637,-676,-677,-678,-679
Dales and Kenoyer 1989: 9, fig. 50; Dales and Kenoyer 1991: 201, fig. 13.12

Cat. no. 91. (also text figure 7.44)

Two wide bangles each made from a single conch shell and carved with a chevron motif.

Material: marine shell, *Turbinella pyrum*
Dimensions: 4.5 cm width, 8.9 x 9.1 cm dia., 5.1 cm internal dia.
Harappa, B 1578
National Museum, Karachi, 54.3554, HM 13828
Kenoyer 1983: fig. 3-18.1

Cat. no. 92. (also text figure 7.45)

Faience bangle made in the shape of a shell bangle or the stylized kidney or womb-shaped motif. Deeply carved cogs or ribbing project along the exterior of the bangle. Traces of blue green glaze are found on the high points and edges, but not in the deeply carved portions. A matching pair was found with this bangle near the large covered building (granary) on Mound F.

Material: blue green faience

Dimensions: 1.4 to 1.75 cm thickness. 7.3 x 8.5 cm width and breadth
Harappa, 13041
National Museum, Karachi, NMP 54.3447

Cat. no. 93. (also text figures 4.15 and 7.47)

Stoneware bangle with highly burnished surface. Wheel made and finished by hand. Because no inscription was carved on this complete bangle prior to firing, we think it may have been a reject; all other examples have short inscriptions.

Material: gray stoneware
Dimensions: 8.6 cm dia., 3.4 cm thickness
Mohenjo-daro, 83-621
Department of Archaeology, Karachi
Halim and Vidale 1984, fig. 69.

Cat. no. 90. (also text figure 7.43)

Cat. no. 92. (also text figure 7.45)

Cat. no. 93. (also text figures 4.15 and 7.47)

Cat. no. 94. (also text figure 7.46)
Bangle made from very fine clay, with tapered edge as on the stoneware bangles. The surface is finely trimmed and burnished, but it is fired to a reddish yellow terracotta color. Made on a wheel and finished by hand.

Material: terracotta
Dimensions: 8.2 cm exterior dia., 1.7 cm width, 5.2 cm interior dia.
Harappa, Lot 525-79
Harappa Museum, H87-534

Cat. no. 95. (also text figure 7.46)
Painted bangle with rounded section, made from very fine clay. This bangle is painted with a reddish black band on the exterior and is fired to a gray color in a reducing atmosphere (without oxygen). The high temperature of the reduction firing has almost turned this terracotta into stoneware. Wheel made and finished by hand.

Material: terracotta
Dimensions: 9.3 cm exterior dia., 1.5 cm width, 5.5 cm interior dia.
Harappa, Lot 508-08
Harappa Museum, H87-383

Cat. no. 96. (also text figure 7.48)
Bangle made from a round, hammered rod bent in a full circle. The space between the ends of the bangle would be pried apart to slip it over the wrist.

Material: copper
Dimensions: 6.13 cm dia.
Mohenjo-daro, DK 3457a
National Museum, Karachi, NMP 51.899, HM 13.809
Mackay 1938: 535, pl. CXL, 60

Cat. no. 97. (also text figure 7.48)
Bangle made from a round, hammered rod bent in a full circle. The space between the ends of the bangle would be pried apart to slip it over the wrist.

Material: copper
Dimensions: 6 cm dia., 0.73 cm thickness
Harappa
National Museum, Karachi, HM 13 710

Cat. no. 98. (also text figure 7.49)
Hollow bangle of hammered sheet gold. The seam lies on the interior of the bangle, and the ends are left open, allowing the bangle to be twisted apart in order to slip it over the wrist or above the elbow, as shown on bronze and terracotta figurines.

Material: gold
Dimensions: 6.53 x 6.07 cm, 0.88 cm wide, .06 cm thickness of gold sheet
Mohenjo-daro
Mohenjo-daro Museum, MM 1382, 50.28/5
Marshall 1931: 529, pl. CLI, A 9

Cat. no. 99. (also text figure 7.49)
Hollow bangle of hammered sheet gold. This bangle was found together with cat. no. 98; they appear to be a pair.

Material: gold
Dimensions: 6.1 x 5.79 cm, 0.86 cm wide, ca. .06 cm thickness of gold sheet
Mohenjo-daro
Mohenjo-daro Museum, MM 1384, 50.40
Marshall 1931: 529, pl. CLI, A 10

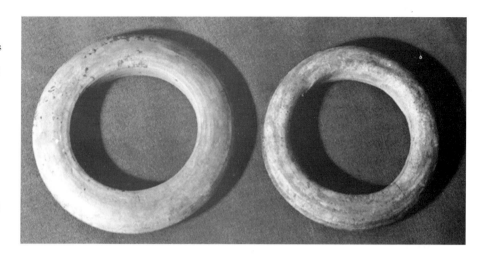
Cat. no. 94 - 95. (also text figure 7.46)

Cat. no. 96 - 97. (also text figure 7.48)

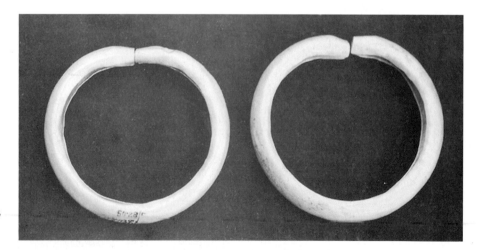
Cat. no. 98 - 99. (also text figure 7.49)

Cat. no. 100. (also text figure 5.24)

Cylindrical drinking glass with concave sides. Finely polished exterior surface with sparkling from internal crystal facets. This unique vessel probably was not made at Mohenjodaro but brought to the city by traders from Baluchistan or Afghanistan.

Material: green feldspar/ Fuchsite
Dimensions: 10.7 cm height, 7.3 cm dia.
Mohenjo-daro, DK 11337 (6)
National Museum, Karachi, 52.1896
Mackay 1938:320, pl. CXVI, 2, CXVII, 8

Cat. no. 101. (also text figure 6.38)

Libation vessel decorated with vermilion-filled incised lines. A single spiraling design is carved around the apex, and a double incised line frames the edge of the orifice. This type of vessel was used in later times for ritual libations and for administering sacred water or medicine.

Material: marine shell, *Turbinella pyrum*
Dimensions: 11.4 cm length, 5.4 cm width.
Mohenjo-daro, DK 8538
Mohenjo-daro Museum, 52.2114, MM 5073
Kenoyer 1983: 183-4, fig. 3-15, 5

Cat. no. 102. (also text figure 6.37)

Large ladle found with burial pottery in a disturbed burial of the Harappan cemetery. Shell ladles were probably used in special rituals for dispensing sacred liquids such as water or oil. A hole in the bottom of the ladle has been repaired with a lead rivet. Corrosion and expansion of the lead has caused the shell to crack. The fact that this object was included with the burial goods indicates that it must have had an important role in the afterlife or perhaps could not be passed on to others due to its strong personal association with the dead individual. No complete burial was associated with this object, so it is not possible to determine if it was used by a man or a woman.

Material: marine shell, *Chicoreus ramosus*
Dimensions: 24.3 cm length, 16.4 cm width
Harappa, Lot 446-01
Harappa Museum, H88-1192
Dales and Kenoyer 1990: 81, figs. 31, 58

Cat. no. 103.

Miniature ladle made from a small shell. The small size may indicate its use for feeding small doses of medicine or for ladling small amounts of sacred liquids during special rituals.

Material: marine shell, *Chicoreus ramosus*
Dimensions: 2.8 cm width, 3.2 cm length
Chanhudaro 2453
Museum of Fine Arts, Boston, MFA 36.2399
Mackay 1943: pl. XC, 13

Cat. no. 104.

Conch shell trumpet. The hole at the apex is roughly chipped, and the exterior is smooth and polished from use. Similar trumpets are still used ritually throughout South and Southeast Asia.

Material: marine shell, *Turbinella pyrum*
Dimensions: 9.66 cm length, 5.1 cm width, 5.6 cm height
Harappa, R2332
Lahore Museum, P501
Kenoyer 1983: 209-10, fig. 3-20,13

Cat. no. 100. (also text figure 5.24)

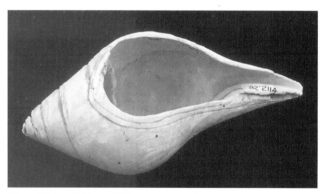

Cat. no. 101. (also text figure 6.38)

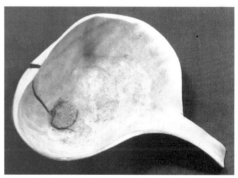

Cat. no. 102. (also text figure 6.37)

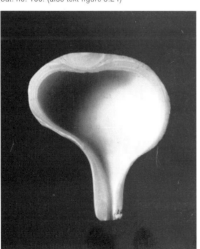

Cat. no. 103. Joint Expedition of the American School of Indic and Iranian Studies and the Museum of fine Arts, 1935-1936. © 1997 Museum of Fine Arts, Boston.

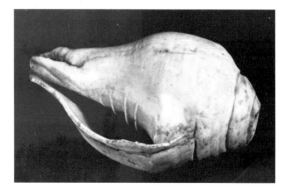

Cat. no. 104.

Cat. no. 105.

Hollow bird figurine used as a whistle. Cream surface with no trace of paint. Hand modeled. Such toys were probably used to amuse children and may represent pet birds such as partridges or doves.

Material: terracotta
Dimensions: 7.8 cm height, 6.5 cm width
Chanhudaro, 3464
Museum of Fine Arts, Boston, MFA 36.2265
Mackay 1943: pl. LIX, 5

Cat. no. 106.

Hollow bird figurine used as a whistle. Cream surface with red painted bands. Hand modeled.

Material: terracotta
Dimensions: 6.5 cm height, 5.2 cm width
Chanhudaro, 1970
Museum of Fine Arts, Boston, MFA 36.2258
Mackay 1943: pl. LIX, 6

Cat. no. 105. Joint Expedition of the American School of Indic and Iranian Studies and the Museum of fine Arts, 1935-1936. © 1997 Museum of Fine Arts, Boston.

Cat. no. 106. Joint Expedition of the American School of Indic and Iranian Studies and the Museum of fine Arts, 1935-1936. © 1997 Museum of Fine Arts, Boston.

Cat. no. 107.

Spherical rattle with cream surface and red brown painted design. Broken examples show that this type of rattle was made from two pieces of clay with tiny clay pellets fired while inside the sphere.

Material: terracotta
Dimensions: 5.5 cm dia.
Chanhudaro, 4735
Museum of Fine Arts, Boston, MFA 36.2735
Mackay 1943: pl. LIX, 9

Cat. no. 108.

Spherical rattle with red brown painted design. These noisy clay rattles may have been used to amuse children, or jugglers may have used to demonstrate their skills.

Material: terracotta
Dimensions: 5.1 cm dia.
Chanhudaro, 4658
Museum of Fine Arts, Boston, MFA 36.2226
Mackay 1943: pl. LIX, 7

Cat. no. 107. Joint Expedition of the American School of Indic and Iranian Studies and the Museum of fine Arts, 1935-1936. © 1997 Museum of Fine Arts, Boston.

Cat. no. 108. Joint Expedition of the American School of Indic and Iranian Studies and the Museum of fine Arts, 1935-1936. © 1997 Museum of Fine Arts, Boston.

Cat. no. 109.

Spinning top or lid. Identical tops made in terracotta are found in great numbers at the larger sites. The tips are often chipped and broken from use. This shell top may have been made by a child of the shellworking community where scraps of shell would have been available. Or it may have been made for the child of a wealthy family, using shell which is more durable than terracotta.

Material: marine shell, species not determinable
Dimensions: 1.5 cm height, 3.2 cm dia.
Chanhudaro, 3409
Museum of Fine Arts, Boston, MFA 36.2383
Mackay 1943: pl. XXIX, 66

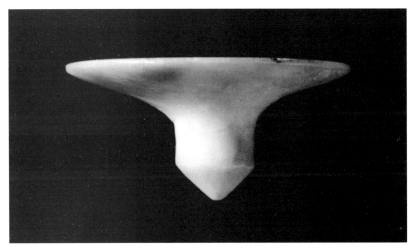

Cat. no. 109. Joint Expedition of the American School of Indic and Iranian Studies and the Museum of fine Arts, 1935-1936. © 1997 Museum of Fine Arts, Boston.

Cat. no. 110. (also text figure 6.12)

Inlay pieces of different designs. Tabular sheet with stepped edges (5092); tabular curved segment incised with intersecting-circle motif (5093); lenticular and concave square pieces for constructing intersecting-circle motif or flower shapes (5094, 5095, 5096, 5097, 5098); womb-shaped fretted design (903, 8081, 8083); intersecting circle design (904); stepped cross (905); fretted petal shape (907); stepped-cross component (912).

Material: marine shell, species not determinable
Dimensions: 3.0 cm to 6.5 cm length
Mohenjo-daro, various contexts
Mohenjo-daro Museum, MM 5092, 5093, 5094, 5095, 5096, 5097, 5098, 903, 904, 905, 907, 912, 8081, 8083
Mackay 1938: pl. CXLI, 10-13, pl. CXLII, 28, 30, 39a, 34

Cat. no. 110. (also text figure 6.12)

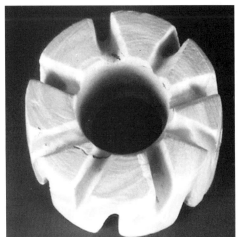

Cat. no. 111. (also text figure 6.10)

Cat. no. 111. (also text figure 6.10)

Shell ring carved with alternating grooves to make a wavy design. This object was probably used for decorating furniture or as part of a composite baton.

Material: marine shell, *Turbinella pyrum*
Dimensions: 1.45 cm height, 2.65 cm dia.
Harappa
Harappa Museum, H90-1777

Cat. no. 112.

Carved ball gaming piece with six sets of double circles on each face of the sphere. Such carved shell balls are found at Mohenjo-daro and Harappa as well.

Material: marine shell, *Turbinella pyrum*
Dimensions: 3.2 cm dia.
Chanhudaro, 2050
Museum of Fine Arts, Boston, MFA 36.2400
Mackay 1943: pl. LIX, 15

Cat. no. 113.

Incised ivory counter from Nausharo with four double circle-and-dot motifs on each side. Possibly used with other counters as gaming dice. Period III, Harappan, 2300-2200 B.C.

Material: ivory
Dimensions: 6.81 cm length, 0.7 x 0.63 widths
Nausharo
Department of Archaeology, Karachi, EBK 5656

Cat. no. 114. (also text figure 6.41)

Carved ivory counter with duck ornament at one end.

Material: ivory
Dimensions: 4.2 cm height, 0.9 cm width
Mohenjo-daro, DK 11330
National Museum, Karachi, NMP 52.1460
Mackay 1938: pl. CXXV, 8

Cat. no. 115. (also text figure 6.41)

Carved ivory counter or stylized figurine with triple circle motifs incised on both faces.

Material: ivory
Dimensions: 7 cm height, 1.5 cm width
Mohenjo-daro, DK 11 330
National Museum, Karachi, NMP 52.1457
Mackay 1938: pl. CXXV, 14

Cat. no. 116. (also text figure 6.41)

Carved ivory counter with double duck-head ornament at one end.

Material: ivory
Dimensions: approx. 4.4 cm height
Mohenjo-daro, DK 8240
National Museum, Karachi, NMP. 52.1458
Mackay 1938: pl. CX, 57

Cat. no. 112. Joint Expedition of the American School of Indic and Iranian Studies and the Museum of fine Arts, 1935-1936. © 1997 Museum of Fine Arts, Boston.

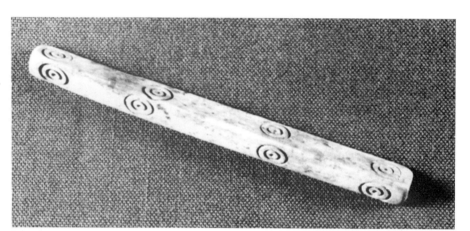

Cat. no. 113.

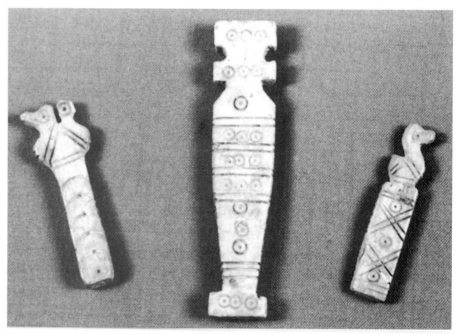

Cat. nos. 114 (right), 115 (center), 116 (left). (also text figure 6.41)

Cat. no. 117. (also text figure 5.30)

Seated male sculpture with shell inlay still remaining in one eye. The braided or combed hair lies back straight, and a plain fillet or ribbon encircles the head and falls down the back of the neck. Two strands of a ribbon or braided hair hang over the shoulder. The stylized ear is a simple cup shape with a hole in the center. The upper lip is shaved and a short, combed beard covers the lower jaw. The forward projecting head and large lips may reflect a specific personality or may be due to the particular style of carving. Slight traces of what may have been a cloak are visible on the back, but the legs are clearly visible and not totally covered with a garment as in other sculptures. The left arm rests on top of the lowered left knee, while the right hand rests on the upraised right leg. This sitting pattern is opposite of that seen on most other sculptures. Other sculptures show the left knee raised and the right knee lowered.

Material: limestone
Dimensions: 33.5 cm height, 16.5 cm width
Mohenjo-daro, DK(i) 419
Mohenjo-daro Museum, MM 432

Cat. no. 117. (also text figure 5.30)

Cat. no. 118. (also text figure 5.1)

Seated male sculpture, "priest-king." Fillet or ribbon headband with circular inlaid ornament on the forehead and similar but smaller ornament on the right upper arm. The two ends of the fillet fall along the back, and although the hair is carefully combed towards the back of the head, no bun is present. The flat back of the head may have supported a separately carved bun as is traditional on other seated figures, or it could have held a more elaborate horn and plumed headdress. Two holes beneath the highly stylized ears suggest that a necklace or other head ornament was attached to the sculpture. The left shoulder is covered with a cloak decorated with trefoil, double circle and single circle designs that were originally filled with red pigment. Drill

holes in the center of each circle indicate they were made with a specialized drill and then touched up with a chisel. Eyes are deeply incised and may have held inlay. The upper lip is shaved, and a short, combed beard frames the face. The large crack in the face may be the result of weathering or the original firing of this object.

Material: low-fired, white steatite
Dimensions: 17.5 cm height, 11 cm width
Mohenjo-daro, DK 1909
National Museum, Karachi, 50.852
Marshall 1931: 356-7, pl. XCVIII

Cat. no. 118b.

Seated male sculpture, "priest-king," cat. no. 118, after initial cleaning showing red pigment in trefoil, double circle and single circle designs on the garment.

Cat. no. 118. (also text figure 5.1)

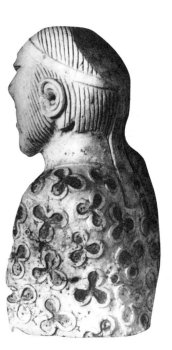

Cat. no. 118b.

Cat. no. 119. (also text figure 5.31)

Seated male figure with head missing. On the back of the figure, the hair style can be partially reconstructed by a wide swath of hair and a braided lock of hair or ribbon hanging along the right side of the back. A cloak draped over the edge of the left shoulder covers the folded legs and lower body, leaving the right shoulder and chest bare. The left arm clasps the left knee, and the hand shows underneath the cloak. The right hand rests on the right knee, which is folded beneath the body.

Material: limestone
Dimensions: 28 cm height, 22 cm width
Mohenjo-daro, L 950
Islamabad Museum
Marshall 1931:358-9, pl. C, 1-3

Cat. no. 120. (also text figure 5.32)

Male head probably broken from a seated sculpture. Finely braided or wavy combed hair tied into a double bun on the back of the head and a plain fillet or headband with two hanging ribbons falling down the back. The upper lip is shaved, and a closely cropped and combed beard lines the pronounced lower jaw. The stylized almond-shaped eyes are framed by long eyebrows. The wide mouth is similar to that of the "priest-king" sculpture. Stylized ears are made of a double curve with a central knob.

Material: sandstone
Dimensions: 13.5 cm height
Mohenjo-daro, DK-B 1057
Mohenjo-daro Museum, MM 431
Dales 1985: pl. IIb; Ardeleanu-Jansen 1984: 139-157

Cat. no. 121. (also text figure 6.33)

Seated ram sculpture fragment, with legs folded underneath the body and ears drooping to the side. A massive beard hangs from the head to the chest.

Material: sandstone
Dimensions: 16.5 cm height, 20 cm length, 12.3 cm width
Mohenjo-daro, U 81 036
Mohenjo-daro Museum, MM 5695
Ardeleanu-Jansen 1987: 59-68

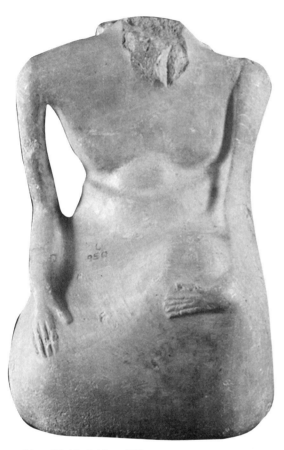

Cat. no. 119. (also text figure 5.31)

Cat. no. 120. (also text figure 5.32)

Cat. no. 121. (also text figure 6.33)

Cat. no. 122. (also text figure 5.3)

Miniature mask of bearded, horned deity. The face is made from a mold and thumb impressions from pressing the clay are visible on the back. The mouth is somber, and the long almond-shaped eyes are open. The short horns arch from the top of the forehead, and two long ears lie against the horns. This peaceful face can be contrasted to the mask from Harappa (cat. no. 123) that shows a ferocious face of what may be this very same deity. Two holes on either side allow the mask to be attached to a puppet or worn as an amulet.

Material: terracotta
Dimensions: 5.3 cm height, 3.5 cm width
Mohenjo-daro, MD 980
Department of Archaeology, Karachi
Dales 1965: 145

Cat. no. 123. (also text figure 5.4)

Miniature mask of horned deity with human face and bared teeth of a tiger. A large mustache or divided upper lip frames the canines, and a flaring beard adds to the effect of rage. The eyes are defined as raised lumps that may have originally been painted. Short feline ears contrast with two short horns similar to a bull rather than the curving water buffalo horns. Two holes on either side allow the mask to be attached to a puppet or worn as an amulet.

Material: terracotta
Dimensions: 5.24 cm height, 4.86 cm width
Harappa
Harappa Museum, H93-2093
Meadow and Kenoyer 1994

Cat. no. 124. (also text figure 5.5)

Mask with open mouth has holes for wooden teeth. Slight ridge forms an eyebrow that ends in a projecting, perforated knob. Half of the mask is reconstructed.

Material: terracotta
Dimensions: 16 cm height, 11 cm width
Mohenjo-daro, XXII NE 2a, MD 1380
National Museum, Karachi

Cat. no. 122. (also text figure 5.3)

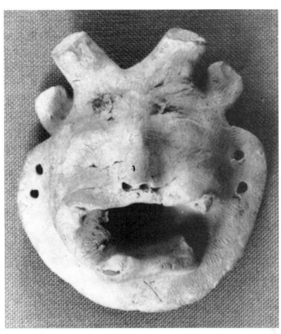

Cat. no. 123. (also text figure 5.4)

Cat. no. 124. (also text figure 5.5)

Cat. no. 125.

Feline mask or puppet, possibly representing a tiger. This hollow figurine has well-modeled eyes, nose and bared fangs. The eyes are not hollow and may have been inlaid.

Material: terracotta
Dimensions: 5.5 cm width
Mohenjo-daro, DK 2380 B
National Museum, Karachi, NMP 50.772
Marshall 1931: 253, pl. XCVI, 6

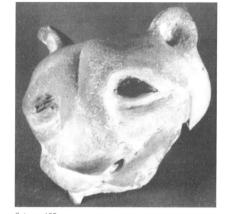

Cat. no. 125.

Cat. no. 126. (also text figure 6.26)

Feline figurine with human male face. The ears, eyes and mouth are filled with black pigment, and traces of black are visible on the flaring beard that is now broken. The accentuated almond-shaped eyes and wide mouth are characteristic of the bearded, horned deity figurines found at Harappa and Mohenjo-daro (cat. nos. 122, 123). This figurine, found in a sump pit filled with discarded goblets, animal and female figurines and garbage, dates to the final phase of the Harappan occupation, around 2000 B.C.

Material: terracotta
Dimensions: 5.5 cm height, 12.4 cm length, 4.3 cm width
Harappa, Lot 5063-1
Harappa Museum, H94-2311

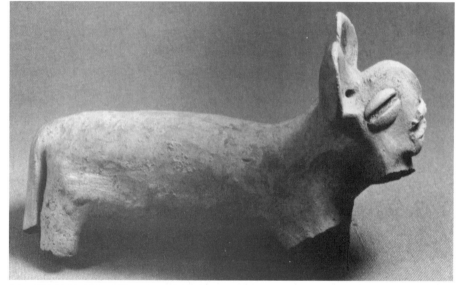

Cat. no. 126. (also text figure 6.26)

Cat. no. 127.

Seated animal figurine with human female head. The manner of sitting suggests that this may be a feline, and a hole in the base indicates that it would have been raised on a stick as a standard or puppet. One other figurine of this type has been discovered from Harappa. The head is identical to those seen on female figurines with a fan-shaped headdress and two cup-shaped side pieces. The choker with pendant beads is also common on female figurines. Hand formed with appliqué.

Material: terracotta
Dimensions: 7.1 cm height, 4.8 cm length, 3.5 cm width
Harappa, 2384
Harappa Museum, HM 2082
Vats 1940: 300, pl. LXXVII, 67

Cat. no. 127.

Cat. no. 128. (also text figure 6.28)

Hollow three-headed animal figurine. The most complete figure is of an elephant with a hollow trunk. Two horns of a water buffalo curve along the cheeks of the elephant, and the bottom jaw of a feline with bared teeth appears at the back of the elephant's head. This complex figure is finely modeled and incised with delicate strokes to portray the character of the elephant. Such multiple-headed animals are depicted on seals (cat. no. 29) and must represent important myths. This object may have been used as a puppet or sacred figure in a cult ritual. Nausharo, Period III, Harappan, 2300-2200 B.C.

Material: terracotta, gray fired
Dimensions: 7.17 cm height, 10.24 cm length, 6.74 cm width
Nausharo, NS 91.02.32.01, LXXXII
Department of Archaeology, Karachi, EBK 7423
Jarrige, C. 1992: 132-5

Cat. no. 129. (also text figure 6.29)

Hollow three-headed animal figurine. This complex figurine depicts a tiger with bared teeth, a bull or buffalo head with punctated hair spots on the forehead, and possibly an elephant with multiple lines outlining the eyes. The tiger's face is finely modeled, but the other animals' features are less refined. This is the second such object found at Nausharo, and although comparable figurines have not been reported from other sites, multiple-headed animals are depicted on seals (cat. no. 29). Nausharo, Period III, Harappan, 2300-2200 B.C.

Material: terracotta, red fired
Dimensions: 6.76 cm height, 6.97 cm length, 4.42 cm width
Nausharo, NS 92.02.70.04
Department of Archaeology, Karachi, EBK 7712
Jarrige, C. 1992: 132-5

Cat. no. 130. (also text figure 6.27)

Animal headed, pot-bellied, ithyphallic human figurine or puppet. A hole for inserting a stick passes through the base and into the lower body. Traces of a large phallus appear on the lower part of the bulging belly. Holes at the shoulder suggest attached and possibly moveable arms.

Material: terracotta
Dimensions: 12.8 cm height
Mohenjo-daro, DK 5472
National Museum, Karachi, NMP 50.517
Mackay 1938: 294-5, 306, pl. LXXVIII, 12

Cat. no. 128. (also text figure 6.28)

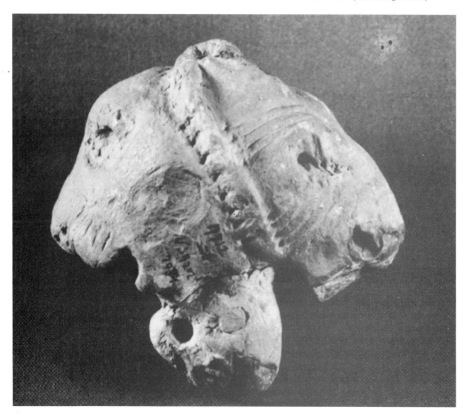

Cat. no. 129. (also text figure 6.29)

Cat. no. 130. (also text figure 6.27)

Cat. no. 131.

Cat. no. 131.

Trumpet-nosed figurine stands with hands covering face. We cannot tell what type of animal or possibly human figure is represented. The hollow trumpet-shaped projection is not seen on other figurines; some experts think it represents a caricature, possibly from a folk tale or ritual.

Material: terracotta
Dimensions: 8.5 cm height
Mohenjo-daro
Mohenjo-daro Museum, MM 790
Wheeler 1968: pl. XXIII

Cat. no. 132. (also text figure 5.14)

Unicorn figurine with joined legs and red-painted design. The horn curves forward as on the seals, and the eyes are applied. This is one of five unicorn figurines found at Chanhudaro. Unicorn figurines have also been found at Mohenjo-daro and at Harappa.

Material: terracotta
Dimensions: 4.64 cm length
Chanhudaro, 4718
Museum of Fine Arts, Boston, MFA 36.2210
Mackay 1943: pl. LV, 11

Cat. no. 133. (also text figure 1.7)

Female figurine with four flowers arranged on the front part of a fan-shaped headdress with cups at two sides and braided edging. This figurine is heavily adorned with a triple-strand choker with pendant beads, a double-strand necklace with central disc pendant, and a triple-strand belt with disc-shaped ornaments.

Material: terracotta
Dimensions: 13.2 cm height
Harappa
National Museum, Karachi, HP 1603

Cat. no. 134. (also text figure 7.14)

Female figurine holding an infant to her left breast. Her hair is arranged in a open fan shape with a punctated headband and a central disc. A narrow necklace hangs along the side of the elongated neck, which is adorned with seven double strands of necklaces. The wide, elongated eyes of the mother contrast with the round eyes of the infant.

Material: terracotta
Dimensions: 10.7 cm height, 4.9 cm wide, 2.25 cm thickness
Mohenjo-daro, DK 8688
National Museum, Karachi, NMP 50.524
Mackay 1938: 277-8, 280, pl. LXXV, 3

Cat. no. 132. (also text figure 5.14) Joint Expedition of the American School of Indic and Iranian Studies and the Museum of fine Arts, 1935-1936. © 1997 Museum of Fine Arts, Boston.

Cat. no. 133. (also text figure 1.7)

Cat. no. 134. (also text figure 7.14)

Cat. no. 135. (also text figure 6.16)

Female figurine heavily adorned with six graduated strands of chokers and pendant bead necklaces. A triple-strand belt supporting a short skirt is closed with a triple-component clasp possibly like the bronze terminals on the massive carnelian bead belts (cat. no. 47). The head has a fan-shaped headdress with braided hair along the edges of what were once cup-shaped side pieces. The head and body may actually belong to different figurines.

Material: terracotta
Dimensions: 18.7 cm height, 9.5 cm width
Mohenjo-daro, DK 2384
National Museum, Karachi, NMP 50.509
Marshall 1931: 338, pl. XCIV, 14

Cat. no. 136. (also text figure 7.20)

Female figurine with double-coiled headdress that rises high above the head. The left arm is raised to the forehead, where a single knobbed ornament hangs. This style of ornament, shown on many other figurines, is still worn by many women in western India and Pakistan today. Ornaments applied around the neck have fallen off. The woman wears a short skirt; the breasts are uncovered, reflecting a style of dress that was common in many areas of the subcontinent during the historical period and still practiced in remote areas.

Material: terracotta
Dimensions: 10.2 cm height, 3.9 cm width, 2.39 cm thickness
Harappa
Harappa Museum, HM 2558
Vats 1940: pl. LXXVII, 52

Cat. no. 137. (also text figure 7.20)

Female figurine with braided or curled locks of hair hanging down the back. A choker with pendant beads and two projecting ear ornaments are similar to those found on other figurines, but the hair style is unique. A single knobbed ornament hanging at the middle of the forehead may represent a type of conical gold ornament found in the jewelry hoards. This figurine, wearing a short skirt, is hand formed with appliqué skirt, breasts, ornaments, eyes and hair.

Material: terracotta
Dimensions: 9.1 cm height, 4 cm width, 2.9 cm thickness
Harappa, Ae 737
Harappa Museum, HM 2397

Cat. no. 138. (also text figure 7.20)

Female figurine with hair twisted into a bun on the side of the head. The ornaments that originally adorned the neck have fallen off, but the short skirt is still in place. Only a few figurines with this type of hair style have been found at Harappa. Hand formed with appliqué skirt, breasts, eyes and hair.

Material: terracotta
Dimensions: 7.1 cm height, 2.9 cm width, 2 cm thickness
Harappa
Harappa Museum, HM 2164
Vats 1940

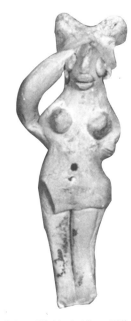

Cat. no. 136. (also text figure 7.20)

Cat. no. 135. (also text figure 6.16)

Cat. no. 138. (also text figure 7.20)

Cat. no. 137. (also text figure 7.20)

Cat. no. 139. (also text figure 7.20)

Female figurine wears a turban with a decorative band around the forehead. A double row of necklaces fits snugly against her chin. She wears a short skirt. Hand formed with appliqué skirt, breasts, ornaments and eyes.

Material: terracotta
Dimensions: 7.9 cm height, 3.4 cm width, 2.3 cm thickness
Harappa
Harappa Museum, HM 2244

Cat. no. 140.

Female figurine with fan-shaped headdress. Fugitive black pigment covers the fan-shaped portion, suggesting that this headdress is made from hair draped over a frame. Hand formed with appliqué eyes, breasts and lips.

Material: terracotta
Dimensions: 7.2 cm height, 5.2 cm width, 3.5 cm thickness
Harappa, Lot 3036-07
Harappa Museum, H90-1615

Cat. no. 141. (also text figure 7.23)

Female figurine with three sets of chokers and necklaces. One of the largest female figurines found at Harappa, it has the common fan-shaped headdress with cups on either side of the head. Traces of black pigment or soot found inside the cups suggest that they were filled with oil and used as a sacred lamp. On the other hand, a sooty black pigment may have been applied to depict black hair. The forward-projecting face is made separately and attached to the body after all of the ornaments had been applied.

Material: terracotta
Dimensions: 14 cm height, 7.8 cm width, 5.8 cm thickness
Harappa, Lot 01-13
Harappa Museum, H87-189
Dales and Kenoyer 1991: fig. 13.15, 1

Cat. no. 139. (also text figure 7.20)

Cat. no. 141. (also text figure 7.23)

Cat. no. 140.

Cat. no. 142. (also text figure 7.21)

Fat woman figurine with turbanlike headdress and appliqué ornaments. Bangles are worn on both wrists and upper arms, ankle bracelets and a choker probably represent beaded ornaments. The right hand is held to the mouth and the left hand clutches the heart, in an expression of amazement that is still typical in the subcontinent today. Nausharo, Period III, Harappan, 2300-2200 B.C.

Material: terracotta
Dimensions: 10.9 cm height, 6.76 cm width, 5.3 cm thickness
Nausharo, NS P, locus I
Department of Archaeology, Karachi, EBK 5125
Jarrige 1986: fig. 25a

Cat. no. 143. (also text figure 7.22)

Figurine of a seated woman grinding grain. The woman wears a choker and looks up; she holds a cylindrical pestle in both hands and rubs it on a flat stone. The edges of the grinding area are raised to keep ground food or grain from scattering. Hand formed from different pieces of clay, with eyes, choker and breasts applied. Nausharo, Period III, Harappan, 2300-2200 B.C.

Material: terracotta
Dimensions: 8.1 cm height, 5.7 cm length, 4.0 cm width
Nausharo, NS/88/II
Islamabad Museum, EBK 6945
Jarrige 1989: pl. XVIIa

Cat. no. 144. (also text figure 7.24)

Female figurine stands with left arm on hip and right hand holding a small bowl in front of the waist. The hair is tied in a horizontal bun hanging low on the back of the neck, and traces of long almond-shaped eyes are visible. Many bangles adorn the upper left arm, and a few bangles are indicated above the right elbow.

Material: copper/bronze
Dimensions: 13.2 cm height, 4.7 cm width
Mohenjo-daro, DK 12728
National Museum, Karachi, NMP 50.883
Mackay 1938: 274, pl. LXXIII, 9-11

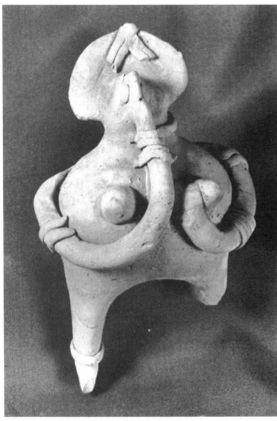

Cat. no. 142. (also text figure 7.21)

Cat. no. 144. (also text figure 7.24)

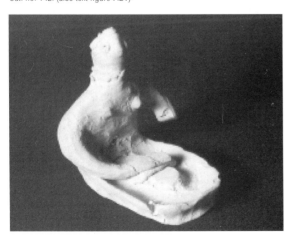

Cat. no. 143. (also text figure 7.22)

Cat. no. 145. (also text figure 7.26)

Male figurine of spear thrower or dancer. Twisting posture and upraised arm suggest a spear may have been held in the right arm. Traces of eyes and nose can be seen, and the hair is arranged in a bun on the back of the head. A turban or long hair is wrapped around the head. A bulging kilt or genitalia and the lack of pronounced breasts suggest that this is a male. The dynamic expression of this figure reflects the high quality of three-dimensional bronze modeling on a miniature scale. The figurine was probably cast, using the lost-wax process.

Material: copper/bronze
Dimensions: 4.1 cm height, 1.7 cm maximum width, 0.6 cm thickness
Chanhudaro
Museum of Fine Arts, Boston, MFA 36.2236

Cat. no. 145. (also text figure 7.26) Joint Expedition of the American School of Indic and Iranian Studies and the Museum of fine Arts, 1935-1936. © 1997 Museum of Fine Arts, Boston.

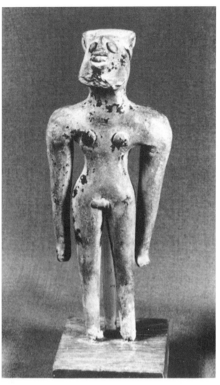

Cat. no. 146. (also text figure 6.17)

Cat. no. 146. (also text figure 6.17)

Nude male figurine or deity with wide, spreading beard wears a broken headdress that may have had two curving horns. The pose is rigid and formal, standing with arms at the sides and feet firmly planted. The eyes, nipples and genitalia are applied, and the entire figure may have been coated with a red brown slip.

Material: terracotta
Dimensions: 14.5 cm height, 5.7 cm width
Mohenjo-daro, DK 3509
National Museum, Karachi, 50.546
Mackay 1938: 271-2, pl. LXXII, 8-10

Cat. no. 147. (also text figure 6.21)

Male figurine or deity with goatlike beard wears a horned headdress that is broken. Almond-shaped eyes and serene mouth are distinctive of the molded masks of a similar horned, bearded deity (cat. no. 122).

Material: terracotta
Dimensions: 9.3 cm height, 8.3 cm width
Mohenjo-daro, DK 7508
National Museum, Karachi, NMP 50.551
Mackay 1938: 282, pl. LXXVI, 18

Cat. no. 147. (also text figure 6.21)

Cat. no. 148. (also text figure 7.25)

Male figurine sits with bent legs extended to the front and knees clasped by both arms. The two legs are joined together forming what appears to be a single leg. Many of these seated male figurines, which were probably used in a special ritual, have been found at Harappa and also at Mohenjo-daro. Highly stylized face with appliqué eyes and incised mouth.

Material: terracotta
Dimensions: 6.3 cm height, 4.41 cm length, 4.6 cm width
Harappa
Harappa Museum, HM 2564

Cat. no. 149. (also text figure 7.25)

Male figurine sits with bent legs extended to the front and the knees clasped by both arms. The eyes, lips and phallus are applied to the hand-formed body.

Material: terracotta
Dimensions: 4.63 cm height, 4.9 cm length, 3.16 cm width
Harappa
Harappa Museum, HM 2560

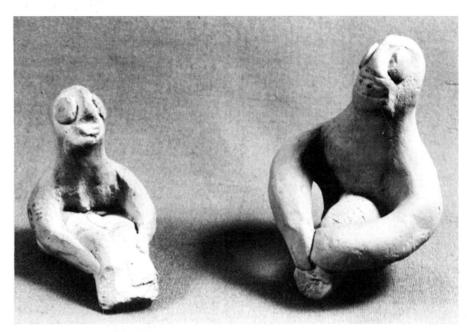

Cat. no. 148, 149. (also text figure 7.25)

Cat. no. 150, 151. (also text figure 7.15)

Cat. no. 150. (also text figure 7.15)

Child figurine wears a turban and a necklace. The hands reach to the sides, and the large feet allow the figure to stand upright without additional support. Traces of red slip indicate that the figurine was probably painted. Hand formed with appliqué.

Material: terracotta
Dimensions: 5.5 cm height
Mohenjo-daro, DK 8734
Mohenjo-daro Museum, MM 1199, 55.114
Mackay 1938: 278, pl. LXXV, 13

Cat. no. 151. (also text figure 7.15)

Child figurine with turban, holding a disc-shaped object, possibly a toy, to its chest. The legs are spread wide, which may indicate it was originally attached to a female figurine. Traces of red slip show that the figurine was originally painted. Hand formed with appliqué.

Material: terracotta
Dimensions: 5.3 cm height, 2.8 cm width, 1.5 cm thickness
Mohenjo-daro, DK 3796
Mohenjo-daro Museum, MM 1204, 50.555
Mackay 1938: 278, pl. LXXVI, 6

Cat. no. 152.

Miniature bed or table with four legs and red painted design on the top. This type of furniture, which can also function as a throne, may have been used either as a toy or actual ritual object.

Material: terracotta
Dimensions: 3.7 cm height, 14 cm length, 10.6 cm width
Chanhudaro, 4507
Museum of Fine Arts, Boston, MFA 36.1973
Mackay 1943: similar to XCI, 6

Cat. no. 153. (also text figure 8.38)

Highly stylized humped-bull figurine, with joined legs and hole in the hump for attaching a cord or copper ring. This distinctive style of bull figurine, with high hump and legs joined is found in the Early Harappan or Kot Dijian period and on into the first phase of Harappan integration. Hand formed with appliqué eyes.

Material: terracotta
Dimensions: 4.7 cm height, 4.7 cm length, 1.8 cm width
Harappa, Lot 3079-01
Harappa Museum, H90-1658

Cat. no. 154.

Humped-bull figurine with legs joined. The joined leg figurines are an earlier style of modeling found at many sites throughout the Indus Valley. Hand formed.

Material: terracotta
Dimensions: 4.1 cm height, 7.8 cm length, 1.8 cm body width, 4.5 cm horn width
Chanhudaro, 487
Museum of Fine Arts, Boston, MFA 36.2212
Mackay 1943: pl. LV, 2

Cat. no. 153. (also text figure 8.38)

Cat. no. 152. Joint Expedition of the American School of Indic and Iranian Studies and the Museum of fine Arts, 1935-1936. © 1997 Museum of Fine Arts, Boston.

Cat. no. 154. Joint Expedition of the American School of Indic and Iranian Studies and the Museum of fine Arts, 1935-1936. © 1997 Museum of Fine Arts, Boston.

Cat. no. 155.

Humped-bull figurine with molded head twisted to the side. The legs were made separated rather than joined together. Hand-formed body and attached head. Eyes are carved with appliqué pupils as on the large hollow bull figurines.

Material: terracotta
Dimensions: 5.23 cm height, 8.59 cm length, 2.92 cm width
Mohenjo-daro, MD 832
Department of Archaeology, Karachi

Cat. no. 156.

Mold for making bull-figurine head which could then be attached to the hand-formed body.

Material: terracotta
Dimensions: 4.4 cm height, 3.7 cm length, 3.2 cm width
Mohenjo-daro, MD 1634
Department of Archaeology, Karachi

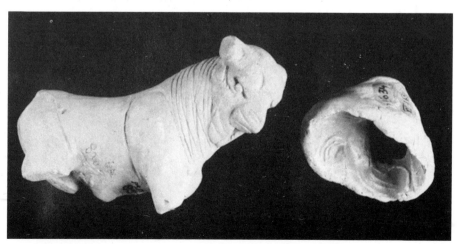

Cat. no. 155, 156.

Cat. no. 157.(also text figure 6.36)

Head of a large humped-bull figurine, with braided halter and inlaid eyes. The broken horns would have extended in a wide curve as shown on seals (cat. no. 9). The original figurine was hollow; portions of such figurines have been found only at Mohenjo-daro, possibly made in the same workshop. The head is partly molded and then touched up with hand modeling, carving and appliqué.

Material: terracotta
Dimensions: 6.2 cm height
Mohenjo-daro, DK 8848
Mohenjo-daro Museum, NMP 50.899, MM 805
Mackay 1938: 310, pl. LXXIX, 33

Cat. no. 158. (also text figure 8.39)

Water buffalo figurine with wide, spreading horns. The head is raised in a manner characteristic of buffalo when they sense danger or prior to attacking. This stance is similar to that depicted on seals (cat. no. 17). Hand formed with appliqué eyes.

Material: terracotta
Dimensions: 5.2 cm height, 9.2 cm length, 2.5 cm width
Harappa, Lot 01-07
Harappa Museum, H87-183
Dales and Kenoyer 1991: fig. 13.14, 4

Cat. no. 159. (also text figure 8.40)

Hollow, seated ram figurine with hole in the center of the back. This unique object may have been used for ritual purposes to hold offerings or a small lamp. Hand formed with punctated and incised designs as well as some appliqué.

Material: terracotta
Dimensions: 9.3 cm height, 12.2 cm length
Mohenjo-daro, DK 9404
National Museum, Karachi, NMP 50.771
Mackay 1938: 188, 640, pl. LXVI, 23

Cat. no. 160. (also text figure 8.26)

Seated ram figurine from a large pin. The pin attachment from below the figurine has broken off since it was originally discovered, but a portion of it stands like a post behind the left shoulder of the ram. This possibly depicts a sacrificial ram tied to a post. Lost-wax casting.

Material: copper/bronze
Dimensions: 5.38 cm height, 5.5 cm length
Mohenjo-daro, DK 10781 AC
National Museum, Karachi, NMP 50.879
Mackay 1938: 300-1, pl. LXXIV, 18-19

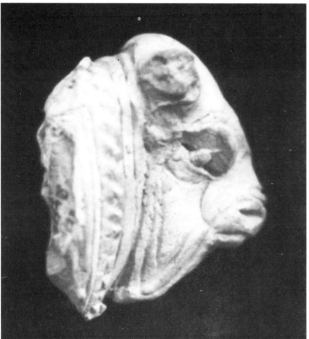

Cat. no. 157.(also text figure 6.36)

Cat. no. 158. (also text figure 8.39)

Cat. no. 159. (also text figure 8.40)

Cat. no. 160. (also text figure 8.26)

Cat. no. 161.

Hollow ram figurine on wheels. The head and body are painted with a hatched design using a light red pigment. One wheel is also painted with four double curved lines that bring to mind the intersecting-circle motif. This type of ram figurine is very common at Chanhudaro but less well represented at other sites. Hand formed with head attached to the hollow body.

Material: terracotta
Dimensions: cart 7.6 cm height, 13 cm length; wheels 7.0 to 7.2 cm dia
Chanhudaro, 4134
Museum of Fine Arts, Boston, MFA 36.2244 (cart) two wheels 36.2245 and 36.2246
Mackay 1943: pl. LVIII, 12

Cat. no. 162.

Movable-head bull figurine. The body and head were not found together, but are approximately the right size for each other. The head is supported by a string passing through a hole in the neck. Many such figurines have been found; they probably represent toys. Hand formed.

Material: terracotta
Dimensions: body, 5.2 cm height, 8.89 cm length, 2.5 cm width; head, 3.5 cm length
Chanhudaro, 3792, 3910
Museum of Fine Arts, Boston, MFA 36.2261 (head) MFA 36.2262 (body)
Mackay 1943: pl. LIX, 1

Cat. no. 163. (also text figure 7.11)

Fighting dog with a projecting collar to protect the throat when attacking other animals. Traditional dog fighting in the rural areas of India and Pakistan involves two or more dogs pitted against a bear or pig. Hand formed with appliqué ornaments.

Material: terracotta
Dimensions: 4.5 cm height, 6 cm length
Mohenjo-daro, DK 9426
Mohenjo-daro Museum, MM 817
Casal 1969: 149

Cat. no. 164. (also text figure 7.12)

Figurine of begging dog with upraised front paws wears a beaded collar. The back legs have been shaped into a stand. Hand formed with appliqué ornaments and eyes.

Material: terracotta
Dimensions: 7.1 cm height, 3.7 cm length, 2.9 cm width
Harappa, Lot 725-01
Harappa Museum, H88-1008
Dales and Kenoyer 1989: fig. 62.1

Cat. no. 161. Joint Expedition of the American School of Indic and Iranian Studies and the Museum of fine Arts, 1935-1936. © 1997 Museum of Fine Arts, Boston.

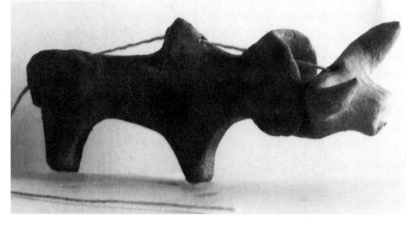

Cat. no. 162. Joint Expedition of the American School of Indic and Iranian Studies and the Museum of fine Arts, 1935-1936. © 1997 Museum of Fine Arts, Boston.

Cat. no. 164. (also text figure 7.12)

Cat. no. 163. (also text figure 7.11)

Cat. no. 165. (also text figure 8.43)

Rhinoceros figurine. The stylized representation of the heavy bumpy skin of the rhinoceros is shown here with appliqué folds and punctated knobs on the skin. Hand formed with appliqué eyes.

Material: terracotta
Dimensions: 6 cm height, 8.5 cm length, 3.1 cm width
Harappa, Lot 57-18
Harappa Museum, H90-283
Dales and Kenoyer 1991: fig. 13.14, 7

Cat. no. 166. (also text figure 8.44)

Elephant head with stylized ears spread wide. Traces of red and white paint bands are visible on the face. Painting elephants, primarily in red and white, for ritual processions is a common practice in traditional India. This figurine may represent a tame elephant or an elephant being marked for sacrifice. Hand formed and incised.

Material: terracotta
Dimensions: 4.8 cm height, 5.4 cm width, 4.6 cm breadth
Harappa, Lot 800-01
Harappa Museum, H87-348

Cat. no. 167. (also text figure 8.46)

Tiger or leopard figurine with incised facial features, including punctated dots on the face that could be whisker marks. This figurine depicts a normal feline without horns or human face and therefore probably represents the actual wild animal. Hand formed with appliqué eyes.

Material: terracotta
Dimensions: 5.7 cm height, 11.9 cm length, 4.5 cm width
Harappa, Lot 59-17
Harappa Museum, H87-339
Dales and Kenoyer 1989: fig. 62.3, Dales and Kenoyer 1991: fig. 13.14, 1

Cat. no. 168. (also text figure 8.47)

Onager or wild ass figurine. The wild ass is still found in Gujarat, India, but it probably was common in the region near Nausharo during the Indus period. Hand formed with pinched mane and punctated eyes. Period III, Harappan, 2300-2200 B.C.

Material: terracotta
Dimensions: 7.43 cm height, 10.5 cm length, 3.74 cm width
Nausharo, NS 91.02.33.01
Department of Archaeology, Karachi, EBK 7711
Jarrige 1990
Harappa Museum, H88-864

Cat. no. 167. (also text figure 8.46)

Cat. no. 165. (also text figure 8.43)

Cat. no. 168. (also text figure 8.47)

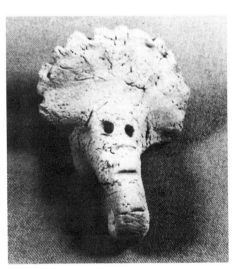

Cat. no. 166. (also text figure 8.44)

Cat. no. 178. (also text figure 3.17)

Large, black-slipped storage jar with narrow base. Wheel thrown in several stages, with molded base.

Material: terracotta
Dimensions: 73 cm height, 47.1 cm maximum dia.
Chanhudaro, 3153, A
Museum of Fine Arts, Boston, MFA 36.2979
Mackay 1943: pl. XXXV, 2

Cat. no. 179. (also text figure 8.7)

Pedestaled jar with flaring rim. This vessel is part of a burial offering of 12 vessels that were arranged at the head and along the side of a male burial (196a) that cut into the edge of the female and infant burial (194a and b). This individual was wearing a steatite necklace and precious beads (no. 67-70). Although undecorated, the vessel is very finely made. The top portion was first thrown on the wheel and after partial drying the vessel was turned over and the base added, again thrown on the wheel.

Material: terracotta
Dimensions: 30 cm height, 12.1 cm maximum dia.
Harappa, Lot 195-03
Harappa Museum, H88-955
Dales and Kenoyer 1991: fig. 13.18

Cat. no. 180. (also text figures 8.12 and 8.13)

Pedestaled jar, with red slip and painted black bands. This is one of 33 pottery vessels placed in the grave of a woman who was buried with her newly born infant (burial 194a and b). The jar had a lid, and the base was attached to the body of the vessel. Only two other vessels in this burial pottery group have similar decorations of red slip and black horizontal bands: a pedestaled globular jar (cat. no. 181) and a pedestaled bowl. The pedestaled jar was wheel thrown in several stages, with attached wheel-thrown base.

Material: terracotta
Dimensions: 36.5 cm height, 21 cm dia.
Harappa, Lot 192-01
Harappa Museum, H88-1189
Dales and Kenoyer 1989: fig. 65A; 1991: fig. 13.18

Cat. no. 178. (also text figure 3.17) Joint Expedition of the American School of Indic and Iranian Studies and the Museum of fine Arts, 1935-1936. © 1997 Museum of Fine Arts, Boston.

Cat. no. 179. (also text figure 8.7)

Cat. no. 180. (also text figures 8.12 and 8.13)

Cat. no. 181. (also text figure 8.12)

Pedestaled globular pot, with red slip and painted black bands. A broken lid was found with this vessel. The three decorated vessels may have been part of the woman's marriage gifts or dowry. This vessel was placed at the head of burial 194a. Wheel thrown with attached base.

Material: terracotta
Dimensions: 25.9 cm height, 29.7 cm maximum dia.
Harappa, Lot 192
Harappa Museum, H88-981/192-15
Dales 1991: fig. 5.1; Dales and Kenoyer 1991: fig. 13.18

Cat. no. 182. (also text figure 8.12)

Large globular pot with no slip, from burial 194a. This type of jar may have been used to hold water or grain. Wheel thrown in several stages, with molded base.

Material: terracotta
Dimensions: 41.6 cm height, 41 cm maximum dia.
Harappa, Lot 192-02
Harappa Museum, H88-884
Dales and Kenoyer 1991: fig. 13.18

Cat. no. 183. (also text figure 8.12)

Shallow bowl with narrow base. Five identical bowls, probably with food offerings, were stacked near the left side of the burial. Wheel thrown off a hump and removed with string cutting.

Material: terracotta
Dimensions: 4.5 cm height, 19.3 cm dia.
Harappa, Lot 192-28
Harappa Museum, H88-865
Dales and Kenoyer 1991: fig. 13.18

Cat. no. 181. (also text figure 8.12)

Cat. no. 182. (also text figure 8.12)

Cat. no. 183. (also text figure 8.12)

Cat. no. 191. (also text figure 8.17)

Deep bowl with wide mouth and flaring rim. The exterior is covered with a red slip and horizontal black bands. Found with a collection of burial pottery in the Harappan cemetery. Wheel thrown with molded base.

Material: terracotta
Dimensions: 27.1 cm height, 32.2 cm maximum dia.
Harappa, Lot 219
Islamabad Museum, H88-1098/219
Dales and Kenoyer 1989

Cat. no. 192. (also text figures 8.16 and 8.17)

Perforated jar found inside a large deep bowl (cat. no. 191). This perforated vessel may have been used in the preparation of beer or other brewed beverages. Wheel thrown and holes punched through from the outside. The base has a larger hole carved in the center.

Material: terracotta
Dimensions: 20 cm height, 8.7 cm maximum dia.
Harappa, Lot 219
Harappa Museum, H88:978/219
Dales and Kenoyer 1989

Cat. no. 191. (also text figure 8.17)   Cat. no. 192. (also text figures 8.16 and 8.17)

Cat. no. 192.

Cat. no. 193. (also text figure 1.4)

Pointed-base goblet with seal impression. The pointed base results from rapid manufacture off a fast wheel and makes it easy for stacking in the kiln. The grooves around the body may serve as a simple decoration, but they also allow for a better grip. Found only in the largest cities and towns, these cups appear to have been used once and then tossed away, as is the case with disposable terracotta cups in the cities of Pakistan and India today. Some of these disposable drinking cups have a seal impression on the shoulder or base and may have been made for specific owners or for specific rituals. Wheel thrown off the hump and string cut base.

Material: terracotta
Dimensions: 15.2 cm height, 12.3 cm maximum dia.
Mohenjo-daro, DK(i) 1073
Mohenjo-daro Museum, MM 1481, 52.2633

Cat. no. 194. (also text figure 1.4)

Pointed base goblet with seal impression. Plain unslipped terracotta with grooves around body. Wheel thrown off the hump and string cut base.

Material: terracotta
Dimensions: 14.7 cm height, 12.3 cm maximum dia.
Mohenjo-daro
Mohenjo-daro Museum, MM 1509

Cat. no. 193. (also text figure 1.4)   Cat. no. 194. (also text figure 1.4)

Cat. no. 195.

Miniature cooking pot with ledge shoulder and flaring rim. Red slip on neck and rim, with unslipped lower body. Wheel thrown.

Material: terracotta
Dimensions: 2.12 cm height, 3.39 cm maximum dia.
Mohenjo-daro, MD 406
Department of Archaeology, Karachi

Cat. no. 196. (also text figure 8.19)

Ledge-shouldered cooking pot with low neck and flaring rim. Red slip on the neck and rim, while the rest of the body is plain, yellowish white surface. Wheel-thrown rim with molded base. Nausharo, Period III, Harappan, 2300-2200 b.c.

Material: terracotta
Dimensions: 20 cm height, 28 cm maximum dia.
Nausharo, NS P7E, XVII /99
Department of Archaeology, Karachi, EBK 5654

Cat. no. 196. (also text figure 8.19) with 195 in lower left.

Cat. no. 195.

Cat. no. 197. (also text figure 8.21)

Cat. no. 197. (also text figure 8.21)

Ledged cooking vessel with high neck and flaring rim. This metal vessel is almost identical to many terracotta cooking vessels and was probably intended for a very wealthy family. It was made by hammering a sheet of copper and raising the hollow base and rim separately. The two pieces were joined together with cold hammering at the ledge. This vessel contained a hoard of copper weapons and tools (see Chap. 8).

Material: copper/bronze
Dimensions: 16.5 cm height, 21 cm maximum dia.
Harappa, No. 277, 13 303 B
National Museum, Karachi, NMP 52.3214
Vats 1940: 85, 384, pl.CXXIV, 27,28

Cat. no. 198. (also text figure 8.22)

Plate with vertical sides. Copper and bronze plates were probably used exclusively by wealthy, upper-class city dwellers. Hammered and raised.

Material: copper/bronze
Dimensions: 4.3 cm height, 30.3 cm dia.,
Mohenjo-daro, DK 10781A
National Museum, Karachi, NMP 52.1028
Mackay 1938: CXVIII, 20

Cat. no. 198. (also text figure 8.22)

Cat. no. 199. (also text figure 9.5)

Dish-on-stand with a hole in the center of the dish that may have been used for a special ritual purpose. The dish is pedestaled on a heavy base with triple ridges. This unique form of vessel was found at the foot of a flexed burial, which had other pottery arranged at the head of the corpse. Dark red slip on the exterior. Cemetery H period, after 1900 B.C. Wheel thrown, with ridges applied to base which was then attached to the dish.

Material: terracotta
Dimensions: 25 cm height, 41.5 cm rim dia., 34 cm base dia.
Harappa
Islamabad Museum, HM 54.3909
Vats 1940, pl. LIII, b, pl. LVII, d, 1

Cat. no. 200. (also text figure 9.4)

Dish or lid with perforation at edge for hanging or attaching to large jar. Dark black paint on deep terracotta red slip. Blackbuck antelope with trefoil design made of combined circle-and-dot motifs, possibly representing stars. Associated with burial pottery of the Cemetery H period, dating after 1900 B.C. Wheel thrown and carved.

Material: terracotta
Dimensions: 17.5 cm dia., 2.5 cm height
Harappa
Harappa Museum, HM 1340, NMP 54-4367
Vats 1940, pl. LXIV, 3

Cat. no. 201. (also text figure 9.1)

Large burial urn with ledged rim for holding a bowl-shaped lid. Dark black paint on deep terracotta red slip. The painted panel around the shoulder of the vessel depicts flying peacocks with sun or star motifs and wavy lines that may represent water. Cemetery H period, after 1900 B.C. Wheel thrown, base possibly molded.

Material: terracotta
Dimensions: 44 cm height, 47 cm maximum dia., 18.5 cm rim dia.
Harappa
Harappa Museum, HM 13547
Vats 1940, similar to pl. LVII, b

Cat. no. 202. (also text figure 9.4)

Small painted globular pot from burial group. Dark black paint on deep terracotta red slip. Leafy vine or banyan leaf design around the neck. Cemetery H period, after 1900 B.C. Wheel-thrown, carved base.

Material: terracotta
Dimensions: 13.8 cm height, 14 cm dia.
Harappa
Harappa Museum, HM 13550
Vats 1940, similar to pl. LVIII, c, 7

Cat. no. 199. (also text figure 9.5)

Cat. no. 200. (also text figure 9.4)

Cat. no. 202. (also text figure 9.4)

Cat. no. 201. (also text figure 9.1)

Cat. no. 203.

Squat pot with bird-and-net motif. Purple brown paint on a red brown surface with white paint highlighting the net design. Hand built using sequential slab construction.

Material: terracotta
Dimensions: 15.2 cm height, 20.7 cm dia.
Harappa, Lot 7505-510
Harappa Museum, H96-3157

Cat. no. 204. (also text figure 2.23)

Squat pot with intersecting-circle motif (shown here before restoration). Purple brown paint on a red brown surface with white painted circles and highlighting. Hand built using sequential slab construction.

Material: terracotta
Dimensions: 16 cm height, 22.8 cm dia.
Harappa, Lot 7505-509
Harappa Museum

Cat. no. 203.

Cat. no. 204. (also text figure 2.23)

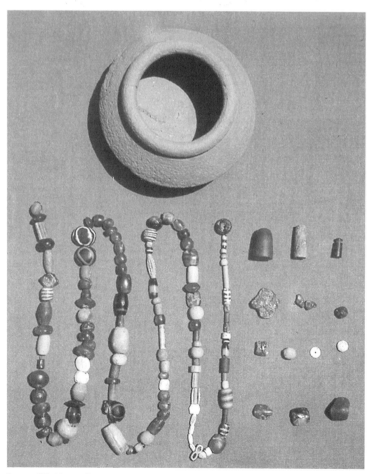

Cat. no. 205. (also text figures 9.6 and 9.7)

Cat. no. 205. (also text figures 9.6 and 9.7)

Small pot with hoard of 133 beads and decorative objects. This vessel was found on the floor of a small room dating to around 1730 B.C., but the wide variety of beads and other objects found inside the pot belong to all periods of Harappan occupation. In addition to carnelian and faience beads, which are the most numerous, the vessel contained a red brown glass bead, the first of its kind from the subcontinent. The pot is wheel formed with a rounded, trimmed base and no surface decoration.

Material: pot, terracotta; beads, agate, steatite, copper, faience, lapis lazuli, amazonite, sandstone, glass
Dimensions: pot, 4.8 cm height, 9.47 cm dia.
Harappa, pot, Lot 7330-500; contents Lot 7330-01 to 133
Harappa Museum, pot, H96-3145; contents, H96-3144

References

Alexandra Ardeleanu-Jansen, "The Therio-morphic Stone Sculpture from Mohenjo-Daro Reconsidered," in *Interim Reports Vol. 2: Reports on Field Work Carried out at Mohenjo-Daro, Pakistan 1983-84 by IsMEO-Aachen University Mission*, ed. Michael Jansen and Günter Urban (Aachen: IsMEO/RWTH, 1987), 59-68.

Roland Besenval, "The 1992-1993 field-seasons at Miri Qalat: New Contributions to the Chronology of Protohistoric Settlement in Pakistani Makran," in *South Asian Archaeology, 1993*, ed. Asko Parpola and Petteri Koskikallio (Helsinki: Suomalainen Tiedeakatemia, 1994), 1: 81-92.

Jean-Marie Casal, *La Civilization de l'Indus et ses Enigmes* (Paris: Fayard, 1969).

George F. Dales, "New Investigations at Mohenjo-daro," *Archaeology* 18.2 (1965): 145-50.

George F. Dales, "Of Dice and Men," *Journal of the American Oriental Society* 88.1 (1968): 14-23.

George F. Dales, "Stone Sculpture from the Protohistoric Helmand Civilization," in *Orientalia Iosephi Tucci Memoriae Dicata*, ed. G. Gnoli and L. Lanciotti (Roma: IsMEO, 1985), 219-24.

George F. Dales, "Some Specialized Ceramic Studies at Harappa," in *Harappa Excavations 1986-1990*, ed. Richard H. Meadow (Madison, Wis.: Prehistory Press, 1991), 61-70.

George F. Dales and J. Mark Kenoyer, "Excavation at Harappa—1988," *Pakistan Archaeology* 24 (1989): 68-176.

George F. Dales and J. Mark Kenoyer, "Summaries of Five Seasons of Research at Harappa (District Sahiwal, Punjab, Pakistan) 1986-1990," in *Harappa Excavations 1986-1990*, ed. Richard H. Meadow (Madison, Wis.: Prehistory Press, 1991), 185-262.

Mohammad A. Halim and Massimo Vidale, "Kilns, Bangles and Coated Vessels: Ceramic Production in Closed Containers at Moenjodaro," in *Interim Reports Vol. 1: Reports on Field Work Carried out at Mohenjo-Daro, Pakistan 1982-83 by IsMEO-Aachen University Mission*, ed. Michael Jansen and Günter Urban (Aachen: RWTH-IsMEO, 1984), 63-97.

Catherine Jarrige, "Les figurines humaines au Baluchistan," in *Les Cités oubliées de l'Indus*, ed. Jean-François Jarrige (Paris: Musée Guimet, 1988), 65-70.

Catherine Jarrige, "Une tête d'éléphant en terre cuite de Nausharo (Pakistan)," *Arts Asiatiques* 47 (1992): 132-35.

Jean-François Jarrige, "Excavations at Mehrgarh-Nausharo," *Pakistan Archaeology* 10-22 (1986): 62-131.

Jean-François Jarrige, "Excavations at Nausharo," *Pakistan Archaeology* 23 (1988): 149-203.

Jean-François Jarrige, "Excavation at Nausharo 1987-88," *Pakistan Archaeology* 24 (1989): 21-67.

Jean-François Jarrige, "Excavation at Nausharo 1988-89," *Pakistan Archaeology* 25 (1990): 193-240.

Jean-François Jarrige, ed. *Les Cités oubliées de l'Indus*. (Paris: Musée Guimet, 1988).

Jean-François Jarrige and Richard H. Meadow, "The Antecedents of Civilization in the Indus Valley," *Scientific American* 243.2 (1980): 122-33.

J. Mark Kenoyer, "Shell Working Industries of the Indus Civilization: An Archaeological and Ethnographic Perspective," Ph.D. diss., University of California at Berkeley, 1983.

J. Mark Kenoyer and Massimo Vidale, "A New Look at Stone Drills of the Indus Valley Tradition," in *Materials Issues in Art and Archaeology, III*, ed. Pamela Vandiver, James R. Druzick, George S. Wheeler and Ian C. Freestone (Pittsburgh: Materials Research Society, 1992), 267: 495-518.

Ernest J. H. Mackay, *Further Excavations at Mohenjodaro* (New Delhi: Government of India, 1938), i text, ii plates.

Ernest J. H. Mackay, *Chanhu-Daro Excavations 1935-36* (New Haven, Conn: American Oriental Society, 1943).

Sir John Marshall, *Mohenjo-daro and the Indus Civilization* (London: A. Probsthain, 1931).

Richard H. Meadow and J. Mark Kenoyer, "Excavations at Harappa 1993: the city walls and inscribed materials," in *South Asian Archaeology, 1993*, ed. Asko Parpola and Petteri Koskikallio (Helsinki: Suomalainen Tiedeakatemia, 1994), 2: 451-70.

Richard H. Meadow and J. Mark Kenoyer, "Excavations at Harappa 1994-1995: New perspectives on the Indus script, craft activities and city organization," in *South Asian Archaeology, 1995*, ed. Bridget Allchin. (New Delhi: Oxford and IBH, 1997).

Anaïk Samzun, "Observations on the Characteristics of the Pre-Harappan Remains, Pottery, and Artifacts at Nausharo, Pakistan (2700-2500 B.C.)," in *South Asian Archaeology, 1989*, ed. Catherine Jarrige (Madison, Wis.: Prehistory Press, 1992), 245-52.

Sayid Ghulam Mustafa Shah and Asko Parpola, *Corpus of Indus Seals and Inscriptions. 2. Collections in Pakistan* (Helsinki: Suomalainen Tiedeakatemia, 1991).

Mohammad Sharif, "Some New Seals from Mohenjodaro and the Evidence of Seal-Making," *Lahore Museum Bulletin* 3.1 (1990): 15-18.

R. E. Mortimer Wheeler, "Harappa 1946: The Defenses and Cemetery R-37," *Ancient India* 3 (1947): 58-130.

R. E. Mortimer Wheeler, *The Indus Civilization*. 3rd ed. Cambridge History of India (Cambridge: Cambridge University Press, 1968).

Bibliography

Achaya, K. T. *Indian Food: A Historical Companion*. Delhi: Oxford University Press, 1994.

Agrawal, Dileep P. and R. K. Sood. "Ecological Factors and the Harappan Civilization." In *Harappan Civilization: A Recent Perspective*, edited by Gregory L. Possehl, 445-54. New Delhi: Oxford and IBH, 1993.

Allchin, Frank Raymond. "The Interpretation of a Seal from Chanhu-daro and Its Significance for the Religion of the Indus Civilization." In *South Asian Archaeology, 1983*, edited by Janine Schotsmans and Maurizio Taddei, 369-84. Naples: Istituto Universitario Orientale, 1985.

Allchin, Frank Raymond, edited by *The Archaeology of Early Historic South Asia*. Cambridge: Cambridge University Press, 1995.

Altekar, A. S. *State and Government in Ancient India* (reprint of 3rd ed. 1958). Delhi: Motilal Banarsidas, 1984.

Amiet, Pierre. "Antiquitiés de Bactriane." *La Revue du Louvre* 3 (1978): 153-64.

Amiet, Pierre. "Iconographie de la Bactriane Proto-Historique." *Anatolian Studies, The British Institute of Archaeology at Ankara* 33 (1983): 19-27.

Ardeleanu-Jansen, Alexandra. "Stone Sculptures from Mohenjo-Daro." In *Interim Reports Vol. 1: Reports on Field Work Carried out at Mohenjo-Daro, Pakistan 1982-83 by IsMEO-Aachen University Mission*, edited by Michael Jansen and Günter Urban, 139-57. Aachen: IsMEO/RWTH, 1984.

Ardeleanu-Jansen, Alexandra. "The Theriomorphic Stone Sculpture from Mohenjo-Daro Reconsidered." In *Interim Reports Vol. 2: Reports on Field Work Carried out at Mohenjo-Daro, Pakistan 1983-84 by IsMEO-Aachen University Mission*, edited by Michael Jansen and Günter Urban, 59-68. Aachen: IsMEO/RWTH, 1987.

Ardeleanu-Jansen, Alexandra. "The Sculptural Art of the Harappa Culture." In *Forgotten Cities on the Indus*, edited by Michael Jansen, Máire Mulloy, and Günter Urban, 167-78. Mainz, Germany: Von Zabern, 1991.

Ardeleanu-Jansen, Alexandra, Ute Franke, and Michael Jansen. "An Approach Towards the Replacement of Artifacts into the Architectural Context of the Great Bath at Mohenjo-daro." In *Forschungsprojekt DFG Mohenjo-Daro: Dokumentation in der Archéologie Techniken Methoden Analysen*, edited by Günter Urban and Michael Jansen, 43-70. Aachen: RWTH, 1983.

Belcher, William R. "Riverine Fisheries and Habitat Exploitation of the Indus Valley Tradition: An Example from Harappa." In *South Asian Archaeology, 1993*, edited by Asko Parpola and Petteri Koskikallio, 1:71-80. Helsinki: Suomalainen Tiedeakatemia, 1994.

Besenval, Roland. "The 1992-1993 field-seasons at Miri Qalat: New Contributions to the Chronology of Proto-historic Settlement in Pakistani Makran." In *South Asian Archaeology, 1993*, edited by Asko Parpola and Petteri Koskikallio, 1: 81-92. Helsinki: Suomalainen Tiedeakatemia, 1994.

Bhan, Kuldeep K. "Late Harappan Gujarat." *Eastern Anthropologist* 45.1-2 (1992): 173-92.

Bhan, Kuldeep K., Massimo Vidale, and J. Mark Kenoyer. "Harappan Technology: Methodological and Theoretical Issues." *Man and Environment* 19.1-2 (1994): 141-57.

Bisht, Ravindra Singh. "Excavations at Banawali, 1974-77." In *Harappan Civilization: A Contemporary Perspective*, edited by Gregory L. Possehl, 113-24. New Delhi: Oxford and IBH, 1982.

Bisht, Ravindra Singh. "A New Model of the Harappan Town Planning as Revealed at Dholavira in Kutch: a Surface Study of its Plan and Architecture." In *History and Archaeology*, edited by B. Chatterjee, 397-408. Delhi: Ramanand Vidhya Bhawan, 1989.

Bisht, Ravindra Singh. "Secrets of the Water Fort." *Down to Earth* (May 1994): 25-31.

Brown, Dale M., ed. *Ancient India: Land of Mystery*. Alexandria, Va: Time-Life Books, 1994.

Burnes, Sir Alexander. *Travels into Bokhara together with a narrative of A Voyage on the Indus.* 4th ed., London: John Murray, 1834; reprint, Karachi: Oxford University Press, 1973.

Casal, Jean-Marie. *Fouilles D'Amri.* Paris: Commission des Fouilles Archaeologiques, 1964.

Casal, Jean-Marie. "Recent Excavations at Pirak. *Archaeology* (October 1970): 343-44.

Chakrabarti, Dilip K. "The Beginning of Iron in India." *Antiquity* 50 (1976): 114-24, 150.

Chakrabarti, Dilip K. "Distribution of Iron Ores and the Archaeological Evidence of Early Iron in India." *Journal of the Economic and Social History of the Orient* 20.2 (1977): 166-84.

Chakrabarti, Dilip K. "Iron and Urbanization: An Examination of the Indian Context." *Puratattva* 15 (1984-85): 68-74.

Chakrabarti, Dilip K. *The External Trade of the Indus Civilization.* New Delhi: Munshiram Manoharlal, 1990.

Chang, Kwang-chih. *Art, Myth, and Ritual: The Path to Political Authority in Ancient China.* Cambridge, Mass.: Harvard University Press, 1983.

Chowdhury, K. A. and S. S. Ghosh. "Plant Remains form Harappa 1946." *Ancient India* 7 (1947): 3-19.

Clark, J. Desmond. "Interpretations of Prehistoric Technology from Ancient Egyptian and Other Sources-Part II." *Paléorient* 3 (1974): 127-150.

Clark, J. Desmond. "Why Change? An Example of the Technology from India's Enduring Past." *Bulletin of the Deccan College* 49 (1990): 83-98.

Casal, Jean-Marie. *La Civilization de l'Indus et ses Enigmes.* Paris: Fayard, 1969.

Cleuziou, Serge. "The Chronology of Protohistoric Oman as Seen from Hili." *Oman Studies*, 63 (1989): 47-78.

Cleuziou, Serge. "The Oman Peninsula and the Indus Civilization: A Reassessment." *Man and Environment* 17.2 (1992): 93-103.

Cleuziou, Serge and Maurizio Tosi, "The Southeastern Frontier of the Ancient Near East," *South Asian Archaeology, 1985*, ed. Karen Frifelt and Per Sørensen (London: Curzon Press, 1989), 15-48.

Cleuziou, Serge, Gherardo Gnoli, Robin Christian, and Maurizio Tosi. "Cachets Inscrits de la fin du IIIe millénaire avant notre ère á Ras' al-Junayz, Sultanat d'Oman." *Académie des Inscriptions & Belles-Lettres, Comptes rendus des séances de l'année* 1994 (April-June 1994): 453-68.

Costantini, Lorenzo. "The Beginning of Agriculture in the Kachi Plain: The Evidence of Mehrgarh." In *South Asian Archaeology, 1981* edited by Bridget Allchin, 29-33. Cambridge: Cambridge University Press, 1984.

Cunningham, Sir Alexander. "Harappa." *Archaeological Survey, Report 1872-73.* (1875): 105-8.

Dales, George F. "New Investigations at Mohenjo-daro," *Archaeology* 18.2 (1965): 145-50.

Dales, George F. "Of Dice and Men," *Journal of the American Oriental Society* 88.1 (1968): 14-23.

Dales, George F. "Stone Sculpture from the Protohistoric Helmand Civilization." In *Orientalia Iosephi Tucci Memoriae Dicata*, edited by Gherardo Gnoli and Lionello Lanciotti, 219-24. Roma: ISMEO, 1985.

Dales, George F. "Some Specialized Ceramic Studies at Harappa." In *Harappa Excavations 1986-1990*, edited by Richard H. Meadow, 61-70. Madison, Wis.: Prehistory Press, 1991.

Dales, George F. and Louis Flam. "On Tracking the Woolly Kullis and the Like." *Expedition* 12.1 (1969): 15-23.

Dales, George F. and J. Mark Kenoyer. *Excavations at Mohenjo Daro, Pakistan: The Pottery.* Philadelphia: University Museum, University of Pennsylvania, 1986.

Dales, George F. and J. Mark Kenoyer. "Excavation at Harappa–1988." *Pakistan Archaeology* 24 (1989): 68-176.

Dales, George F. and J. Mark Kenoyer. "Excavation at Harappa–1989." *Pakistan Archaeology* 25 (1990): 241-80.

Dales, George F. and J. Mark Kenoyer. "Summaries of Five Seasons of Research at Harappa (District Sahiwal, Punjab, Pakistan) 1986-1990." In *Harappa Excavations 1986-1990*, edited Richard H. Meadow, 185-262. Madison, Wis.: Prehistory Press, 1991.

Dennell, Robin W., Linda Hurcombe, Rogan Jenkinson and Helen Rendell. "Preliminary Results of the Palaeolithic Programme of the British Archaeological Mission to Pakistan, 1983-1987." In *South Asian Archaeology, 1987*, edited by Maurizio Taddei, 17-30. Rome: IsMEO, 1990.

Dhyansky, Yan Y. "The Indus Valley Origin of a Yoga Practice." *Artibus Asiae* 48.1-2 (1988): 89-108.

Dikshit, K. N. "The Legacy of Indus Civilization in North India." *Puratattva* 21 (1991): 17-20.

Dupree, Louis, ed. *Prehistoric Research in Afghanistan 1959-1966*. ns 62.4. Philadelphia: The American Philosophical Society, 1972.

During-Caspers, Elizabeth L. C. "Harappan Trade in the Arabian Gulf in the Third Millennium B.C." *Mesopotamia* 7 (1972): 167-191.

Durrani, Farzand A. "Excavations in the Gomal Valley: Rehman Dheri Excavation Report No. 1." *Ancient Pakistan* 6 (1988): 1-232

Durrani, Farzand A., Ihsan Ali, and George Erdosy. "Seals and Inscribed Sherds of Rehman Dheri." *Ancient Pakistan* 10 (1995): 198-233.

Erdosy, George. "City States of North India and Pakistan at the Time of the Buddha." In *The Archaeology of Early Historic South Asia*, edited by Frank Raymond Allchin, 99-122. Cambridge: Cambridge University Press, 1995.

Erdosy, George. "The Prelude to Urbanization: Ethnicity and the Rise of Late Vedic Chiefdoms." In *The Archaeology of Early Historic South Asia*, edited Frank Raymond Allchin, 73-98. Cambridge: Cambridge University Press, 1995.

Fairservis, Jr., Walter A. "Excavations in the Quetta Valley, West Pakistan." *Anthropological Papers of the American Museum of Natural History* 45 (part 2) (1956).

Fairservis, Jr., Walter A. *Excavations at the Harappan Site of Allahdino: The graffiti: a model in the decipherment of the Harappan script*. New York: American Museum of Natural History, 1977.

Fairservis, Jr., Walter A. "The Origin, Character and Decline of an Early Civilization." In *Ancient Cities of the Indus*, edited by Gregory L. Possehl, 66-89. New Delhi: Vikas, 1979.

Fairservis, Jr., Walter A. "Allahdino: An Excavation of a Small Harappan Site." In *Harappan Civilization*, edited by Gregory L. Possehl, 107-12. New Delhi: Oxford and IBH/ AIIS, 1982.

Fairservis, Jr., Walter A. "The Script of the Indus Valley Civilization." *Scientific American* 248.3 (1983): 58-66.

Fairservis, Jr., Walter A. "Cattle and the Harappan Chiefdoms of the Indus Valley." *Expedition* 28.2 (1986): 43-50.

Fairservis, Jr., Walter A. "The Decipherment of Harappan Writing. Review of Tamil Civilization: Indus Script Special Issue," *The Quarterly Review of Archaeology 1986*, 4.3-4 (fall 1988): 10.

Fairservis, Jr., Walter A. and Franklin C. Southworth. "Linguistic Archaeology and the Indus Valley Culture." In *Old Problems and New Perspectives in the Archaeology of South Asia*, edited by J. Mark Kenoyer, 133-41. Madison, Wis.: UW-Madison Department of Anthropology, 1989.

Fentress, Marcia A. "The Indus "Granaries": Illusion, Imagination and Archaeological Reconstruction." In *Studies in the Archaeology and Palaeoanthropology of South Asia*, edited by Kenneth A. R. Kennedy and Gregory L. Possehl, 89-97. New Delhi: Oxford and IBH, 1984.

Flam, Louis. "Recent Explorations in Sind: Paleography, Regional Ecology and Prehistoric Settlement Patterns." In *Studies in the Archaeology of India and Pakistan*, edited by Jerome Jacobson, 65-89. New Delhi: Oxford and IBH, 1986.

Flam, Louis. "Fluvial Geomorphology of the Lower Indus Basin (Sindh, Pakistan) and the Indus Civilization." In *Himalayas to the Sea: Geology, Geomorphology and the Quaternary*, edited by John F. Shroder, Jr., 265-87. London: Routledge, 1991.

Flam, Louis. "Excavation at Ghazi Shah, Sindh, Pakistan." In *Harappan Civilization: A Recent Perspective*, edited by Gregory L. Possehl, 457-67. New Delhi: Oxford and IBH, 1993.

Francfort, Henri-Paul. *Fouilles de Shortugaï Recherches sur L'Asie Centrale Protohistorique*. Paris: Diffusion de Boccard, 1989.

Fuchs, Steven. *The Gonds and Bhumia of Eastern Mandla*. New York: Asia, 1960.

Gensheimer, Thomas R. "The Role of Shell in Mesopotamia: Evidence for Trade Exchange with Oman and the Indus Valley." *Paléorient* 10.1 (1984): 65-73.

Gentelle, P. "Landscapes, Environments and Irrigation: Hypotheses for the Study of the 3rd and 2nd Millenniums." *Man and Environment* 10 (1986): 101-10.

Gould, Harold. *Caste and Class: A Comparative View*. Reading, Mass.: Addison Wesley Modular Publication, 1971.

Gould, Harold. *The Hindu Caste System*. Delhi: Chanakya, 1987.

Greenhill, B. *Boats and Boatmen of Pakistan*. South Brunswick and New York: Great Albion Books, 1971.

Gulati, A. N. and A. J. Turner. *A Note on the Early History of Cotton*. Bulletin 17, Technological Series 12. Bombay: Indian Central Cotton Committee, 1928.

Halim, Mohammad A. and Massimo Vidale. "Kilns, Bangles and Coated Vessels: Ceramic Production in Closed Containers at Moenjodaro." In *Interim Reports Vol. 1: Reports on Field Work Carried out at Mohenjo-Daro, Pakistan 1982-83 by IsMEO-Aachen University Mission*, edited by Michael Jansen and Günter Urban, 63-97. Aachen: RWTH-IsMEO, 1984.

Harris, David R. "Settling Down: An Evolutionary Model for the Transformation of Mobile Bands into Sedentary Communities." In *The Evolution of Social System*, edited by J. Friedman and M. J. Rowlands, 401-17. Pittsburgh: University of Pittsburgh, 1978.

Helms, Mary W. *Craft and the Kingly Ideal: Art, Trade, and Power*. Austin: University of Texas Press, 1993.

Hemphill, Brian E. and John R. Lukacs. "Hegelian Logic and the Harappan Civilization: An Investigation of Harappan Biological Affinities in Light of Recent Biological and Archaeological Research." In *South Asian Archaeology, 1991*, edited by Adalbert J. Gail and Gerd J. R. Mevissen, 101-20. Stuttgart: Steiner, 1993.

Hemphill, Brian E., John R. Lukacs, and Kenneth A. R. Kennedy. "Biological Adaptations and Affinities of Bronze Age Harappans." In *Harappa Excavations 1986-1990*, edited by Richard H. Meadow, 137-82. Madison, Wis.: Prehistory Press, 1991.

Hiebert, Fredrik T. "Production Evidence for the Origins of the Oxus Civilization." *Antiquity* 68 (1994): 372-87.

Hiebert, Fredrik T. "South Asia from a Central Asian Perspective." In *The Indo-Aryans of Ancient South Asia: Language, Material Culture and Ethnicity*, edited by George Erdosy, 192-205. Berlin: de Gruyter, 1995.

Jansen, Michael. "City Planning in the Harappa Culture." In *Art and Archaeology Research Papers*, no. 14 (December), edited by Dalu Jones and George Michell, 69-74. London: AARP, 1978.

Jansen, Michael. "Settlement Patterns in the Harappa Culture." In *South Asian Archaeology 1979*, edited by Herbert Härtel, 251-69. Berlin: Dietrich Reimer, 1980

Jansen, Michael. "Architectural Remains in Mohenjo-Daro." *Frontiers of the Indus Civilization*, edited by Braj Basi Lal and S. P. Gupta, 75-88. Delhi: Books and Books, 1984.

Jansen, Michael. "Preliminary Results on the "Forma Urbis" Research at Mohenjo-Daro." In *Interim Reports Vol. 2: Reports on Field Work Carried out at Mohenjo-Daro, Pakistan 1983-84 by IsMEO-Aachen University Mission*, edited by Michael Jansen and Günter Urban, 9-21. Aachen: IsMEO/ RWTH, 1987.

Jansen, Michael. *Mohenjo-Daro: City of Wells and Drains, Water Splendour 4500 Years Ago.* Bergisch Gladbach: Frontinus Society Publications, 1993

Jarrige, Catherine. "Les figurines humaines au Baluchistan," *Les Cités oubliées de l'Indus*, edited by Jean-François Jarrige, 65-70. Paris: Musée Guimet, 1988.

Jarrige, Catherine. "Une tête d'éléphant en terre cuite de Nausharo (Pakistan)." *Arts Asiatiques* 47 (1992): 132-35.

Jarrige, Catherine. "The Mature Indus Phase at Nausharo as Seen from a Block of Period III." In *South Asian Archaeology, 1993*, edited by Asko Parpola and Petteri Koskikallio, 1:281-94. Helsinki: Suomalainen Tiedeakatemia, 1994.

Jarrige, Jean-François. "Towns and Villages of Hill and Plain." In *Frontiers of the Indus Civilization*, edited by B. B. Lal and S. P. Gupta, 289-300. New Delhi: Books and Books, 1984.

Jarrige, Jean-François. "Continuity and Change in the North Kachi Plain (Baluchistan, Pakistan) at the Beginning of the Second Millennium B.C." In *South Asian Archaeology, 1983*, edited by Janine Shotsmans and Maurizio Taddei, 35-68. Naples: Istituto Universitario Orientale, 1985.

Jarrige, Jean-François. "Excavations at Mehrgarh-Nausharo," *Pakistan Archaeology* 10-22 (1986): 62-131.

Jarrige, Jean-François, ed. *Les Cités oubliées de l'Indus*. Paris: Musée Guimet, 1988.

Jarrige, Jean-François. "Excavation at Nausharo." *Pakistan Archaeology* 23 (1988): 149-203.

Jarrige, Jean-François. "Excavation at Nausharo 1987-88." *Pakistan Archaeology* 24 (1989): 21-67.

Jarrige, Jean-François. "Excavation at Nausharo 1988-89." *Pakistan Archaeology* 25 (1990):193-240.

Jarrige, Jean-François. "The Final Phase of the Indus Occupation at Nausharo and its Connection with the Following Cultural Complex of Mehrgarh VIII." In *South Asian Archaeology, 1993*, edited by Asko Parpola and Petteri Koskikallio, 1:295-314. Helsinki: Suomalainen Tiedeakatemia, 1994.

Jarrige, Jean-François and Richard H. Meadow. "The Antecedents of Civilization in the Indus Valley." *Scientific American* 243.2 (1980): 122-33.

Jarrige, Jean-François and Marielle Santoni. *Fouilles de Pirak*. Paris: Diffusion de Boccard, 1979.

Jarrige, Jean-François. "Economy and Society in the Early Chalcolithic/Bronze Age of Baluchistan: New Perspectives from Recent Excavations at Mehrgarh." In *South Asian Archaeology, 1979*, edited by Herbert Härtel, 93-114. Berlin: Dietrich Reimer, 1981.

Jarrige, Jean-François. "Chronology of the Earlier Periods of the Greater Indus as seen from Mehrgarh, Pakistan." In *South Asia Archaeology, 1981*, edited by Bridget Allchin, 21-28. Cambridge: Cambridge University Press, 1984.

Jarrige, Jean-François. "Excavations at Nausharo." *Pakistan Archaeology* 23 (1988a): 149-203.

Jarrige, Jean-François. "Les Cités oubliées de l'Indus: Introduction." In *Les Cités oubliées de l'Indus*, edited by Jean-François Jarrige, 13-37. Paris: Musée National des Arts Asiatiques Guimet, 1988.

Jarrige, Jean-François and Monique Lechevallier. "Excavations at Mehrgarh, Baluchistan: Their Significance in the Prehistoric Context of the Indo-Pakistan Borderlands." In *South Asian Archaeology, 1977*, edited by Maurizio Taddei, 463-536. Naples: Istituto Universitario Orientale, 1979.

Jenkins, Paul Christy. "Continuity and Change in the Ceramic Sequence at Harappa." In *South Asian Archaeology, 1993,* edited by Asko Parpola and Petteri Koskikallio, 1:315-28. Helsinki: Suomalainen Tiedeakatemia, 1994.

Joshi, Jagat Pati and Asko Parpola. *Corpus of Indus Seals and Inscriptions. 1. Collections in India.* Helsinki: Suomalainen Tiedeakatemia, 1987.

Karve, Irawati. *Hindu Society—An Interpretation.* Poona: Deccan College, 1961.

Kennedy, Kenneth A. R. "Have Aryans Been Identified in the Prehistoric Skeletal Record from South Asia?" In *The Indo-Aryans of Ancient South Asia: Language, Material Culture and Ethnicity,* edited by George Erdosy, 32-66. Berlin: de Gruyter, 1995.

Kenoyer, J. Mark. "Shell Working Industries of the Indus Civilization: An Archaeological and Ethnographic Perspective." Ph.D. diss., University of California at Berkeley, 1983.

Kenoyer, J. Mark. "Shell Working Industries of the Indus Civilization: A Summary." *Paléorient* 10.1 (1984): 49-63.

Kenoyer, J. Mark. "The Indus Bead Industry: Contributions to Bead Technology." *Ornament* 10.1 (1986): 18-23.

Kenoyer, J. Mark. "Socio-Economic Structures of the Indus Civilization as Reflected in Specialized Crafts and the Question of Ritual Segregation." In *Old Problems and New Perspectives in the Archaeology of South Asia,* edited by J. Mark Kenoyer, 183-92. Madison, Wis.: UW-Madison Department of Anthropology, 1989.

Kenoyer, J. Mark. "The Indus Valley Tradition of Pakistan and Western India." *Journal of World Prehistory* 5.4 (1991): 331-85.

Kenoyer, J. Mark. "Urban Process in the Indus Tradition: A Preliminary Model from Harappa." In *Harappa Excavations 1986-1990,* edited by Richard H. Meadow, 29-60. Madison, Wis.: Prehistory Press, 1991.

Kenoyer, J. Mark. "Harappan Craft Specialization and the Question of Urban Segregation and Stratification." *Eastern Anthropologist* 45.1-2 (1992): 39-54.

Kenoyer, J. Mark. "Ornament Styles of the Indus Tradition: Evidence from Recent Excavations at Harappa, Pakistan." *Paléorient* 17.2 -1991 (1992): 79-98.

Kenoyer, J. Mark. "Experimental Studies of Indus Valley Technology at Harappa." In *South Asian Archaeology, 1993,* edited by Asko Parpola and Petteri Koskikallio, 1:345-62. Helsinki: Suomalainen Tiedeakatemia, 1994.

Kenoyer, J. Mark. "Faience from the Indus Valley Civilization." *Ornament* 17.3 (1994): 36-39, 95.

Kenoyer, J. Mark. "Early City-States in South Asia: Comparing the Harappan Phase and the Early Historic Period." In *The Archaeology of City-States: Cross Cultural Approaches,* edited by Deborah L. Nichols and Thomas H. Charlton. Washington, D.C.: Smithsonian Institution Press, 1997, in press.

Kenoyer, J. Mark. "Ideology and Legitimation in the Indus State as Revealed Through Public and Private Symbols." *Pakistan Archaeologists Forum* 4.1-2 (1995): 81-131.

Kenoyer, J. Mark. "Interaction Systems, Specialized Crafts and Culture Change: The Indus Valley Tradition and the Indo-Gangetic Tradition in South Asia." In *The Indo-Aryans of Ancient South Asia: Language, Material Culture and Ethnicity,* edited by George Erdosy, 213-57. Berlin: de Gruyter, 1995.

Kenoyer, J. Mark. "Shell Trade and Shell Working during the Neolithic and Early Chalcolithic at Mehrgarh." In *Mehrgarh Field Reports 1975 to 1985 - From the Neolithic to the Indus Civilization,* edited by Catherine Jarrige, Jean-François Jarrige, Richard H. Meadow and Gonzaque Quivron, 566-581. Karachi: Department of Culture and Tourism, Government of Sindh and the French Foreign Ministry, 1995.

Kenoyer, J. Mark and Heather M.-L. Miller. "Metal Technologies of the Indus Valley Tradition in Pakistan and Western India." In *The Emergence and Development of Metallurgy,* edited by Vincent C. Pigott. Philadelphia: University Museum, University of Pennsylvania, 1997, in press.

Kenoyer, J. Mark and Massimo Vidale. "A New Look at Stone Drills of the Indus Valley Tradition." In *Materials Issues in Art and Archaeology, III*, No. 267. edited by Pamela B. Vandiver, James R. Druzik, George S. Wheeler and Ian Freestone, 495-518. Pittsburgh: Materials Research Society, 1992.

Kenoyer, J. Mark, Massimo Vidale, and Kuldeep K. Bhan. "Contemporary Stone Bead Making in Khambhat India: Patterns of Craft Specialization and Organization of Production as Reflected in the Archaeological Record." *World Archaeology* 23.1 (1991): 44-63.

Khan, F. A. "Excavations at Kot Diji." *Pakistan Archaeology* 2 (1965): 13-85

Kohl, Philip L. "The Balance of Trade in Southwestern Asia in the Mid-Third Millennium B.C." *Current Anthropology* 19.3 (1978): 463-92.

Kutzbach, John E. and COHMAP Members. "Climatic Changes of the Last 18,000 Years: Observations and Model Simulations." *Science* 241 (August 1988): 1043-52.

Lal, Braj Basi. "The Two Indian Epics Vis-a-vis Archaeology." *Antiquity* 55 (1981): 27-34.

Lal, Braj Basi. *Some Reflections on the Structural Remains at Kalibangan*. Simla: Indian Institute of Advanced Study, 1978.

Lal, Braj Basi. "Kalibangan and the Indus Civilization." In *Essays in Indian Protohistory*, edited by D. P. Agrawal and D. K. Chakrabarti, 65-97. Delhi: B. R. Pub. Corp., 1979.

Lal, Braj Basi and K. N. Dikshit. "The Giant Tank of Shringaverapura," *The Illustrated London News* (January, 1982): 59.

Lamberg-Karlovsky, Clifford Charles. "Trade Mechanisms in Indus-Mesopotamian Interrelations." In *Ancient Cities of the Indus*, edited by Gregory L. Possehl, 130-37. New Delhi: Vikas, 1979.

Lechevallier, Monique and Gonzaque Quivron. "Results of the Recent Excavations at the Neolithic Site of Mehrgarh, Pakistan." In *South Asian Archaeology, 1983*, edited by Janine Schotsmans and Maurizio Taddei, 69-90. Naples: Istituto Universitario Orientale, 1985.

Leshnik, Lawrence S. "The Harappan "Port" at Lothal: Another View." In *Ancient Cities of the Indus*, edited by Gregory L. Possehl, 203-11. New Delhi: Vikas, 1979.

Lucas, Alfred. *Ancient Egyptian Materials and Industries (4th ed. revised)*. London: Arnold, 1962.

Lukacs, John R. "On Hunter-Gatherers and Their Neighbors in Prehistoric India: Contact and Pathology." *Current Anthropology* 31.2 (1990): 183-86.

Lukacs, John R. "Biological Affinities from Dental Morphology: The Evidence from Neolithic Mehrgarh." In *Old Problems and New Perspectives in the Archaeology of South Asia*, edited by J. Mark Kenoyer, 75-88. Madison, Wis.: UW-Madison Department of Anthropology, 1989.

Mackay, Ernest J. H. *Further Excavations at Mohenjodaro*. New Delhi: Government of India, 1938.

Mackay, Ernest J. H. *Chanhu-Daro Excavations 1935-36*. New Haven, Conn.: American Oriental Society, 1943.

Mahadevan, Iravatham. "The Sacred Filter Standard Facing the Unicorn: More Evidence." In *South Asian Archaeology, 1993*, edited by Asko Parpola and Petteri Koskikallio, 1:435-45. Helsinki: Suomalainen Tiedeakatemia, 1994.

Mainkar, V. B. "Metrology in the Indus Civilization." In *Frontiers of the Indus Civilization*, edited by B. B. Lal and S. P. Gupta, 141-51. New Delhi: Books and Books, 1984.

Marshall, Sir John. *Mohenjo-daro and the Indus Civilization*. London: Probsthain, 1931.

Masson, Charles. *A Narrative of Various Journeys in Baluchistan, Afghanistan and the Punjab*. London: Bently, 1842.

McCarthy, Blythe and Pamela B. Vandiver. "Ancient High-strength Ceramics: Fritted Faience Bangle Manufacture at Harappa (Pakistan), ca. 2300-1800 B.C." In *Materials Issues in Art and Archaeology*, No. 185, edited by Pamela B. Vandiver, James R. Druzik, and George S. Wheeler, 2: 495-510. Pittsburgh: Materials Research Society, 1990.

Meadow, Richard H. "Prehistoric Subsistence at Balakot: Initial Considerations of the Faunal Remains." In *South Asian Archaeology, 1977*, edited by Maurizio Taddei, 275-315. Naples: Istituto Universitario Orientale, 1979.

Meadow, Richard H. "Animal Domestication in the Middle East: a Revised View from the Eastern Margin." In *Harappan Civilization: A Contemporary Perspective*. 2nd ed. edited by Gregory L. Possehl, 295-320. New Delhi: Oxford and IBH, 1993.

Meadow, Richard H. "A Camel Skeleton from Mohenjo Daro." In *Frontiers of the Indus Civilization*, edited by B. B. Lal and S. P. Gupta, 137-40. New Delhi: Books and Books, 1984.

Meadow, Richard H. "Continuity and Change in the Agriculture of the Greater Indus Valley: The Palaeoethnobotanical and Zooarchaeological Evidence." In *Old Problems and New Perspectives in the Archaeology of South Asia*, edited by J. Mark Kenoyer, 61-74. Madison, Wis.: UW-Madison Department of Anthropology, 1989.

Meadow, Richard H. "Prehistoric Wild Sheep and Sheep Domestication on the Eastern Margin of the Middle East." In *Animal Domestication and its Cultural Context*, edited by Pam J. Crabtree, D. V. Campana, and K. Ryan, 24-36. Philadelphia: University Museum, University of Pennsylvania, MASCA, 1989.

Meadow, Richard H. "Animal Domestication in the Middle East: A Revised View from the Eastern Margin." In *Harappan Civilization: A Recent Perspective*. 2nd ed., edited by Gregory L. Possehl, 295-320. New Delhi: Oxford and IBH, 1993.

Meadow, Richard H. "The Origins and Spread of Agriculture and Pastoralism in South Asia." In *The Origins and Spread of Agriculture and Pastoralism in Eurasia*, edited by David R. Harris, 390-412. Washington, D.C.: Smithsonian Institution Press, 1996.

Meadow, Richard H. and J. Mark Kenoyer. "Excavations at Harappa 1993: The City Walls and Inscribed Materials." In *South Asian Archaeology, 1993*, edited by Asko Parpola and Petteri Koskikallio, 2:451-70. Helsinki: Suomalainen Tiedeakatemia, 1994.

Meadow, Richard H. and J. Mark Kenoyer. "Excavations at Harappa 1994-1995: New Perspectives on the Indus script, Craft Activities and City Organization." In *South Asian Archaeology, 1995*, edited by Bridget Allchin. New Delhi: Oxford and IBH, 1997, in press.

Mellaart, James. *The Neolithic of the Near East*. New York: Scribner's, 1975.

Misra, Virendra N. "Indus Civilization and the Rgvedic Saraswati." In *South Asian Archaeology, 1993*, edited by Asko Parpola and Petteri Koskikallio, 2:511-26. Helsinki: Suomalainen Tiedeakatemia, 1994.

Misra, Virendra N. and S. N. Rajguru. "Palaeoenvironment and Prehistory of the Thar Desert, Rajasthan, India." In *South Asian Archaeology, 1985*, edited by Karen Frifelt and Per Sørensen, 296-320. London: Curzon Press, 1989.

Moorey, Peter Roger Stuart. *Materials and Manufacture in Ancient Mesopotamia: The Evidence of Archaeology and Art*. Vol. S237. Oxford: BAR International Series, 1985.

Mughal, M. Rafique "The Harappan Settlement Systems and Patterns in the Greater Indus Valley (circa 3500-1500 B. C.)." *Pakistan Archaeology* 25 (1990): 1-72.

Mughal, M. Rafique "The Consequences of River Changes for the Harappan Settlements in Cholistan." *Eastern Anthropologist* 45.1-2 (1992): 105-16.

Mughal, M. Rafique "Jhukar and the Late Harappan Cultural Mosaic of the Greater Indus Valley." In *South Asian Archaeology, 1989*, edited by Catherine Jarrige, 213-22. Madison, Wis.: Prehistory Press, 1992.

Oldham, R. D. "On Probable Changes in the Geography of the Punjab and Its Rivers." *Journal of the Asiatic Society of Bengal* 55.2 (1887): 305-67.

Parpola, Asko "The Indus Script: A Challenging Puzzle." *World Archaeology* 17.3 (1986): 399-419.

Parpola, Asko. *Deciphering the Indus Script*. Cambridge: Cambridge University Press, 1994.

Parpola, Asko. "Deciphering the Indus Script: a Summary Report." In *South Asian Archaeology, 1993*, edited by Asko Parpola and Petteri Koskikallio, 2:571-86. Helsinki: Suomalainen Tiedeakatemia, 1994.

Parpola, Asko. "Indus Script." In *The Encyclopedia of Languages and Linguistics*, edited by R. E. Asher and J. M. Y. Simpson, 1669-70. Oxford: Pergamon Press, 1994.

Parpola, Simo, Asko Parpola, and Robert H. Brunswig. "The Meluhha Village: Evidence of Acculturation of Harappan Traders in Late Third Millennium Mesopotamia?" *Journal of the Economic and Social History of the Orient* 20.2 (1977): 9-165.

Pelegrin, Jacques. "Lithic Technology in Harappan Times." In *South Asian Archaeology, 1993*, edited by Asko Parpola and Petteri Koskikallio, 1:587-98. Helsinki: Suomalainen Tiedeakatemia, 1994.

Perkins, Dexter. "The Fauna of Aq Kupruk Caves: A Brief Note." In *Prehistoric Research in Afghanistan (1959-1966)*, edited by Louis Dupree. 73. ns 62.4. Philadelphia: The American Philosophical Society, 1972.

Possehl, Gregory L. *Kulli: An Exploration of an Ancient Civilization in South Asia*. Durham, N.C.: Carolina Academic Press, 1986.

Possehl, Gregory L. "African Millets in South Asian Prehistory." In *Studies in the Archaeology of India and Pakistan*, edited by Jerome Jacobson, 237-56. New Delhi: Oxford and IBH and AIIS, 1987.

Possehl, Gregory L. "Revolution in the Urban Revolution: The Emergence of Indus Urbanism." *Annual Review of Anthropology* 19 (1990): 261-82.

Possehl, Gregory L. "The Harappan Civilization in Gujarat: The Sorath and Sindhi Harappans." *Eastern Anthropologist* 45.1-2 (1992): 117-54.

Possehl, Gregory L. "The Date of Indus Urbanization: A Proposed Chronology for the Pre-urban and Urban Harappan Phases." In *South Asian Archaeology, 1991*, edited by Adalbert J. Gail and Gerd J. R. Mevissen, 231-49. Stuttgart: Steiner, 1993.

Possehl, Gregory L. *Radiometric Dates for South Asian Archaeology*. Philadelphia: University of Pennsylvania Museum, 1994.

Possehl, Gregory L. and M. H. Raval. *Harappan Civilization and Rojdi*. New Delhi: Oxford and IBH and AIIS, 1989.

Postgate, J. Nicholas. *Early Mesopotamia: Society and Economic at the Dawn of History*. London: Routledge, 1992.

Potts, Daniel T. *The Arabian Gulf in Antiquity: From Prehistory to the Fall of the Achaemenid Empire*, vol. 1. Oxford: Clarendon Press, 1990.

Potts, Daniel T. "South and Central Asian Elements at Tell Abraq (Emirate of Umm al-Qaiwain, United Arab Emirates), c. 2200 BC-AD 400." In *South Asian Archaeology, 1993*, edited by Asko Parpola and Petteri Koskikallio, 2:615-28. Helsinki: Suomalainen Tiedeakatemia, 1994.

Pracchia, Stefano, Maurizio Tosi, and Massimo Vidale. "On the Type, Distribution and Extent of Craft Industries at Mohenjo-daro." In *South Asian Archaeology, 1983*, edited by Janine Shotsmans and Maurizio Taddei, 207-47. Naples: Istituto Universitario Orientale, 1985.

Prasad, Kameshwar. *Cities, Crafts and Commerce under the Kusanas*. Delhi: Agam Kala Prakashan, 1984.

Prasad, Kameshwar. "Urban Occupations and Crafts in the Kusana Period." In *Essays in Ancient Indian Economic History*, edited by Brajadulal Chattopadhyaya, pp. 111-20. New Delhi: Munshiram Manoharlal, 1987.

Quivron, Gonzaque "The Pottery Sequence from 2700-2400 BC at Naushero, Baluchistan." In *South Asian Archaeology, 1993*, edited by Asko Parpola and Petteri Koskikallio, 2:629-44. Helsinki: Suomalainen Tiedeakatemia, 1994.

Ramanujan, A. K. "Toward an Anthology of City Images." In *Urban India: Society, Space and Image*, edited by Richard G. Fox, 224-44. Durham, N.C.: Duke University, 1971.

Rao, Shikarpur Raganatha. *Lothal: A Harappan Port Town (1955-62)*, vol. 1. Memoir No. 78. New Delhi: Archaeological Survey of India, 1979.

Rao, Shikarpur Raganatha. "A "Persian Gulf" Seal from Lothal." In *Ancient Cities of the Indus*, edited by Gregory L. Possehl, 148-52. New Delhi: Vikas, 1979.

Rao, Shikarpur Raganatha. *Lothal: A Harappan Port Town (1955-62)*, vol. 2. Memoir No. 78. New Delhi: Archaeological Survey of India, 1985.

Ratnagar, Shereen. *Enquiries into the Political Organization of Harappan Society*. Pune: Ravish, 1991.

Reddy, Seetha N. "On the Banks of the River: Opportunistic Cultivation in South India." *Expedition* 33.3 (1991): 18-26, 76-77.

Samzun, Anaïk. "Observations on the Characteristics of the Pre-Harappan Remains, Pottery, and Artifacts at Nausharo, Pakistan (2700-2500 B.C.)." In *South Asian Archaeology, 1989*, edited by Catherine Jarrige, 245-52. Madison, Wis.: Prehistory Press, 1992.

Santoni, Marielle. "Potters and Pottery at Mehrgarh during the Third Millennium B.C. (Periods VI and VII)." In *South Asian Archaeology, 1985*, edited by Karen Frifelt and Per Sørensen, 176-85. London: Curzon Press, 1989.

Sarianidi, Victor. "Recent Archaeological Discoveries and the Aryan Problem," In *South Asian Archaeology, 1991*, edited by Adalbert J. Gail and Gerd J. R. Mevissen, 252-63. Stuttgart: Steiner, 1993.

Sen, Samarendra Nath and Mamata Chaudhuri. *Ancient Glass and India*. New Delhi: Indian National Science Academy, 1985.

Scharfe, Hartmut. *The State in Indian Tradition*. Leiden: Brill, 1989.

Sellier, Pascal. "The Contribution of Paleoanthropology to the Interpretation of a Functional Funerary Structure: The Graves from Neolithic Mehrgarh Period IB." In *South Asian Archaeology, 1989*, edited by Catherine Jarrige, 253-66. Madison, Wis.: Prehistory Press, 1992.

Shaffer, Jim G. "The Later Prehistoric Periods." In *The Archaeology of Afghanistan: From Earliest Times to the Timurid Period*, edited by Frank Raymond Allchin and Norman Hammond, 71-90 ff. London: Academic Press, 1978.

Shaffer, Jim G. "Bronze Age Iron From Afghanistan: Its Implications For South Asian Protohistory." In *Studies in the Archaeology and Palaeoanthropology of South Asia* edited by Kenneth A. R. Kennedy and Gregory L. Possehl, 41-62. New Delhi: Oxford and IBH, 1984.

Shaffer, Jim G. "The Indo-Aryan Invasions: Cultural Myth and Archaeological Reality." In *The People of South Asia: The Biological Anthropology of India, Pakistan, and Nepal*, edited by John R. Lukacs, 77-90. New York: Plenum Press, 1984.

Shaffer, Jim G. "One Hump or Two: The Impact of the Camel on Harappan Society." In *Orientalia Iosephi Tucci Memoriae Dicata*, edited by Gherardo Gnoli and Lionello Lanciotti, 1315-28. Rome: IsMEO, 1988.

Shaffer, Jim G. "The Indus Valley, Baluchistan and Helmand Traditions: Neolithic Through Bronze Age." In *Chronologies in Old World Archaeology*. 3rd ed., edited by Robert Ehrich, 1:441-64. Chicago: University of Chicago Press, 1992.

Shaffer, Jim G. "Reurbanization: The Eastern Punjab and Beyond." In *Urban Form and Meaning in South Asia: The Shaping of Cities from Prehistoric to Precolonial Times*, edited by Howard Spodek and Doris Meth Srinivasan, 53-67. Washington, D.C.: National Gallery of Art, 1993.

Shaffer, Jim G. and Diane A. Lichtenstein. "Ethnicity and Change in the Indus Valley Cultural Tradition." In *Old Problems and New Perspectives in the Archaeology of South Asia*, edited by J. Mark Kenoyer, 117-26. Madison, Wis.: UW-Madison Department of Anthropology, 1989.

Shaffer, Jim G. and Diane A. Lichtenstein, "The Cultural Tradition and Palaeoethnicity in South Asian Archaeology." In *The Indo-Aryans of Ancient South Asia: Language, Material Culture and Ethnicity*, edited by George Erdosy, 126-54. Berlin: de Gruyter, 1995.

Sharif, Mohammad. "Some New Seals from Mohenjodaro and the Evidence of Seal-Making," *Lahore Museum Bulletin* 3.1 (1990): 15-18.

Shah, Syed G. M. and Asko Parpola. *Corpus of Indus Seals and Inscriptions. 2, Collections in Pakistan*. Helsinki: Suomalainen Tiedeakatemia, 1991.

Singh, Purushottam. "The Narhan Hoard of Punch Marked Coins (A Preliminary Report)." In *The 10th International Congress of Numismatics in London*, edited by I. A. Carradice, 465-69. London: International Association of Professional Numismatics, 1986.

Singh, Ravindra N. *Ancient Indian Glass: Archaeology and Technology*. Delhi: Parimal Publications, 1989.

Sollberger, E. "The Problem of Magan and Meluhha." *Bulletin of the London Institute of Archaeology* 8-9 (1970): 247-50.

Srinivasan, Saradha. *Mensuration in Ancient India*. Delhi: Ajanta, 1979.

Stacul, Giorgio. "Harappan Post Urban Evidence in the Swat Valley." In *Frontiers of the Indus Civilization*, edited by B. B. Lal and S. P. Gupta, 271-76. New Delhi: Books and Books, 1984.

Stech, Tamara and Vince C. Pigott. "The Metals Trade in Southwest Asia in the Third Millennium B. C." *Iraq* 48 (1986): 39-64.

Swynnerton, Charles. *Folk Tales from the Upper Indus*. Reprint. Islamabad: Institute of Folk Heritage, 1978.

Vats, Madho Sarup. *Excavations at Harappa*. Delhi: Government of India Press, 1940.

Vidale, Massimo. "Specialized Producers and Urban Elites: on the Role of Craft Industries in Mature Harappan Urban Contexts." In *Old Problems and New Perspectives in the Archaeology of South Asia*, edited by J. Mark Kenoyer, 2:171-82. Madison, Wis.: UW-Madison Department of Anthropology, 1989.

Vidale, Massimo. "On the Structure and the Relative Chronology of a Harappan Industrial Site." In *South Asian Archaeology, 1987*, edited by Maurizio Taddei and Pierfrancesco Callieri, 203-44. Rome: IsMEO, 1990.

Weber, Steven A. *Plants and Harappan Subsistence: An Example of Stability and Change from Rojdi*. New Delhi: Oxford and IBH, 1991.

Weber, Steven A. "South Asian Archaeobotanical Variability." In *South Asian Archaeology, 1989*, edited by Catherine Jarrige, 283-90. Madison, Wis.: Prehistory Press, 1992.

Wheeler, R. E. Mortimer. "Harappa 1946: The Defenses and Cemetery R-37," *Ancient India* 3 (1947): 58-130.

Wheeler, R. E. Mortimer. *The Indus Civilization*. Cambridge: Cambridge University Press, 1953.

Wheeler, R. E. Mortimer. *The Indus Civilization* 3rd ed. Cambridge: Cambridge University Press, 1968.

Wilhelmy, Herbert. "Das Urstromtal am Ostrand der Indusebene und das Sarasvati-Problem." *Zeitschrift fur Geomorphologie* Supplement 8 (1969): 76-93.

Willey, Gordon R. and P. Phillips. *Method and Theory in American Archaeology*. Chicago: University of Chicago Press, 1958.

Witzel, Michael. "Rgvedic History: Poets, Chieftains and Polities." In *The Indo-Aryans of Ancient South Asia: Language, Material Culture and Ethnicity*, edited by George Erdosy, 307-52. Berlin: de Gruyter, 1995.

Woolley, Sir Leonard. *Excavations at Ur*. London: Ernest Benn, 1955.

Wright, Rita P. "New Perspectives on Third Millennium Painted Grey Wares." In *South Asian Archaeology, 1985*, edited by Karen Frifelt and Per Sørensen, 137-49. London: Curzon Press, 1989.

Wright, Rita P. "The Indus Valley and Mesopotamian Civilizations: A Comparative View of Ceramic Technology," in *Old Problems and New Perspectives in the Archaeology of South Asia*, edited by J. Mark Kenoyer, 1:145-56. Madison, Wis.: UW-Madison Department of Anthropology, 1989.

Wright, Rita P. "Patterns of Technology and the Organization of Production at Harappa." In *Harappa Excavations 1986-1990*, edited by Richard H. Meadow, 71-88. Madison, Wis.: Prehistory Press, 1991.

Index

Chanhudaro, 136; razor, pin and pincers, 128; saw, 158; saw for shell working, 96; vessels, 156
bronzeworkers, modern, 19
Buddha, 105
Buddhism, 26, 179; swastika, 108
Buddhist civilization, culture, 18, 19; rituals, 119; stupa and monastery, Mohenjo-daro, 56; stupas, 21, 23; texts, 20
buffalo, water (see also water buffalo), 38
buffalo-horned deity, 46
buildings, orientations of, 52; private/domestic (see also houses), 58; public, 52, 58, 62
bull, figurines, 118; motif, Mehrgarh, 39; seal, 15; humpless, short-horned, 86; short-horned, on seals, 85; tiger-man-plant, 112
bun hair style, on men, 136
burial customs, changes over time, 16; Regionalization Era, 43
burial, offerings, Cemetery H, 175; ornaments, Mehrgarh, 39; pottery, 120, 122; pottery, Harappa, 148, 153; rituals, Cemetery H, Harappa, 174; matri-local, 133; with shell bangles, 107
burials, 122; Mehrgarh Neolithic, 38; of children, Cemetery H, 175; social and ritual status, 122
Burnes, A., 20, 27
button seals, 88; Mehrgarh, 45
cake, terracotta, 45
calendars, Arabic, Chinese, Mesopotamian, 53
camel figurines, with riders, 177
camel, two-humped Bactrian (*Camelus bactrianus*), 40, 89, 167
canister, stoneware manufacture, 75
caper (*Capparis decidua*), 169
caravans, 89
caravansarai, Harappa, 55
cardamom, 170
cardinal directions, 52
carnelian inlay, pendant, 141
carnelian, 96; bead, burial offering, 123; decorated, 97; Early Historic, 181; etched, 143; long biconical, decorated, long faceted, 40, 97; resources, 92; bleached, 143
carp, 168
carpenters, 129
carpetmaking, 128, 149
carpets, 159
cart, terracotta, 90; two-wheeled, 40, 89
carved rocks, northern Pakistan, 109
caste, 59, 131
catfish, 168
cattle, 26, 35-38, 164; on seals, 84
cavalry, 179
cedar (*Cedrus deodara*), deodar tree, 57, 122
cemeteries, 18
cemetery, 144; at Harappa, 122
Cemetery H, 172; culture, 174; burial pottery, 174
cenotaph, no trace, 122
Central America, 33
Central Asia, 17, 28, 89, 96, 174; gold source, 96
centrifugal force, 151

ceramic, manufacturing, 129; production, 149; technology, 151
ceramics, see also pottery
ceremonies, public, 83
Chagai hills, lapis lazuli source, 96
Chalcolithic period, 38
Champa, 180
Chanhudaro, 177; beadmaking, 160; bronze male figurine, 136; long biconical carnelian beads, 161; painted pottery, 14; seals, 74; unicorn figurine, 87
chatter-marks, 152
chaupat, 120
checker-board design, 108
chert weight, manufacture, 149
chert, grey black, 35; knapping, 34; sickle, 34, 35; stone tools, 33
chevron motif, on shell bangles, 144
Chicoreus ramosus, spiny Murex marine shell, 94, 95
chiefdoms, Early Historic, 179
childbirth and childhood, 132
children's toys, figurines, 134
China, 17, 28, 33
Chinese, calendar, 53;pilgrims, 20
chipped stone tool-making, 149
chipping technique, for bead perforation, 160
chisels, copper, 158, 159
chlorite, carved containers, 96
Cholistan, 27
Chota Nagpur plateau, 177, 180
chronology, chart, 24
chutneys, 169
cinnamon, 169
circle-and-dot motif, 108
circular brick platforms, Harappa, 65
cisterns, 53, 58; stone-lined, 59
citadel, Dholavira, 53; Mohenjo-daro, 23, 56
cities, hinterland, 50; Indus, 15; modern, 19; Sumerian, 24
citrus fruits, 169
city, 49-67; government, 81; planning, 52; states, Early Historical period, 50; walls, 53
city-state, independent, 100; Early Historic, 178-179
civic control, 56
clams, 168
clans, 83
clarified butter, ghee, 164
classes, social or ethnic, 44; stratified, 43
clay marbles, 133; tag, 83; unfired containers, 37
climate, 30
cloak, male sculpture, 137; spotted, depicted on stone sculptures, 101
cloth, preserved on silver or copper objects, 128
clothing, depicted on stone sculptures, 101; worn by men, 137
cloves, 170
coastal communities, Balakot, 168
cobra, on seals, 85
coconut, 169
coercion, through trade and religion, 99
coffin burials, Cemetery H, 175
coffin, wooden, 122
coiffure, female figurine, 36

coins, 182
college, Mohenjo-daro, 62
colonnades, brick, Mohenjo-daro, 63
colorant, faience, 157
coloring beads, Early Historic, 180
columella, 119
comic, figurine, 116
commemorative mementos, 116
commercial weaving, 128
common people, 149
compartmented buildings, Mehrgarh, 41
complex technologies, 150
conch shell bangles, 182
conch shell, trumpets and libation vessels, 182; trumpet, 119, 130
cone-shape gold ornament, 142
conflict, human, 82
conical gold ornament, forehead, 134
conical stone objects, 110
constricted cylindrical drill, 160, 180
containers, unfired clay, 37
continuity, shell bangles, faience, 178; examples of, 182
control of crafts, 44; direct and indirect, 149
control, civic, 56; of trade, 98-99
cooking oils, 169
cooking pot(s), 151, 155; bronze, aluminum, 156; heavier, Pirak, 178; traditions, 168; miniature, 133
copper, 40, 96; arsenical, 158; bangles, 146; bead, burial offering, 123; bead, Mehrgarh Neolithic, 38; blades, curved razor, 128; crude, refined, alloyed, 158; drill, 160; drill, tubular, 176; hoard, Harappa, 158; metallurgy, 158, 180; metallurgy, Early Historic, 180; mining regions, 158; mirror, 159; objects, 177; ore, source areas, 94; ores, 149; razor, carpet making, 159; seals, 73; smelting, 158; spears and knives, 42; tablet, 112; tablet, Harappa, 75; tablets, 158; tablets, Mohenjo-daro, 74; tools, 159; vessels, 156; copper/bronze, metallurgy, 149; mirror, grave offering, 123; ram figurine, 158; tools and weapons, 76; weapons, 158
copperworking, 55
cord, twisted, 129
cores, prismatic, 34
coriander, 169
cortex, 34
cottage industry, pottery, 152
cotton, 163; fabrics, 159
cottonseed oil, 169
courtyard, 58
cowrie shell, dice, 120
craft activity areas (see also workshops), 53
craft specialization, 149
crafts, control of, 44, 149; specialized, 17
craftsmanship, Indus, 18
cremation urn, 172
cremation, Cemetery H, 175
crocodile, gharial, 114; on seals, 85
crop failure, 174
crops, summer and winter, 38
cross-breeds, cattle, 164
cross-dressing, 137

independent professionals, 128
India, 14, 28, 30, 183, modern cities, 19, peninsular, 17
Indian elephant (*Elaphus maximus*), 166
indigo (blue), dye, 137
indirect percussion, 34
Indo-Aryan, language family, 26, 78, 179; speaking peoples, 19, 174
Indo-Gangetic tradition, 26, 179
Indrapat (Delhi), 180
Indus, alloying, 158; boats, 90; cities, 15; cities, decline, 173; civilization, discovery, 20; craftsmanship, 18; deities, 118; delta, 30, 168; fabrics, 128; faience, strong, 157; goblet, disappears, 178; looms, no depictions, 159; region, 49; religious integration, 118; river, 27; technical qualities, 18; traders, 91; weights, in Mesopotamia, 98
Indus script, 41, 69; stoneware bangles, 145; undeciphered, 16; seals and impressions, in Mesopotamia, 98
Indus (Valley) Tradition, 25, 26, 173
Indus Valley, 17, 33, 173
Indus Valley civilization, 15, 25; origins, 16; settlements, 17
ingots, bun-shaped copper, 94, 158
inlaid woodwork, 149
inlay, gold and steatite, 141
inscription(s), (see also script, seals, tokens, tablets, writing), 75-76; large, Dholavira, 53-54; post-firing (graffiti), 75
Integration Era, 25, 26, 49
Integration Era, Indo-Gangetic tradition, 179
integration of society, role of writing, 77
intensification, subsistence practices, 178
interaction and exchange spheres (see also trade), 40
intermediary communities, in trade, 97
internecine warfare, 182
intersecting-circle motif(s), 14, 108, 153; at Harappa, 45; inlay and impressed, 109
invention, of writing, 77
inverse indirect percussion, 34, 35
Iran, 174
iron oxide, red ochre, 153
iron, production 180, 182; technology, 27; weapons, 179
irrigation, 38, 163; technology, 42
Islam, 181
ithyphallic caricatures, 116
itinerant performers, 130
ivory, 38; carving, 129; rods, carved dice, counters, 120; seal, Rehman Dheri, 45; workers, modern, 19; ritual offering stand, 86; source areas, 96
jackal figurine, 165
jackfruit, 169
Jain architectural traditions, glazed tiles, 181
Jainism, 26, 179
jamun (*Syzygium cumini*), 169
Jansen, M., 52
jar, black-slipped, 72
Jarrige, J.-F., 36
jasper, 96
jasper, orbicular, 143; with eye patterns, 142

jati, caste, 131
Jericho, 35
Jerruk, 33
jewelry, 139; hoard, 135, 140; hoard, Allahdino, 138
Jhukar Phase, 177
Jhukar seals, 84,178
joker, figurine, 116
jugglers, 133
jujube (*Zizyphus jujubata*), 38, 169
jungle fowl, (chicken) figurine, 165
Kabul river and pass, 28
Kachi plain, 37, 173, 177
Kalibangan, 42, 46; cylinder seal, 118; plowed field, 163; seals, 74, 84
kama, 81
Karachi coast, marine shell, 94
Karachi, dried fruits vendor, 169
Kashmir, 28
Khambhat, 34, 161
kharif, summer or fall crop, 163
Kharoshthi script, 78
kidney design, 109
kidney-shaped ornament, with inlay, 141
Kili Gul Mohammed, 36
kilns, 129; pit and updraft, 151; small and large, 42
Kish, 24
knives, copper, 42
kohl/eye liner, 45
Kot Diji Phase, bricks, 56; Regionalization Era, 39, 49, 152
Kot Diji, fortified, 42; horned deity motif, 46; wall, 44; style, cooking pots, 155
Krishna, 182
Kunal, jewelry hoard, 138
Kushana Period, 82
Kutch, 27, 28, 96, 168; carnelian source, 96; conch shell, 182
Lahore, 20
Lambis, sp., 119
lance head, copper, 159
landlords, 17
language "X", 78
languages, Dravidian, Indo-Aryan, etc., 78
langur, long tailed monkey, 131
lapidary arts, 182
lapis lazuli, 39, 43, 96, 139; bead, burial offering, 123; resources, 93, 96
latrines (see also toilets), 42, 60
lattice, 58
law and order, 17
lead, 158; rivet, 119
leaders, political, 81; spiritual, 17
leather workers, 130
legacy, Indus Valley Civilization, 180
legitimize power, 115
lemon, 169
lentils, 169
leopards, 114, 167
Levant, 35
Lewis, J., 20
libation vessel, shell, 119
lime, 169
linguists, 17
linseed oil, 169
liquor manufacturers, 130
lizardite beads, 128, 140

Localization Era, 25, 173, 179
logograph, 71
logosyllabic (morphemic) writing system, 71
long braid, male and female figures, 136
long carnelian beads, 160; wide belt, 134
loom and loom weights, 159
lost-wax casting, 135, 158
lota (water jar), 60
Lothal, 182; Arabian Gulf style seal, 97; gaming board, 121; reservoir, 163; sealings from burned storehouse, 84; seals, 74
lower town, Dholavira, 53
Lukacs, J., 38
macaque, monkey, 131
mace head, stone, marble, 42, 159
Mackay, E. J. H., 161
madder (red), dye, 137
Magan, 98
magicians, 133
Mahabharata, 29, 179; battle, 182
Mahadevan, I., 86
Mahua flower (*Madhuca indica*), 169
Makran, 30; coast, 43; conch shell, 182
Malang, Sufi mystic, 182
male, burials, 123; burial with shell bangle, 124; children, desire for, 132; deity, 112; deity, seated in yogic position, 113; sculptures, clothed, 137; torso, Harappa, 129; virility, 111;
male figurines, 111; nude, 137; with tiger beard, 167; with turbans, headbands, 136; with ornaments, 137; with infant, 44
Malwa plateau, 179
man (men), fighting short-horned bull, 115; spearing each other, 118; wearing bangles, 146;
manganese, black, 153
mango, 169
manhood, 136
manufacture of shell bangles, 94-96
manufacturing process of stoneware bangles, 75
manuscripts, palm leaf, 79
many-faced deity, 112
map, Indus Valley sites and trade routes, 50
marine shell resources, 92, 94
market exchange, 98
market, Harappa, 55
markets, 58
Markhor goat, 118; on seals, 85
Marshall, J., 21
masks, 133; terracotta, 82, 83
mass production, 155; of pottery, 152
Masson, C., 20
mastic, 141
mat-weaving, 129
Mathura, 180
matri-local burial, 133
matted hair, male and female figures, 136
Mauryan Empire, 23, 26, 179
Mauryan kings, 81
measures, standardized, 26
medicinal preparations, 119
medicine(s), 168; dried fruits, 169; herbs, 170

planning, city, 52

plant(s), foods, processing, 35; motifs, 112; wild and domestic, 26, 35-38

plastered, pottery, 156

platforms, circular brick, at Harappa, 65, 66; bathing, 60

Pleiades (*krittikah*), 52; script sign, 79

Pleistocene glacial period, 35

Pliny the Elder, 181

plow, Banawali, 163

plowed field, Kalibangan, 163

plum, 169

Po-fa-to, 21

pointed-base goblet, 120, 154

points, bone, 42

poisoned arrows, 166

Polaris/North Star, 52

political leaders (see also rulers), 81

political organization, 100

polluted, vessels for food preparation, 155

pollution, water, 59

polychrome geometric designs, Pirak, 178; jar, Mehrgarh, 32; painting, pottery, 153

pomegranate, 35, 169

population, Mohenjo-daro, 50

porters, 89

post firing graffiti, Harappa, 69

postal relay station, Harappa, 55

pot-bellied figurine, 116

potter's wheel, 151; marks, relation to Indus script, 41, 70; 129

potter(s), modern, 19; Mohammad Nawaz, 151

pottery, discs, game, 132; kilns, 42; kilns, Mound E, 152; production, 42; workshops, 152; black-slipped jar, 72; chaff-tempered (early), 26; disposable, 17; easily polluted, 155; greyware, 41; hand-built, 45, 151; handmade and basket-impressed, 36; painted, 17, 40, 43, 152; plain, wheel formed, 151; polychrome, 32; house replicas, 57, 58

Potwar plateau, 33

power, 43-45; legitimize, 115; role of writing in, 77; symbols of, 45, 81; walled city as symbol of, 65

Prakrit dialects, 78

Prayag (modern Allahabad, India), 29

prayer beads, 181

praying figure, 112

Pre-pottery Neolithic A, 35

precious, metals, stones, 139; metalworking, 149; stones, 43, 96

preconditions for state-level society and urbanism, 40-45

predicting the future, 120

pregnant women, 134

pressure-flaking, 34

priest, 115

priest-king sculpture, 18, 80, 100, 137

priestesses, female attendants, 106

privacy, 58

private buildings, 58

private symbols, 107

procession, seven robed figures/worshipers, 104, 106

processions, 83

procreation, 111-112

prostitutes, 130

protective womb, 109

proto-Dravidian, 78

proto-Shiva, seal, 112

public, assembly area, 62; buildings/structures, 52, 58, 62; ceremonies, 83; rituals, 115; symbols, 107; washing area, 128; wells, 60

pulses, 163

punch-marked coins, 182

Punjab, 20, 179

Punjab Phase, Late Harappan, 174

puppeteer, 83, 116

puppets, terracotta, 82; religious myths, 133

purity, of kitchen, 155; of water, 59

quarries, chert, 34

quartzite, grinding stones, 161

quern, sandstone, 150

rabbit, on seals, 85; terracotta figurine, 165

rabi, winter or spring crop, 163

race, oxcarts, on-track betting, 130

radiocarbon dates, 25

railway bed, 20

railway engineers, 20

rainy season, 30

Rajasthan, 27, 43; copper ore, 94; irrigation canals, 163

Rajgrha, 180

Rakhigarhi, 49, 127

ram, figurine, copper/bronze, 158; sculpture and figurine, 118

Ramayana, 179

Rangpur Phase, 174

ranking, of occupational and craft specialists, 43; of raw materials, 156

Rann of Kutch, 28, 178

Ras' al-Junayz, 97

rattle, terracotta, 130, 133

Ravi river, 27

raw material(s), imported and local, 149; partly processed, 149; resources, 40, 91

rebus principle, 78

reciprocal exchange, 98

rectangular seal, Mohenjo-daro, 73

red dogs, wild, 130

red ochre (iron oxide), 153

red pigment, 119

red pigment, female figurine, Naushara, 44

red sandstone, male torso, 129

red vermilion, figurine decoration, 141

red-and-white eye beads, imitation, 142

red-dog, from Meluhha, 98

reed house, with seated deity, 113

refugees, 174

Regionalization Era, 25, 39-45

Rehman Dheri, 45; horned deity motif, 46; potter's marks, 69

religion, used for coercion, 99

religious, art, 105; festivals, 91; functions, great bath at Mohenjo-daro, 64; integration, Indus, 118; order, 81

replica, storage jar, 151

reservoirs, 53, 58

resource areas, 91

retaining walls, 41

rhesus, monkey, 131

rhinoceros (*Rhinoceros unicornis*), 166; on seals, 84; terracotta figurine, 166

rice, 26, 163, 170, 173, 178, 180

Rig Veda, 24, 29, 78, 179

rings, 109; toe and finger, Allahdino, 138

ringstones, 53, 57, 109; Mohenjo-daro, Dholavira, 54

ritual, buildings, 58; figurines, 131; games, 76, 120; headdress, 124; narratives, 114; object/offering stand, seals and ivory replica, 85-86; offering stand, 119; offering stand, design on gold fillet, 139; ornament, stoneware bangle, 145; pottery, 120; purity, 155; sacrifices, 170; specialists, 128; status, burials, 122; utensils and paraphernalia, 119

rituals, Vedic, 86

river banks, agriculture, 163

Riwat, 33

rock crystal, 181

rock quartz, 157; Early Historic, 181

rock salt, 169

Rohri hills, chert quarries, 33, 34, 43

Rojdi, endless-knot motif, 108

Rome, 64, 181

roof, house, 56

rosewood (*Dalbergia latifolia*), 122

royal cemetery of Ur, 97

royal storerooms, 182

royal titles, on seals, 84

rulers, 149; and trade, 99; control by, 99-100; depictions of, 100-102; of the Indus, 17, 81-104; seals of, 83-84; stone images of (Kushana Period), 82

ruling elites, 127, 158

Rupar, seals, 74

sacred, brazier on seals, 86; conch shell, 182; symbols, 107; symbols, on unicorn pendant, 18; tree, 62; water, 119

sacrifice, domestic and wild animals, 118; human, 119; thirteenth, 106; votive figurines, 118

Sage Agastya Muni, 182

Sahiwal, milk buffalo, 164

Sahni, D. R., 22

Sahyadripar mountain range, 30

sailboat, 90

salt, 169

sanctuary, 105

Sanghao cave, 33

sanitation, 58-60

Sanskrit, 78

Saraswati, abandoned settlements, 173; dried-up river, 178; region, 49; river, 27, 173

Sargon of Akkad, 98

Satpura mountain range, 30

Saurashtra, 53, 174; marine shell, 94

saw, 158; copper/bronze, 96, 159

scented oils, 130

schist, green, carved containers, 96

script, Brahmi, 78; deciphering, 78-79; disappearance, 77-78; Indus, 41, 69-80; invention of Indus script, 70; Kharoshthi, 78; logographic, 71; proto-Elamite, 70

sculptural schools, 129

sculpture(s), bronze, 135; Hindu, 82; male torso, 129; stone, of humans, 62, 82, 100-102

sea salt, 169

Credits

All photographs of artifacts and archaeological sites in Pakistan are presented courtesy of the Department of Archaeology and Museums, Government of Pakistan. Except as indicated below, all photographs and illustrations are by the author, Jonathan Mark Kenoyer.

Department of Archaeology and Museums, Government of Pakistan: figure 6.8; cat. nos. 31, 32, and 33, photographs by Jyrki Lyytikkä for the University of Helsinki, all three photographs courtesy of Asko Parpola.

Archaeological Survey of India: figures 1.9, 1.12, 1.13, 3.8, 3.9, 3.10, 3.11, 6.32.

National Museum of India: figure 6.18, photograph by Erja Lahdenperä for the University of Helsinki, courtesy of Asko Parpola.

J.-F. Jarrige, French Archaeological Mission: figures 2.8, 2.9, 2.11, 2.12, 2.14, 2.18, photographs by C.Jarrige

Harappa Archaeological Research Project: photographs by Richard H. Meadow, figures 4.1, 4.5, 4.8a, 4.11, 5.4, 5.11, 6.3, 6.5, 6.24, 6.34, 8.4, 8.31; photographs by George F. Dales, figures 5.5, 5.13, 8.20; photographs by George Helms, figures 6.7, 6.43, 7.1.

University of Pennsylvania Museum: figures 5.26, 5.27.

Museum of Fine Arts, Boston: figures 1.1, 5.14, 7.26, 8.31, 8.32, 8.33 and all catalogue photographs of Chanhudaro objects.

Louvre, Paris: figure 1.15,photographs by Pierre and Maurice Chuzeville

William R. Belcher: figure 8.49.
Patrick Craig: figure 7.41.
Chris Sloan: figure 3.19.
Elizabeth J. Walters: figure 7.29.

The design of this catalogue was produced entirely with PageMaker 6.0 software on Macintosh Power-PC computers at David Alcorn Museum Publication Design, Blairsden, California,

Output by **Delta Dot** (Pvt.)Ltd.,Karachi,on Ultre 94E Imagesetter of Heidelberg Prepress Div.

The families of type used for headlines, body text, and captions throughout this catalogue are ITC Fenice in its roman, italic, bold, and bold italic forms, in addition to Helvetica in its condensed, condensed light, and condensed bold forms.

The catalogue was Thread stitched and bound by Al-Rehman Paper Crafts, Karachi.